Literature and History
in the Age of Ideas

Literature and History in the Age of Ideas

Essays on the French Enlightenment
Presented to
George R. Havens

Edited by
Charles G. S. Williams

Ohio State University Press

Copyright © 1975 by the Ohio State University Press
All Rights Reserved.
Manufactured in the United States of America

Library of Congress Cataloguing in Publication Data

Main entry under title:
Literature and history in the age of ideas.

English or French.
Includes index.
CONTENTS: Davidson, H. M. Fontennelle, Perrault, and the realignment
of the arts.—Brumfitt, J. H. Historical pyrrhonism and Enlightenment historiography in France.—Williams, C. G. S. The Diamond of Courtoisie and
the Dragonnades of 1681: Valincour's Vie de François de Lorraine.—[etc.]—
A bibliography of the writings of George R. Havens (p.
1. French literature—18th century—Addresses, essays, lectures. 2. Enlightenment—Addresses, essays, lectures. 3. France—Intellectual life—Addresses,
essays, lectures. 4. Havens, George Remington, 1890-   —Bibliography. I.
Williams, Charles G. S., ed. II. Havens, George Remington, 1890-
PQ263.L5   914.4'03'34   74-23240
ISBN 0-8142-0193-8

Table of Contents

TABLE OF CONTENTS

Foreword

During his long and productive academic life, Professor George Remington Havens has been blessed with many close friends, devoted colleagues, and faithful students, many of whom would have been better qualified than I am to present this volume and the man it is meant to honor. For although it has been my pleasure to become acquainted with George Havens on the occasion of those meetings at which lovers of the French eighteenth century are fond of gathering, in the Statlers and Hiltons that are our substitutes for La Briche, La Chevrette, La Grandval, or Les Délices of yore, he is really known to me almost exclusively through his publications, letters, and his reputation.

It seems safe to conjecture, therefore, that the editor of this volume has wished on the one hand, to assign the task of writing the foreword to one of the many in the world who have been the so-to-speak anonymous beneficiaries of Professor Havens's good works; and on the other hand, that he has probably also intended to make sure that the impeccable standards of historical objectivity for which Professor Havens is so justly famous not be distorted on this occasion by close personal bonds of affection, or adumbrated by excessive sentimentality.

Be that as it may, the following remarks result perforce not from subjective experience but from a dispassionate examination of the record. To put it another way, their author was left with no choice but simply to try to behave like a historian when writing about a man who is himself one. In this sense at least, "tout est pour le mieux dans le meilleur des mondes possibles."

Nor ought this aphorism be thought to be the sign of an altogether ironical, let alone cynical, attitude. The faith in progress, which is related to Panglossian caricatural optimism, was shared by many of the writers whom Mr. Havens has spent his life studying. Yet it has, as we know, fallen into disrepute since. No doubt it was excessive in its heyday; but so is today the discredit it suffers. Friends and admirers of Professor Havens can fortunately find evidence for reborn faith by simply observing the progress achieved during his lifetime by the two causes to which he has most contributed in person: the university that he has served and the field of scholarship that he has cultivated.

In grateful recognition of his leading role in making his academic home one of the great universities of this country, and its Department of Romance Languages one of the truly distinguished ones, the Ohio State University awarded him in 1965 the honorary degree of Doctor of Humane Letters, with a citation from which the following excerpt speaks to the first consideration above:

> A stalwart champion of higher education and academic excellence, he has made many contributions as scholar, teacher, director, counselor, and animator of productive research. He has provided sound judgment, resourcefulness, and unflagging energy as a leader at the departmental, college, and university levels. The Graduate School, the University Library, and the University Press are greatly indebted to him for his ceaseless, ardent, and cogent efforts in their behalf.

In more than one way, Professor Havens has carried his service to the Ohio State University beyond the call of duty. During the years following his retirement in 1961, he accepted, for instance, to write a chronicle of his own department from the early days of the university to its centenary in

1970. The seventy-two-page mimeographed *History of the Department of Romance Languages at the Ohio State University* that resulted from his archival work is incidentally a far more readable and arresting piece of writing than one would be led to assume from its title alone or from its private printing.

A few years before Ohio State conferred upon him the Doctorate of Humane Letters, in 1959 the University of Michigan had already selected Mr. Havens for the same high academic honor, thus testifying that his beneficial influence had been felt beyond the confines of his own campus. Nor should it be assumed that this gesture was merely the effect of some sort of good-neighbor policy between adjoining states, for there is nothing regional, let alone parochial, about Professor Havens's reputation. Indeed, regardless of his unswerving loyalty to the university on whose faculty he has served for forty-two years, he has also taught at no fewer than eight other institutions.

At the time of his initial appointment at Ohio State, in 1919, as a young graduate from Amherst College (Class of 1913), he had already taught at the Riverview Military Academy of Poughkeepsie, at the Mt. Vernon Collegiate Institute of Baltimore, and at Indiana University. He had also found time to do war service at Plattsburg and Camp Taylor, and to work in France after the Armistice with the *Foyer du Soldat* at Poitiers, Angoulême, and Ham. And no sooner had he settled in Columbus than Princeton tried—unsuccessfully—to lure him away. Moreover, during his career at Ohio State, he has served as visiting professor for the summer on the faculties of Johns Hopkins, Columbia, Chicago, the University of California, and the University of Pennsylvania.

Once we add to this record his long and active involvement in the affairs of the Modern Language Association—to limit this selective inventory to his strictly professional activities—we marvel all the more at the volume, variety, and sustained quality of his scholarly publications, for a complete list of which the reader is referred to pages 387–98 of this book. For if those of us who tend nowadays to be skeptical about progress in general can at least take heart in observing the continuous advance, during the last half-century, of American scholarship dealing with the French Enlightenment, this comforting phenomenon is in no small measure directly attributable to George R. Havens.

When he received in 1917 the Ph.D. degree from the Johns Hopkins University for his thesis *The Abbé Prévost and English Literature,* he had almost no predecessor on this continent for this kind of scholarship in which he was going to excel. Thus his life corresponds precisely to a period of unprecedented development and prosperity for the very studies to which he has devoted himself. He belongs to the generation of the pioneers; and the reason our field of scholarship so thrives nowadays is because theirs was also a generation of giants.

Two of them, above all others, although slightly younger than Professor Havens, must be mentioned here. They have been closely associated with him in their work, and remain indissolubly linked with him in the idyllic and exalting dream-world that we of the later generations conjure in our imagination of the nascent state of eighteenth-century French studies in the United States at the time of World War I and shortly thereafter. Also they were kind and charitable enough to come to the rescue of this hapless chronicler. Realizing that he had been asked to practice the most treacherous genre after that of introducing the president of the United States, that of the foreword, and so under unusually adverse conditions, since he could not leaven his remarks, according to the strict ritual that governs the genre, with personal anecdotes, these two other members of the generation of giants have shared with him some of their memories, and thus provided him with the most precious documents in his research.

The first of these gentlemen, Ira O. Wade, Emeritus Professor of French at Princeton, whose tribute and contribution appears in this volume, recalls that "among my academic friends George is my oldest and for my money my most reasonable one." And Mr. Wade goes on reminiscing thus:

> He was completing his graduate work in Hopkins when I arrived in 1914 as a Freshman. We lived in the same rooming house, ate in the same student pension, went for walks almost daily into Druid Hill Park as we exchanged a very artificial conversation in order to keep our French fluid. These were the mechanics of student life however. George, who was a little older and very sensible, was invaluable in keeping me a little steady. I have always been thankful for those days with him and more than grateful for his company.

As for the other member of this noble trio, Emeritus Professor Norman L. Torrey of Columbia University, rather than add his own scholarly study to our collective endeavor, chose to couch his contribution in the more personal genre, eminently congenial to all faithful *dix-huitiémistes*, of the familiar letter:

> I first met George at a MLA meeting at Harvard in 1925, when I gave a paper on Voltaire and the English Deists. I announced my hope of going to Russia to check, under the auspices of a newly established cultural relations exchange. George said he had had the same idea, so we labored together among Voltaire's books in Leningrad in the summer of 1926. The next year we gave a joint report on Voltaire's library at the MLA meeting and then published our joint endeavors in *PMLA* and the *Fortnightly Review*.
>
> When I told George that my work schedule at Yale was so heavy that I couldn't write up any more articles, he came down on me hard, saying that I *had* to write if I hoped to have a career. I followed his advice. Ever since, he has been my mentor, my judicious and friendly critic.
>
> Among other ties, we both owed a great debt to Gustave Lanson. He published George's early articles on Rousseau in *RHL* and encouraged him in many ways. I visited Lanson at the École Normale and told him of my idea of working on Voltaire and the English Deists. He not only was enthusiastic but gave me many helpful hints for procedure. George was

Lanson's foremost ardent supporter and defender this side of the Atlantic.

My friendship with George Havens over a span of nearly fifty years has been a treasured memory. The thoroughness and high standards of his scholarship and his complete honesty are matched only by his ingrained modesty.

Testimonies by eyewitnesses are of singularly high value, as Voltaire discovered when working on his *Siècle de Louis XIV*, even when they cannot help but be also testimonials. From the firsthand experience of these two lifelong friends and confreres of George Havens, we could sketch a portrait of the man we are honoring; and we could also understand how the features that would appear in this portrait—modesty, honesty, seriousness, hard work, sound judgment—qualified him so well for his pioneering role.

Now, should there be among scholars and critics of the later generations some who, considering themselves—even with some justice—to be pioneers in their own right, should be skeptical about the claims to this status of a scholar whose methods of research, inspired by Lanson, they would consider old-fashioned, their skepticism ought to be easily dispelled by the following two considerations, one quite concrete, the other more theoretical.

The first simply has to do with Professor Havens's scholarly writings. Let us take a few examples from a long list.

To publish in 1921 a thesis entitled *The Abbé Prévost and English Literature* was bold to the point of temerity, both because it illustrated the still very new methods of what was then becoming known as comparative literature, and because Prévost's stature in those days did not begin to compare to that to which it has now been raised.

To travel in 1926 from Columbus to Leningrad in order to take a look at Voltaire's library was not only a remarkably imaginative venture, but must also have been especially at that date a real adventure, not unworthy perhaps of comparison with Diderot's long ride to the same city a century and a half earlier.

xiv

To publish in 1946 the first critical edition of Rousseau's first major work was not only an innovative and courageous undertaking but one of lasting influence. When the same text was edited again in 1964 in the Pléiade *Œuvres complètes* series, the editors of the volume in which it appeared felt it necessary to refer no fewer than fifty-three times to George Havens in their notes.

To edit in 1951 the first critical bibliography of French eighteenth-century literature, jointly with Donald F. Bond, was again an unprecedented accomplishment, which to this date has not been superseded.

And so it goes. Examples of this kind seem to indicate that the originality and value of scholarship do not necessarily have to rest on the invention of new methods of approach, but can result from a diligent and intelligent application of tried-and-true methods to new objects of inquiry, provided these are chosen with good taste and good judgment.

In the new *Querelle des Anciens et des Modernes* that has in the last few years divided and stimulated practitioners of literary history and criticism, as in the older one, the winners tend to be those whose intellectual powers prevail, regardless of the side they have chosen.

But one should not succumb to the temptation of pedantry, especially when writing about a man so free himself of this vice of our profession. It is, however, admittedly harder to avoid all pomposity when reviewing the career of a man whose renown is greater than one's own, and especially when one is charged with the responsibility of spokemanship for so broad, distinguished, and ardent a group of admirers and friends.

And since we, somewhat belatedly, are trying to apply the brakes on rhetoric and platitudes, let us also try to resist another temptation. As we look back in nostalgia at the golden age when the young Amherst graduate was one of the earliest American scholars to break into print in those seemingly impregnable bastions of French academic life the *Revue d'histoire littéraire de la France* and the *Revue de littérature comparée*, let us not sigh tearfully about "the good old days," and philosophize on the irreversibility of time. Not only because many of us were not there to bear witness to the legendary goodness of those bygone days, but more importantly because this is not a story of rise and decline or of lost paradises. The line linking students and teachers is an uninterrupted one in which we play both roles in succession as in that of the generations. The advance of scholarship is a sinuous but a continuous one.

Not all of us, bound together in this volume as we are in honoring a great teacher and a great scholar, are addicted to the same methodological predilections or to the same literary tastes. Nor have we all taken Professor Havens's courses, or written dissertations under his guidance. But we have all been his readers, and have benefited in the process; and all of us, students and teachers of literature and history in the Age of Ideas, are in his debt.

This book perhaps has no other unity, but none other would be more fitting.

Georges May

Preface

The title of this volume, *Literature and History in the Age of Ideas*, will immediately suggest to those familiar with the writings of George R. Havens the title of his intellectual history *The Age of Ideas: From Reaction to Revolution*. It will also suggest for those who know the "livingness" of that history, which vividly illustrates the principle that "ideas live only in people," one preoccupation of his scholarship. Textual and bibliographical scholarship, analyses of the genesis of individual works and of the evolution of ideas, have led always to the broadest historical and humanistic focuses in Professor Havens's scrutiny of the doctrine of the *Encyclopédie* —that men are only what ideas have made them. His preoccupation in that scrutiny has constantly been to clarify the complex interactions of books and ideas, in eighteenth-century Frenchmen's rethinking of their past, their present, and their future directions, with the men, the material conditions, and the institutions of a France evolving "from reaction to revolution." With the scope and diversity that the general topic of this volume has been given by its contributors— from essays in bibliography, on the conditions of the book trade, in the history of science and of political theory, general considerations of historical writing and literary genres, the evolution of the Enlightenment and its heritages, to the series of essays on individual works of *philosophes* and men of letters—a number of orders of presentation would have been possible. The most prudent arrangement might well have been, following Bayle's example, an alphabetical one.

The essays in this volume have been arranged, however, perhaps less prudently, but in the spirit of *The Age of Ideas*, by subject in a broadly chronological order. The essays on Voltaire, whose presence is, moreover, very often felt in the volume, on Rousseau, and on Diderot, have been grouped together, nonchronologically, as have been three essays on books, which are further linked by the common but diversely illustrated subterfuges of clandestinity. A first grouping of essays, whose subjects and chronology suggest "Beginnings" in an Age of Ideas, designated itself naturally in those essays that examine the new alignment of the arts and the new rhetoric of the *Querelle des Anciens et des Modernes*; the new history that emerges from the pyrrhonist and humanist traditions; the consolidation of experimental science and of Newton's influence in France; Montesquieu's transformation of journalistic sources into the satiric art of *Les Lettres persanes*; the making of a *philosophe* in that intellectual circle around Jean Bouhier, from the late 1720s to the 1730s, in which Cuenz worked toward a synthesis resembling Voltaire's during the Cirey years. Similarly, the four concluding essays of the volume suggested quite as naturally the heading of "Heritages," as they examine the ideological and creative reactions of Lamartine and of Stendhal to the heritages of the Enlightenment, readership of French texts in the American eighteenth century, and conclude with a personal essay on the conscience of the Enlightenment. But what was less clear, if headings were to be given, was the point at which "Beginnings" as a section was to end or that at which "Heritages" was to begin. The majority of the essays that treat Voltaire, Rousseau, and Diderot, tendencies of thought or trends in literature, explore beginnings—of individual thought to come into contact with itself, of literary creativity to find its expressive resources, and of both to mobilize the tactics of clandestine organization and public challenge. The ever-present "beginnings" of all authentic intellectual activity and artistic creation preclude finally—as do the "heritages" of this Age of

Ideas situated in the continuity of traditions of other ages of ideas—all but the most hypothetical subdivisions.

At each stage in the planning, editing, and completion of this volume, I have found nothing but good will, good wishes, and good advice. I wish especially to thank Professor Otis Fellows and Professor Georges May for their wisely practical advice and generous encouragement. The encouragement and assistance of the chairman of the Department of Romance Languages, Professor David Griffin, of Professor John Rule of the Ohio State Department of History, of Dr. Richard Armitage, Professors Eleanor Bulatkin, and Walter Meiden, and of Mr. Weldon Kefauver and Mr. Robert Demorest of the Ohio State University Press, have also greatly aided my completion of this book. It has been a privilege and a great personal pleasure to edit and to offer this volume of studies from former students, colleagues, and friends, to Professor Havens and to offer to students of the eighteenth century in France the bibliography of his writings to date. The project of this volume of studies was born in conversations with the late Robert Mitchell, professor of French at the University of Pittsburgh, whose work with Professor Havens on Voltaire's *Mahomet*, long in revision, was to have enriched this collection of essays. His death before the project took shape has deprived me of the keen-minded discussions of it he certainly would have engaged in and saddens all of his colleagues who looked forward with pleasure and confidence to reading his final positions in those now interrupted discussions.

C.G.S.W.

Literature and History
in the Age of Ideas

Fontenelle, Perrault
And the Realignment of the Arts

HUGH M. DAVIDSON

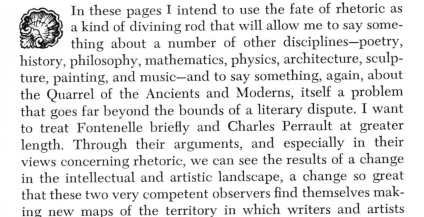 In these pages I intend to use the fate of rhetoric as a kind of divining rod that will allow me to say something about a number of other disciplines—poetry, history, philosophy, mathematics, physics, architecture, sculpture, painting, and music—and to say something, again, about the Quarrel of the Ancients and Moderns, itself a problem that goes far beyond the bounds of a literary dispute. I want to treat Fontenelle briefly and Charles Perrault at greater length. Through their arguments, and especially in their views concerning rhetoric, we can see the results of a change in the intellectual and artistic landscape, a change so great that these two very competent observers find themselves making new maps of the territory in which writers and artists and thinkers do their work.

What are we talking about specifically? The answer is, I think, productive techniques, kinds of knowledge, mental categories: all abstract and ambiguous entities—though no less real for that. Indeed, these abstractions are deceitful, for they gather about themselves concrete myths, imagery, and even kinds of pathos. They form one factor in seventeenth-century creative activity, certainly not the only one, but one that is indispensable. (In art, as in metaphysics, what is necessary may very well not be sufficient.) In other words, in dealing with disciplines and categories, I do not mean to overlook or to undervalue other factors more in tune with our own reflexes, like the experience of the author (with its conscious and unconscious elements), tragic reactions to the human condition, idealism, paths to freedom, *honnêteté, mondanité, crise de conscience, lumières,* and other such principles that we apply in interpreting classical and postclassical literature. My point is that Fontenelle and Perrault seem unable to think without having recourse to the ideas and techniques that I am about to treat.

One further preliminary remark. The history of intellectual and artistic disciplines has to grapple with an extraordinarily complex and unstable reality, made up of varying dosages of choice, logic, chance, and fashion. More precisely: in speaking of a realignment of the arts I do not mean to suggest an abrupt shift, because on close examination one usually finds continuity. Clearly a trend lies behind the *Digression sur les Anciens et les Modernes* and the *Parallèle des Anciens et des Modernes.* General interest in science, for example, had been growing for several decades. The success of Lémery's *Cours de chimie* (1675) inspired Fontenelle to remark that "il se vendit comme un ouvrage de galanterie ou de satire." Mme de Grignan was an enthusiastic Cartesian. Boileau pictures thus Mme de la Sablière:

> Un astrolabe à la main, elle a dans sa gouttière
> A suivre Jupiter passé la nuit entière.
> *(Satire* 10.429-30)

There is a lot of evidence of a more serious kind that one might adduce.

The sixteen pages of the *Digression* (1688) contain a startling demotion of rhetoric and poetry. The general question has to do—as we all know—with the relative position of the Ancients and Moderns. Fontenelle answers it, to his own satisfaction, at least, by comparing men to trees: if nature produces trees as tall today as in ancient times, there is no reason to suppose that the creative powers she distributes to men are weaker in the present than in the past. I have not used in

4

this "proof," says Fontenelle pointedly, flights of eloquence: "J'ai cru que le plus court était de consulter un peu sur tout ceci la physique, qui a le secret d'abréger bien des contestations que la rhétorique rend infinies" (p. 164).

A few paragraphs later Fontenelle does something quite radical: turning to psychology and the faculties of the soul, he assigns eloquence and poetry mainly to the imagination, and then physics, medicine, and mathematics to reasoning ("raisonnement"). By this one stroke the intellectual seriousness and respectability of rhetoric is undermined. Generally speaking, in the seventeenth century, for a discipline to be dependent on imagination is a bad sign: Pascal, Spinoza, and Malebranche, to cite three notable examples, agreed in thinking it the mistress of error. And again, we must consider Fontenelle's *additive* notion of the way in which sciences and arts are constituted. At any moment they consist of a collection or sum of views ("un amas de vues") and rules. If we accept this, he can lead us to another unflattering conclusion: eloquence and poetry require only a limited number of these views and rules in order to reach their perfection as arts, whereas physics, medicine and mathematics are composed of an infinite number of views.

Fontenelle sums everything up devastatingly:

> Pour ce qui est de l'éloquence et de la poésie, qui font le sujet de la principale contestation entre les anciens et les modernes, quoiqu'elles ne soient pas en elles-mêmes fort importantes, je crois que les anciens en ont pu atteindre la perfection, parce que, comme j'ai dit, on la peut atteindre en peu de siècles. (p. 167)[1]

Here we see the specific terms (*éloquence* and *poésie*) in which he understands the central issue of the Quarrel and how he will deal with it, unblinkingly. In Greece and Rome excellence in public speaking led to the highest honors and positions. But that is all changed; rhetoric has no such utility now. As for poetry, well:

5

La poésie au contraire n'était bonne à rien, et ç'a été toujours la même chose dans toutes sortes de gouvernements; ce vice-là lui est bien essentiel. (p. 168)

Even if one allows for irony in this judgment, it hurts.

As we put down the *Digression*, we know that we have left behind the notion—inscribed in the program of the Academy and often echoed on many levels of what was said and thought in the seventeenth-century literature that we call classical—the notion of rhetoric as a basic and unavoidable discipline, as the cornerstone of a *quadrivium* made up of eloquence, poetics, history, and philosophy: in Fontenelle's hands it has been narrowed to oratory, tied to the imagination, assimilated to poetry, shown to be irrelevant to the facts of political life, and set in invidious contrast with other disciplines.

In some ways it is hard to imagine two works more different than Fontenelle's pamphlet and the four ample volumes of Perrault's *Parallèle des Anciens et des Modernes*. But the relationship is obvious: Perrault elaborates in the latter what is sketched in the former. (And he is also continuing, of course, to develop themes from his poem *Le Siècle de Louis le Grand*, which had caused a sensation when read to the Academy in 1687.) His undertaking is spread over the period from 1688 to 1697: in 1688 the first volume (containing the first two of what was to be a set of five long dialogues) appeared, to be followed in 1690, 1692, and 1697 by volumes completing the series. Within the framework of a two-day visit to Versailles —that *image de notre siècle*, as he says—Perrault shows us a Président, an Abbé, and a Chevalier, who examine first the "préjugé" in favor of the Ancients, then the status of the arts and sciences as divided into (1) architecture, sculpture, and painting; (2) eloquence and poetry; and (3) a mixed but important bag, ranging from astronomy to gardening and cooking, with a final bit on fireworks. For my purposes it seems best to start *in medias res*, with the question of eloquence.

6

From that we can work out toward a view of Perrault's "système," as he calls it from time to time.

Like Fontenelle, Perrault is capable at moments of using rhetoric in the narrow sense of oratory, but for the most part he reverts to a broad conception: rhetoric is once more the basis of *belles-lettres*. The Abbé, the Président and the Chevalier discuss, à propos of eloquence: Plato and Aristotle—not as philosophers, not as two great sources in any theorizing about rhetoric, but as writers, and their works are judged as examples of expository discourse; the histories of Thucydides and Livy; dialogues (here they praise Pascal's *Lettres provinciales*); fables; novels; allegories; literary correspondence; Demosthenes and Cicero; Theophrastus and La Bruyère; the speeches of Le Maistre; and sermons. In short, the area over which rhetoric presides directly is that of expression in prose. Moreover, it would not be hard to show that Perrault carried over into the dialogue on poetry the ideas and terms used in the discussion of prose.

Now in the decades when what we call "classical doctrine" and "classical taste" were developing, we often find in critical statements both narrow uses and broad uses of the terms *rhetoric* and *eloquence*. Where, then, is the realignment of the arts promised in my title? The transition that I wish to indicate amounts to this: the superiority of an essentially verbal culture is now debatable in the face of achievements in the nonverbal spheres of plastic arts and music, and in the sciences of nature, where words are less important than things. Rhetoric, and poetry along with it, must in this emergent situation find their proper place. Of course, in line with his thesis, Perrault defends them in their modern state, but what makes his thought particularly interesting is not so much his defense as the attempt that he makes to integrate these formerly supreme arts into his picture and not simply to demote them or to juxtapose them alongside the other arts and sciences. I do not want to oversystematize the *Parallèle*, but there is evidence for this organizing tendency.

For example, the Président opens the discussion of poetry on a sharp note by saying flatly that modern poets can never equal the beauties that one sees in the ancients, because *la fable et les fictions*, which form the most beautiful parts of poetry, cannot be used in a vital way by modern poets. The Abbé counters with a definition:

> La poésie n'est autre chose qu'une peinture agréable, qui représente par la parole tout ce que l'imagination peut concevoir, en donnant presque toujours un corps, une âme, du sentiment et de la vie aux choses qui n'en ont point. (pp. 285-86, 7-8)

This reminds us at once of the phrase from Horace, *ut pictura poesis*, an idea that Perrault takes very seriously; and used as a principle, it obviously can unify, in spite of differences in media, two great areas of creative activity.

But more important, I think, is the fact that essential analogies of poetry, painting, and rhetoric are involved here. Perrault finds three elements in painting: lines, by which one gives to figures their characteristic images; shadings ("les jours et les ombres"), by which the painter causes the objects shown to take on relief and volume; and colors, the natural colors of things, by which he achieves true and complete likenesses. These elements have their counterparts in language. You will note in the following lines the unmistakable references to the main topics of rhetoric.

> Les mêmes choses se rencontrent dans l'art qui conduit la parole: les termes simples et ordinaires dont on se sert dans le langage le plus commun, sont comme le premier trait et la première délinéation des pensées que l'on veut exprimer; les mouvements et les figures de la rhétorique, qui donnent du relief au discours, sont les jours et les ombres qui les font avancer ou reculer dans le tableau: et enfin les descriptions ornées, les épithètes vives, et les métaphores hardies sont comme les couleurs naturelles dont les objets sont revêtus et par lesquelles ils nous apparaissent tels qu'ils sont dans la vérité. (p. 286, 8-9)

8

We have, therefore, two parallel sequences: lines, chiaroscuro effects, and colors matched with common terms, figures, and verbal ornaments.

Actually, in the earlier dialogue on architecture, sculpture, and painting, Perrault had laid the groundwork for a far-reaching integration of all the arts. Lines, shadings, and colors were there, but his distinction of the three parts of a painting came out somewhat differently.

> Pour bien me faire entendre, il faut que je distingue trois choses dans la peinture: la réprésentation des figures, l'expression des passions et la composition du tout ensemble. (p. 153, 209)

These three topics—figures, passions, composition—appear in one guise or another throughout most of the rest of the dialogue. They guide Perrault in analyzing particular works (*The Pilgrims of Emmaus* by Veronese and *The Family of Darius* by Lebrun) and in sketching a history of painting as well as in setting up parallels with other arts, such as music or eloquence. Each of the three parts of painting corresponds to a psychological power.

> Car il faut remarquer que comme la peinture a trois parties qui la composent, il y a aussi trois parties dans l'homme par où il en est touché, les sens, le cœur, et la raison. (p. 154, 213)

And so the delineation of objects with their colors strikes the eye agreeably; the expression of feelings in the attitudes and faces of the figures touches the heart; and, in the picture taken as a whole, gradations of light, shade, and proportion please reason.

The Abbé adds: "Il en est de même des ouvrages de tous les autres arts" (p. 154, 214). He keeps up for a while this process of arranging things in chains of proportions. In music, sounds and voices appeal to the ear, expressive changes in the voices to the heart, and the harmony of the parts to the mind. In eloquence, the diction and gestures affect the senses, the figures win the heart, and the general plan or economy of the speech satisfies the mind. Such is the key to his unifying scheme: three aspects of art and three aspects of the human psyche are distinguished; the two lists are seen to correspond; and on the side of art, one arrives at a synoptic view that links the arts by analogies, while at the same time, on the side of man, one arrives at a corresponding table of effects and pleasures.

Another kind of unity appears in a comparison of the two paintings. The Abbé admits that Veronese's picture is very beautiful, but, he adds,

> comme un tableau est un poème muet, où l'unité de lieu, de temps et d'action doit être encore plus religieusement observée que dans un poème véritable, parce que le lieu y est immuable, le temps indivisible, et l'action momentanée, voyons comment cette règle est observée dans ce tableau. (p. 156, 223)

Veronese's people are assembled in the same place, but they do not cooperate in a single action; the painter seems to have put them together arbitrarily, whereas Lebrun does everything in a more regular fashion.

> Je ne crois pas que nous ayons aucun de ces reproches à faire au tableau de la famille de Darius. C'est un véritable poème où toutes les règles sont observées (p. 157, 226-27).

And so, the Horatian formula turns out to be reversible: *ut poesis pictura.*

There is one last area to be added to this "système": the sciences. Perrault does not have a neat map of this sector. In it lie parts of philosophy—logic, morals, metaphysics, physics—and mathematics and those spectacularly successful modern arts or sciences—like navigation, geography, astronomy—that depend on accurate observation and precise measurement. What Perrault does in order to bring these fields into line with

10

the other arts we have been discussing makes a complicated story that I can only refer to here. Suffice it to say that, in his mind, these renewed and corrected disciplines, clearly superior in their modern forms to what the Ancients had, may be reduced to ensembles of *vues* and *règles,* of conclusions and of techniques. And so we find ourselves using once more the same vocabulary that served in analyzing eloquence, poetry, sculpture, architecture, painting, and music. (Fontenelle had used this vocabulary, too.)

Now it might seem that rhetoric, which by its shifting relative position has given us some insight into the restructuring of an ensemble of disciplines, would now go out of the picture in the treatment of natural and other sciences. That is not the case, however. Perrault's definition—and then redefinition—of rhetoric will show what I mean.

> Pour y procéder avec ordre je crois que nous devons commencer par convenir de ce que c'est que l'éloquence. Cicéron que nous reconnaissons tous pour un excellent maître en donne plusieurs définitions. L'éloquence, dit-il, consiste à parler avec abondance et avec ornement; l'orateur, dit-il ailleurs, n'est autre chose qu'un homme de probité qui parle bien, et dans un autre endroit il dit qu'être éloquent c'est savoir dire des choses qui persuadent. (p. 190, 41)

The Chevalier makes immediately one of his little jokes: "Je crois que Cicéron a fait la première de ces définitions pour lui-même: car il parle fort abondamment" (p. 190, 41-42). Then the Abbé (i.e., Perrault), in a decisive move inspired in great part—I am convinced—by the *Art de penser* or *Logique* of Port-Royal, leaves all those definitions behind.

> Je voudrais donc que l'éloquence en général ne fût autre chose que l'art de bien parler selon la nature du sujet que l'on traite, et selon les lieux, les temps et les personnes. (p. 190, 42-43)

This way of conceiving rhetoric establishes in one sentence the general perspective in which all the dialogues of the *Pa-*

11

rallèle become truly intelligible, and by the same token, the perspective in which the exact sciences will be treated. Rhetoric involves itself in a work of mediation between specialists in the arts and sciences—who must be allowed their technicalities wherever necessary—on the one hand, and on the other, readers who are not *savants*, whose times, places, and persons must be taken into account. What I am saying is that the realignment of the arts and sciences toward which Fontenelle to some degree and Perrault in a much ampler way are moving includes rhetoric (1) as one among many elements in the system and (2) as a pervasive instrument that is needed if the system itself is to be brought into being and made accessible. In the second case we have the comprehensive art of expression once more, but not exactly in the sense favored by earlier, more "classical" theorists. In the earlier phase of the discussion, when it was the basis of *belles-lettres*, rhetoric sought to guide writers who had something to *create* in writing; in its new role it provides a relevant line of thought to those who have something to *communicate* in writing.

If at times we are very conscious of the weaknesses and superficialities of the *Parallèle*, we must on the whole recognize the skill, tact, and good humor that inform it. Anecdotes, facts, erudition, contemporary allusions: the author knows how to use them all in realizing his plan. He and his public were struggling with the original form of what we have come to know in the twentieth century as the problem of the "two cultures," one mainly verbal and inventive and the other scientific and investigative. By 1688 the latter had become so imposing that some kind of mutual adjustment was required. Indeed, Perrault does more than bring the "two cultures" together, since he is *au courant* of what has happened in a third area, that of the plastic arts. In the context of use and enjoyment he unifies the arts by referring their effects to a certain image of man—with his powers of sense, feeling, and reason; and in the context of production he unifies both arts and sci-

12

ences by referring them again to man—specifically, to taste
and imagination for the arts and to reason and sense for the
sciences.

In short, what Perrault did in the *Parallèle* was to illustrate
—at times brilliantly—a kind of encyclopedic thinking that
makes of him a worthy forerunner of Diderot and his collabo-
rators. Like them, he saw the possibility of drawing up an inventory of knowledge that would discriminate, unify, and
popularize.

1. My quotations from Fontenelle are taken from Robert Shackleton's
edition of the *Entretiens sur la pluralité des mondes* and the *Digression
sur les Anciens et les Moderns* (Oxford: Clarendon Press, 1955); those from
Perrault are taken from the *Parallèle des Anciens et des Modernes en ce qui
regarde les arts et les sciences* as reprinted in 1964 by Eidos Verlag München.
With introductory material by H. R. Jauss and M. Imdahl, it forms volume
2 of the series "Theorie und Geschichte der Literatur und der schönen
Künste." Page references given in the text are to this reprint (first series)
and to the original edition.

Historical Pyrrhonism and
Enlightenment Historiography in France

Historical Pyrrhonism has always been with us; but if it has been most succinctly summarized in the twentieth century in the famous words of Henry Ford, it was most fully expounded, at the end of the seventeenth, by Pierre Bayle, above all in his *Dictionnaire historique et critique*. If the crisis of doubt about the reliability of history can be assigned to any period, it is to the decades that precede and follow the year 1700. Here, I wish to examine the reasons for this crisis and to consider some of the ways in which the early eighteenth century tried to surmount it, thus paving the way for the major historical writings of the Enlightenment. The subject is a vast one, and what follows can do little more than offer guidelines for a more thorough study yet to be undertaken.

If the art of history is as old as Herodotus, the science of history dates largely from the Renaissance and the Reformation. Serving at first as the handmaiden of theological and political controversy, it rapidly emancipated itself. By the end of the seventeenth century it was capable of dictating, at times, to its former masters.

In the seventeenth century the French contribution to the development of this science was outstanding. The compilations of Duchesne and Baluze opened the way to new knowledge of the Middle Ages, and the lexicographical studies of Du Cange offered a new key to the interpretation of rediscovered texts. The Bollandist *Acta Sanctorum* and the Benedictine *Annales* showed that even hagiography could be critical. It was a disagreement between these two religious orders that led Mabillon, in his *De re diplomatica*, to produce the first textbook of the new science of diplomatics. His companion, Montfaucon, was soon to perform a similar service for Greek paleography.[1] Meanwhile, chronology was becoming exact enough to challenge the authority of the biblical text itself; archaeology and numismatics advanced sufficiently for a historian at the end of the seventeenth century to write a universal history "proved" by evidence derived from them,[2] and this evidence was of a nature to silence even the otherwise skeptical Hardouin.[3]

Potentially, these developments were of great importance. Yet they were developments in the auxiliary sciences, in the tools of the historian's trade, rather than in the writing of history itself. The seventeenth-century *érudit* often stuck to lexicography or genealogy or concentrated on the compilation of texts. He was perhaps right to do so, for it was to the accurate establishment of texts that many of the new critical methods most naturally led. They did not provide criteria for assessing whether what the text said was true; still less did they offer guidelines for the development of historical explanation or the construction of historical narrative. Nor were the *érudits* unaware of their limitations. The learned Jansenist Tillemont, for example, spoke of his own *Histoire des empereurs* as merely a preparatory compilation for the work of the real historians, the "génies les plus beaux et les plus élevés" who could not be expected to "arrêter le feu qui les anime" to indulge in laborious discussions of minor points of fact.[4] Many others made a similar absolute distinction between the erudite critic and the historian proper.[5] For no one in the seventeenth century doubted that Clio was a muse.

The devotees of the muse meditated their mistress with varying degrees of strictness and with varied success. But they have enough in common to be classed together, in opposition both to the *érudits* and to the "philosophic" historians of the eighteenth century, as belonging to what has been

16

termed the "humanist" school of historiography. They took as their models the historians of antiquity (particularly Livy and Sallust) and as their theoretical guides the writings of Lucan and Cicero. Cicero's discussion of history in his *De Oratore* is constantly referred to as an authority and could well serve as an introduction to most seventeenth-century historical writing.[6]

The humanist historians had two types of aim: didactic and artistic. In theory, at any rate, the former was by far the more important. Men must "voir dans l'histoire, comme dans un miroir, l'image de leurs fautes," wrote Saint-Réal.[7] The Jesuit Le Moyne and the Cartesian Cordemoy express similar sentiments.[8] So, too, of course, do many eighteenth-century writers such as Fénelon and Rollin.[9] The *philosophes* themselves do not abandon this concept, though with them the "lessons" of history become social and political. They had been political, too, in an earlier age, but as La Bruyère remarked, "les grands sujets" were taboo in Louis XIV's reign; and historiography, in the main, ceased to provide a forum for the discussion of social or political issues.

If the historian could not study society, he could study man. A consequence of the relative interdiction of political themes was a greater interest in human nature—a tendency closely linked with the psychological interests of the salons and of the masters of classical literature. It is symptomatic, perhaps, that Louis XIV could choose Racine and Boileau as his royal historiographers. Theorists of "humanist" historiography took a similar view. Saint-Réal made a direct attack on political history and called his own method "une anatomie spirituelle des actions humaines."[10] Rapin urged the historian to concentrate on the study of motives—especially the more curious and unusual ones.[11] Another Jesuit, Le Moyne, even insisted on the alliance of history and poetry,[12] thereby provoking the scornful comments of Bayle.[13]

The danger implicit in this is obvious. If history is a school of politics, it must strive for factual accuracy, for without that no "lesson" can be valid. But if the lesson of history is to be

17

moral and psychological, such accuracy is not essential. Provided that the portrayal of character is true to life, the narrative of events, though it should be *vraisemblable*, has no need to be *vrai*. The dividing line between history and the historical novel tends to disappear. "Pourvu que l'on suive la vraysemblance dans les choses douteuses, on instruit autant ceux qui lisent l'histoire que si on disoit la vérité," says Cordemoy.[14] Historians like Varillas, Saint-Réal, and Vertot put this view into practice, manipulating the facts of history with the same freedom as Racine.[15] They are further encouraged to do so, moreover, by the emphasis that the theorists place on form. "La forme qu'on doit donner à l'histoire est ce qu'elle a de plus essentiel," says Rapin;[16] and Fénelon, though in many ways he exemplifies a new spirit, re-echoes this view when he states that "la principale perfection d'une histoire consiste dans l'ordre et dans l'arrangement."[17] Voltaire, of course, can still say something very similar,[18] but fortunately he is incapable of following his own advice. Moreover, "form" in the eighteenth century is no longer so formal as it was in the seventeenth, when a strict reliance on classical models seemed obligatory and imaginary portraits, harangues, debates, and other stylized rhetorical devices were *de rigueur*. Le Moyne, perhaps the most "literary" of the theorists, insists that "harangues are necessary in history"; and Rapin, though somewhat more skeptical, has no objection to a few "petits discours à propos."[19]

All these psychological and literary preoccupations leave little room for a concern for factual accuracy. D'Alembert relates the following story of Varillas.

> On représentoit à un historien du dernier siècle, connu par ses mensonges, qu'il avoit altéré la vérité dans la narration d'un fait; "cela se peut, dit-il, mais qu'importe? le fait n'est-il pas mieux tel que je l'ai raconté?"[20]

And Vertot's reaction to the belated arrival of the documents he needed—"J'en suis fâché, mais mon siège est fait"—has become proverbial.

18

Of course, the "humanist" historians could, and often did, search for the facts. The search, however, did not always take them very far. Daniel, writing his *Histoire de France* at the beginning of the eighteenth century, shows some evidence of the new critical spirit. Yet he could still write, in the Introduction to that work:

> La Citation des Manuscrits fait encore beaucoup d'honneur à un Auteur. J'en ai un assés grand nombre. Mais je dirai de bonne foi que cette lecture m'a donné plus de peine qu'elle ne m'a procuré d'avantage.[21]

Moreover, the first part of Daniel's statement is not altogether true, for the historians are constantly being warned against the bad taste of displaying too much erudition. Saint-Réal objects to "un grand nombre de Dates, de Noms, et d'Evénemens."[22] Cordemoy admires Herodotus because "il n'apporte rarement les preuves de ce qu'il dit" and asserts of such proofs that "comme elles interrompent toujours la narration, elles sont toujours fort désagréables."[23] Even Fénelon insists that the good historian "retranche toute dissertation où l'érudition d'un savant veut être étalée."[24] Indeed, the conflict between a desire to demonstrate one's accuracy and a resolve to avoid the pedantic display of erudition remains a characteristic of much eighteenth-century historiography.

Thus, while the "antiquarian" historian was acquiring new skills, "popular" history was approximating more and more to the historical novel. It is hardly surprising that this state of affairs produced growing uncertainty and growing skepticism.

Nor was an appeal to the philosophers likely to help remove these doubts. Skepticism about history, as about much else, was characteristic of the *libertins* such as La Mothe le Vayer, whose *Du peu de certitude qu'il y a dans l'histoire* expressed doubts on many traditional beliefs and, more generally, on the veracity of historians who were so often moved by a desire to flatter, or by national prejudice.[25] Truth, moreover, was not his unique concern, for he was humanist enough to say of history that "je l'estimois principalement comme celle qui faisoit les propres fonctions de la Philosophie morale."[26] Here was no way out of the dilemma. Moreover, Cartesianism, increasingly the dominant force in French philosophical thought, was even more radical in doubting the value of the study of history. In the *Discours de la méthode* Descartes himself warned:

> Lorsqu'on est trop curieux des choses qui se pratiquaient aux siècles passés, on demeure ordinairement fort ignorant de celles qui se pratiquent en celui-ci.[27]

"Les sciences des livres" were less likely to produce truth than were "les simples raisonnements que peut faire naturellement un homme de bon sens touchant les choses qui se présentent."[28] Malebranche, if anything, went even further;[29] and Vico, writing nearly a century after the *Discours*, could still complain of the crippling effect of Cartesian thought on historical studies.[30]

"Philosophy" and history were thus at odds; and if Bossuet, in his *Discours sur l'histoire universelle*, appeared for a time to have squared the circle by uniting Augustinian teleology with some aspects of more modern scientific thought, his vision and eloquence could not for long cover up the fact that his compromise was no longer acceptable.[31]

The stage was set for Bayle who, more than any other individual, gave substance to the concept of historical Pyrrhonism. Bayle re-echoed the doubts of Descartes and La Mothe le Vayer, but seemed to go even further when, in the *Critique générale de l'histoire du Calvinisme*, he asserted that:

> Je ne lis presque jamais les Historiens dans la vue de m'instruire des choses qui se sont passées, mais seulement pour savoir ce que l'on dit dans chaque nation et dans chaque parti sur les choses qui se sont passées.[32]

It is true that he later modified this view to the extent of admitting that one would at least be sure that there had been a battle of Jarnac,[33] but this was scant consolation.

20

However, if, like Descartes, Bayle doubted the value of historians, unlike Descartes he still kept on reading them. The results of his studies are visible, above all, in the *Dictionnaire historique et critique*, which in both form and content constitutes the greatest manifestation of historical Pyrrhonism. To demonstrate the truth of this statement would be impossible in an article of this nature, and in any case the task has been performed before.[34] Here it is enough to say that Bayle's "atomization" of history ancient and modern and his merciless demonstration of its errors and uncertainties constitute the essential document of the "bankruptcy of history" of which Paul Hazard has left so lively an account.[35]

It would, of course, be a mistake to see in the publication of the *Dictionnaire* the manifestation of a unique moment of crisis. Historical Pyrrhonism lived on into the eighteenth century. It was not until 1738 that Beaufort effectively demolished the myths of early Roman history,[36] and Voltaire still felt the need to publish a work entitled *Le Pyrrhonisme de l'histoire* in 1769. It is equally true that the answers to some of Bayle's problems would be derived from the technical achievements of his predecessors and that answers to others were being formulated by contemporaries such as Saint-Evremond or Fontenelle. The *Dictionnaire* was not, strictly speaking, a watershed. For the purposes of this article, however, it may serve as such. Henceforth we shall turn our attention to efforts to create a "new" history.

Insofar as the problems involved were methodological, their solution was in part to be found in increased contact between the "humanist" historians and those *érudits* who were already in possession of relatively sophisticated methods. Probably the most important of the institutions that favored such contacts was the Académie des Inscriptions, which, though founded by Colbert, only became important after it had received its royal charter in 1701. Its membership was predominantly scholarly, but its debates had repercussions beyond the narrow world of the antiquarians. Fréret's views on the historical origin of the French and Levesque de

Pouilly's *Dissertation sur l'incertitude des premiers siècles de Rome* were to provoke a wide measure of debate.[37] Moreover, the Académie also contained men like Vertot, most famous for his "siège fait" and for his racy but untrustworthy histories of revolutions. And if Vertot was not altogether at home in this scholarly company, he made every effort to become so, making many contributions to the early proceedings of the Academy.[38]

Increasing concern for scholarly method was to be found elsewhere. Fleury's *Histoire ecclésiastique* of 1691 was a not very critical compilation, but the *Discours* that accompanied it demanded careful citation of contemporary authorities and a close scrutiny of these according to methods that he proceeded to describe.[39] Daniel's *Histoire de France* of 1703 was in many ways an even more unreliable work, but in his preface he showed a real concern with critical method, criticizing harangues as untrue, insisting on the accurate citation of sources, and demanding the unanimous agreement of his authorities before accepting any fact as established.[40] The theorists, moreover, reinforced this attitude. Lenglet du Fresnoy, for example, in his *Méthode pour étudier l'histoire*, which first appeared in 1713 but was later greatly augmented and frequently reprinted, devoted a whole chapter to the discussion of the "Précautions qu'il faut apporter dans la lecture des historiens" and further chapters to the exposition of critical rules. De Juvenel, in his *Principes de l'histoire* of 1733, was far more concerned with critical method than was any seventeenth-century theorist and gave a long and careful list of "les marques les plus évidentes de supposition ou de suspicion."[41] Le Long, in his *Bibliothèque historique de la France*, attributed the improvement he saw in historical writing to "le secours de la saine critique."[42]

Yet this increased awareness of the importance of critical method, significant though it was, could not in itself constitute an adequate foundation for a new historiography. Without the presence of other factors, it could indeed merely have

22

served to reinforce Bayle's Pyrrhonism. Some more positive
sense of purpose was necessary if the historian was not merely
to end up collecting disconnected facts. If the details of
events and the motives of individuals were to remain forever
uncertain, as Voltaire, following others, was repeatedly to
maintain,[43] then narrative history had to find a new form.

Indications as to the nature of this new form are to be
found in the work of one who owes much more to *libertin*
skepticism than to the new methodology of the scholars.
Saint-Evremond's *Réflexions sur les divers génies du peuple
romain* of 1695 attempts to explain Roman history in terms of
its various *génies*; in terms, that is to say, which are mainly
psychological, but which are concerned with the psychology
of the group rather than with that of the individual. Fontenelle, in theory at any rate, calls for a similar approach, insisting that the most "philosophic" and most worthwhile history is "l'histoire de l'esprit humain."[44] In works like his essay
De l'origine des fables he makes one of the earliest significant contributions toward a psychological solution of a problem with which the eighteenth century was to continue to
wrestle[45]—that of the explanation of mythology.

However, this increased awareness of group psychology—
though it is clearly an ancestor of Montesquieu's *causes mo-
rales*—has less immediate impact on the development of a
new approach to history than has the reintroduction into the
field of historical speculation of La Bruyère's "forbidden subjects"—politics and religion.

Fénelon could not be called a political historian, but his
discussion of history in the *Lettre à l'Académie*, published in
1716, illustrates the way in which political opposition can
lead to the formulation of new questions. In many ways Fénelon is a "humanist" who insists on artistic excellence in history and opposes the display of critical erudition. Yet other
aspects of his work strike a newer note. His demand for the
accurate portrayal of what he calls "il costume," even though
it is an echo of Plutarch, implies a desire to see the historian

23

entering into the spirit of the age he is describing to a greater extent than was the case with most of the "humanists."[46] When he turns to discuss the history of France, he shows particular interest in constitutional problems and, in particular, in the relationship between the different estates of the realm and the way these relationships have developed.[47]

It is with Boulainvilliers rather than Fénelon, however, that historiography begins, once again, to become a vehicle of political propaganda. Though only published posthumously in 1727, his *Histoire de l'ancien gouvernement de France* is a product of the turmoil caused by the defeats of the War of the Spanish Succession. Its defense of an idealized feudalism and its insistence that this was the "natural" and therefore right form of government for France spark a controversy in which Dubos, Montesquieu, and later even Mably are to join.[48] Of course, this use of history is not without its dangers, as Voltaire, for example, was to point out.[49] Yet it is nevertheless fruitful in creating a new interest in social history. Boulainvilliers's work claims to be "une histoire de France qui proposerait plutôt celle du génie des Princes et du Gouvernement, que celle des événements."[50] And if he does not quite fulfill his promise, he does so sufficiently for his biographer Renée Simon to assert that he rather than Voltaire is the true father of modern historiography.[51]

With his *Vie de Mohamed*, published in 1730, Boulainvilliers also made a significant contribution to that opposition to Christian orthodoxy which was to be another outstanding feature of Enlightenment historiography. By this time, however, this movement of opposition was already well under way. If one had to choose a starting point for it, one could hardly do better than go back to Fontenelle's *Histoire des oracles*, which set out to refute the belief that the oracles of pagan antiquity were inspired by devils. With a fine command of an essentially Cartesian method, an all-pervading skepticism, and a constant use of irony, Fontenelle first examined and destroyed the evidence on which the traditional belief was based and

24

then proceeded to offer a more natural explanation in terms of the trickery of priests and the gullibility of men. If he showed the same skeptical attitude to human motives as did Bayle, he was not satisfied, as Bayle often was, with skeptical conclusions, but pressed on to positive results. Indeed, if his subject was not limited in scope and remote from contemporary problems, and if his material (adapted from Van Dale) was not secondhand, one might be tempted to call the *Histoire des oracles* the first work of Enlightenment historiography.

Yet these limitations are important, and similar doubts could be raised about any work written in the first two decades of the eighteenth century. If all the techniques and approaches that were to characterize the new historical writing were now to hand, they had still to be put to work.

At the threshold of Enlightenment historiography proper stand two works that have stood the test of time, that demonstrate the triumph of historical thinking over Pyrrhonism, and yet that could hardly be more dissimilar: Voltaire's *Histoire de Charles XII* and Montesquieu's *Considérations sur les causes de la grandeur des Romains et de leur décadence.* If Voltaire had not lived to become the most prolific of *philosophe* historians, the *Histoire de Charles XII* might not deserve this place of honor, for though it enshrines a "philosophic" message (the folly of aggressive war); though it contains brief but masterly analyses of political and social conditions in different countries of Europe; and though (in places at any rate) it shows Voltaire's deep concern for reliable firsthand sources, it is still in many ways a superb adventure story rooted in the "humanist" tradition.[52]

The *Considérations*, on the other hand, must stand on its own feet since it is the only great work of Montesquieu's that can be described as "a history." However, it has no need of support from elsewhere. It is true that it lacks some of the characteristics often associated with "enlightened" historiography. The strong streak of skepticism that Voltaire never loses is hardly found here. Montesquieu accepts what his authorities tell him, as one critic puts it, "like a jurist."[53] His views of historical causation have not yet acquired the subtlety that characterizes *De l'Esprit des lois*, and he can use climatic determinism as a convenient method of explaining the inexplicable, as he does, for example, in speaking of the bravery of the Macedonians.[54] Yet despite its limitations, this is the first great work of "philosophical" history. Montesquieu's thesis, that the very determining factors that led to the growth of the small city-state were equally responsible for the collapse of the great empire, may be questioned. What cannot be questioned is the fact that this is the first great work in which all other factors are subordinated to this type of causal explanation.

With these two works, historical writing may be said to have regained its assurance. If Bayle could have read them, they would not have silenced all his doubts; but they would have shown him that historiography could be more than just the imaginative creation of poets or the negating atomization of his own critical method.

1. On the general course of development of seventeenth-century historiography, and particularly the work of the *érudits*, see E. Fueter, *Geschichte der neueren Historiographie* (Munich and Berlin, 1936); J. W. Thompson, *A History of Historical Writing* (New York, 1942); A. Molinier, *Les Sources de l'histoire de France*, vol. 5 (Paris, 1901); G. Monod, "Du progrès des sciences historiques," *Revue historique* 1 (1876); L. Traube, *Vorlesungen und Abhandlungen zur Paläographie und Handschriftenkunde* (Munich, 1909); the studies devoted to Mabillon in the *Archives de la France monastique*, vol. 5 (Paris, 1908).

2. Bianchini, *La Istoria universale, provata con monumenti, e figurata con simboli degli antichi* (Rome, 1697).

3. For an account of these developments, see A. Momigliano, "Ancient History and the Antiquarian," *Journal of the Warburg and Courtauld Institutes* 13 (1950): 285-315.

4. See P. Hazard, *La Crise de la conscience européenne* (Paris, 1942), Notes et Références, p. 36.

5. E.g., Père Daniel, *Histoire de France* (Paris, 1729), Preface, p. lxxxvii.

6. Cicero, *De Oratore*, especially Bk. II, ch. 15. Lenglet du Fresnoy notes (*Méthode pour étudier l'histoire* [Paris, 1729], Preface) that Rapin's

Instructions pour l'histoire (Paris, 1677) are nothing more than a commentary on Cicero. The eighteenth-century humanists still appeal to his authority: e.g., Le Vassor, *Histoire du Règne de Louis XIII* (Amsterdam, 1720), Preface; F. de Juvenel, *Principes de l'histoire* (Paris, 1733), p. 167.

7. C. V. de Saint-Réal, *De l'usage de l'histoire, Œuvres* (The Hague, 1722), 1:72. See also the preface to his *Conjuration des Espagnols contre Venise*, 4:141.

8. P. Le Moyne's *De l'histoire* (1670) devotes a chapter to proving this. Cordemoy also emphasizes it in his *Divers traitez de métaphysique, d'histoire, et de politique* (Paris, 1691).

9. See Fénelon, *Lettre à l'Académie*, ed. A. Cahen (Paris, 1899), p. 110, and H. Ferté, *Rollin, sa vie, ses œuvres, et l'université de son temps* (Paris, 1902), p. 337.

10. See G. Dulong, *L'Abbé de Saint-Réal* (Paris, 1921), pp. 104-5.

11. Rapin, *Instructions pour l'histoire*, pp. 35, 63-8.

12. Le Moyne, *De l'histoire*, devotes a chapter to showing that "Wit is the first quality of the historian."

13. *Pensées diverses sur la comète*, ed. Prat (Paris, 1939), 1:32.

14. See Dulong, *Saint-Réal*, p. 327.

15. This is shown by Dulong's examination of all three in his *Saint-Réal*. In Vertot's case it is also amusingly revealed in the *Vie de l'auteur*, which precedes the 1737 edition of his *Histoire des révolutions arrivées dans le gouvernement de la république romaine*.

16. Rapin, *Instructions*, p. 26.

17. Fénelon, *Lettre à l'Académie*, p. 115.

18. See Brumfitt, *Voltaire Historian* (Oxford, 1958), p. 161.

19. Rapin, *Instructions*, pp. 81-3.

20. D'Alembert, *Discours sur la meilleure méthode d'écrire l'histoire* (Paris, 1761), p. 193.

21. Daniel, *Histoire de France*, Preface, p. lii.

22. Saint-Réal, *Œuvres*, 1:3.

23. Cordemoy, *Divers traitez de métaphysique, d'histoire, et de politique*, p. 35.

24. Fénelon, *Lettre à l'Académie*, p. 112.

25. La Mothe le Vayer, *Œuvres* (Dresden, 1756), 5:441 ff.

26. Ibid., 4:282.

27. Descartes, *Discours de la méthode*, ed. Gilson (Paris, 1947), p. 6.

28. Ibid., pp. 12-13.

29. *De la recherche de la vérité* (1674). See especially Bk. II, Pt. II, chs. 4 and 5.

30. See Vico, *Autobiography*, trans. Fisch and Bergin (Ithaca, N.Y., 1944), p. 130.

31. See the excellent chapter on Bossuet in P. Hazard, *La Crise de la conscience européenne*, pp. 203 ff.

32. Bayle, *Œuvres diverses* (The Hague, 1722), 2:10.

33. Ibid., p. 12.

34. See, for example, the studies by Delvolvé, Cazes, Lenient, Robertson, and Cassirer's *The Philosophy of the Enlightenment.*

35. *La Crise de la conscience européenne*, pp. 30 ff.

36. *Dissertation sur l'incertitude des cinq premiers siècles de l'histoire romaine.*

37. On Fréret's contribution, see A. Thierry, *Œuvres* (Paris, 1859), 4:33-35; on that of Levesque de Pouilly, R. Flint, *Historical Philosophy in France* (Edinburgh, 1893), pp. 255 ff.

38. The first volumes of the Academy's *Mémoires* contain a number of contributions from him, including one on "harangues" (3:83 ff.) in which he contrives to sit uneasily on the fence.

39. See particularly pp. 8 and 12 of the 1771 Paris edition of the *Discours.*

40. Daniel, *Histoire de France*, Preface, pp. li-lii.

41. De Juvenel, *Principes de l'histoire*, pp. 168-69.

42. Le Long, *Bibliothèque historique de la France* (Paris, 1769-78), l:xv.

43. See Brumfitt, *Voltaire Historian*, p. 137.

44. Fontenelle, *Œuvres* (Paris, 1818), 1:106, 232.

45. See J.-R. Carré's edition of *De l'Origine des fables* (Paris, 1932); on the 18th century's interpretation of mythology, Frank E. Manuel's *The 18th Century Confronts the Gods* (Cambridge, Mass., 1959).

46. Fénelon, *Lettre à l'Académie*, p. 119.

47. Ibid., pp. 124-26.

48. For an account of this controversy, see Brumfitt, *Voltaire Historian*, pp. 63-65.

49. See, for example, the article "Histoire" in the *Dictionnaire philosophique*, ed. Moland, 19:356.

50. *Histoire de l'ancien gouvernement de France*, Preface. Boulainvilliers amplifies his views in, for example, his *Lettre à Mlle Cousinot sur l'Histoire de France.*

51. R. Simon, *Henri de Boulainvilliers* (Paris, 1942), p. 46.

52. See Brumfitt, *Voltaire Historian*, pp. 9 ff.

53. Fueter, *Geschichte der neueren Historiographie*, p. 383. Sorel in his *Montesquieu* (Paris, 1889, p. 56) makes a similar point about Montesquieu's acceptance of Livy.

54. Montesquieu, *Œuvres* (Paris, 1866), 1:21.

The Diamond of *Courtoisie* and the
Dragonnades of 1681: Valincour's
Vie de François de Lorraine

CHARLES G. S. WILLIAMS

I. Valincour, Historian and Humanist

 Jean-Baptiste Henri du Trousset de Valincour (1653-1730) became *historiographe du roi* after serving a willing apprenticeship under his friends Racine and Boileau. During the 1690s he accompanied Racine in the field on occasion, by his own choice, to witness at firsthand the military events that Racine and Boileau had been commissioned to chronicle.[1] Although by 1699 he had enjoyed in society for almost two decades success as a poet and literary critic, the same year of his official charge brought him the principal recommendation for election to Racine's place in the Académie.[2] Eight years after his death, the *Armorial général de la France* paid an eloquent tribute to the man of letters whose career culminated in that charge. "Les grands talens de feu M. de Valincour, & son génie heureux dans tous les genres de littérature, lui méritèrent l'honneur d'être choisi par le feu Roi Louis XIV pour écrire les Annales de son Règne. Il sacrifia à cet Ouvrage la plus nombreuse partie de ses veilles."[3]

Voltaire, who respected Valincour's probity and academic eloquence without finding much éclat in his career, ranged his predecessor as *historiographe* among the "do nothings."[4] A letter from Valincour to Noailles seeking aid in obtaining work space at Versailles for his research and writing, however, reveals that a not inconsequential part of each working day

31

was reserved for that task.[5] But whatever the fruits of his labors, the writing perished in the conflagration that destroyed his retreat at Saint-Cloud in 1726. Anecdote has it that Valincour's man, sent to fetch the history especially, returned from the flames with a bundle of court gazettes.[6] It is generally destruction of Racine's or Boileau's contributions to the history that is regretted. And for some commentators the fire would seem, less regrettably, to have destroyed all claims for Valincour's consideration as a historian. Good reasons are to be found, however, in the evidence of his mind and method that the surviving historical writing gives, to regret the loss of his contributions to the history of the reign quite as much as one must those of his more illustrious colleagues.

It is unlikely that Valincour, educated at Clermont, received there the prize awarded later to Voltaire, a copy of Davila's history of the civil wars, which might conveniently have offered a first step toward concentrated work on his biography of Guise.[7] His training there, overseen in part perhaps by no less a prose stylist than Bouhours,[8] did initiate him into the "beautés de l'Histoire" and the art of oratory that he demonstrated later in widely appreciated eulogies of Racine and of Boileau in the Académie. The impetus to seek felicity of expression, ease, and elegance in the kind of non-oratorical prose that distinguishes his life of Guise may well have come also from the author of *Du bel esprit*. The master later praised the *Vie*, but a more telling compliment was Bussy's recommendation of it to one of his correspondents.[9] A hard judge of men of letters' efforts to write about men of arms, neither satisfied with the historiographical appointments of Racine and Boileau nor enthusiastic over Bouhours's own biography of Pierre d'Aubusson, Bussy awards the prize to the pupil rather than the teacher—complimenting him indirectly by supposing the anonymously published *Vie* to have been the work of a former soldier—Saint-Evremond.

Fontenelle also admired the *Vie* and gave, in fuller description of its qualities than they have yet had, reasons for both its appeal to men like Bussy and its broader achievement as historical writing. After judging this history by his fellow academician "plus convenable à ses talents et à son caractère" than was his earlier verse, Fontenelle praises the *Vie* as a

> petit morceau d'histoire qui remplit tout ce qu'on demande à un bon historien; des recherches qui, quoique faites avec beaucoup de soin, et prises quelquefois dans des sources éloignées, ne passent point les bornes d'une raisonnable curiosité; une narration bien suivie et animée, qui conduit naturellement le lecteur, et l'intéresse toujours; un style noble et simple, qui tire ses ornements du fonds des choses, ou les tire d'ailleurs bien finement; *nulle partialité pour le héros, qui pouvait cependant inspirer de la passion* à son écrivain.[10]

These qualities of brevity and animation of narrative, sobriety of tone, modest but affirmative probity in research, and impartiality in its presentation seem to have recommended the *Vie* to Voltaire. Voltaire's listing of it for Sir Everard Fawkener among the twenty "best books I know in regard to history" produced by Frenchmen (Best. 4240) and its use by historians from Bayle through the nineteenth century bear witness to the real presence of those qualities whose praise could be thought suspect in Fontenelle's semi-official history of members of the Académie des Sciences. The qualities praised by Fontenelle look forward, in their own way, to distinctive aspects of Voltaire's own writing of history. Their presence in Valincour's earliest history, the erudition and concision of analysis of his later naval history highly acclaimed by Eugène Sue,[11] his outspokenly precise historical appraisal of both the state of Europe and of French naval affairs for Fleury in 1726,[12] and his final denunciation of eulogies passing as history[13] promise much and justify disappointment that no more of his historical writing was completed or has survived. But the *Vie* has never been accorded the attention that its qualities merit it in this history, within Valincour's career as it may be seen to be oriented toward the Enlightenment,

33

and perhaps most significantly for that orientation in its treatment, in 1681, of an inflammatory subject that could gain the respect of Voltaire.

II. In Search of the *Vie*

There is no direct documentation to reveal either Valincour's reasons for writing the *Vie* or the genesis of the history. Reasons are suggested, however, by the book itself and the qualities praised by Fontenelle, whereas external events in the historian's career and especially in the affairs of the church not previously considered cast light upon the genesis of the history.

Since Mabre-Cramoisy's notice promises a series of similar lives "de tous les grands hommes du siècle passé & de celuy-cy," it is quite probably a publisher's venture that was initially responsible for Valincour's *Vie*. The subject later in the century of several fictional works, Guise's person and dramatic career were unquestionably the stuff of an attractively saleable book. Valincour was a good "risk" in this venture that he most probably accepted with interest and pleasure. His lively and irreverent *Lettres à Mme la marquise de *** sur le sujet de la Princesse de Clèves*, published in 1678 also by Marbre-Cramoisy, had demonstrated both his ability to produce a best-selling book and his extensive and thoughtful acquaintance with the period and the sources of its history that were Mme de Lafayette's. Although he shows interest and originality in literary criticism,[14] Valincour's first interest, in history, orients his remarks to problems of the relationship of history and fiction, of Mme de Lafayette's characterization, narrative technique, and style in terms of the demands made on the knowledgeable reader of history. Notable among sources of knowledge were Brantôme's lives of distinguished captains, which were published only twelve years earlier. Valincour savored Brantôme's style, respected his principles, and took the lives as a major source for the *Vie*.[15]

34

The *Vie*, stamped with the same independent critical spirit that enlivened the dialogues on the novel, was in fact attractive to men like Bussy and sold more widely than has been acknowledged. Several printings, including a pirated one and an English translation by Ferrand Spence, all in 1681,[16] constituted no real failure and brought the volume to a fairly large number of readers. But there are a number of indications that Valincour himself was not seeking to capitalize finally on current vogues of biography and pseudo-biographical fiction and that he had other reasons than sales to a broader audience for writing the *Vie* as he did. The drama and psychological portraiture that had made the fortune of a Mézeray and continued to make that of writers of historic fiction are much subdued and generally schematic. High seriousness of concern is conveyed by a sobriety of tone and a style that are almost bleakly *incolores*. With an aristocratic scorn for Parisians' political fickleness also apparent, the *Vie* is little calculated to appeal to the wider audience that would have brought it extensive reprinting.

The historical interest and knowledge of the period of the Wars of Religion, very much a part of Valincour's preoccupations from 1678, are again displayed near the end of his official career. In 1725 he took the opportunity of a *Discours* welcoming Président Portail to the Académie to develop at length the virtues of *litterae humaniores* and to celebrate the tempering of the letter of the law by the spirit of humane magistrates formed by their study of them. To this celebration is added denunciation of the fanaticism of the Ligue and specific praise for those members of the magisterial class who, he believed, had undertaken to combat it by composing the *Satire Ménipée*, "Satire ingénieuse, qui couvrant d'un ridicule amer & judicieux, la folie & l'insolence des Ligueurs, retint tant de bons François dans les sentiments de respect & de fidélité qu'ils doivent à leur Prince légitime."[17]

At this date what had been a scandal to the mind of Montesquieu's intellectual Persian was no less scandalous to Valincour, unmitigatedly disgusted by the fanatical factionalism firing the *Unigenitus* controversy to the point that he feared both for the community of the faithful within France and the weakening of the church before the challenge of the East. Having failed in his own practical efforts to be a voice of mediating reason in this controversy,[18] his letters to Cardinal Gualterio—and through him to the Curia—repeatedly deplore in the tone of a concerned and reasonable Catholic layman the dogmatic factionalism and fanaticism that kept the controversy and its threats alive throughout his lifetime.[19] The *Discours* of 1725 is both an appeal to the reason of enlightened magistrates and a tribute to them that echoes at the end of his career homage paid to Michel de l'Hôpital in the *Vie*. The state of religious controversy by April 1681, which recalled to men of the day the more violent prejudices of the Ligue,[20] suggests that Valincour made his *Vie* also a plea for reasoned mediation and a denunciation of fanaticism, which in its own way might "retenir de bons Français."

By 1679, when Locke recorded in his journal that about three hundred Protestant churches had been destroyed in France in the last two decades, aspiration to unification of the French church had been seriously compromised by the proliferation of restrictive edicts harassing places of worship, ministers, and the faithful of the Protestant community. If in June of 1680 Pellisson optimistically predicted "l'extinction prochaine de l'hérésie en France,"[21] opinion on the means of achieving it was yet in 1681 much divided in print. While one Gallican extremist recommended the violence of separation from Rome as key to the *Moyens sûrs et honnestes pour la conversion de tous les hérétiques*, Maimbourg provided his usual use of history as apology for power.[22] Arnauld, on the other hand, in his *Apologie pour les catholiques*, endorsed the pacific moderation of Pellisson's tested policy of tax dispensations and monetary indemnities for abjuration. But more expeditious and violent tactics had already begun to replace Pellisson's plans. In the first months of 1681, Maril-

36

lac implemented in Poitou the menacing and ruinous tactic of garrisoning of troops as pressure to abjure. "La seule vue de ces troupes," it was said without any suggestion of abuses, "déterminait les esprits à écouter plus volontiers la voix des pasteurs qu'on leur envoyait."[23] Well before Louvois adopted it as policy in the summer of 1685, duress or its threat "avait gêné autant qu'il pouvait l'œuvre de rapprochement des esprits, d'abord par les dragonnades de Marillac, odieuses aux protestants les mieux disposés."[24] These measures threatening to resolve once for all the question "Réunion ou dragonnades?"—with especially violent words from the Assemblé du clergé,[25] hostile policy of the Le Telliers, and new rigor of the king responding to pressures of international politics—led in turn to a hardening of opposition by the Protestant community. The extreme point was being approached when repulsion of any suggestion of conferences for the purpose of reasoned mediation of concessions put an end to the real possibility of reunion.

Mme de Maintenon, Valincour's future protectress and friend, protested to little avail the general policy of harassment and expressed the belief, also in 1681, that in the matter of Huguenots' conversion "il faudroit ne rien oublier pour les gagner par douceur." Henri Daguesseau (of whom Valincour left an admiring prose portrait) wrote from Languedoc that "le zèle de la Religion ne doit pas aller jusqu'à l'injustice."[26] But this moderation was not shared by all zealous ladies of piety or intendants with force of arms at their disposal. The irenic direction taken by Bossuet, in the attempts of his *Exposition* (1668-71), *Conférence avec Claude* (1678), and *Histoire des variations* (begun in 1681), to liquidate purely verbal matters of controversy standing in the way of reunion, may have seemed on the point of being no longer open to a hardened factionalism refusing discussion and insisting on differences. Reasoned mediation and reason itself appeared in danger of coming to a standstill.

It is in this climate of religious and political controversy,

37

extremism, civil disturbance, and stalemate that Valincour's *Vie* was published. Whether or not this history published by Bossuet's printer was planned to demonstrate its author's worth to the prelate who was later his spiritual adviser,[27] and who was just beginning the *Histoire des variations*, its implied views are Bossuet's. The *Vie* was no impediment to Valincour's advancement shortly after its appearance to a position in the entourage of the young Toulouse, which most probably would have required the approval of Bossuet.[28] Bossuet's opinions as a member of the special council exploring the possibilities of reunion were from 1666 moderate, politic, and reasoned.[29] He had predicted in 1662 the glory of Louis's success, celebrated later in the *Oraison* for Le Tellier, but through tempered means: "Il aurait la gloire d'étouffer l'hérésie elle-même par un sage tempérament de sévérité et de patience."[30] When the Coadjuteur d'Arles insisted in 1675 that "entière destruction de l'hérésie" be immediately implemented, he received no answer from Bossuet. And in his eloquent *Sermon sur l'unité de l'Eglise* he pleaded for a cessation of all spirit of contention and reaffirmed his desire to safeguard the unity of the Gallican church through a spirit of irenism that should animate the 1681 Assemblée du clergé. Several months earlier in the same year, Valincour, more modestly and indirectly in his *Vie*, seems to have presented the same plea.

What most probably began as a publishing venture and pure enjoyment for the man of letters almost certainly underwent thoughtful genesis as Valincour, by training a humanist and by temperament an admirer of the *Politiques*, became increasingly mindful of the troubled state of France and aware that writing a life of Guise constituted a political act with incendiary potentiality. As a fledgling academician he later celebrated Louis's zeal from 1697 to 1699 to "affermir de plus en plus la véritable religion, par son exemple & par son autorité."[31] In old age he affirmed categorically to Bouhier that "jamais des sujets soulevés contre leur souverain ne peuvent avoir raison," since "nous sommes dans un Royaume et non dans la République de Platon; or, qui dit Roi et sujets dit d'un côté le droit de commander, de l'autre le devoir et même la nécessité d'obéir. . . . C'est le seul bon parti à prendre en tout temps et surtout dans les temps fâcheux."[32] The younger man certainly felt in 1680-81 much the same and that "right" lay on the side of François de Lorraine and the "cause" of the Triumvirat. But the story is, significantly, not so simply told. Following the critical spirit that is always a mark of his writing and guide in the *Vie* to those qualities praised by Fontenelle, Valincour renounced all explicit propaganda, dogmatism or pragmatism, that could be construed as an apology for violent destruction of "heresy" by power.

Like D'Aubigné and De Thou, Bayle and Voltaire, Valincour regretted that for the sake of "bons Français" Guise's last words to his son—"Souvenez-vous de moy, sans désirer de venger ma mort, puis que Dieu nous commande de pardonner à nos ennemis"—fell on deaf ears. The *Vie* ends with the facts of a contrary reality: "Jamais une seule mort n'a tant fait couler de sang, ni entraisné un si grand nombre d'illustres victimes." With this reality in mind, Bayle later described in the Guises "un mélange de bonnes et de mauvaises qualités . . . propre à bouleverser un état." Valincour had already found this *mélange* dramatically presented in a question of La Renaudie that De Thou transcribed: "Demeurons d'accord que le Duc de Guise a fait glorieusement toutes choses dans la guerre; mais les choses qu'il a faites sont-elles de si grande conséquence, qu'elles puissent récompenser & les pertes & les deffaites qu'on a reçues dans le Royaume par sa funeste ambition, & qui ont ouvert le chemin aux maux qui estoient déjà prêts d'y entrer, & que ces Princes y ont appelez?"[33] It is this question that the historian explores and focuses in his biography of François de Guise.

III. THE SHAPE OF A LIFE: *gloire souillée— souillure du préjugé?*

In form, Valincour's life of a great soldier offers few surprises. "Ce n'est pas l'histoire que j'écris, mais une vie," he asserts, echoing Plutarch. The humanist adopts an outline traditional to the genre—"vie, œuvres, portrait"—and concentrates his narration on battles and diplomacy.

Moving toward final eulogy, the account of the soldier's soldier "born" at Metz and extinguished at Orléans does so in its own terms. The traditional miscellany of the final portrait begins with a description of popular reaction to Guise's assassination. "Les Catholiques disoient qu'ils avoient perdu leur protecteur, & regarderent sa mort comme un Martyre qu'il avoit souffert pour la défense de la Foy." To the popular mind, kept in constant focus, the historian juxtaposes his own reflection on the evidence: "Il eût toutes les qualitez qui ont jamais fait les plus grands Heros" (p. 164). Rather than the heroism of a martyred knight of the church cut down in his predestined mission of defense of the faith by a fanatical "heretic," Guise is finally eulogized as "le Seigneur le plus honneste de son siecle" (p. 146)—the picture of the soldier of honor and humanity and the "bon Français" that radiates from Brantôme's *Vie de M. de Guyze le grand.*

But in this history we are not in the realm of Bossuet's *oraison* formulas describing a Le Tellier "*toujours* semblable à lui-même, *toujours* supérieur à ses emplois." "Il faut avoûër que tous les temps de la vie des grands hommes ne se ressemblent pas," the historian generalizes, facing the follies of Guise's Italian campaign, "une guerre qui paroissoit manifestement injuste."[34] When it becomes a matter of civil war, he declares: "On ne peut lire sans horreur ce qui fut dit en ce temps-là, & ce qui a esté escrit depuis" (p. 95). Final qualification of method is neither apologetic nor defensive. "Si ses ennemis luy ont reproché quelque chose, *c'estoit moins* à luy qu'il s'en falloit prendre, qu'au malheur de son siecle, & aux desordres qui sont arrivez durant son temps" (p. 165). Personal interventions by the historian call for understanding of particular circumstances and stress the fact that sources distorted by personal jealousy, popular idealization, and partisan passion render even more elusive any real understanding of the already complex matters of human motivation and historical causation. The historian does not ask for total absolution (as the words underscored [italics above] indicate). Nor does he claim to have the final truth of this life. His combative tone issues instead a claim to have gone beyond polemic and to have moved toward the truth of this life in itself and within the context of its time.

In these terms the career is made to indicate an evolution, three distinct phases in the eleven years whose changing perspective must be viewed before the significance of the life may be seen and judged. First (pp. 13–71), military glory from Metz to Calais, redeeming Italy and establishing Guise's reputation, consecrates the lieutenant-général as "Conservateur du Royaume." With the death of Henri and accession of the pathetic François II the scene changes (pp. 71–121) as the man embroiled in court life and civil administration emerges. New position and power for the Guises, likened to the "Maires du Palais," require a new perspective as events lead to the formation of the Triumvirat in opposition to Condé. As Guise moves (pp. 122–64) from the "signal de la rébellion" that is Condé's possession of Orléans to his own death there, by way of Blois, Tours, Bourges, Rouen, Paris, and Dreux, the skills and qualities of both soldier and "courtier" are viewed against the reality of civil war.

Two-fifths of the *Vie* is given to what had become for men of letters by 1681 the fine art of description of *art militaire*.[35] The armature of the *Vie* is the series of battles already enumerated by Brantôme with first place in praise given to Metz. Valincour's thirty-two-page description of Metz is as precise and pertinent as that which is found in Lavisse: the eye-witness account he usually seeks, here the diffuse *Mémoire* by Salignac,[36] is reduced to clear chronology and narrated with scarcely less animation than Bossuet's account of Rocroi. Appreciating Brantôme's expansive tribute to Guise, Valincour follows to the letter its concluding remark—"Bref, qui voudra bien mettre en ligne de conte tout ce qui s'est faict en ce siège, dira et conffessera que ç'a esté le plus beau siège qui fut jamais."[37] After elaboration he confirms this judgment soberly: Guise "fit une infinité d'autres reglemens, qui peuvent servir de modele à ceux qui se trouveront en de pareilles occasions."

The "model" serves a complex function in the *Vie*. Careful technique in "model" military description shows Guise's "model" art of war, the thoroughness established at Metz— of reconnaissance, strategic deployment and maneuver, and post-armistice reconstruction, which came to characterize his military genius more than did incisiveness and speed of attack and withdrawal. Technical precisions are accompanied by other generalized advice for the commander—delegation of subordinate command, treatment of mercenaries in combat and negotiation and of civilians facing war. But description is not purely technical and pragmatic. The chef d'oeuvre functions in a manner not unlike that of the first chef d'oeuvre in Sainte-Beuve's biographical method. Cohesion of detail in a plan constituting a chef d'oeuvre and revealing the emerging genius yields also the presence of a powerful man. In place of the myth of Providence's special favor, which Guise's "miraculous" victories and recoveries suggested in the popular mind and beyond,[38] Valincour visualizes Guise's control and natural command as causes explaining successes. Nothing is beyond him in planning, "rien est au-dessous de luy" in work necessary to implement it. For all involved at Metz, Guise is the ideal—"un égal, mais un égal d'un prestige supérieur," both for the soldier who "voulait sentir qu'une pensée supérieure organisait son sacrifice"[39] and for the subordinate commander who wished fitting opportunity and recognition for those qualities of *courtoisie* that Brantôme most admired.[40]

As Valincour felt and presented it, war is for men like Guise what it was for Brantôme—a superior mode of life, conception of existence, and source of morality. "Jeunes guerres" reveal personality and character that do not change in "normal and natural" circumstances. Brantôme agreed with La Brosse that "qui a faict parestre son courage et valeur en la chaleur de la jeunesse, il ne le perd jamais, quelque vieil aage qu'il face, si ce n'est par une grand' disgrace." For him, Guise was "très-bon en sa jeunesse, très-brave, très-courageux et très-généreux; bref, telz en jeunesse que sur l'aage, et telz sur l'aage qu'en jeunesse."[41] Part of Guise's prestige at Metz, the qualities of "*clémence, courtoisie, douceur & miséricorde,*" Brantôme found greatly promising for the rest of the career. The whole series of anecdotes recounted by Valincour, at Metz and in military activity throughout the *Vie*, all exemplify these different manifestations of a soldier's noble code that unaltered deserves in final eulogy "à faire connoistre le caractere de son esprit & de son humeur."

The qualities of heart and mind seen in the observance of the soldier's noble code, described by "honorable men," serve as criteria for judgment both of actions in the last phases of Guise's career and the verisimilitude of their description by other historians. It is not only in the enthusiasm of Brantôme or the celebratory verse of Michel de l'Hôpital that the historian found the exemplary qualities of the hero of Metz; "*clémence*" and "*douceur*" he found acknowledged in one of the most likely, responsible sources of contradiction, in D'Aubigné.[42] Valincour will thus be able to see Guise acting during the civil war with concern for injury to his countrymen, when precautions against looting were taken by him to spare the Rouennais, for example, because he had seen Guise's concern for the material and spiritual well-being of the citizens of Metz. A *massacre* at Vassy is a psychological improbability that facts can be seen to illuminate in other terms than those of an armed charge against unarmed Huguenots evoked by some Protestant historians. When it is a question of public proclamation that soldiers demanding favors after the death of Henri II will suffer death, Valincour will no more than Brantôme consent to believe Guise directly responsible in what was the Cardinal de Lorraine's violent policy.[43] He had seen too vividly from Metz to Calais the soldier's *courtoisie*, the respect it offered and received, to believe in its subordination to fiscal necessity. Similarly, he will not give as the truth a self-serving ambition that allegedly motivated Guise's fatal slowness in aiding Thermes at Gravelines. "Je ne puis croire ce que dit un Auteur célebre qu'il [Guise] affecta ce retardement pour donner lieu à cette défaite qu'il regardoit comme l'augmentation de son autorité" (p. 70). Again, insisting typically on the evaluation of evidence as well as on psychological verisimilitude, when Guise is said to have plotted the assassination of Condé, Valincour judges that "quoy-que le seul recit de cette histoire la fasse paroistre incroyable, principalement à l'égard de Guise qui n'estoit pas capable de conseiller un assassinat; j'ay cru estre obligé de la rapporter icy comme je l'ay trouvée écrite dans les Historiens de ce temps-là" (p. 97).

Critical sense gives value to impartiality. There is critical reaction to anonymous broadsides, partisan distortion, and generally dismissed foreign sources[44] by the historian who wants to gain both a reasonably true view and a hearing for it. But opposition comes also to "un Auteur célebre," De Thou, to whom he owes much in method and critical procedure. The table of contents of Du Ruyer's translation[45] of De Thou's *Histoire* contains almost an exact outline for the *Vie*. If the armature of military events and portrayal of Guise's noble code reflect agreement with Brantôme, Brantôme's *cursus honorum* in war scarcely changes focus with the reality of civil war, and his "socioeconomic defense" of it (if serious) is totally outside Valincour's humanist orientation.[46] Forever the diamond of *courtoisie*, the beauty of a Spanish charger in motion, Guise is for Brantôme that enviable man who changes events by his actions, the man whose presence in scarlet and black and luster in chivalry set off or expose the merits and faults of a Coligny, a Condé, a Navarre. Ambition that might taint *courtoisie* by political self-interest is constantly denied. De Thou's *Histoire* is a middle ground for the historian between the extremes of praise and detraction. Valincour found (for example, in the transcription of La Renaudie's deposition at Nantes) a steady focus on the infamous ambition of the Guises and the movements of power politics summarily dealt with by Brantôme, a presentation of evidence thus similar to his own, and a justification to reexamine the *Histoire* itself critically. He found, as Mézeray had, "l'historien De Thou que les bons Français ne doivent jamais nommer sans préface d'honneur."[47] For the hearing that he wished on Guise, the historian might thus have described his method as Voltaire does his in a characteristic passage of *Le Siècle de Louis XIV*, a method similar also to Bayle's tactical preparation for just attention to his point of view.[48] After particular critical evaluation, he opposes as sources De Thou, D'Aubigné, and Bèze, which a hard critic—say a Jurieu—might admit unquestionably, to those like Brantôme and Carle, for example, which he would not.

In his account of the Italian campaign and the first ambiguous signs of "le naturel ambitieux" and political manipulation that belong to Act I of this dramatic life and after decisive peripeteia become compromising in the later stages of the career, Valincour's *Vie* suggests less the techniques of popular sermon or fiction than it does a discreet adaptation of Corneille's dramaturgy. Guise's career as it is shaped in the *Vie* is not without some resemblance to the drama of Corneille's Horace. Like the dramatist, the historian will leave complex the historical personality and the motivation/causation when extraordinary virtue under stress of extraordinary circumstances becomes humanly ambiguous. The king's favor, the consecration as *Conservateur du Royaume* by both Parlement and Parisians when Guise returned from Italy to the panic in the aftermath of the national crisis of Saint-Quentin, and the transformation of the soldier's soldier of Metz into the national hero by the events of 1558–59, all crystallize the hero before the event that brings final consolidation of that power, the death of Henri II, closes Act II of the drama.

Along with the ambition and politics of the Italian campaign, one other fact is recorded in exposition of the "model" of Metz that prepares the dramatic highpoint of the last phase of Guise's career, the extraordinary circumstances and "testing" by the reality of civil war that might constitute for a classical dramatist the continued action of a fourth act. At Metz, Guise "ordonna une Procession générale pour rendre graces à Dieu; & pour achever cette cérémonie par un Sacrifice agréable, il fit brusler publiquement tous les Livres de Luther qui se trouverent dans la ville." Although there is no direct commentary, Valincour significantly follows De Thou and omits Salignac's observation that this ceremony took place "sans scandale d'aucun."[49] By the time of the ambivalent last phase of Guise's career—by Act IV, as it were—the questions that will create its dramatic ambiguity have been indirectly but certainly implied. Ambition of the king's man and "le seigneur le plus honnête de son siècle"—or the demagogue's drive to power and pretensions to a crown? Piety from *miséricorde* and humanity—or fanaticism in an outward show of that kind which Bayle will shortly denounce in his *Pensées diverses sur la comète*? With these questions there is also the incrimination of men swayed by fear and the prestige of power to support violence, the "peuple trop crédule," "peuple furieux," denounced by Voltaire in *La Henriade* (2.26-28). Are they not endorsing that disorder which they wish to prevent? "A Paris, le Prevost des Marchands & les Eschevins allerent au-devant de Guise, & le peuple le receût *comme un homme envoyé du Ciel* pour conserver sa Religion" (p. 117).

When the field is left for the court, there are always threats of that disgrace which Brantôme envisaged, a new set of extraordinary circumstances in which the soldier is no longer entirely the hero unanimously acclaimed in the field. Valincour implies, first in the miscalculations and misfortunes of the Italian Campaign and then after the death of Henri II, what Lucien Romier later stated: "François de Lorraine n'était pas un politique. Pur type soldat, [il avait] le génie et le tempérament de son art, avec une sorte de naïveté dans la pratique des choses non militaires."[50] His talents and true *gloire* are the soldier's; ambition and thoroughness do not work in the context of power struggle when Catherine and Montmorency, Coligny, Condé, Navarre, and Cardinal de Lorraine more than anyone, exert wills of their own that are determined by other codes which force Guise into a different position and light. There is no doubt that the true, military *gloire* is *souillée* in Valincour's narration, and there are suggestions from his account of Metz on that this is the result of what Voltaire might call *souillure du préjugé*. Polemical, impassioned evidence is from the death of Henri II on given more hearing. The spectacle of being manipulated and of a lapse from former virtue is felt by outside observers. Hence, with loss of control comes loss of admiration and division of opinion in polemics that may still only be the result of ever-present jealousy of the great but that have additional justification and significance.

With the accession of François II there is what Corneille might call a "suspension agréable" before the last actions and denouement of the drama: "Jamais les Guises ne s'estoient veûs si proche de leur ruine, & jamais ils ne se virent si élévez. Il sembloit que toutes choses eussent conspiré pour les rendre maistres du Royaume" (pp. 74-75). The figures around Guise remain, suggestively, shadowy and thereby vaguely conspiratorial and menacing, abstract terms in a struggle that may be seen to pit simplistically the good (fighting for king and church) against the bad (those rebels fighting for themselves). Only Cardinal de Lorraine, emphasizing his importance, is given some fullness of life. Yet this simplicity of interpretation, partly political orientation and in part the result of classical economy in composition, does not leave Guise in his ideals and *gloire* any the less compromised in the ambiguous contexts of power struggle and civil war. Lorraine is not the "fiend from Hell" (nor is Catherine the "Italian dissembler") excoriated by D'Aubigné. He is shown rather as the timid man Brantôme describes,[51] acting from weakness with a brashness and aggressive violence that are clearly presented

47

as compensatory, misguided emulation of his brother. Emulation in the field by men of arms may have noble results, but this sibling rivalry brings nothing but compromising ignominy when, as Brantôme admits, the man of ambition to power in the cardinal takes precedence over the man of the church. Valincour does not simply follow the line of chroniclers, from Villehardouin on, who absolve responsibility and compromise in leaders by the presence of *mauvais conseillers*. As men commanding admiration and hatred, Guise and his brother are antithetical. But eschewing the lengthy antithesis that could constitute a rhetorical "beauté de l'Histoire," it is more subtly similarity of the hero and "anti-hero" of the same blood that the historian suggests. The cardinal is the incarnation of the infamous ambition of the Guises, ambition shared by François, legitimately directed in the field by the soldier's qualities but darkened in the spheres of the cardinal's actions. Rather than an absolute antithesis to Guise, the cardinal is presented as the embodiment of his worst quality. A similar function is given to the "rebels." Their use of religion as a pretext for struggle to power and their apparent blind indifference to the injury done to sovereign and to France represent the temptations and ambiguous reality of Guise in his worst or most questionable moments.

After all the psychological probing and interpretation, there remains at the center of the drama the image of François II, made to ask the Guises pathetically: "Qu'ay-je donc fait à mon peuple pour l'obliger à me vouloir tant de mal? . . . Ne seroit-il point à propos que vous retirassiez? (p. 83). However "right" the defense of king and church by them, the facts remain of disorder, of a suffering France, of a king doubtfully served by them in life and neglected scandalously in the honors of burial.[52]

It is in recounting the details of an alleged master plan whereby the Guises sought supreme affirmation of power by liquidation of the entire royal family that Valincour records his general feeling of horror over confrontations of power using religion as a pretext. "On ne peut lire sans horreur ce qui fut dit en ce temps-là, & ce qui a esté écrit depuis. Que les Guises craignant les ressentimens du Roy de Navarre, & jugeant d'ailleurs que leur autorité ne seroit jamais tranquille ni assûrée tant qu'il resteroit un Prince du Sang pour la contester, ils avoient entrepris de s'en défaire" (p. 95). The historian of Metz knows a Guise "doux et modéré," incapable of such action, who "eut toûjours une affection tres-pure & tres-sincere pour la Religion Catholique" (p. 104). But it is precisely because he was "doux et modéré," the historian acknowledges, that Guise "se rendoit complice des violences & des emportmens de son frere, en ne les empeschant pas, & souvent en l'aidant à executer des desseins auxquels il auroit deû s'opposer" (p. 78). What is true of Guise's passive responsibility in seconding his brother's pretensions to the papacy in the Italian campaign, as Valincour interpreted it from anti-Guise and anti-papal sources, is also true for Vassy and more generally for events leading to the First War of Religion.

At Vassy, primary responsibility may fall on "une troupe de ces gens insolens & inutiles qui sont toûjours à la suite des Grands, & qui ne témoignent jamais l'attachement qu'ils ont à leur Religion qu'en outrageant ceux qui n'en sont pas (p. 113). In this outbreak of violent intolerance, insults are fast followed by rocks as "domestiques" of Guise avenge an accidental blow he had suffered. It is the Guises' doubtful fortune to arouse passionate admiration and hatred, in the fickle crowd, "aisé à effrayer [et] qui pour l'ordinaire se consolent aussi aisément qu'ils s'affligent."[53] But clearly the historian asserts that men of arms, at Vassy or in Marillac's *dragonnades*, as many feared in 1681,[54] should not allow their code of honor to be debased by the modes of feeling and violent intolerance of lesser men, who become all too soon an unprincipled mob.

Even if he has the misfortune of being a catalyst of violence, a man like Guise faced with this "malheur et désordre" has the same passive responsibility in loss of control that he has to bear in tacit consent to the cardinal's violent actions.

For this responsibility there will be the repentance of final general confession. But the historian suggests that something more efficacious might have preceded it. Active participation in the cardinal's violence is made more precise in the historian's account of the Conjuration d'Amboise and its aftermath. He deplores the violence of recriminations following Amboise that so moved the young D'Aubigné, whose emotion he transfers and focuses dramatically in the reaction of François II. But he also deplores the design of the princes to assume power and the dissimulation of Condé. "La liberté de conscience qu'ils demanderent ne leur servit que pour couvrir leurs intentions d'un titre specieux & pour grossir leur parti, en y attirant les Huguenots, qui haïssoient mortellement les Guises, *dont ils avoient toûjours esté persecutez*" (p. 79). The fault lies on both sides and incriminates both parties in the causes of war. And once again, of importance for the fanaticism to come, the blame must be shared by the "public, qui dans ses malheurs ne cherche qu'à trouver de qui se plaindre" (p. 78). Both sides lose, as might similar divisions in 1681 if violence in a struggle for political power replaces any reasoned mediation of real issues of religion troubling France.

After Amboise, "quelque soin que prissent les Guises pour persuader au Roy que cette conspiration ne regardoit que sa personne & celle de ses freres, ils ne pouvoient empescher qu'il n'entendist parler quelquefois de l'aversion qu'on avoit pour eux" (p. 83). As for Condé, "sans doute le Chef des conjurez, s'estant plaint avec cette audace qui imite si bien l'innocence de ce qu'on avoit voulu donner au Roy de méchantes impressions de sa conduite, . . . il s'offroit de le [Guise] démentir à la point de l'épée." In Valincour's account this is not a *défi* to a duel of honor. It is a gross ruse that Guise counters politically with another. Smarting yet from this and dissatisfied with Montmorency's report that the Conjuration "ne regardoit point la personne du Roy comme ils [les Guises] le vouloient faire croire," the Guises are justified by him to Parlement in what may be seen to be terms of pure violence: "Si les Seigneurs particuliers ne pouvoient sans honte souffrir qu'on fist insulte à leurs domestiques . . . il n'estoit pas étrange que le Roy eust pris une vengeance exemplaire de l'entreprise qu'on avoit osé faire contre les premiers Ministres de son Estat" (p. 87). The ally of policy, always presented as more violent than Guise, already puts into question the very existence of the Triumvirat—Act IV of Guise's drama—formed in part, the historian makes it clear, as a safeguard of personal power vis-à-vis the princes and Coligny. There is no doubt that Valincour lauds the principle of this alliance of 6 April 1561, but he takes care to show that the reconciliation of Guise and Montmorency at Chantilly, where they remained until the coronation of Charles IX, did not put an end either to personal ambition or to the tension of factions. He repeats with the detail of a Saint-Simon a quarrel over precedence at the coronation, and reflects: "Ne pouvant plus souffrir le mépris public qu'on faisoit de la Religion, ni peut-estre la diminution de son autorité, Guise se retira chez luy, après s'estre plaint à la Reine de la protection qu'elle donnoit aux Huguenots" (p. 110). The Triumvirat, Valincour concedes, was an "entreprise qui a conservé la Religion Catholique" (p. 122); but because of it civil war, "très funeste à tous les deux partis," is the final reality, compromise, and denouement of the drama of the *Vie*.

Valincour emphasizes the fact that the aftermath of Amboise incriminates Parlement, which after Amboise—or in 1681 or in the mid-1720s—may be a hope for mediation and order. "Le Parlement écrivit une Lettre au Roy sur ce qui venoit d'arriver, & une autre à Guise, dans laquelle on luy donnoit le nom glorieux de Conservateur de la Patrie. Quelques services qu'il eust pû rendre à l'Estat en cette rencontre, la reconnoissance du Parlement parut extraordinaire, & un peu au dessous de la dignité d'une si grande compagnie" (p. 88). With factions in political stalemate after persecution and violence, and with Parlement justifying violence in a manner that endorses its future use and foreshadows the Guise Parle-

51

ment,[55] the breakdown of all reasoned institutional mediation of real problems that might be feared in the first quarter of 1681 is made visible in Valincour's tensely dramatic presentation of the Assemblée de Fontainebleau, 15 August 1560 (pp. 89–91). Again blame lies on both sides. "Les esprits estoient trop eschauffez, & ni les uns ni les autres ne vouloient l'accommodement qu'ils faisoient semblant de chercher. Les Guises estoient bien résolus de ne rien épargner pour conserver leur puissance; & les autres déterminez à tout entreprendre pour la détruire, & pour se mettre en la place de leurs ennemis" (p. 89). Foredoomed to failure, this confrontation of violent language inviting future violence and adjourning without accomplishment is in Valincour's account a model warning for the present. He presents a warning against association with fanaticism and violence, which tarnished the *gloire* of a heroic soldier of the past and may again debase soldiers become *dragonnades*. With this warning is a plea for present reasoned mediation of real problems that, replacing factionalism and civil violence, will avoid the undermining and erosion of principle by impassioned policy and violent intolerance that had prepared, and then issued from, the acts of the Ligue.

In his account of Guise's death Valincour, insisting on his documentation, reports—as always without rhetorical display of his own—what he found to be in Guise an easy, natural eloquence. "Je rapporteray icy quelques-unes de ses dernieres paroles, non pas telles que je les auray imaginées, comme font la pluspart des Historiens, mais comme elles ont esté écrites par l'Evesque de Riés, qui l'assista jusqu'au dernier soupir."[56] But there is a significant reordering of his source. Guise is made to turn first to Catherine with the most important counsels the *Vie* has to offer "bons Français" of 1681.

Il luy conseilla d'employer toutes choses pour faire la paix, que c'estoit le seul moyen d'appaiser les troubles qui divisoient la France; qu'Elle sçavoit bien qu'il ne luy avoit jamais donné d'autre conseil; que dans le temps mesme où il croyoit se devoir rendre maistre d'Orleans, il avoit esté d'avis qu'on fist de nouvelles propositions d'accommodement aux Huguenots; et qu'enfin tous ceux qui conseilloient la guerre, n'estoient ni bons François, ni bons serviteurs du Roy. (p. 158)

In Marillac's tactics Valincour may have felt already what Voltaire will express to the Swiss pasteur Vernes—that the *dragonnade* "a fait le malheur du siècle" (Best. 12705)—and have begun to express a reaction to violent intolerance that looks forward directly to the bolder and more explicit commentary on it five years later of Bayle's *Contrains-les d'entrer.* He may well have been aware that, from the mid-1670s and especially from 1679 through the first quarter of 1681, Louis XIV had little by little arrived at a hardened policy that was becoming resigned to violence and that in the matter of unification of the faith this tendency ran counter to the progress already made in method and effectiveness of religious controversy. He was certainly aware that the dazzlingly effective results of violent "conversion" might very quickly obscure the example of that progress he saw in Bossuet and its slower alternatives through "l'empressement que tout le monde avait de voir ce grand ouvrage achevé."[57] "Bulletins de victoire" began, in February, to appear regularly in the *Gazette de France.* The men of arms, intendants or soldiers, who might be given to violence; pious ladies more rigorous than Mme de Maintenon; magistrates less enlightened than Daguesseau; members of both confessions to whom Bossuet shortly was to offer the message of his sermon on church unity—all these persons responsible for both force of opinion and its violent direction are among the most likely audience for the kind of book Valincour was writing and seem to be precisely those persons for whom its method and message were intended. If Benoist could record, by the end of 1681, that "honnêtes gens" of the court condemned Marillac's policy for its threat to the integrity of men of arms and the violence of the man himself,[58] Valincour's life of Guise may have played some effective part in influencing the direction of that opinion. But whatever the reality of its effectiveness, the *Vie* is an act of faith in the efficacy of history, "sage conseillère des princes," by a humanist who makes his history a political act conceived with intellectual probity.

1. Racine to Boileau, 24 juin 1692, *Œuvres* ed. Mesnard (Paris, 1865), 7:55; Valincour to Legendre, 5, 13 juin 1693, *Normandie* 10 (1895): 201.

2. Chapelle, *Recueil . . . de l'Académie* (Paris, 1699), p. 136.

3. *Registre Premier* (Paris, 1738), 2:575.

4. *Nouvelles considérations sur l'histoire, Œuvres historiques*, ed. Pomeau (Paris, 1957), p. 49.

5. *RHLF* 10 (1903): 672.

6. T. Tastet, *Histoire des quarante fauteuils* (Paris, 1855), 3:39.

7. LA VIE/DE/FRANCOIS/DE LORRAINE/DUC DE GUISE/A PARIS/ Chez Sebastien Mabre-Cramoisy . . . /M.DC.LXXXI./Avec privilège de sa Majesté/ 16 avril/. 1 vol. in 12. 174 pp. All quotations are from this printing.

8. On the problematic evidence of the exact training by Bouhours, see Valincour, *Lettres à Madame la marquise* (Tours, 1972), Introduction, pp. iii-iv.

9. Bouhours cited by Lachèvre, *Bibliographie des recueils collectifs* (Paris, 1901-5), 3:121; Bussy, letter of 1 janvier 1686, *Correspondance*, ed. Lalanne (Paris, 1858), 5:486.

10. *Eloges* (Paris, 1825), 2:252-3. Emphasis added.

11. E. Sue, *Histoire de la Marine française* (Paris, 1836), 4:38-39.

12. Memoirs published by Monmerqué, *Mémoires du marquis de Vilette* (Paris, 1854).

13. E.g., letters of 19 novembre and 1 décembre 1729 to Bouhier, *RHLF* 31 (1924): 400-401.

14. See G. Genette, "Vraisemblance et motivation," *Communications* 10 (1968): 5-21.

15. For his personal appreciation and reservations, see letter of 22 décembre 1729 to Bouhier, *RHLF* 31 (1924): 402.

16. Variations in format and pagination reveal at least three printings.

17. *Recueil . . . de l'Académie* (Paris, 1724-5), p. 136.

18. See J. Louail, *Histoire du livre des Réflexions et de la Constitution* (Amsterdam, 1723), 1:371-72.

19. E.g., from 1717 to 1725: Britism Museum Add. MSS. 20395, pp. 8, 13v, 15v, 25v, 36v, 42, 45v, 60, 61v, 101v, 112, 130v, 133, 176, 226.

20. See Jean Orcibal, *Louis XIV et les protestants* (Paris, 1951), p. 24.

21. Orcibal, pp. 77, 176 for the letter of 29 juin 1680 to Innocent XI. The harassment is exhaustively detailed by E. Benoist, *Histoire de l'Edit de Nantes* (Delft, 1695), vol. 4.

22. Cologne, 1681; Maimbourg, "Epistre au Roy," *Histoire du luthé-*

ranisme (Paris, 1681). See the reaction to his politics of G. Burnet, *History of the Rights of Princes* (London, 1682).

23. Mme de Caylus, quoted by Orcibal, p. 108. On the realities, see Benoist, 4:274-82.

24. Orcibal, p. 83.

25. Especially notorious was J.-B. Adéhmar de Monteil de Grignan, Coadjuteur d'Arles, whose violent remonstrance of 1675 circulated in England (Beinecke Library British Tract, 1677/C28). The remonstrance to the king after the Assemblée of July 1680 was widely denounced. See Burnet, pp. 95-97; Benoist, 4:413; Orcibal, p. 23.

26. Maintenon, letter of 28 septembre 1681, *Correspondance*, ed. Langlois (Paris, 1935), 2:405; Daguesseau, quoted by Benoist, 4:383. For Valincour's portrait of him see P. Adry, ed., *La Princesse de Clèves* (Paris, 1807), 2:332-35.

27. See Bossuet, *Correspondance*, ed. Urbain (Paris, 1925), 14:109-27, 129-51, 218-19; H. Busson, *La Religion des classiques* (Paris, 1948), pp. 410-11.

28. On the problem of the exact date, between 1681-83, of Valincour's appointment and Bossuet's part, see Fontenelle, *Eloge*, p. 253; A. Cazes, ed., *Lettres à Madame la marquise* (Paris, 1926), Introduction, pp. 34-35.

29. See A. Rébelliau, *Bossuet historien des protestants* (Paris, 1891), pp. 70-73, 76-77; A.-G. Martimort, *Le Gallicanisme de Bossuet* (Paris, 1953), p. 280; J. Truchet, *Politique de Bossuet* (Paris, 1966), pp. 22, 46, 188.

30. Quoted by Orcibal, p. 23.

31. Final panegyric of the reign, *Discours de réception à l'Académie* (Paris: Coignard, 1699), pp. 13 ff., elaborates the year's set subject for eloquence: "Sur la piété du Roy & sur l'attention qu'il a eue aux interests de la Religion dans le dernier traité de Paix."

32. Letters of 19 août and 3 mai 1728, *RHLF* 31 (1924): 376, 393.

33. De Thou, *Histoire des choses arrivées de son temps*, tr. Du Ruyer (Paris: Courbé, 1659), 2:90-91.

34. Description of the Italian campaign (pp. 53-60) is strongly antipapal but in calculated contrast to the virulence of Régnier de la Planche.

35. See R. Zuber, *Les "Belles infidèles" et la formation du goût classique* (Paris, 1969), p. 209.

36. Bertrand de Salignac, *Le Siège de Metz* (Paris, 1552).

37. Brantôme, *Œuvres*, ed. Lalanne (Paris, 1864), 4:189.

38. Physical recovery as "quelque chose de miraculeux," pp. 6, 167, following the *Mémoires de Martin et Guillaume du Bellay* (ed. Bourilly [Paris, 1919], 4:313-14).

39. On the ideal, see Zuber, *Les "Belles infidèles,"* pp. 208-9, and Michelet, *Histoire de France* (Paris, 1879), 15:188.

40. See Robert Cottrell, *Brantôme: The Writer as Portraitist* (Geneva, 1970), pp. 123-49.

41. Brantôme, *Vie*, pp. 318, 279-80.

42. *Histoire universelle*, ed. Ruble (Paris, 1880), 2:143-44.

43. P. 77; Brantôme, *Vie*, pp. 223-25.

44. E.g., pp. 12, 52.

45. See above, n. 33.

46. *Vie de l'Admiral de Chastillon, Œuvres*, 4:328-34.

47. Quoted by Saint-Beuve, *Causeries* (Paris, 1857), 7:224.

48. Voltaire, *Œuvres historiques*, ed. Pomeau, pp. 889-90. Cf. the critical evaluation of method by J. H. Brumfitt, *Voltaire Historian* (London, 1958), pp. 23, 188; J. Solé, *Bayle polémiste* (Paris, 1972), p. 19.

49. P. 44. See *Le Siège de Metz*, Coll. Petitot, 23:401; De Thou, 1:628.

50. L. Romier, *Les Origines politiques des guerres de Religion* (Paris, 1913), 2:119.

51. Pp. 55, 72; Brantôme, *Vie*, pp. 229, 276.

52. Pp. 99-100 repeat the famous "Tanneguy du Chastel, où es-tu?" anecdote, seemingly from De Thou, 2:175.

53. Pp. 62, 131.

54. See Orcibal, pp. 72-74.

55. On the Parlement's "persistent hostility" to Huguenots and Guise's use of it, see J. H. Shennan, *The Parlement of Paris* (London, 1968), pp. 211-12; on the Guise Parlement, pp. 225-27.

56. Lancelot de Carle, *Lettre de l'Evesque de Riez. . .* , (Paris, 1563).

57. Orcibal, p. 109.

58. See Benoist, *Histoire de la Révocation*, 4:503; Orcibal, pp. 73-74, on the general reaction and Louvois, Arrêt du 19 mai.

The *Journal des Sçavans* and
The *Lettres Persanes*

ALESSANDRO S. CRISAFULLI

Letter 108 of the *Lettres persanes* is an amusing indication of the merits as well as the shortcomings of the literary periodicals of the early eighteenth century. Usbek-Montesquieu first states that these publications seem very popular to him; then he gives an idea of the numerous books that they reviewed and abstracted: "La paresse se sent flattée, en les lisant: on est ravi de pouvoir parcourir trente volumes en un quart-d'heure."[1] But he criticizes the journalists for talking only of the new books to the neglect of the old, and for being too careful not to pass judgment on the works analyzed for fear of bringing upon their heads the wrath of sensitive authors. The result, according to Montesquieu, is that they are very boring, for they begin by insipidly praising the subject of the books and then proceed to the praises of the authors. In complaining thus, Montesquieu had in mind those editors who expressed the policy (not always adhered to) of being entirely noncommittal about the works of which they gave an account. The *Journal des Sçavans*, for instance, during the first years of its publication, had apparently taken the liberty of judging the merit of the books it summarized; but it had to give this practice up because it found that "on s'en plaignit . . . comme d'un attentat sur la liberté publique, et qu'on dit que ce serait exercer une espèce de tyrannie dans l'Empire des Lettres, que de vouloir s'attribuer le droit de juger des ouvrages de tout le monde. C'est ce qui fit résoudre à n'user plus de critique dans le Journal, mais

59

au lieu de censurer les livres, de s'attacher à les bien lire pour en pouvoir donner un extrait plus exact au public."[2]

Montesquieu's criticism does not, of course, represent his serious opinion of the periodicals of his day; far from finding them boring, he read them regularly and with profit. His familiarity with periodical publications is revealed not only by his facetious criticism but also by the many notes from them still found in the *Pensées* and the *Spicilège*, two of the notebooks he drew from in writing his works. The sources presented here concern the *Journal des Sçavans* and the *Lettres persanes* and have been chosen to show how Montesquieu modified the material borrowed in order to shape it or adapt it to his artistic purposes.

Letter 89, dealing with man's desire for glory and the degree to which it motivates the subjects of different nations, shows that Montesquieu was already speculating about the principles of the republican, monarchical, and despotic forms of government that he was later to expound in the *Esprit des lois*. In singling out for greatest praise the behavior of republican subjects, he utilizes a passage from the *Journal des Sçavans* for the year 1685, one of the volumes that he had certainly read and abstracted, as can be seen from the *Pensées*.[3] The various tokens of honor used by the Romans are there summarized from a Latin book on the prizes awarded by Rome for military achievements: "Pour les récompenses, comme le seul désir de la gloire rendait braves les Romains, si nous en croyons leur histoire, le prix des victoires les plus signalées, n'était ordinairement que l'honneur du triomphe, un surnom, une couronne de laurier ou de chêne, une louange ou une statue dans une place publique" (13 [1685]: 20).

In fashioning his own version of the passage, Montesquieu says: "Mais le sanctuaire de l'honneur, de la réputation et de la vertu, semble être établi dans les républiques et dans les pays où l'on peut prononcer le mot de patrie.[4] A Rome, à Athènes, à Lacédémone, l'honneur payoit seul les services les plus signalés. Une couronne de chêne ou de laurier, une statue, un éloge, étoit une récompense immense pour une bataille gagnée, ou une ville prise" (pp. 228–29).

The single sentence from the *Journal des Sçavans* lacks the scope and the stylistic qualities of the passage Montesquieu composed for his purpose. Concerned not merely with Rome but with other examples of the republican form of government as the ideal state, he constructed three sentences that express his admiration with a significant pattern of rhythm and sounds. The first sentence, entirely original, strikingly conveys Montesquieu's feeling with a triad of anaphoric phrases, "de l'honneur, de la réputation et de la vertu," with a concentration of *r* sounds, and with the alliteration of the *p*'s. The ternary rhythm recurs, with a meaningful counterpart and echo, at the beginning of the second sentence through the specific mention of the three most famous republican states of antiquity, arranged in ascending order corresponding to the length of their names: "A Rome, à Athènes, à Lacédémone." The rest of the second sentence is a restructuring of the main clause of the original: "le prix des victoires les plus signalées n'était ordinairement que l'honneur du triomphe." The changes, achieved by the personification of "honneur" and its function as subject of "payoit" and by the substitution of the more general word "services" for "victoires," result in a more concise clause punctuated with alliteration: "l'honneur payoit seul les services les plus signalés." For his third and concluding sentence, Montesquieu borrowed two phrases: "une couronne de laurier ou de chêne" and "une louange ou une statue," but he transformed them by slight syntactical and semantic changes. In the first phrase, he simply reversed the order of the two nouns; in the second, besides, he replaced one of the nouns with a synonym and dropped the conjunction. The switch of "chêne" and "laurier" results in the juxtaposition of "chêne" and "couronne" with a more notable echo effect and in the placing of "laurier," a more substantial word, at the final, stressed position of the phrase. The other phrase, "une statue, un éloge," continues, with the added emphasis of

61

the asyndeton, the binary rhythm of the first. Thus the modified phrases, "une couronne de chêne ou de laurier, une statue, un éloge," are perfectly fitted into the last part of sentence, Montesquieu's own thought, expressed by binary combinations with rhyme and assonance: "récompense immense . . . bataille gagnée . . . ville prise."

In this same 1685 volume Montesquieu found a curious little story about an extraordinary blind man who "jouait même aux cartes, et gagnait surtout beaucoup, quand c'était à lui à faire, parce qu'il connaissait au toucher quelles cartes il donnait à chaque joueur" (13 [1685]: 433). This oddity, reported with a sense of wonder, becomes the nucleus and the climactic point of Letter 32, in which Rica amusingly describes his visit to the Hospice des Quinze-Vingts. Without knowing that the Hospice is an institution for the blind, Rica observes that its inmates were quite cheerful and that some were playing cards and other games. He leaves the place at the same time as one of them who, having heard him ask for the way to the Marais, offers to take him there and expertly guides him through the hazards of Paris traffic. Upon reaching his destination, Rica wants to know more about his guide and asks him who he is: "—Je suis aveugle, Monsieur, me répondit-il. —Comment! lui dis-je, vous êtes aveugle? Et que ne priïez-vous cet honnête homme qui jouoit aux cartes avec vous de nous conduire?—Il est aveugle aussi, me répondit-il: il y a quatre cents ans que nous sommes trois cent aveugles dans cette maison où vous m'avez trouvé" (p. 85).

In this example the creative process is directed toward a comic effect. The astonishing idea of a blind man's skill at cards is developed into a little scene between Rica, moved by curiosity, and his blind guide, acting with self-assurance and pride. His revelation: "Je suis aveugle," springs a surprise that is prolonged in Rica's repetition of it in question form and with a change of subject: "Comment! . . . vous êtes aveugle?" and echoed with increasing irony in the rejoinder: "Il est aveugle aussi." But that is not the end of the word play; it

62

continues with: "il y a quatre cents ans que nous sommes trois cents aveugles."[5]

Another strange idea derived from the *Journal des Sçavans* is exploited in Letter 51, a satirical treatment of the manners, laws, and government of Russia. In the summary of an English account of Russia, Montesquieu's attention was drawn to a passage dealing with the marriage contract: "Il [l'auteur] en remarque plusieurs particularités fort plaisantes. Il dit qu'un des articles qu'un père fait toujours mettre dans un contrat lorsqu'il marie quelque fille est que le mari ne la fouettera jamais . . . " (7 [1679]: 265). Montesquieu rewrote the passage thus: "Quoique les pères, au contrat de mariage de leurs filles, stipulent ordinairement que le mari ne les fouettera pas; cependant on ne sçauroit croire combien les femmes moscovites aiment à être battues; elles ne peuvent comprendre qu'elles possèdent le cœur de leur mari, s'il ne les bat comme il faut" (p. 132).

The passage from the abridgment of the English book concerns only the article in the marriage contract. Montesquieu, with a concessive clause, subordinates this odd fact to another curious piece of information from other sources: the desire of Russian wives to be beaten by their husbands in order to have the assurance of being loved.[6] The combination results in a witty statement that sets the legalized wishes of the fathers against the perverse and unnatural inclination of their daughters. Montesquieu thus achieves another example of incongruity and surprise similar to that of the blind men who behave normally. But the artistic exploitation of this source goes beyond the ironical contrast set up between Russian fathers and daughters. Montesquieu, resorting to the letter-within-a-letter device, which appears several times in his fiction,[7] imagines that a Russian wife is writing to her mother to complain about her misfortune: her husband does not love her because he does not beat her! And she envies her lucky sister who gets a beating every day and recalls that, when she was a child, it sometimes seemed to her, that her father loved her mother too

63

much! The letter-within-a-letter device involves, moreover, the process of comic dramatization observed in Letter 32. The blind man acting like a person with normal sight and the Russian wife who wants to be beaten speak and act for themselves, each motivated by pride, though in different situations.

Montesquieu's most substantial borrowing from the *Journal des Sçavans* is in Letter 78. It is a strange anecdote about the value the Spaniards and the Portuguese attach to the mustache. It was drawn from an account of a Spanish book on Portuguese colonies in Asia,[8] and is the second of two amusing stories about conquerors: "Ce qu'on raconte de Jean de Castro, qui était un autre de ces premiers conquérants n'est pas moins agréable que l'autre paraît surprenant. Ce bon homme se trouvant en un extrême besoin d'argent se coupa une de ses moustaches, et sur ce gage précieux demanda aux habitants de Goa vingt mille pistoles; elles lui furent prêtées, et peu de temps après il les rendit avec beaucoup de fidélité, et dégagea sa moustache" (5 [1677]: 215–16). Montesquieu relates the anecdote as part of a letter ridiculing the Spanish and the Portuguese concept of honor: "Quant à la moustache, elle est respectable par elle-même, et indépendamment des conséquences; quoiqu'on ne laisse pas quelquefois d'en tirer de grandes utilités, pour le service du Prince et l'honneur de la nation, comme le fit bien voir un fameux général portugais dans les Indes: car, se trouvant avoir besoin d'argent, il coupa une de ses moustaches et envoya demander aux habitans de Goa vingt mille pistoles sur ce gage; elles lui furent prêtées d'abord, et dans la suite il retira sa moustache avec honneur" (p. 201).

Montesquieu's version is more concise as a result of his eliminating certain details and changing the order of the phrase "sur ce gage"; but more significant, artistically, are the additions and adjustments he made in order to set the anecdote in a new context. He once again made use of a letter-within-a-letter, inserted this time in a letter by Rica to Usbek and plausibly attributed to a Frenchman traveling in Spain.[9] The anecdote occupies a conspicuous place at the end of the first part of the Frenchman's satire. He associates the mustache in a curious manner with eyeglasses, noting that gravity is the most salient national characteristic of the Spaniards and the Portuguese and that it is displayed in two principal ways: "par les lunettes, et par la moustache." After ridiculing the practice of wearing glasses as a vain show of learning, the biased French observer goes on with ironical logic to talk about the mustache, making a distinction between its intrinsic value and its possible usefulness to ruler and nation, and ending with a remarkable illustration. The general's deed in cutting off his mustache and the mustache itself assume mock-heroic proportions in the new, satirical setting created for the story by Montesquieu. The elaborate preparation for its ironical retelling is evident in the syntactical links *quant à, quoique, comme, car* that mark the flow of the irony in a carefully constructed period.

These examples of borrowing from the *Journal des Sçavans* show Montesquieu the skilled writer at two levels of literary creation: in the first example he structures a moving, expressive passage by modifying the syntax of a sentence that stimulated his feeling and imagination and combining it with ideas and words of his own. In the other passages he uses his creative imagination at the level of both style and structure. The extraordinary blind man, the stipulation that Russian brides should not be beaten, the anecdote about the Portuguese general's valuable mustache are just curiosities in the contexts in which Montesquieu found them. He dramatized them comically by placing them in new contexts: a snatch of dialogue and letters-within-letters. In these cases he developed, and gave form and emotional intensity to, the ludicrous potential of his sources.

---

1. *Lettres persanes*, ed. Antoine Adam (Geneva, 1954), p. 273. All page references are to this edition and will be indicated henceforth after each quotation.

2. *Journal des Sçavans*, Amsterdam ed., 5 (1677): 166. The spelling of all quotations from the *Journal* has been modernized; all references, indicated henceforth after each quotation, are to the Amsterdam edition. Jean Le Clerc, the editor of three periodicals, likewise protested, on several occasions, his impartiality and his practice of praising rather than censuring authors. His *Bibliothèque choisie*, he asserts, "est pleine de louange des habiles gens, qui m'ont donné occasion de parler de leurs ouvrages. . . . Je n'ai rien dit de désavantageux à personne, qu'après en avoir été violemment outragé . . . " (*Bibliothèque choisie*, 19 [1709]: 376-77). Cf. also 21 (1710): 1-2; and his *Bibliothèque universelle*, 1 (1686): Preface.

3. *Œuvres complètes* (Paris: Pléiade edition, 1949), 1: 1188.

4. Montesquieu does not at the time of the *Lettres persanes* distinguish between *honneur* as the exclusive principle of the monarchical form of government and *vertu* as that of the republican form.

5. The letter closes with a similar effect of irony reinforced by repetition with a variation and a chiastic arrangement: "Mais il faut que je vous quitte: voilà la rue que vous demandiez: je vais me mettre dans la foule; j'entre dans cette église, où, je vous jure, j'embarrasserai plus les gens qu'ils ne m'embarrasseront" (p. 85). In thus concluding the letter, Montesquieu recalls, as all commentators point out, Cotolendi's *Lettre d'un Sicilien*. Speaking also of the blind in Paris and the institution of the Quinze-Vingts, the Sicilian ends with a detail about their begging in the churches and the trouble they cause by their noise. Montesquieu's superior wit and creativity are evident in the play with the word *embarrasser*, which is not used by Cotolendi.

6. The traveler Adam Olearius, *Voyage . . . en Moscovie, Tartarie et Perse*, trans. A. de Wicquefort, 2 vols. (Paris, 1659), and John Perry, *Etat présent de la Grande Russie*, translated from English (La Haye, 1717), are Montesquieu's main sources for his letter on Russia. The statement that Russian wives like to be beaten comes most likely from Olearius, who mentions with some skepticism all the travelers before him who speak of it. But neither he nor Perry reports the curious article in the marriage contract to which Montesquieu refers.

7. The device is first used in Letter 28 and besides Letter 51 is repeated in 78, 130, 142, 143 and 145. In Letters 28 and 51, the opening sentence is the same: an actress complains to Rica: "Je suis la plus malheureuse fille du monde"; the Russian wife echoes: "Je suis la plus malheureuse femme du monde."

8. *Asia portuguesa de Manuel de Faria y Sousa cavallero de la Orden de Christo y de la Casa Real*, Tome 2. E. Carcassone found the story of de Castro's mustache in a life of the general by Freyre de Andrada; but the details are different. See *Lettres persanes*, ed. E. Carcassone (Paris: Les Textes Français, 1929), 2:193.

9. French-Spanish animosity, dating back to the end of the sixteenth century, continued to rise in the seventeenth and the eighteenth. It is significant that the source of most of Letter 78 is a Frenchwoman's biased and spurious account of Spain, Mme d'Aulnoy's *Relation du voyage en Espagne* (1691).

From London to Lapland:
Maupertuis, Johann Bernoulli I
And *La Terre applatie*, 1728-1738

When Maupertuis left Paris for London late in May of 1728, he carried letters of introduction to Sir Hans Sloane, successor to Isaac Newton in the presidency of the Royal Society, and *associé étranger* of the Académie royale des Sciences. In a brief letter of 22 May, the botanist Bernard de Jussieu says he would have liked to accompany Maupertuis "qui porte cette lettre." Just over three months later, 4 September, Maupertuis writes from Paris, thanking Sloane for courtesies and kindnesses, in particular that he has been admitted as a Fellow of the Royal Society. Thus the "six months" usually assigned to the visit to England is an exaggeration, and Maupertuis's exposure to science and life in London must be limited to about twelve weeks in June, July, and August of 1728.

There seems to be no record of what Maupertuis did during those weeks. The usual educated visitor would see the Tower, St. James's Palace, some of the new Wren churches, and most particularly St. Paul's, at that time brilliantly white since its completion in 1710. Of special interest would be Sloane's house in Bloomsbury and his rich botanical garden in Chelsea, as well as the Royal Observatory, where Flamsteed had worked with notable results until his death in 1719. The Journal of the Royal Society records his presence at two meetings, 23 May and 27 June, both old style; on 20 June he was proposed as Fellow by the mathematician Abraham de Moivre, and a week later he was ballotted and elected. Because

69

the Society did not usually meet during July and August, it is unlikely that he attended other sessions. There must have been other occasions where he could gather firsthand impressions of Newtonian scientists, a breed of men such as he had not met before. Pierre Brunet says that one cannot exaggerate the scientific importance of this visit, "qui apparaît vraiment décisif dans l'orientation ultérieure des travaux de Maupertuis."

However, the influence exerted on Maupertuis by English culture in general was much less profound than that felt by Voltaire, whose contemporary sojourn *outre-Manche* extended from 1726 to some time in 1729. The mathematician seems to have felt no impulse to learn English. Most of those he met would be more or less fluent in French or Latin; the education and travel of the young Englishman of those days gave him some skill in languages. Sloane, for instance, had been in Paris and Montpellier in 1683-84, and had been given a medical degree by the shadowy university in Orange. Pierre Desmaizeaux, with whom he later exchanged letters, and de Moivre were both Huguenot refugees; a letter to William Jones, also a mathematician (1 September 1729), was written in Latin. Cromwell Mortimer, one of the secretaries of the Society, at this time editing the *Philosophical Transactions*, would be using both French and Latin in his daily occupations.

All the evidence indicates that Maupertuis's purpose in visiting England was quite different from that of the exile Voltaire. As a professional scientist of standing among his colleagues, his use of time was subject to the standards expected of an academician as well as to the strictures of his conscience. On the other hand, Voltaire was an amateur in every sense of the word; a product of the Jesuit educational system as well as of the libertine society of the French Regency, he had wide and uncoordinated interests, and followed his whim into almost every corner of English life. The intellectual chaos of his *Letters Concerning the English Nation* makes his position as a dilettante quite clear. In contrast, Maupertuis was no amateur of human affairs like Voltaire; he showed no interest in British politics or religious variations, or in literature, the theater, or history, so far as his subsequent writings indicate. He was a scientist, a mathematician, convivial and a good mixer in social gatherings, but he was not seriously interested at this time in anything beyond his mathematics and his own branch of the physical sciences.

In 1728 the work of Newton was already known in French scientific circles, even if not accepted as sound theory. Newton had been named one of the first eight *associés étrangers* on the reorganization of the Académie in 1699; the *Principia* had been reviewed in the Netherlands soon after publication, and discussed in the *Acta Eruditorum* of Leipzig in the 1690s. The second edition of the *Principia* had been sent in 1714 to Fontenelle, secretary of the Académie des Sciences; to the Abbé Jean Paul Bignon, in charge of the Bibliothèque du Roi; and to the Académie, to which institution went also six copies of the third edition in 1728. The more accessible *Opticks* had been analyzed in ten sessions of the Académie by Etienne François Geoffroy in 1706, and a copy of the English edition sent to Varignon in 1718. Pierre Coste's translation of this work (Amsterdam, 1720, and Paris, 1722) was presented to the Académie in 1722.

Meanwhile, the resistance of the Cartesians was growing; a widely read book by the Abbé Philippe Villemot, *Nouveau système ou nouvelle explication du mouvement des Planètes* (Lyon, 1707) had appeared, offering arguments regarded as trivial by such leading Cartesians as Johann Bernoulli and Leibniz, but still influential among the reading public who found the *tourbillons* easy to understand. It cannot be denied that many Frenchmen and others hesitated to accept the idea that an Englishman who had shown no great respect for the academies and scientists of the Continent could possibly develop a theory that would put the vortices to rout. Science was still a matter of belief and unconscious prejudice for the majority, and it would take much education and liberation of

71

spirit to accept the view that truth has no nationality and demands no patriotism.

Maupertuis was a Newtonian before he left France, but he gained confidence in England from the discovery that an entire academy of intelligent men was convinced that the Cartesian cosmos of vortices, nearly unanimously accepted in France, was without foundation in observed fact or confirmation in mathematical or physical theory, was, in fact, a figment of the imagination, a useless substitute for a sound theory of the universe. For British scientists Newton's universe, subject to the operation of simple laws capable of mathematical expression, made much more sense, even if it seemed to depend on the acceptance of the possibility of gravitational attraction over immense distances and the denial of a theory of orbital motion by means of impulses in a plenum. This reciprocal attraction exerted by bodies remote from one another, an "occult quality" as the French were inclined to call it, was the chief obstacle to the understanding of Newtonian physics on the Continent, and it took much discussion and a monumental experimental effort to overcome this particular stumbling block. When he returned to France, even more convinced that Newton was right, Maupertuis was determined to produce the evidence that would persuade his colleagues that their views needed revision. To this end, he began a series of theoretical investigations, to be followed by observations, that resulted ultimately in the recognition of the new physical theory as fundamental to the understanding of the shape and motions of the solar system and its components, as well as to geodetics and navigational science.

Maupertuis's movements in the months that followed his return to Paris are unrecorded. He seems to have paid a short visit to Montpellier, probably for his health, a recurrent problem. Late in 1729 he was in Basel, to study with Johann Bernoulli (1667–1748), an *associé étranger* of the Académie des Sciences, and one of the leading mathematicians of Europe. This was an important move on the part of the younger scientist: Bernoulli was, among all the thinkers of the day, the man whose views had to be met with the maximum of precision in argument, for he was an outspoken adversary of Newton and a leader in the development of the theory of the Cartesian vortices. The record of this challenge to the accepted system of the Académie is found in the copious correspondence that passed between the friendly antagonists, preserved in the library of the University of Basel, on which this essay is largely based.

Fortunately for the historian, the massive Bernoulli collection is quite literally a *Briefwechsel*, an exchange of letters, in which those sent by Maupertuis can be read in the light of replies drafted by the Bernoullis, Johann I and II, thus permitting an understanding of their individual interests as well as of their contrasting personalities. Comments on third persons are frequent, the elder Bernoulli's caustic references to some of Maupertuis's associates adding spice to pages of mathematical calculations. In view of the inadequacy of most publications from the correspondence of Maupertuis, and the destruction in 1915–16 of the bulk of his papers left in the hands of La Condamine, the Basel collection offers perhaps the best available unexploited source of information concerning the latter part of Maupertuis's career and the development of his work as scientist and public figure.

Well before Maupertuis's visit, Jakob (1654–1705) and Johann Bernoulli had welcomed foreign students to Basel and to their house up the hill from the university. In the Engelhof, in recent years a pension much used by students, Jakob Bernoulli had formed, as Fontenelle says in his *éloge*, "des Assemblées et une espèce d'Académie" in which he performed experiments, "ou le fondement ou la preuve des calculs géométriques," thus becoming the first to establish in Basel "cette manière de philosopher, la seule raisonnable, et qui cependant a tant tardé à paraître." Johann continued this hospitable device for promoting the sciences, and Maupertuis would revisit the house several times in the next thirty years,

73

although there is reason to believe that his way of life, developed in the lively society of a brief career in the *mousquetaires gris* and the cafés of Paris, was not entirely to the taste of the elder Bernoullis, firmly Protestant and supporters of the Peterskirche round the corner from their house. But in spite of differing tastes, gifts and services were exchanged between Maupertuis and his friends; spectacles were sent from Paris for the older couple, and extra copies of Johann Bernoulli's award-winning dissertation of 1730, *Nouvelles Pensées sur le système de Descartes*, printed at Maupertuis's expense. Bernoulli balanced the account by comments and suggestions for Maupertuis's mathematical productions, his constructive criticism being of considerable importance to the younger man.

The *Philosophiae naturalis Principia mathematica*, commonly called the *Principia*, was published in 1687, and Bernoulli's critical comments appeared soon after in the *Acta Eruditorum* of Leipzig. The substance of them was repeated from time to time in publications and correspondence; their author was clearly piqued that Newton had not deigned to refute the criticism nor to act on it in preparing the second edition. Everything that passed between Maupertuis and Bernoulli in later years has to be read in the light of this basic opposition. Each hoped to bring the other to his own point of view; Bernoulli held that the stellar universe was full of a very subtle matter arranged in whirlpools that shared their motion with planets, satellites, and even suns, fundamentally the system of vortices or *tourbillons* invented by Descartes with much elaboration as the refined observations of astronomers and the mathematical requirements might demand, whereas Maupertuis worked from the basis of a universe of celestial objects in motion in an essentially empty universe permitting free movement except as the attraction of other mass objects might intervene. For this Newtonian scheme of things Maupertuis saw that one of the most interesting problems would be the determination of the shape of a rotating body in its own field of gravitation, assuming a degree of fluidity in its matter and a speed of rotation sufficient to produce tangential force great enough to affect its shape without causing it to fly apart.

The two systems were mutually incompatible: no compromise was possible between the universe full of vortices and a solar system consisting of planets and satellites unconnected by a material medium moving freely in orbits determined by their tangential inertia and the gravitational force of the sun. Bernoulli held for the one, Maupertuis for the other; they could understand each other's calculations, respect each other's integrity, if not their basic assumptions. They recognized that the positions to which each clung were sincerely held and would not be abandoned without some final physical demonstration, argument and mathematical proof not being enough to break the other's faith in his own interpretation of the phenomena.

During 1729 and 1730 Maupertuis had begun work on the theory of spheroids rotating in their own field of gravity, and had kept Bernoulli in touch with his developing calculations. On 11 June 1731 he writes that his "pièce sur les sphéroïdes et sur les anneaux" is nearing completion, the rings in questions being suggested by the rings of Saturn first observed by Huygens and announced in 1658, since when they had been a matter of much speculation. Acting on advice from Bernoulli, Maupertuis has put his dissertation in Latin, because he believed "qu'elle seroit mieux reçue en Angleterre qu'ici; j'ai envie de l'envoyer aux *Transactions philosophiques*"; an argument based on Newtonian theory would be more welcome in London than in Paris. Bernoulli is now asked to examine the article for its geometry and for its Latin as well:

> Corrigez donc, Monsieur, effacez, ajoutez ce que vous jugerez à propos, et ne me refusez pas ce plaisir. Je ne veux point lire cette pièce dans nos assemblées, où il y a des gens que le seul mot d'attraction épouvante.

75

Bernoulli returns the *pièce* on 26 June, describing it as "très beau, et très bien écrit en latin"; he has made some corrections, suggesting especially a word to describe Saturn's rings as *fluentum*, defined as "un amas de matière fluide qui coule doucement et avec une vitesse uniforme," rather than *effluvium*, which would indicate an outpouring as from a spring or a comet's tail. Accepting the correction, Maupertuis has sent (30 July 1731) his dissertation to England, "la doctrine qui y est répandue étant un peu obieuse dans ce pays-ci . . . où l'on croit que les tourbillons expliquent tout sans s'embarrasser des couleuvres qu'il faut dévorer pour les concilier avec les phénomènes."

Maupertuis sent his *pièce* to Sloane on 9 July, with a letter in which he repeated his thanks for election to the Royal Society and expressed the hope that his contribution would be accepted for publication in the *Transactions*. Appearing in England, it would need to contain no defense of the theory of gravitation because that was accepted by everyone, whereas in France, as he repeats in a letter to Bernoulli, such a development would be badly received, adding,

> quant à faire ma cour à mes compatriotes, je ne crois pas que l'amour de la patrie doive gêner le moins du monde les opinions purement philosophiques. Et quelque respect que j'aie pour l'Académie, je ne voudrois pas qu'elle exigeât de moi aucun sacrifice sur ces sortes de choses, quelque chose qui en pût arriver. . . . Je ne serois jamais de tel ou tel sentiment par politique, et l'Académie ne l'exige pas non plus.

Publication of such things went a little faster in his day than in ours, but in September he had had no word from Sloane that his article had been received. However, on 27 March 1732 his essay on spheroids had been seen and approved by the mathematician John Machin, one of the secretaries of the Royal Society, and early publication was planned. In a letter to Cromwell Mortimer, Maupertuis expressed his pleasure at the approval of his purely mathematical solution of a problem that in time would affect the observational sciences; not only was he aware of the empirical British spirit, but he knew that his work would have important bearings on the mapping of the earth and so on navigation as well. At this time he submits a "petit scholion" that will make it clear that he does not regard "comme des déterminations vrayes et exactes ce que je dis dans les deux problèmes . . . sur la forme des sphéroïdes et des anneaux," because he fears that some readers may be prejudiced against him for finding other proportions for the two diameters of the earth (polar and equatorial) than those calculated by Newton: "Ce grand homme n'a point d'admirateur si zélé que moi," a statement that perhaps has a modicum of *politique* in it, in spite of a previous protestation to Bernoulli.

In number 422 of the *Philosophical Transactions*, "for the months of January, February, and March," of 1732, Maupertuis's paper was published: "De Figuris quas Fluida rotata induere possunt Problemata duo; cum conjectura de Stellis quae aliquando prodeunt vel deficiunt; et de Annulo Saturni." And in spite of his anxieties over French views about Newtonian thought, he published in the same year in Paris his *Discours sur les différentes figures des astres, où l'on essaye d'expliquer les principaux phénomènes du ciel*, a little book that offered two years before Voltaire's *Lettres philosophiques*, a readable and accurate account of the principles of the theory of gravitation. Some twenty-six years later, justice was done: in his *Histoire des mathématiques* of 1758, J. E. Montucla of the Académie des Sciences would credit Maupertuis with a large part in a "révolution presque subite et générale dans la manière de penser," created by his "exposition lumineuse . . . de la théorie de l'attraction dans son livre *de la Figure des Astres.*"

Relations between the elder Bernoulli and Maupertuis continued more or less evenly through the next two years. In September 1732 Maupertuis asked permission to communicate two of Bernoulli's papers to the Académie, mentioning the interest taken by François Nicole (1683-1758) and Alexis-Claude Clairaut (1713-65) in Bernoulli's investigations. A little later, expressing his wish to see Bernoulli in Paris occupying the post of astronomer, he adds:

> Nous ne sommes pas dans un temps où l'on puisse espérer que le ministre paye des gens tels que vous et leur donne les pensions qu'il leur faudrait. . . . Cela étoit bon dans les années magnifiques du règne de Louis XIV.

But the fundamental difference over Newtonian physics was not forgotten. On 26 April 1733 Bernoulli remarks that he still finds it better to explain phenomena of movement by impulsion than by Newton's obscure concept of attraction; there may even be an element of pique in this attitude, deriving from Newton's indifference to Bernoulli's comments on the *Principia* and the failure to correct "errors" in that book in its later editions of 1713 and 1726. He recognizes the influence of Newton on the younger generation, both in France and in England, when he describes them as "sectaires . . . indiscrets jusqu'à tel point qu'ils prétendent qu'on doive approuver aussi les bévues sur cela seul qu'elles viennent de Mr. Newton."

Meanwhile, the search for objective observational support for the opposing views continued. Jacques Cassini had spent the summer of 1733 in measuring a degree of longitude between Paris and Saint Malo, on which Maupertuis remarks that "de sa mesure résulteroit encore que la terre seroit allongée; mais je crois qu'il manque à tout cela bien des choses pour pouvoir rien assurer." A letter of Bernoulli's about this time refers to Cassini's visit to Landau, a town in the Palatinate under French control; this visit was doubtless in connection with the general mapping of France then in progress. Already, 17 February 1734, Maupertuis speaks of a decision to send an expedition to the west coast of South America to measure a degree along a meridian crossing the equator; but the astronomers, Bouguer and La Condamine, cannot leave so soon, because "nos escadres ont autre chose à faire que des observations astronomiques." In a letter of 8 May 1735 Bernoulli expresses surprise that "Messieurs vos Amériquains" are still in Paris, and he continues

> Mais, dites moi, Monsieur, les Observateurs ont-ils quelque prédilection pour l'un et l'autre des deux sentiments? car s'ils sont portés pour la Terre applatie, ils la trouveront sûrement applatie; si au contraire ils sont imbus de l'idée pour la terre allongée, leurs observations ne manqueront pas de confirmer son allongement: le pas du sphéroïde comprimé pour devenir allongé est si insensible, qu'il est aisé de s'y tromper, si on veut être trompé en faveur de l'une ou l'autre opinion. Toutefois supposé que les observations décident contre moi, je me suis déjà muni d'une réponse convenable, qui me mettra à l'abri de toute objection; ainsi j'attendrai de pied ferme le résultat des observations Américaines.

One notices an almost religious fervor with which Bernoulli clings to his point of view: one is tempted to recall the early theologian's "Credo quia absurdum."

Finally, on 12 September 1735, Maupertuis writes from "Turi" (Thury, where the Cassinis had an estate, whence they took their title?) that the Lapland expedition is planned:

> Nous allâmes il y a 15 jours à Versailles comme nous faisons tous les ans, présenter le volume de nos Mémoires au Roy, à la Reyne et aux Ministres; on y parla beaucoup d'un voyage vers le pôle dont il avoit été question dans nos assemblées. M. de Maurepas vint quelques jours après à l'Académie et nous annonça que le Roy avoit ordonné ce voyage. On ira dans le Golfe de Bothnie mesurer quelques degrés et faire des observations sur la longueur du pendule, etc. On sçaura peut-être aussy tost par ce voyage que par celuy du Pérou quelle figure a la Terre: car si elle est aussy allongée que m. Cassini le pense, la différence entre un degré de latitude en ce pays-là et un degré vers Paris doit être sensible. Comme je dois faire ce voyage je vous prie, Monsieur, d'avoir la bonté de penser à ce que nous pouvons faire de mieux et de m'envoyer vos Reflexions. Les distances sur le Terrain se mesurent assez seure-

ment avec des quarts de cercle tels que ceux qu'on emporte de 2 et 3 pieds de rayon, mais l'opération délicate c'est celle de la différence en latitude ou la différence de distance d'une mesme étoile au zénit, aux deux extrémités de la distance mesurée sur Terre. On prend comme vous sçavez cette différence avec quelque secteur de 10 ou 12 pieds de rayon; mais malgré l'énormité de l'instrument on a encore bien de la peine à parvenir à l'exactitude qu'il faut pour établir une différence entre les degrés. Comme le voyage du Nord se fera avec le même appareil que celuy du Pérou et que nous sommes les maîtres de porter tant d'instruments que nous voudrons, faites moy la grâce de me dire ce que vous me conseillez là-dessus, et quand mesme il arriveroit que nous trouvassions la Terre applatie, je vous promets de rendre le prix pour vous si on vous le redemande.

C'est asseurément une très belle chose que fait la France au milieu d'une grande guerre, d'envoyer aux deux bouts du Monde mesurer la Terre. J'espère donc Monsieur, que vous me feres part de quelqu'une de vos industries qui s'étendent à tout et que vous me mettres en état de faire sur cela un ouvrage auquel les Anglois ny autres n'auront rien à dire soit qu'il les justifie soit qu'il les condamne. Cleraut sera du voyage et nous allons l'un et l'autre passer les vacances chez M. Cassini pour nous exercer à l'Astronomie.

In a lengthy reply to this letter (13 October 1735) Bernoulli expresses his surprise:

J'ai appris avec étonnement le voyage du nord, auquel vous êtes destiné avec Monsieur Clairaut. . . . Pour avouer la vérité, je ne vous croyois assez routiné en fait de pratique pour les observations; vous et moi, nous sommes plus faits pour le cabinet à y vaquer aux méditations; cependant votre adresse naturelle et un peu d'exercice que vous allez vous donner chez Mr Cassini vous mettra en peu de temps au fait de la pratique pour devenir observateur adroit et habile. Mais quant à Mr Clairaut je n'ai pas si bonne espérance qu'il puisse bien réussir dans l'art de faire des observations à cause de sa myopie. . . . qui n'est point du tout propre pour cet exercice.

The letter is long, but it indicates a good deal of thought on the part of Bernoulli. He confesses his lack of experience in observational astronomy, as he had been hampered from childhood with weak eyes. He goes on to suggest a point of reference well above the surface of the earth in order to

> attraper le véritable moment du passage de l'étoile par le méridien. . . . J'ai donc pensé qu'on pourroit remédier en quelque façon à cet inconvénient, si on pouvoit avoir un point visible et immobile sinon dans le ciel, au moins d'une élévation fort haute au-dessus de la Terre, mais où trouvera-t-on un tel point, puisque les sommets des plus hautes montagnes comme celui du Pic (de Ténériffe), n'ont guère de hauteur perpendiculaire plus grande que d'une lieue, ce qui est trop peu sensible par rapport au demi-diamètre de la Terre: il me semble qu'on pourroit se servir à ce dessein (je hasarde cette idée mais à condition que vous ne vous en moquiez pas) des aurores boréales qui sont fort fréquentes dans les pays septentrionaux où vous allez; il y en a qui doivent être fort hautes, témoin celle de 1726 qui fut vue dans presque toute l'Europe et dont la hauteur réelle suivant le calcul de Mairan surpassa la distance de 230 Lieues.

Bernoulli could not leave the suggestion without its mathematical development, proceeding to accept the hypothesis that the aurora, composed of circular bands parallel to the equator that, having their highest point at the meridian, would allow spectators at different points on a given meridian to make exact calculations of their difference in latitude. One may reasonably doubt if Bernoulli had observed the northern lights; he does not seem to have realized the extreme difficulty of finding a point in their shimmering beauty on which one could fix a telescopic sight long enough to establish angular measurements. It is quite possible that the long passage on the aurora that occurs near the end of the *Relation du voyage fait par ordre du Roy au cercle polaire*, published by Maupertuis after the return from Lapland (Paris, 1738), was inserted to answer Bernoulli's well-meant suggestion. In another paragraph Bernoulli discusses the merits of the Gulf of Bothnia for such observations as Maupertuis and his colleagues had in mind. Its northerly position, the extent of the

81

body of water and the long meridian available for measurement, the relatively straight western coast between Gävle and Nora, the absence of tides, all would facilitate observations and make results more useful. Bernoulli adds that for observing the aurora one should choose positions as near water level as possible, when the sea is calm. A final paragraph on these matters offers a series of questions still of scientific interest:

> Voilà, Monsieur, bien au long mes pensées sur cette affaire; vous direz peut-être que j'en parle comme l'aveugle des couleurs; j'en tombe d'accord, mais vous me les avez extorquées. Souvenez vous en voyageant de faire aussi des observations sur l'inclinaison de l'aiguille aimantée, sur la grandeur de la réfraction horizontale des astres, sur les hauteurs moyennes du Baromètre à la surface de la mer, sur la pesanteur de ses eaux et sur d'autres curiosités qui doivent se trouver différentes dans les pays du Nord de celles de nos climats tempérés.

Bernoulli expects that this letter will find Maupertuis "chez Mr Cassini," to whom he sends his compliments, "en lui demandant pourquoi à son retour de voyage de Landau (qu'il fit l'année passée pour mesurer les degrés parallèles de Paris) il n'a pas voulu nous honorer de sa presénce comme on m'avait fait l'espérance."

The first months of 1736 were spent by Maupertuis and his colleagues in preparation for their expedition, not only in calculations and programming the work to be done, but in arranging for the various instruments necessary for their innumerable observations. Perhaps the most imposing of these was the nine-foot telescopic sector made with consummate accuracy by George Graham of London, and sent by sea to Stockholm and thence to Torneå, at the mouth of the river of that name, whose valley was to be the site of their activities. Graham had also made the clock for the timing of observations, as well as some of the pendulums of different types by which Richer's experiments made at Cayenne sixty years before were to be repeated under different latitudes.

82

Letters to Bernoulli in these months reflect his great interest in the expedition as well as that exhibited by Jacques Cassini; the credibility of these two men depended appreciably on the results Maupertuis would bring home. Bernoulli expected a maximum of accurate measurements, over as long an arc of the meridian as possible, to which requirement Maupertuis replies that the expedition cannot expect to make observations through ten degrees of latitude, and that

une telle précision n'est guère espérable et nous n'en avons pas besoin: jamais on n'aura les dimensions de la Terre avec la dernière exactitude, et je crois qu'il suffira pour ses habitants de savoir en général la grandeur, et qu'elle est allongée ou applatie et à peu près les bornes de sa figure. Or pour trouver cela il suffira, je crois, de trouver entre le premier degré de latitude et celui que nous allons mesurer, une différence assez considérable pour qu'elle ne puisse pas être attribuée aux erreurs commissibles dans les opérations, et si la Terre a la figure que M. Cassini lui attribue il doit y avoir entre ces deux degrés une différence d'environ 1500 Toises et si ceux de Pérou et nous mesuraient un intervalle de 2 ou 3 degrés les différences seraient deux ou trois fois plus grandes. Si la Terre a donc quelque figure qui s'écarte autant de la sphérique dans l'un ou l'autre sens que celle-là, son allongement ou son applatissement sera sûrement décidé à moins qu'on ne suppose que son Méridien diffère sensiblement de l'ellipse et que sa courbure ait des augmentations et diminutions alternatives dans chaque quart de sa circonférence. Nous partons la semaine de Quasimodo pour nous rendre à Dunkerque où je pourrais encore recevoir votre réponse si vous ne tardez point à la faire. . . . Je ne doute point que vous n'ayez une manière de concilier votre système sur l'inclinaison des orbites avec l'applatissement de la Terre s'il a lieu. Je suis si accablé d'affaires que je n'ai point pu avoir l'honneur de vous écrire plus souvent. Je suis toujours mon cher ami avec les sentiments les plus tendres,

Votre très humble et très obéissant serviteur

Maupertuis.

There is no need here to recount the adventures of Maupertuis and his colleagues between their departure from Dunkerque on 2 May 1736 and their return to France more than a year later. Maupertuis published a full account in his *Relation du voyage . . . au cercle polaire* (Paris, 1738) giving abundant detail of the methods adopted, the difficulties encountered, and the various means of transportation utilized, including one of the earliest references in French to the use of skis, which the scientists did not attempt. Their ship reached Stockholm on 21 May, and Maupertuis arrived at Torneå on 18 June, a region he was not to leave until nearly a year later. In the meantime, the expedition had set up eight signal beacons for triangulation on mountains along some sixty miles of the valley, had made innumerable observations of the angles of the triangles thus established, and had moved the heavy Graham sector and pendulum by boat and sled from Torneå to the northern end of their triangulation at Kittis and back again, meanwhile suffering from the cold and privations of a region very far from the comforts of Paris. No record of the extremes of cold experienced seems to have been kept; it was most probably out of the lower range of their thermometers. Maupertuis's own account of this year is recommended to anyone who delights in travel literature from another epoch, in parts of the world where tourists do not yet commonly go.

A letter dated "Sur le Zuidersee 11 Aoust 1737" gives us the best picture of Maupertuis on his return from what the eighteenth century somewhat generously described as "le Pôle." This letter could not convey the precise conclusions reached by the scientists, which had to be reserved for communication to Maurepas and the Académie Royale des Sciences; but there is no doubt that the tone of the letter, and its precise reference to the average result of observations of the pendulums, gave Bernoulli a very clear idea of what the final result would be. A note of quiet confidence exudes from the passages we quote:

> Les temps, les lieux, les plaisirs, les peines, ne me feront jamais vous oublier, mon cher Monsieur, et quelque longtemps

84

qui se soit passé, sans que j'ai eu le plaisir de vous écrire, je conserve toujours pour vous les mêmes sentiments où j'étais lorsque j'avais le bonheur de vous voir et de vous entendre, et j'ai cru que vous pardonneriez mon silence à la vie que j'ai menée en Lapponie.

Nous voici de retour, et je n'ai pas pu attendre à être à Paris pour vous dire quel a été le succès de notre voyage, quoique je ne puisse vous faire part du résultat de notre opération, avant que j'en aie rendu compte au Ministre et à l'Académie. Je vous dirai seulement que nous avons été assez heureux pour vivre, et même nous bien porter pendant un an dans la zone glacée, ou sur ses confins; que nous y avons mesuré sur la glace du Fleuve de Torneå une distance de 7400 toises, qui mesurée deux fois, ne nous a donné que 4 pouces de différence; que cette distance nous a servi de Toise pour mesurer par des Triangles un arc du Méridien de 57 1/2 minutes, qui a un tiers dans la zone glacée; et que le petit nombre et la disposition de nos triangles, et enfin l'excellence de l'instrument avec lequel nous avons observé la différence des deux Zéniths qui terminent notre arc, et la précision qui s'est trouvée dans cette opération répétée par deux étoiles différentes ne nous laissent rien à souhaiter. J'espère que tout le monde sera content de ce travail, et que la question sur la figure de la Terre sera pour jamais décidée. Je ne vous parlerai point de la vie qu'il nous a fallu mener pour parvenir à cette fin heureuse, des froids, des peines, des fatigues, des périls, tout est passé, et sur 15 personnes que j'avais à conduire, il n'y en a pas eu un de mort, ni de malade. M. Celsius Professeur de l'Astronomie à Upsal était de notre compagnie, et le Roi vient de le récompenser les services qu'il nous a rendus, par une Pension de 1000 livres. Je crois qu'on peut démontrer qu'en comptant les erreurs de la mesure sur la Terre et celles qu'on peut avoir commises pour déterminer par les étoiles l'amplitude de notre arc, il est impossible que l'erreur totale passe 50 toises, et qu'il est moralement sûr qu'elle en est bien éloignée. C'est là dans l'instrument avec lequel nous avons pris la distance de l'étoile au zénith une précision presque incroyable, mais dont on conviendra lors qu'on le connaîtra, et qu'on verra les vérifications que nous en avons faites. C'est un secteur de 9 pieds de rayon, et qui ne porte que 4 1/2 degrés, fait à Londres par M. Graham et auquel l'excellence de la construction, le microscope, et toutes les commodités donnent un grand avantage sur des instruments qui seraient beaucoup plus grands.

85

> Nous avons fait aussi dans la zone glacée plusieurs expériences sur la pesanteur, et toutes nous ont fait voir qu'elle est dans ces pays considérablement plus grande qu'à Paris; mais il nous est arrivé des choses assez remarquables. Pour être plus sûrs d'apercevoir les plus petites différences qu'il est difficile de déterminer par la mesure actuelle des Pendules, et pour éviter aussi les objections qu'on fait sur les pendules appliqués aux horloges, outre deux horloges faits exprès pour ces expériences, nous avons fait faire plusieurs pendules simples, de différentes figures et de différentes matières dont nous avons éprouvé le temps des oscillations à Paris; quelques-uns de ces pendules étaient des globes attachés à une verge de fer, les autres pour être plus invariables étaient de grosses barres de fer d'environ 4 1/2 pieds et de 1 1/2 pouce de diamètre, tous oscillants si librement, qu'ils pouvaient conserver le moindre mouvement pendant 8 et 10 heures et quelques-uns pendant plus de 20. Tous ces instruments nous ont donné des augmentations différentes de pesanteur.

Maupertuis offers further comment on the behavior of pendulums and concludes by saying that he is proceeding to Paris at once, where he hopes to have word from Bernoulli.

The next letter in the sequence is not Bernoulli's reply, which has been lost and the draft most probably destroyed, but the announcement by Maupertuis of the formal result of the expedition:

> J'ai reçu, mon cher Monsieur, votre lettre du 26 Août, à mon arrivé à Paris, et puis vous dire maintenant que la Terre est applatie; et que cet applatissement même est si considérable qu'il est impossible que les erreurs qu'on auroit pû faire en approchent. . . . Il est bien vrai que cette nouvelle a fait de la peine à M. Cassini, mais elle n'en a pas moins été démontrée dans l'Académie. Quant à ce que vous dites qu'il eût dû venir lui-même assister à cette mesure, il n'a tenu qu'à lui, mais je ne crois pas que quand il y auroit été, les choses en eussent été mieux faites.

This letter, dated 8 September 1737, is mostly devoted to a reply to a number of rather acrid comments Maupertuis found in Bernoulli's of 25 August, of which the first dealt with the absence of Cassini from the expedition. Other points raised by Bernoulli were that the base line should have been measured a third time, that it should not have been established on the inclined plane of a river, that the Cassinis had made four measurements that did not accord with the Lapland results, that the members of the expedition were all prejudiced in favor of "l'applatissement," that finally Bernoulli himself should have been invited but was omitted as a Lutheran while Celsius who is Lutheran was included and finally rewarded by Louis XV. These captious comments brought replies in detail. The measurement of the base line was performed twice with ample checking at every stage, and the difference of four inches was not important in view of the considerable length involved. The base may have been inclined, but that makes no difference because such a variable may be allowed for; Cassini's measurements in France may have indicated a different result, but they were two and not four and "le nombre ne fait rien à l'affaire."

As for the accusation of prejudice, Maupertuis adds:

> Quant à ce qu'on pourroit croire que la préoccupation pour l'un ou l'autre Système pût avoir part au résultat qu'on trouve sur l'allongement ou l'applatissement, nous qui étions une compagnie entière, composée même de différentes Nations, avons bien moins cela à craindre, que ceux qui seuls ont retrouvé ce que leurs Pères et Grands Pères avoient trouvé. Je ne crois pas même encor malgré cela qu'il fût permis de faire aucun soupçon de cette espèce, qui attaque l'honneur des gens, et si quelqu'un s'en avisoit, on n'y pourroit opposer que le Mépris.

And when it comes to the final point, on Bernoulli's introduction of the issue of religion, Maupertuis does not conceal his annoyance:

> Il est vrai que M. Celsius est Luthérien, et Luthérien fort de mes amis; il nous a rendu de fort bons services dans notre ouvrage, et il étoit juste et honorable que le Roy l'en récom-

pensât. Pour vous, mon cher Monsieur, je n'ai garde de croire que vous parlez sérieusement, lors que vous dites que vous seriez venu avec nous, si je vous avez invité; c'étoit une proposition que je n'aurois jamais osé vous faire. Mais ce qu'il y a de certain, c'est que la Diversité de religion n'étoit d'aucune conséquence dans notre expédition, et qu'elle n'étoit ni Sainte, ni Croisade, nous n'allions ni pour Conquérir le Pays, ni pour Convertir les gens.

There does not seem to have been anything in this letter to offend a scientist; the chief points raised by Bernoulli had been answered one by one, and while Maupertuis conceded nothing, it could not be denied that he had seen the work done on the site, and could speak with an authority of a sort to which the sedentary Bernoulli was not accustomed. Maupertuis referred in this letter to a disagreement with Clairaut about pendulums, and finally expressed a willingness to defer to the younger scientist's view, "et quand je suis seul d'un avis différent du sien, je n'ai pas grande opinion du mien," a statement that may very well have pricked the notoriously thin skin of the recipient of the letter. Maupertuis's conclusion quickly covers up the irritant; he sends compliments to Madame Bernoulli, conveys those of his father to Bernoulli—for whom the elder Maupertuis had been looking after some business details—mentions a mathematician he has met in Upsala, and closes with the usual compliments of the eighteenth century.

This letter, however, did little to pacify Bernoulli, whose theory of the universe was being destroyed by the application of the principles of his much disliked Newton. A letter, also lost and of which no draft has been preserved, must have been written in the latter part of September; Maupertuis refers to it in a letter to Johann Bernoulli II (1710-90), at this time becoming one of the French scientist's closest friends and to whom we shall refer as "Jean," in which he says "Je suis très sensible à la manière dont Monsieur votre Père en use avec moi, et à la lettre remplie de sarcasmes que j'en ai reçue; s'il croit ne m'avoir pas offensé, il se trompe bien."

Maupertuis did not reply to this missing letter before the end of the year; under the date of 31 December 1737 he writes:

Il y a déjà quelque temps, Monsieur, que j'ai reçu votre écrit d'aimables rémonstrances: quoique j'y aie trouvé plusieurs choses qui pourroient me faire de la peine, et qui me jetteroit dans de grandes discussions si j'entreprenois de les détailler ici et qui ne seroient point du tout capables de rétablir entre nous la bonne intelligence que je souhaitte qui y soit; comme j'ai cru appercevoir dans cet écrit quelques marques d'amitié, j'y ai été plus sensible qu'à tout le reste, n'ayant jamais rien souhaité plus ardemment que de trouver un peu d'amitié dans un homme pour qui j'ai autant d'estime que pour vous.

It is apparent from this letter that Maupertuis had not replied fully to the earlier letter from Bernoulli, that of 25 August. The discussion over religious differences was still open, and Maupertuis's refusal to pass one or two problems to Clairaut was still a sore point with Bernoulli. A witty and perhaps too pointed remark at this juncture may have been an allusion that Bernoulli took to heart: "Monsieur Clairaut comme bien d'autres, aura peut-être le défaut de sacrifier de petits devoirs d'amitié à l'envie de passer pour grand géomètre." But Maupertuis seems here to be making a serious effort to mend his fences with Bernoulli, stopping short of flattery, but paying the kind of respect that younger men of the new century appropriately owed their seniors who had opened the way to the new world of mathematical physics. The Cartesian view died hard, old friendships cooled, and the correspondence between the two mathematicians became less frequent, somewhat more formal, and less satisfactory on either side.

Signs of the cooling of friendship begin to be apparent soon after the final decision of the Académie on the shape of the earth. In his letter of 31 December 1737 Maupertuis had taken up one by one the grievances of Bernoulli, admitting his failure to respond to an invitation to visit Basel as well as his neglect to express thanks for assistance in a problem concerning pendulums. He keeps his letter brief, for

> une réponse plus complette pourroit peut-être réveiller les altercations, pour lesquelles j'ai un éloignement infini, ne souhaitant que paix et amitié, surtout de vous, que je considère infiniment. C'est dans ces sentimens que je vais commencer la nouvelle année, que je vous souhaite remplie de bonheur, tant pour vous que pour Madame Bernoulli, et pour toute votre famille.

The correspondence becomes less warmly intimate, and occasionally ironically distant as Maupertuis turns more and more to exchange letters with Johann II, his friend Jean. The final note seems to be found in a few lines of a letter of 12 April 1739, in which Bernoulli chides Maupertuis for not instructing Mme du Châtelet more precisely in the theory of *les forces vives*, saying,

> Je m'étonne, Monsieur, que depuis si longtemps que vous connoissez cette Dame philosophe, vous ne lui ayez pas donné de meilleures instructions sur cette importante matière. Je m'apperçois bien que Mr de Voltaire croupit dans la même erreur, mais je le lui pardonne, car il a épousé les sentimens de Newton et des Anglois en général, il n'ose donc pas être plus clairvoyant qu'eux.

After which he closes the discussion of their disagreement by saying he has never doubted Maupertuis's friendly feelings toward him, and that

> ce qui de ma part peut avoir excité ces nuages, c'est je vous jure, uniquement mon imprudence et point du tout ma volonté; c'est donc votre extrême délicatesse, votre sensibilité qui y a contribué le plus. Mais sans accuser ni l'un ni l'autre de nous, laissons dissiper ces nuages. . . .

And he ends with protests of a continuation of the esteem of his family and his own "dévouement parfait."

90

There are just six more letters from Maupertuis to Bernoulli in these papers, and no drafts of letters in the other direction. After Maupertuis's invitation to Bernoulli to come to Berlin as a member of the reorganized Academy there, and the rejection of this offer, correspondence seems to have ceased, and Maupertuis's relations with Basel must be studied in his letters to Jean.

With Maupertuis's announcement of the findings of the Lapland expedition to the Académie des Sciences and to the chief exponent of the theory of the elongated earth, we come to the denouement of this half-century of intellectual drama: fifty years separate the publishing of the *Principia* from the return from Lapland. There was little need to await the return of *Messieurs les Amériquains* from their prolonged travels in the Pacific Ocean, the Andes, and Brazil. The results of measuring an arc of a meridian north from Torneå offered sufficient evidence of *la Terre applatie*.

Yet in spite of the unhappy posture of Johann Bernoulli after 1737, his importance to the whole enterprise must be recognized. He had a significant influence in the development of Maupertuis, encouraging him from the beginning of their friendship in the most flattering terms, criticizing his work, offering suggestions for its improvement, singling him out from among French mathematicians of the day for the most friendly and helpful treatment. The correspondence that passed between the two from the time of Maupertuis's first visit to Basel deserves publication in its entirety and careful study for what it may contribute to the history of science, the personal aspect of the biography of two men, and the influence of personal idiosyncrasies on intellectual relations. Bernoulli was representative of the best traditions of seventeenth-century mathematics, rigorous in method, inventive in thought, although working as he admitted in his study, without reference to observational astronomy or application to innovation in the technical arts.

In those ways, his wisdom, his experience and that of the members of his family, were of great value to Maupertuis. One cannot read the *Relation du voyage . . . au cercle polaire* and the other texts associated with it in connection with the correspondence that passed between the two men without sensing the debt owed to the older savant. The Lapland expedition gained because Maupertuis, who was in large part responsible for it, had to face the intellectual positions taken by Bernoulli, perhaps less by his positive suggestions than by the necessity of meeting his objections to it in detail and his criticism of its postulates.

Taken as a whole, this episode, springing from an idea in the mind of a mathematician, and conducted to a successful conclusion with the cooperation and sometimes lively criticism of a man of similar interests and occasionally diametrically opposed views, who knew that his position would meet shrewd argument and precisely observed fact, is perhaps the event that did most to consolidate the position of Newtonian physics as a central element in the movement known as the Enlightenment. The scientists—Maupertuis, Clairaut, La Condamine, and Bouguer and their colleagues—knew that the natural world could not be understood from libraries and laboratories, or from measurements taken in the central provinces of France. Such facts had to be determined by observations made at extreme points on the earth's surface, sometimes under it, sometimes involving considerable expense of effort and time and the facing of great hardships. They knew also that these arduous experiences, accompanied by accumulated precise calculations, would lend authority to the conclusions finally presented to the scientists and academies of Europe. Their determinations would be interpreted and popularized and pass into the literature of generations yet unborn. Voltaire's *Micromégas* was but a hint of what the stimulus of Newtonian space would do for poets, whether André Chénier in his *Hermès*:

Je vois l'être et la vie et leur source inconnue,
Dans les fleuves d'éther tous les mondes roulants;
Je poursuis la comète aux crins étincelants,
Les astres et leurs poids, leurs formes, leurs distances;
Je voyage avec eux dans leurs cercles immenses.
Comme eux, astre, soudain je m'entoure de feux;
Dans l'éternel concert je me place avec eux:
En moi leurs doubles loix agissent et respirent;
Je sens tendre vers eux mon globe qu'ils attirent;
Sur moi qui les attire ils pèsent à leur tour.
Les éléments divers, leur haine, leur amour,
Les causes, l'infini s'ouvre à mon œil avide.

or Shelley, in whose poems the Newtonian universe is the tacitly accepted stage on which the action takes place, perhaps most clearly expressed in his *Ode to Night*:

Palace-roof of cloudless nights!
Paradise of golden lights!
   Deep, immeasurable, vast,
Which art now, and which wert then
   Of the Present and the Past,
Of the eternal Where and When,
   Presence-chamber, temple, home,
   Ever-canopying dome,
Of acts and ages yet to come!

Glorious shapes have life in thee,
Earth, and all earth's company;
   Living globes which ever throng
Thy deep chasms and wildernesses;
   And green worlds that glide along;
And swift stars with flashing tresses;
   And icy moons most cold and bright,
   And mighty suns beyond the night,
Atoms of intensest light.

Under the impact of such imagery, the vortices, dreamed up on the desk of another mathematician, disappear without trace except as a historical curiosity. Science continued its perpetual revolution, ceasing even more to be something learned

93

from books or calculated by deduction from accepted systems, and increasingly recognized as an on-going process in the hands of professionals who undertake difficult and sometimes hazardous quests among the realities of immense distance and mass, time and energy, where the authority of traditional philosophy has no power, and the world lies open to new and even radical innovation of method and theory. This is the kind of world in which Maupertuis's prophetic *Lettre sur le progrès des sciences* was born, typical of the *mouvement philosophique*, the most significant contribution of the eighteenth century to the ages that follow.

The Bernoulli-Maupertuis correspondence is in the Öffentliche Bibliothek der Universität Basel; quotations from it have been taken from a transcript made by a secretary of the Bernoullikommission for me with the permission of the late Dr. Otto Spiess. A few quotations are derived from the correspondence of Hans Sloane and others in the British Museum.

"De Figuris quas fluida rotata induere possunt, Problemata duo; cum conjectura de Stellis quae aliquando prodeunt vel deficiunt; et de Annulo Saturni. Authore Petro Ludovico De Maupertuis, Regiae Societatis Londinensis, et Academiae Scientiarum Parisiensis Socio" was published in the *Philosophical Transactions*, no. 422, for January, February and March, 1732, pp. 240-56. The letter to William Jones, "Parisiis 1ª Sept. 1729," was published by S. P. Rigaud from the collections of the Earl of Macclesfield, in *Letters of Scientific Men*, I, London, p. 281.

The *Œuvres de Mr de Maupertuis* have been used in the four-volume edition published by J. M. Bruyset in Lyon, 1756. The *Degré du Méridien entre Paris et Amiens*, 8vo (Paris, 1746), has a useful introduction, presumably by Maupertuis, in which the Graham sector is described in detail and illustrated on a folding plate.

There is no secondary literature dealing with the present aspect of this episode. If Pierre Brunet had known of the material in London and Basel, this study would have been unnecessary. His useful books, *Maupertuis*, 2 vols. (Paris, 1929) and *L'Introduction des idées de Newton en France* (Paris, 1931) have been of much help, as have Roger Hahn's *Anatomy of a Scientific Institution* (Berkeley, Calif., 1971) and I. Bernard Cohen's article, "Isaac Newton, Hans Sloane, and the Académie royale des Sciences" in the *Mélanges Koyré* (Paris, 1964).

Notes on the Making of a
Philosophe: Cuenz and Bouhier

IRA O. WADE

Everyone interested in the intellectual development in France during the first half of the eighteenth century knows of the collection of letters that Président Bouhier assembled, chiefly from the late twenties to the middle forties. They have been the subject of a very pleasantly written book by Emmanuel de Broglie, which has attempted to present a series of essays upon the relationships between the Président at Dijon and his correspondents throughout France, usually with generous selections from each (Valincour, Olivet, Le Blanc, Marais, Passionei, and Caumont, and many others of a lesser order of importance who have been treated more casually).[1] The letters themselves serve to demonstrate a special interest on the part of the letter-writer or a commentary upon some important contemporary event, or, very often, an observation upon an outstanding contemporary person. The most informative parts of Broglie's work are undoubtedly the two chapters dealing with the correspondence between Bouhier and Marais, but the others are not to be treated lightly either, since taken together they constitute in their modest way a sociological portrait of the time. I myself have profited in recent years from the minor exchange that took place between Bouhier and Valdruche, in regard to Voltaire's intellectual activities at Cirey.

Many years ago, in fact, it seemed to me that the full collection of these Bouhier papers, which are now at the Bibliothèque Nationale,[2] would be very helpful in furnishing us

97

with some interesting insights into Voltaire's activities not only of a literary but a political, religious, and moral nature as well, if one wished to take the time to sort out these matters. Indeed, after I had copied the Le Blanc letters as a test case of how they might be used in establishing this background to a period, Mrs. Monod-Cassidy came out with her thesis on Le Blanc,[3] the first part of which showed how effectively this material of Le Blanc could be utilized for these purposes, and the second part of which was a very careful editing of this correspondence. I should add that my close friend Professor Havens knew about these activities and, as in so many other enterprises of like nature, made his contribution to them, too, before any of us.[4]

I confess that my own preoccupation in all these more important moves of my colleagues has practically always been to ferret out in what way these documents and studies tell us something more about Voltaire and his "doings." I have insisted, for instance, upon the importance of Valdruche's remarks concerning Voltaire. Coming at the moment of the Cirey retreat when Voltaire was making some effort to conceal his movements, and also to some extent his thoughts, even the low-key observations of a local *avocat* who was obviously favorably impressed with the new arrival could conceivably add something to our knowledge of the newcomer. This kind of secondary correspondence concerning Voltaire has not always found its way into the Besterman correspondence. Indeed, there is really no reason why it should have done so, since Mr. Besterman had a stupendous job in taking care of Voltaire's massive production. Nonetheless, I kept telling myself without doing very much about it that if somebody in this computer age wanted to bring together all this personal commentary upon Voltaire and his thought and his works, it could do much to enlighten us about the "real" Voltaire. I venture to add my little *marotte* that the "real" Voltaire I am talking about is the "poet turned *philosophe*"—and that event

98

happened precisely at the peak of the Bouhier correspondence, that is to say, sometime between 1738 and 1744. Naturally, anybody who can throw any light upon that event in my humble but interested opinion deserves a hearing.

Just how far we can go with this "hearing" is unknown, because we really have not made the experiment. Perhaps if I may be permitted here to make a modest beginning, "à titre d'essai," as we used to say when we didn't know whether we had something important to say or not, I can at least start someone who is young and vigorous thinking upon the subject. One point that appeared to me extremely important about Voltaire's intellectual development was the way he turned first from poetry to history. I confessed all along that I did not understand too well how that happened. I could understand that the *Histoire de Charles XII* was a "new" kind of history. I was astounded, however, to realize that the *Lettres philosophiques* were a perfectly logical development of the *Charles XII*. It was merely this "new" history further developed. I made the deduction that the *Siècle de Louis XIV* and the subsequent histories could be expected to carry forward this "new" history. This deduction, though it seemed to me not illogical, did not work too well when I tried to adjust the purpose of each work with the development of the "new" theory of history. Because, specifically, if the *Charles XII* presented the portrait of a country ruined by its king and his government, and the *Lettres philosophiques* was the blueprint of a country that was advanced in civilization and the portrait was presented to the French to show them how they could "advance" their civilization, was the *Louis XIV* devised to be an example of a king who ruined his country as did Charles XII, or of a king who built a civilized nation as did Peter the Great; or was it a demonstration of the way a nation develops all the aspects of its civilization as Voltaire had just demonstrated with his blueprint of the English? Had Voltaire hit upon a new way of writing satirical, moral, political,

99

or cultural history? If so, which kind was the *Siècle de Louis XIV*? The question is by no means an idle one, although I admit that my handling of it was none too edifying.

There is no doubt, though, as to where I stand. I believe that history for Voltaire was the transition between poetry and philosophy; that is, he became a *philosophe* by running upon a difficult problem in history, and he solved it not "poetically" but "philosophically." Of course, it could have been solved "poetically": Homer did long before Voltaire.

Unfortunately, what I believe is not enough. Where is the evidence? Logic requires that the *Louis XIV* be presented as a glorious age highly developed in civilization—one of the four great ages of man, in fact. But another logic requires that the *Louis XIV* be presented as a king who ruined his country. One could easily be persuaded that the early drafts of the *Siècle* were modified. Valdruche, one of Bouhier's correspondents gave us a hint (which I quoted)[5] that such was indeed the case. Here is another passage from the Goujet-Bouhier correspondence,[6] of 26 August 1739, that lends some confirmation to the Valdruche statement:

> Il se prépare [Voltaire] à donner son histoire de Louis-le-Grand et du Sauzet me mande qu'il en a déjà une partie entre les mains et qu'il va mettre l'ouvrage sous presse. Un homme avec qui je suis fort lié m'a dit qu'il avait lu la plus grande partie de cette histoire et qu'il y avait trouvé un défaut dominant, c'est que l'auteur y attaque *Dieu et le Roi*. On assure que Mr. de Voltaire, mieux conseillé, a passé depuis l'éponge sur ces différents endroits. . . .

However, it is not the making of a "new" historian that concerns me here. What I am interested in doing is describing, defining, or delineating a *philosophe* as he actually existed in Voltaire's day. This is not an easy task: what usually happens when we undertake this enterprise is that we either accept a portrait of the type as it was given in the century, or we compose a synthetic portrait made up of selected definitions culled

100

at random, or finally, we imagine ourselves as the *philosophe* and wind up by describing ourselves. I see nothing inherently evil in any of these methods, nor do I condemn anyone who picks his hero of the time and calls him "the *philosophe*," as the time ultimately attributed the title to Diderot. The only thing that sends me into a modest towering rage is to be told that "of course, a *philosophe* is not a philosopher." Since Cuenz's only claim to fame is that he is a *philosophe* becoming a philosopher and since he marks out step by step how it was done to his friend Bouhier, he could, I suppose, be used to reduce the blood pressure of one Enlightenment student, even if it is at the expense of raising the pressure of scores of others.

To make my point, though, I am forced to make three simple statements that have grown out of my more recent studies: (1) the French Enlightenment is above everything else (pagan, modern, scientific, and so on) "*philosophique*"; (2) it was made philosophical by the *philosophes*; (3) they are the natural descendents of the free-thinkers on the one hand and the European philosophers of the seventeenth century on the other. The difference between free-thinker and philosopher in the seventeenth century is that the former is more likely to adopt as his goal, modes, that is to say attitudes, of philosophy (skepticism, stoicism, epicureanism, or naturalism), whereas the philosophers stick more readily to formal branches of philosophy (theology, metaphysics, physics, ethics) and treat their subject more analytically and systematically. There are places where this distinction breaks down, of course, but in general this was the distinction. The *philosophe*, being the descendent of these two groups has to devise some way to merge the two operations. He usually does this by adopting a formal branch of philosophy as the core of his thinking (as when Voltaire in the *Traité de métaphysique* proclaimed "je ramène tout à la morale") and tries to make his attitude conform to his core. Or the *philosophe* would sometimes adopt an attitude toward a particular branch

101

of knowledge and try to make other branches of knowledge conform to that attitude (for example, skepticism in history to skepticism in natural history to skepticism in theology). The result of this forming and conforming was the production of movement. What made thought move for a *philosophe* was ideas; he preferred for them to be "free," but if they had to conform to situations that curtailed their freedom, he settled for their "livingness." In this way the *philosophe* created the myth that ideas are more alive than men and in reality are the *only* guarantee for the "livingness" of men. Moreover, after 1750, the doctrine of the *Encyclopédie* became that men are only what ideas have made them.

One of the problems in the organization of thought at the beginning of the Enlightenment is how the intelligent but nonprofessional philosopher could make a synthesis of the philosophers whose systems were so numerous and so contradictory in the seventeenth century. Because the key to the problem of the development of thought from the seventeenth to the eighteenth century certainly involves the reaction of the enlightened thinker of the eighteenth century, who is going to be known as a *philosophe*, to the systematic *philosophe*, to the systematic philosophers. Succinctly put, the quality of Voltaire's thought can only be assessed against the development of thought in the preceding epoch. What he came to think and how he came to organize it into what has been qualified generally as unphilosophical can be understood only by reference to the twelve major philosophers— Bacon, Hobbes, Galileo, Descartes, Gassendi, Pascal, Spinoza, Malebranche, Leibniz, Locke, Newton, and Bayle—with whom he had to deal before organizing his philosophy. And the same would be true of the philosophies of Montesquieu, Rousseau, and Diderot.

In fact, the seventeenth century presents an abundance of individual philosophers, who in their peculiar way express the philosophical tendencies of their milieu, whether it be English, French, German, or Hebrew. In addition, these philosophers had to contend with currents of philosophical thinking that came from antiquity and, because of the peculiar situation of the time, persisted: skepticism, stoicism, epicureanism, and naturalism. Each of these modes of thinking not only had its adherents but opposed each of the others with a vitality that was only exceeded by the opposition of the individual philosophers the one to the other. The thing to remark, however, is that each mode of ancient philosophy entered into the composition of each modern seventeenth-century philosopher and gave color and tone to his system, and many times there were conflicts of two or more modes in the systematic organization of a single philosophy. Nor was this variety of ancient philosophy the sole factor of disorganization. The philosophers of the seventeenth century tended to become scientists or political theorists; or sometimes, as in the case of Hobbes, both scientists and political theorists; or, as in the case of Pascal and Leibniz, scientists, theologians, and political theorists. This phenomenon that was taking place in philosophy was undoubtedly brought about by the shift from the dominance of theology, which was supposed to embrace all these subjects as secondary fields of interest, to the dominance of philosophy, which took over these subjects (including theology itself) as no longer secondary but primary fields of interest.

The consequence of this diversity can be seen in the struggle between the ancient and modern, between theology and metaphysics, between theology and science, or between metaphysics and science, or even between natural science and the science of man. The dilemma of an uncomplicated, but intelligent, individual trying to make some headway in the face of these massive oppositions can only be surmised. It is not an easy matter to trace the reactions of each one of the seventeenth-century philosophers to the complications of philosophic thought of the time. This has never been done, as far as I know, in any consistent way. On the other hand, we have studies upon Voltaire and Leibniz, or Voltaire and Bayle, or Diderot and Descartes, but the authors of these studies find it sufficient to study the reactions of Voltaire and Diderot to one of these philosophers without further complicating matters by adding ten or eleven others. Voltaire's situation, however, required that he divide his attention between the whole complex of seventeenth-century philosophy. The problem with him was that his enlightened development demanded consideration of the possibilities attendent upon a synthesis of the thought of all these worthies.

It is fairly easy to work out a timetable of Voltaire's acquaintance with the various principal philosophers, although we are not too sure about certain specific details. His first serious consideration of one of them began with Malebranche in 1723. He himself confessed in 1738 in a letter to the editor of *Pour et contre* that he had in front of him at that moment a copy of the *Recherche de la vérité*, whose Book 3 had been amply annotated by himself fifteen years before. Professor Mason[7] finds that the first overt reference to Bayle was made in a note to *La Ligue*, dated 1723; two years later, in 1725, he owned a copy of the *Dictionnaire historique et critique*. In 1724 a letter from Bolingbroke undertook to direct Voltaire away from Malebranche and Descartes to Locke and Newton: "Si vous lisez *l'Essay sur l'Entendement humain*, vous lisez le livre que je connois le plus capable d'y [to the discovery of truth] contribuer. Si vous n'y trouvez que peu de choses, prenez garde que ce ne soit votre faute. Il est sûr que vous n'y trouverez pas les profondeurs de Descartes ni le sublime de Mallebranche" (Best. 185). Bolingbroke added that they both exceeded the limits of scientific reasoning and have been superseded by the Huyghens and the Newtons. Bolingbroke remarked further that Descartes and Malebranche, although profound, were really not philosophers but poets. The English lord asserted that more important as philosophers were Huyghens and Newton. Implied in his statement was the thought that Voltaire would be well-advised to replace his enthusiasm for Descartes and Malebranche by serious study of Locke and Newton. We do not really have

104

any firm evidence that Voltaire really knew Descartes at this date, June 1724. The works of Descartes, however, that are still in his library are dated 1723 (*Les Principes de la philosophie*), 1724 (*Discours de la méthode*), 1724–25 (*Lettres qui traitent de plusieurs belles questions, concernant la morale, la physique, la médecine, et les mathématiques*), 1724 (*Les Méditations métaphysiques*), 1726 (*Les Passions de l'âme, Le Monde, ou traité de la lumière, et la Géométrie*). The way these dates are bunched around the Bolingbroke letter is very suggestive. Clearly, only one—the *Principes*, which incidentally Descartes regarded as the textbook of his philosophy —preceded the Bolingbroke advice, but the rest are between the letter and Voltaire's arrival in England.

One would be fairly safe in assuming that he had a speaking acquaintance with Descartes, Bayle, and Malebranche before the English sojourn (1726–29). He was, however, too much engaged with poetry and drama to give any very serious attention to the three. In England he gained apparently the same sort of superficial speaking acquaintance with Bacon, Newton, and Locke. In all probability it was not very profound, although he does seem to have read Pemberton's *Introduction to Sir Isaac Newton's Philosophy* in manuscript while in England. In the years immediately following the English sojourn, 1729–33, he devoted himself to rather active investigation in Newton's philosophy as preparation for the letters on Newton in the *Lettres philosophiques*. A major portion of his time was nonetheless given to a careful study of Locke's *Essay concerning Human Understanding*. His correspondence with Cideville and Formont indicate that he perused the *Essay* three different times during these early thirties, and that dissatisfaction with Locke's solutions, which he thought were too timid, was what led him to undertake the *Traité de métaphysique*. Since between 1734 and 1739 he made three separate drafts of the *Traité*, he obviously was deeply engaged with Locke. Since he brought out the *Philosophie de Newton* in 1738 and a third part in 1740, he was just as deeply engrossed in Newton. In addition, he had become acquainted with Wolff through Frederick by 1736. Wolff was a follower of Leibniz. Mme du Châtelet devoted half of her *Institutions de physique* to Leibniz and the second half to Newton. The third part of the *Eléments de la philosophie de Newton* was a selection of certain philosophical, scientific subjects ("De Dieu, De l'espace et de la durée, De la liberté dans Dieu, De la liberté dans l'homme, De la religion naturelle, De l'âme, Des premiers principes de la matière, Des monades, and De la force active"), and gave a comparison of the way Descartes, Leibniz, and Newton regarded these subjects. Hence Voltaire was now, by 1740, drawn into a close consideration of Leibniz. He knew at this time at least (1738) the *Théodicée* and Desmaizeaux's two volumes on Leibniz that included the text of the discussion between Leibniz and Dr. Clarke. Moreover, Voltaire had now (1736–40) become deeply interested in certain "philosophical" subjects: the nature of God, the immortality of the soul, the nature of matter, thinking matter, free will, happiness, friendship, and good and evil. All these special subjects were treated by Bacon, Descartes, Malebranche, Bayle, Leibniz, Newton, and Locke, so that a whole raft of philosophers had gotten into the picture, including Pascal. Two important philosophers missing in the schedule, though, are Hobbes and Spinoza. Not much definite information can be adduced here as to when Voltaire became seriously acquainted with them. A note in the *Notebooks* giving the main points of Spinoza's philosophy apparently dates from the Cirey period, but we are not too sure. We have always assumed that his view on Spinoza was founded upon Bayle's article in the *Dictionnaire* and that acquaintance with Bayle may be taken as acquaintance with Spinoza, but we must not go as far as that.

Voltaire's self-transformation from a poet into a *philosophe* is, as can be divined from the above timetable, a rather complicated affair, destined in fact to become much more complicated before he had completed his course. A relatively simple example of the same phenomenon can be seen in the case of a more or less normal contemporary citizen of Neuchâtel: Cuenz. He is what might be called "un illustre inconnu," but he is not totally unknown. Broglie has given him a very brief paragraph:

> Avec Cuentz de Neufchâtel, Bouhier soutient aussi une discussion en règle sur des sujets philosophiques; celui-là était un partisan décidé des idées de Locke, et le Président avait à jouer ici le rôle contraire, c'est-à-dire à modérer les idées de son correspondant et à défendre les droits du spiritualisme cartésien, que tout Français instruit de cette époque avait été élevé à respecter.[8]

Charles Des Guerrois in his biography of Bouhier[9] stressed that though the Dijon Président spent forty-six years of his life in the eighteenth century, he reminds one almost exclusively of a seventeenth-century man, not at all of Voltaire's time. Des Guerrois explains that this impression comes from Bouhier's interest in the philosophers. But we have just seen in the Voltaire timetable that Voltaire had that interest, too. Des Guerrois's next remark is more appropriate: "Bouhier discute avec M. Cuenz les plus épineuses questions philosophiques, celui-là est un métaphysicien, occupé à radouber ses systèmes, et Bouhier veut bien entrer en discussion avec lui, se lançant dans les pures questions métaphysiques: la corporéité de l'âme, l'existence plus ou moins prouvée des substances immatérielles, etc. [sic]." This up to the present constitutes, as far as I know, all we know about Cuenz. It could be shortened, I suppose, to the remark that Cuenz had a philosophical discussion with Bouhier between 1736 and 1744. I might add, precisely at the time when Voltaire was preoccupied with the task of organizing his thought.

In a letter of 9 April 1738, the would-be philosopher of Neuchâtel explained to his Président friend at Dijon that, having taken up the subject of metaphysics many years be-

107

fore, he had first had to choose between Descartes and Gassendi. Soon, a study of Bayle's article "Rorarius" in the *Dictionnaire historique* had complicated the situation by introducing Leibniz and Malebranche and a choice had become necessary between *"causes occasionnelles"* and preestablished harmony." Chance had brought Cuenz and Bourguet together in Neuchâtel. The latter, who was now a correspondent of Président Bouhier, had been a correspondent and was now an ardent disciple of Leibniz. Acquaintance with Bourguet led Cuenz to a whole series of discussions on metaphysical subjects. Cuenz acknowledged that his new friend Bourguet was a zealous partisan of Leibniz, just as he was an enthusiastic follower of Locke. Indeed, Bourguet, said Cuenz, in an effort to convert him to Leibniz, had given him some of the German philosopher's articles that he had never had the opportunity to study. But, added Cuenz, "Je fus moins de temps à reconnaître qu'il pourrait bien perdre ses peines avec moi." Cuenz's casual remarks about his relation with Bourguet and the way they had involved him in choices between Descartes and Newton as well as between Malebranche, Leibniz, and Locke recall rather vividly the discussions that were taking place at the same time between Voltaire and Mme du Châtelet concerning Descartes, Leibniz, and Newton. The experiences of the two couples show to what extent the reputation of Descartes was still sustained in certain circles in 1738 and confirm the tendency of both Mme du Châtelet and Voltaire to start any debate concerning Leibniz with Descartes's position. The point, however, should be made that whereas the opposition that had to be resolved by Voltaire and Mme du Châtelet lay between Newton and Leibniz, the opposition that had to be resolved by Cuenz and Bourguet lay between Locke and Leibniz.

It was in his long letter to Bouhier of 9 April 1738 that Cuenz gave a detailed account of his entry into seventeenth-century philosophy. Though the section is not short, it is worthy of some attention, not only because it presents a human situation that must have been characteristic of many thinkers between 1720 and 1746, but because it also strikingly sums up the dilemma of Voltaire:

M'étant trouvé à Paris depuis 1722 et ayant quelquefois eu plus de loisir même que je n'eusse souhaité, cette curiosité naturelle à l'homme de savoir ce qu'il est et la grande réputation de Descartes me portèrent à commencer par ses *Méditations.* . . . Mais il me parut que ce grand philosophe était allé un peu trop loin: je ne savois pas avant lui, que ce fût une opinion dont il falloit se défaire, *que le corps existe.* Depuis il m'est tombé entre les mains l'excellent traité de Mr. Locke de *l'Entendement humain* qui m'a donné de toutes autres lumières. J'estime qu'on ne réussira guère à devenir bon métaphysicien, à moins qu'on n'adopte ses principes et surtout ce qu'il dit concernant l'origine de nos idées. Enfin, après les *Méditations* de Descartes, j'ay leu sa méthode, et ai été fort surpris de voir, qu'après avoir si divinement bien raisonné, dans les premières trois parties, il soit tombé comme dans une espèce de délire à la quatrième, où il parle de la nature de l'âme, et où il paraît qu'il y a autant de sophismes ou de paralogismes qu'il y a des mots. J'ai ensuite parcouru *le Traité de l'esprit* du médecin La Forge, et quelques ouvrages du Père Malebranche, dans lesquels ce philosophe met dans tout son jour le système des *causes occasionnelles.* Le premier m'a paru un pauvre raisonneur, et le système du second n'est qu'une espèce de fatalisme, au moins j'estime qu'avec les intentions du monde les plus pures, ce philosophe chrétien auroit de la peine à se défendre qu'il n'en résulte que Dieu est l'auteur du péché. Je crois qu'à peu près on en peut dire autant du système de M. de Leibniz, qui à ce qu'il me semble, n'a relevé (l'esprit) que pour le faire retomber de l'autre côté. Il me paraît que M. Bayle, dans quel esprit Dieu le sait, a trop flatté cette âme présomptueuse, et qu'en la flattant, il n'a fait que lui ficher plus avant dans sa tête son système chimérique. Ce philosophe, où il raisonne sur l'âme ou sur les formes des bêtes comme il les appelle, tenait le vray entre ses mains, mais comme cela arrive souvent aux plus grands esprits, il a passé le vray, et plus il l'a passé, plus il s'en est éloigné.
J'ai fait des remarques sur les différens auteurs, de même sur quelques écrits du Dr. Clarke, de M. Leclerc, et en particulier le traité de M. Ditton, où dans son supplément, il combat le

sentiment de M. Locke, que *Dieu a peu joindre originairement la capacité de penser à quelques parties de la matière.* Ces remarques m'ont conduit insensiblement à penser que du débris des trois systèmes connus, on pourrait imaginer à former un quatrième plus simple, qui seroit à couvert de toutes les objections qui ont été faites ici contre les autres en le fondant principalement sur ces deux principes, qu'un être non étendu et purement spirituel, capable du sentiment, de la puissance et de toutes les modifications est une contradiction palpable, et qu'il suffit de distinguer les êtres qui existent en *visibles et palpables* et en invisibles et impalpables à nos sens grossiers, hypothèse très aisée à concilier avec la révélation et avec les grandes fins qu'elle nous propose et plus propre que toute autre à fermer la bouche aux Phyrrhonniens et aux esprits forts.

These rather lengthy quotations from Cuenz's letter of 9 April 1738 could be supplemented by the very long letter of 4 June 1738 (f. fr., 24410, ff. 255–63). This latter letter is accompanied in time by veritable philosophical dissertations that resemble closely those of Voltaire in the *Traité de métaphysique*: there is one on the nature of God, another on the immortality of the soul and its nature, a third on free will, and a fourth on good and evil.

Bouhier replied to Cuenz's initial letters in a letter in which he grants to his Neuchâtel friend the right to make hypotheses if he wishes. He nonetheless denies that he wants to separate metaphysics from physics, which Cuenz had tried to do (f. 255ᵛ). He notes there are difficulties in Cuenz's notion that God is something else than a spirit. He adds, though, that he is not at all upset by the notion that God has created man as a machine, and he ends his letter by affirming that the system of the union of the soul and body, especially that adopted by Leibniz in the doctrine of preestablished harmony, despite the fact that it is supported by very important individuals, seems filled with insurmountable difficulties. Returning to the problem of the nature of God, Bouhier remarked that Cuenz had implied that God was composed of material substance to which Cuenz replied (f. 267) that such was indeed his idea:

110

"Dieu est un Etre réel et étendu dans sa manière incompréhensible d'exister (non pas matériel et corporel ou composé
comme les corps de la matière que nous connaissons) mais
dont la nature nous est absolument inconnue." To substantiate this point of view that skirts so close to Spinoza, Cuenz
quotes from (of all things) Newton, *Principes*, scholies gén-
éraux, pp. 482, 483: "*Virtus* (Puissance) dit en parlant de la
nature divine ce grand homme, après le bon sens, *sine sub-
stantia subsistere non potest*," and added: "C'est précisément
mon système." It must be noted that Cuenz wanted particularly to avoid the accusation of adopting the God of Spinoza.
He stresses that his concept of the Deity is that He is extent
and immense, and He is all-powerful, omniscient, and omni-
present, but he does not wish to identify Him with the universe as does Spinoza:

> Dieu est immense, en ce que rien ne le borne, ni ne peut le
> borner. Aucun être ne peut le borner activement. Si l'univers
> le borne passivement, c'est que Dieu a bien voulu se borner
> Lui-même, dans ce sens, et on sentira aisément que c'est sans
> préjudice de son étendue réelle, quelqu'elle soit.

His example of an immense substance that fills the universe
is the sun with sunlight. Finally, he endeavors to strengthen
this point of view by passages from the Bible. Cuenz protests
that it is impossible to think of a spiritual non-extended Being
and an immense Being at the same time. He sees very clearly
that if he accepts that God is everything that exists and everything that exists is God, he slips immediately into Spinozism.
He attempts to avoid this difficulty by quoting from Houtteville's *Essay sur la Providence*.

As for the nature of the soul, Cuenz adopts the view that
it is immortal without being able to explain how its immortality occurs. He affirms his belief that God acts by mediate
as well as immediate ways. As Creator and Preserver of the
universe, he acts through general laws that he has established.
These general laws are known to us only imperfectly. He acts

111

also through immediate intervention, what we call a miracle. We know miracles only by faith. Cuenz adds that to understand these actions, one has to know "la matière, le plein et le vide, et la nature de nos idées." He promises to explain them in the forthcoming treatise he is projecting. He adds the remark: "Le moindre de mes embarras est d'accorder tous mes principes avec la Révélation (f. 270ᵛ)." He reverts over and over to the problem of the immortality of the soul. He admits that the difficulties are extreme, especially because of recent discoveries in biology, which embarrass him: Andry's *Traité de la génération des vers*, for instance, and Réaumur's *Histoire des insectes*.

Cuenz sent to his Dijon friend at this time an "Abrégé" of his views on free will (ff. 274–77). He concluded that seeing that man depends upon God, and upon an infinity of physical causes, he is not a free being. Therefore, the real freedom of man can only consist in aiming at limited, fixed goals:

> Ce qu'on appelle communément liberté de l'homme n'est dans le fond autre chose qu'un pouvoir *in abstracto* inhérent à sa nature, qu'il a de décider dans les occasions entre cette inclination naturelle et les suggestions de sa raison éclairée. Se déterminer pour la première, c'est abuser de ce pouvoir; se décider selon la raison éclairée, c'en est faire un bon usage.

It is from this capacity or power that the duty of man is derived: a duty that consists in cultivating his reason. He thereby acquires all the knowledge necessary to him in order to perform his duties toward God, his neighbor, and himself. If he will listen to his reason enlightened by his knowledge, he can lead a life in conformity with these positive duties. In this sense, man is free:

> L'homme est donc proprement responsable de l'usage qu'il fait de sa faculté de connaître, et de sa volonté de se déterminer, et d'agir en conséquence de ses connaissances acquises. Si l'homme est coupable, c'est 1⁰ pour n'avoir pas par sa faute

112

acquis les connaissances qui lui étaient nécessaires; 2⁰ pour n'avoir pas suivi le Dictamen de sa raison éclairée.

Cuenz insists that freedom is "exemption de nécessité et de contrainte." It is true, he admits, that man depends upon a thousand different circumstances that control him. But he has notwithstanding to know his duty to God, to his fellow men, and to himself. Cuenz maintains that given the wisdom and goodness of God, the freedom of man is assured.

The response of Bouhier to these views on the nature of God, the immortality of the soul, and free will can be found on ff. 303–5 of the correspondence. Bouhier acknowledges that although in his youth he had plunged into metaphysical speculations, he now finds so many uncertainties in them among the first-rate philosophers that he has pretty nearly renounced the study of metaphysics and hence is unfamiliar with recent works in this field. On the subject of innate ideas, however, he confesses that he is of Locke's opinion. On the problem of the nature and immortality of the soul, he is aware of so many difficulties that he would advise the suspension of judgment and adherence to the general opinion in which all have been reared. He concedes, nonetheless, that there is nothing contrary to religion in the belief that the soul is material, since such a view had been adopted by the early Christian Fathers. On the other hand, he sees no objection to the view that God can make our soul immortal and capable of receiving rewards and punishments. None of that runs counter to Christianity. He adds that notwithstanding these concessions, he fails to understand why Cuenz insists that "une substance inétendue est un être de raison." That view would make God's immateriality "une chimère." Only the out-and-out materialists would dare adopt such an attitude. Bouhier objects likewise to the distinction between "matière subtile" and "matière grossière." Calling subtle matter "esprit" does not solve the difficulty, though; it is still matter. A better solution, he suggests, would be the assertion "l'âme est une modification de la matière faite d'une manière imperceptible par l'Etre Suprème qui lui a donné la faculté de penser, d'apercevoir, etc., d'où il s'ensuit qu'elle est mortelle de sa nature" but made immortal by the Will of God. Bouhier supports this view by references from Dodwell. Finally, he suggests that Cuenz will do well to consult Beausobre's *Histoire du manichéisme* on the problems of free will, good and evil, and the nature of God.

The activity of Cuenz about 1738–40 became extraordinarily diverse. It is clear that he was not entirely satisfied with his solutions to the problem upon the nature of God because of his tendency to skirt Spinozism despite his every effort to avoid that result. Cuenz turned to Bayle's *Réponse aux questions d'un provincial* (*Œuvres diverses*, 3:940–42) where Bayle undertakes to clarify the nature of God. It was an apt selection for him to make. I cannot here enter into Bayle's discussion. A mere run-down of the subjects will show how they embrace the core of Cuenz's problems in three folio pages:

> Preuves de son immatérialité (De Dieu); Conséquences de ce dogme opposées à des vérités qu'on ne peut abandonner (*cf.* Les raisons qui prouvent l'immatérialité de Dieu, prouvent aussi l'immatérialité de tous les êtres pensans); Difficulté sur l'âme des bêtes; Et sur la liaison locale de l'âme de l'homme avec le corps; Impossibilité d'accorder l'immatérialité de Dieu avec son immensité; Les Cartésiens ne lèvent point la difficulté; Selon quelques Chrétiens les preuves de l'immatérialité de l'âme ne convainquent point; Selon M. Locke l'essence de la substance spirituelle et corporelle nous est inconnue; Objections contre ce sentiment (*cf.* . . . je ne vois point que l'on puisse dire qu'il y ait dans la matière quelque attribut incompatible avec la pensée, ni qu'il y ait dans l'âme quelque attribut incompatible avec l'étendue); Si l'étendue est distincte de la matière, elle ne peut rendre la matière étendue.

Acquaintance with Bayle's handling of these subjects produced two effects upon Cuenz. They forced him first of all to adopt an attitude that differs somewhat from Voltaire's optimistic point of view in 1738. In Cuenz's opinion man is more inclined to evil than to good. He asserts that man has need of a revelation and experience. Man consequently is not in this respect free; he needs absolutely God's grace. These views are closer to those of Bayle than to those of Voltaire in 1738. Cuenz concludes nonetheless that in spite of everything, man must have the power to attain the good; otherwise God cannot be good, wise, and just. This conclusion was also Voltaire's in 1738.

Cuenz's dilemma between the wisdom of God and the evil of man is what led Bouhier to suggest Beausobre's *Histoire du manichéisme.* Cuenz followed the suggestion of his Dijon friend and, as Voltaire on a later occasion, turned to Manichaeism and to Beausobre's book. Similarly, Voltaire wrote to M. Formey, 2 January 1752: "J'ai lu, toute la nuit, *L'Histoire du Manichéisme.* Voilà de la théologie réduite à la philosophie." On 13 July 1740 (ff. 306–7) Cuenz quotes Beausobre to support his view that man's errors can be attributed more to the obscurity in which the Deity has left certain matters than to man's evil nature. That view, Cuenz maintains, is not counter to the teachings of Christianity. He asserts that Mani's doctrine is very similar to his own view. "Je ne crois pas," he wrote, "que ceux qui l'ont condamné ayent substitué quelquechose de mieux digéré, de plus clair, et de plus évident. . . ." In this letter of 12 December 1740 he now explains that "faire de Dieu un Etre inétendu, c'est traiter Dieu comme un point mathématique," and that would be blasphemy. He argues still that God's immensity implies real extent. He objects nonetheless to having this extent interpreted as extended matter, for fear of falling into Spinozism. "Je ne crois pas," he wrote, "que Dieu remplisse physiquement tout l'espace immense." He acknowledges, though, that he can say nothing specific about God's presence in the universe and nothing about the "figure de l'Etre divin." He, nonetheless, expresses his conviction that "du centre de son essence, de sa nature, de son étendue réelle, il voit tout, il éclaire tout, il dirige et gouverne tout; rien ne peut arriver, sans qu'il ne le voye et qu'il ne le veuille, ou qu'il ne le permette."

Bouhier in his reply (f. 325) admits that God's immensity does not mean that He occupies all space. That interpretation can only lead to Spinozism. He adds that we have no conception of a spiritual substance, and we haven't the foggiest notion how a spiritual being can occupy the whole universe and even surpass infinity. He adds sententiously that there are many things in nature we cannot understand: the infinite divisibility of matter, space, infinity. Nonetheless, he feels sure that the world did not organize itself, that there must accordingly be a Superior Being, that this Being cannot be matter. He insists that we know absolutely nothing about His nature, and concludes that the substance of Divinity is different from material substance.

About 1738 Cuenz became acquainted with Algarotti's *Neutonianismo*. He wrote Bouhier that he had been weighing the accusation that Newton had reintroduced the occultism of Aristotle into physics, and he now feels certain that he can explain how this accusation originated. He has decided to make an "abrégé" of his system and to send it to Sloane and the Royal Society. This he did after having first submitted the "abrégé" to Osterwald and to Werenfels. "Tous ces messieurs m'ont fait des objections, auxquelles j'ai tâché de satisfaire du mieux que j'ay pû." In the letter of 4 June 1740, to Bouhier, he announced that Sloane had judged his *Abrégé de métaphysique* worthy of being submitted to the Royal Society. A theologian had been appointed to report upon it. His report "hemmed and hawed," said Cuenz, but he had found nothing contrary to reason, to religion, or to philosophy. Cuenz had now decided to turn the "Abrégé" into a book. At the same time, he began publishing articles in the *Journal Helvétique* (4 July 1740): "On Happiness," "On Conjugal Love," "On Friendship," and an "Essay on Free will." These are some of the subjects treated in Voltaire's *Discours*

116

en vers sur l'homme. Bouhier having obviously offered some suggestions, Cuenz promised (11 July 1740) to try to clarify his views. He adds: "Le but de mon ouvrage étant de faire taire les esprits forts incorrigibles et de ramener les pyrhoniens de bonne foi par rapport à cette matière." On 14 July 1740 he announced that he was working upon the commentary upon Bayle. He explained on 10 February 1741 that the bringing together of all these letters, explanations, replies, commentaries, "abrégés," will make four volumes, in-8°. Shortly thereafter, he informed Bouhier that he now had enough text to make five or six volumes. "J'examine tous les systèmes," he stated, "et hypothèses qu'y ont paru jusqu'à présent, et ferai voir qu'ils conduisent tous à établir celui dont il est question, comme le plus probable au moins" (f. 332). On 10 June 1741 he announced he is now studying Cudworth. And he cites the passage in Locke's *Essay* where the Englishman maintains that we will never know whether a "material spirit" can think or not. It was the theme song in all of Voltaire's treatment of Locke.

Cuenz now explains (ff. 335ᵛ-38) the layout of his book, to be called *Système nouveau*: two letters on Bayle (one a commentary on what he says about the immateriality of God, the other on chapters 112 and 141 on the continuation of his *Pensées sur la comète*. Cuenz promised a third chapter on Cudworth's intellectual system, as printed in the first ten volumes of Le Clerc's *Bibliothèque choisie*. These three chapters are to constitute the second volume; the first volume will be devoted to an apology for Locke. A third volume will be composed of the essay sent to Sloane with the commentary that was made by the Royal Society.

Having received volume one, Bouhier wrote, 20 February 1742, that he would have preferred to have Cuenz begin by destroying the three systems that dominate modern thought in order to erect his own system "sur les ruines." He would have advised a brief presentation of Cuenz's stand so that one would know right off what he intended to propose. Bouhier

117

now rejects the notion of "extended Spirit" as a definition of the Deity, and he refuses, having been raised in the opposite opinion, to support the notion of the materiality of the soul. He confesses, nonetheless, that he knows no arguments that will justify that opinion.

Cuenz's book was eventually published in 1742 under the title *Essai d'un sistème nouveau concernant la nature des êtres spirituels, fondé en partie sur les principes du célèbre Mr. Locke, philosophe anglais dont l'auteur fait l'apologie* (4 vols., Neuchâtel, 1742). A copy now exists at the Bibliothèque Nationale. In the *Discours préliminaire,* Cuenz undertakes to give a plan of his work and the history of its development. He confesses the idea of writing Locke's apology was occasioned by an attack against the English philosopher in Prévost's *Pour et contre.* He admits that he welcomed this occasion, since it gave him the opportunity to express his own opinions on the nature of the soul. He states that he is firmly opposed to the doctrine of the pure spirituality of the soul, that is, its absolute non-extension. He places alongside this view the systems of occasionalism (from Malebranche) and preestablished harmony (Leibniz). In short, he admits that he is now opposed to Descartes, Malebranche, and Leibniz. These systems, he says, encourage free-thinkers and skeptics, stating at the same time that he intends to establish his criticism of these systems upon his doctrine: "C'est sur ce fondement que je me propose de raisonner sur les systèmes des causes occasionnelles et de l'harmonie pré-établie" (p. xi). These two interpretations he now calls inconceivable and contradictory. He professes more respect for the "famous" Descartes, but adds that he is not at all persuaded of the verity of his system. Finally, his attitude toward Leibniz is likewise chiefly negative:

> Je crois que l'on en peut dire autant de l'illustre M. de Leibnitz. Son système de l'harmonie, sa *Théodicée* font beaucoup plus d'honneur à la subtilité de son esprit et à sa vaste érudition qu'ils ne servent à l'avancement de la vérité. (p. xiv)

118

He gives a fairly succinct outline of the subjects that he proposes to treat: the limits of our knowledge, the preliminary principles upon which we reason, the nature of Being considered in general; the nature of God, the origin and nature of power and movement, the vacuum, matter, substance, accident, attribute, and mode; the distinction of man and animal, the origin and nature of all our ideas, free will, miracles. All of these subjects were likewise treated by both Voltaire and Mme du Châtelet. One of the subjects Cuenz promises to treat fully is the nature of the soul and its relationship with the body. He confesses that he is particularly interested in the problem of extension and nonextension of the soul. He is very critical of those who use the geometrical method to build a metaphysics: "L'usage que Spinoza en fit dans son *Ethique* en fait connaître le danger" (p. lxxii). To this condemnation, he adds that of Wolff and Leibniz. Finally, it should be noted that he quotes from the "illustre Mme du Châtelet." And well he might, because they are precisely the subjects under discussion at Cirey between 1735 and 1746.

Cuenz takes advantage of his dialogue here with Bouhier to give the outstanding points that he thinks he has made in the *Système nouveau* (f. 345): There is no way to obtain a clear notion of a Being who is absolutely devoid of extent. He can, in fact, be only a figment of the imagination. One can only conclude that the soul has a real extent. This extent which has a reality in the soul consists in a spiritual body—invisible, impalpable, indivisible, and immortal. The active and passive power of the soul has been breathed into it by God. This divine breath is not a substance, it is a mode. The soul comes into the world as a simple animal with unfulfilled potentialities. As these potentialities become realities, they unite first to become internal senses, which combine with external senses, and this combination in turn furnishes the wherewithal for the development of reason and the making of a personality. Though man begins by being an animal, he ultimately distinguishes himself from all other animals by a

119

more refined organization, by speech, by the ability to produce abstract ideas. "Cette différence est établie en vertu des causes finales." Cuenz insists, however, that all the ideas of the soul have a reality of their own. Its immortality is established upon God's "Toute-puissance" and his "Véracité." The Supreme Being, therefore, must also have an extent that is a reality, "mais d'une manière incompréhensible à nos lumières." Nonetheless, space that is God's domain really exists, and movement has its source in the Deity. Space and movement combined, the source of active and latent power, is "un pur don de Dieu." It imparts to all living beings their perceptivity and their motivity. These beings are consequently free. In a letter of 11 March 1742 Cuenz proposes that one understands by the word "matter" the same sort of thing we see in the word "color"; that is, it is and is not simultaneously, it has the appearance of reality and a reality or, as he says, there is a matter "en tout sens très parfaite" and another matter that is "raw" matter.

Having organized his thought in the four volumes of the *Système nouveau*, it was subjected to some fairly rough treatment in the *Journal Helvétique* for May-June, 1742, and Cuenz naturally felt constrained to defend his ideas. Here Cuenz takes up Trembley's discoveries and Bonnet's discussions of their importance. Cuenz saw in them confirmation of his system. He insists that had his system not been invented, the Spinozists would have taken them over to prove the validity of their system. Cuenz thereupon in the November-December 1742 number of the *Journal Helvétique* inserted two letters in which he utilized Trembley's discoveries to support his views. To Trembley and Bonnet he now adds Réaumur, and takes a decisive step in rejecting Descartes's theory of animal automatism.

Cuenz was as astounded by these discoveries as Réaumur, or Trembley whom he had trained, or Voltaire, because the problem is presented for these "*germes*," as Cuenz called them, as for a human being. The point I want to make in con-

120

cluding is that the extraordinary impact of these discoveries in biology that Cuenz takes as confirmation for his philosophy and Voltaire seems to have taken so lightly as confirmation for his *Micromégas* is really the same problem. I am convinced that Cuenz had never heard of *Micromégas*, and as far as I can tell, Voltaire never heard of Cuenz and his *Système nouveau*. Cuenz took his text, therefore, not from Voltaire but from Réaumur, whom he quoted:

> Loin, ce me semble, qu'on doive avoir quelque peine à accorder que la génération des pucerons se puisse faire d'une manière si simple, on ne doit être embarrassé de ce que, pour opérer la génération des autres animaux, une voye plus composée a été prise par Celui qui ne saurait manquer de choisir les moyens les plus parfaits et les plus convenables (f. 377).

Cuenz's comment should be read with *Micromégas* in mind:

> Ce sentiment paraît très probable, comme il est très digne de la justesse de l'esprit et de la grande perspicacité de notre illustre observateur. Mais les questions reviennent: Quel est l'ouvrier de ces germes ou de ces Embrions? Quel est le principe de vie qui anime ces petits êtres? Il est très évident que la chère de ces germes est entièrement passive ici. Elle ne sait, ni ne sent, au moins activement, ce qu'elle fait, si tant est qu'elle agisse véritablement en ces occasions. Ne faut-il donc pas convenir que, comme le dit notre auteur lui-même, *qu'un si grand ouvrage n'a pû être fait que par l'intelligence par excellence*? Mais comment pouvons-nous concevoir que cet ouvrier tout-puissant le fait? Ce ne peut être, comme j'ai dit, qu'au moyen d'un certain mécanisme qu'il a établi dans la nature, et d'une force qui émane immédiatement de lui et qui après avoir opéré d'une manière qui nous sera à jamais inconnue, au moins en cette vie. L'organization complète de ces êtres, de ces embrions, les anime et leur donne les facultés qui leur conviennent.

Cuenz calculates that Réaumur's *pucerons* multiply fabulously. He asks therefore if God is busied with making each a soul? "Ces âmes, supposé qu'elles existent réellement, que sont-elles? Quelle est leur nature? Que deviennent-elles? Quelle est leur destinée?"

We must now record one final bit of information. In spite of the feverish activity of my friend Cuenz, despite four volumes of his philosophy, the numerous articles of the *Journal Helvétique*, the seemingly interminable correspondence with his friend Bouhier and his unwavering confidence in his system—which does not seem to me to differ materially from the views of Voltaire as one finds them in the Cirey Period and especially in the *Traité de métaphysique*, the section on metaphysics in the *Eléments*, and the *Discours en vers sur l'homme* —the *philosophe* from Neuchâtel announced to the *philosophe* of Dijon, in October 1744, that he had not sold twenty copies of his work. He added, laconically, "selon les apparences, je n'ai rien de mieux à espérer pour l'avenir." Nonetheless, like the true *philosophe* he had become, he added: "Cela n'empêche pourtant pas que je ne continue de travailler à un supplément qui sera une pièce des plus fortes." Apparently, once a *philosophe*, always a *philosophe*. Cuenz, however, had to get his personal satisfaction from the approval of his Dijon friend. On 21 December 1744 he wrote to Bouhier: "Je suis extrêmement flatté de la bonne opinion qu'a de mon ouvrage philosophique un juge aussi compétent et aussi éclairé comme vous êtes, Monsieur; Je sens bien qu'indépendamment des grandes difficultés qu'il y a dans la chose même, par rapport à la prévention qu'il y a dans les esprits, et aux passions qui tyrannisent les hommes, le tems présent n'est pas fort propre, pour donner cours à un ouvrage de cette nature." Never did a *philosophe* make so ill-timed a prophecy. It could be that the only philosophical defect a *philosophe* has is that he lacks a spirit of prophecy. He just has no vision of the future, otherwise he would not have gone to the edge of the abyss and plunged into the French Revolution. However that may be, this fervent follower of Locke finishes as a modest disciple of Leibniz, and a casually interested dabbler in Spinozism, just as Voltaire did. In the same letter of 21 December 1744, he wrote: "Quant à l'hypothèse des animalcules, Leibniz si je ne me trompe, est celui qui s'est approché le plus du but, mais il resterait à satisfaire à beaucoup de difficultés." The *philosophes* may not have been good prophets, but they surely understood the philosophers—the immediate philosophers of the past.

1.   Emmanuel de Broglie, *Les Portfeuilles du Président Bouhier et fragments de correspondance littéraire* (Paris, 1896).

2.   Fonds français MSS. 24409-24421. Subsequent references will be given in the text.

3.   H. Monod-Cassidy, *Un Voyageur-philosophe au XVIIIe siècle: L'Abbé Jean-Bertrand Le Blanc* (Cambridge, Mass., 1941).

4.   G. R. Havens, "The Abbé Le Blanc and English Literature," *MP* 18 (1920): 423-41.

5.   I. O. Wade, *The Intellectual Development of Voltaire* (Princeton, N.J., 1969), pp. 257-58. See also pp. 352-53 and *passim*.

6.   Bibliothèque Nationale, fonds français MS. 24411, ff. 300-75.

7.   H. T. Mason, *Pierre Bayle and Voltaire* (London, 1963).

8.   E. de Broglie, *Les Portfeuilles*, p. 298.

9.   Charles Des Guerrois, *Le Président Bouhier: sa vie, ses ouvrages, et sa bibliothèque* (Paris, 1855).

Sur les *Mémoires* de Voltaire

C'est devenu un lieu commun de la critique que de
s'étonner de la fortune curieuse subie par les œuvres
de Voltaire. Toutes celles qui firent sa réputation durant sa vie, toutes celles qui furent le plus discutées et cri-
tiquées après sa mort, sont à peu près tombées dans l'oubli;
La Henriade, La Pucelle, Zaïre, Mérope, malgré les qualités
qu'on veut bien encore leur reconnaître, n'ont plus de public. Les ouvrages historiques se lisent encore avec intérêt,
mais sans susciter d'enthousiasme. Ce que nous aimons aujour-
d'hui, ce sont les *Contes,* la *Correspondance,* les *Mélanges.*
Voltaire, le poète, est devenu Voltaire l'ironiste, et le champion du pathétique, celui qui avait le secret de faire pleurer
ses contemporains, est pour nous, après deux siècles, le démo-
lisseur le plus vif et le plus gai que jamais littérature ait connu. Chose curieuse, et que je me borne à signaler en passant,
car elle ne touche pas à mon sujet, le nom et le prestige
de Voltaire n'ont pas été affectés par cette révolution
et les jugements portés sur lui, en bien ou en mal, n'ont guère
varié, quoique ce soit une tout autre œuvre que l'on admire
ou que l'on déteste.

C'est donc le polémiste, le combattant, le styliste en prose
qui retient désormais notre attention. Or, il se trouve, dans
cette catégorie si justement appréciée, un ouvrage de premier ordre qui, tout en ayant une certaine réputation, n'a
jamais pourtant connu un véritable succès. Il s'agit des *Mémoires,* ou pour respecter le titre exact, qui a cette longueur

125

chère au dix-huitième siècle: *Mémoires pour servir à la vie de M. de Voltaire, écrits par lui-même.*

Ce n'est pas chercher à être paradoxal que de soutenir que ces *Mémoires*, assez peu connus, sont d'un grand intérêt historique et, du point de vue littéraire, valent les meilleurs contes. Ils datent de 1759, c'est-à-dire qu'ils ont été écrits peu de temps après *Candide*, au moment où la verve de Voltaire est à son apogée. D'où vient alors qu'ils soient passés à ce point inaperçus?

Cela tient d'abord et surtout aux circonstances. De son vivant, Voltaire n'a jamais laissé paraître le livre. A la différence des autres ouvrages gardés sous clef, il n'y a jamais eu de fuite pour celui-ci, ce qui, par parenthèse, semblerait assez prouver que quand il ne voulait pas permettre la diffusion d'un écrit, il savait le garder secret. Cependant, il y a une tradition qui veut qu'en 1768 le manuscrit lui ait été dérobé par La Harpe, mais, soit que l'histoire soit inexacte, ce que je pense, au moins en ce qui concerne les *Mémoires*, soit que La Harpe se soit rendu compte qu'il s'exposait à de graves dangers en publiant un texte très subversif par ses personnalités, l'ouvrage ne fut soumis à aucun libraire.

En effet, sous l'insouciance et la légèreté des propos, se cache un pamphlet des plus audacieux en ce sens qu'il présente sous un jour peu flatteur les personnages les plus en vue de la scène européenne, à commencer par le roi de Prusse, Frédéric II. Il ne s'agit plus ici d'êtres fictifs, que l'auteur anime et ridiculise à sa guise, auxquels il prête les aventures les moins croyables et les plus scabreuses. Non, sur le tempo même des contes, de ce ton enjoué qui fait accepter les attaques les plus fortes, il dévoile l'intimité d'un puissant souverain, à une époque où un monarque n'avait aucune commune mesure avec un simple citoyen, il n'hésite pas à juger et à condamner d'un mot les principaux courtisans de Versailles, ou du moins ceux avec qui il a eu des démêlés, il parle des maîtresses du roi de France, bref il manque aux bienséances pour notre plus grand amusement. Pour qui sait l'horreur qu'inspirait aux gouvernements de l'Ancien Régime tout ce qui pouvait ressembler à une critique, même indirecte, il est facile de comprendre pourquoi Voltaire n'a jamais envisagé la publication clandestine d'un pareil livre: l'anonymat n'aurait pas suffi à le protéger.

Ce fut donc pour le public de 1784 une véritable surprise que la parution de ces *Mémoires,* dans des éditions furtives, faites visiblement à la hâte et qui fourmillent de fautes d'impression et de lecture. Personne, sauf quelques initiés, n'avait entendu parler de ce livre, et l'on n'imaginait pas qu'un auteur aussi audacieux que Voltaire, qui disait ce qu'il avait envie de dire et faisait imprimer tout ce qu'il venait d'écrire, eût gardé par devers lui, inédit, un texte de cette importance.

Or, en 1784, Frédéric II est encore vivant; de ce fait, les attaques dirigées contre lui, et qui sont les plus nombreuses, sont celles qui frappent le public et font croire aux commentateurs à une vengeance posthume de Voltaire qui n'a jamais pardonné au roi de Prusse l'aventure de Francfort. Nous verrons ce qu'il faut penser de cette opinion des contemporains. Le livre fit du bruit, mais moins qu'on aurait pu le croire; il venait trop tard. La plupart des personnages étaient morts, les événements semblaient lointains; ce n'était plus cette réaction choquée et amusée qu'obtenaient les productions de Voltaire de son vivant. Les nouvellistes en parlent tous, mais sur un ton modéré. Et Frédéric, toujours aussi habile, se garde bien de lui assurer un succès de scandale en le faisant interdire par la police. Peut-être d'ailleurs s'était-il rendu compte que le portrait fait par son ancien ami, malgré les traits perfides dont il était émaillé, ne lui faisait pas un si grand tort.

On peut donc affirmer que cette publication quasi clandestine n'obtint pas l'attention qu'elle aurait eue quelques années plus tôt sous une forme mieux soignée. L'ouvrage est donc à peu près inconnu du public lorsqu'il paraît pour la première fois dans une version acceptable. C'était dans la collection dite de Kehl des *Œuvres complètes* de Voltaire. Et bien entendu le texte passa presque inaperçu au milieu de cette avalanche de volumes. C'était d'autant plus un enterrement de première classe que les éditeurs, peu soucieux de s'attirer les reproches des personnes mentionnées dans les *Mémoires* ou de leurs héritiers, l'avait relégué au tome 70. Depuis, il a toujours été repris dans les recueils d'*Œuvres complètes*, et Dieu sait si ces recueils ont été nombreux pour Voltaire. Mais de telles éditions monumentales n'aidaient que peu à la diffusion d'un volume qui avait souffert d'un lancement défavorable. C'est seulement en 1886 que la Société des Bibliophiles donne une édition séparée des *Mémoires* avec une bonne introduction. Au total, il existe à ma connaissance six éditions du livre, dont la dernière remonte à 1965. Toutes ont été assez rapidement épuisées, ce qui laisse supposer qu'elles n'ont pas été tirées à un très grand nombre d'exemplaires. Voilà pourquoi, à mon avis, les *Mémoires*, malgré leurs qualités, n'occupent pas une place plus marquante dans l'œuvre de Voltaire. Bien qu'uniques en leur genre, ils se sont trouvés en quelque sorte assimilés aux facéties, aux dialogues, à toutes les fusées volantes qui vont sortir de l'usine de Ferney, et auxquels on rend volontiers hommage, sans trop les connaître.

Il reste deux chances de survie à un texte classique que le grand public boude, l'école et les travaux d'érudition. Malheureusement les *Mémoires* n'ont fait l'objet d'aucune édition scolaire, alors qu'il y en a je ne sais combien du *Siècle de Louis XIV*. Quant aux chercheurs, ils n'ont guère accordé d'attention à ce petit livre. Les historiens dans l'ensemble ont dédaigné un écrit que sa gaîté rendait suspect; le document leur a paru manquer par trop de gravité, ce n'est pas ainsi que s'exprime en général un témoin digne de foi. Certes, rares sont ceux qui ont nié la valeur historique des *Mémoires*, mais plus rares encore sont ceux qui les ont vraiment mis à contribution. Répétant les commentaires des premiers lecteurs, on n'a voulu y voir qu'un texte systématiquement dénigrant et une assez vilaine vengeance différée. Une fois de plus il convient de remarquer combien, chaque fois qu'une explication fait tort à Voltaire, elle est facilement adoptée. Seul de tous

128

les critiques, Paul Souday a osé affirmer nettement à quel point la vérité historique était respectée dans cet écrit de propagande:

> Il [Voltaire] a toujours eu le souci du vrai dans ses ouvrages d'histoire et même de polémique, d'abord parce que c'est beaucoup plus intéressant et qu'établir la vérité est le plus vif des plaisirs de l'esprit . . . , ensuite parce qu'un polémiste qui s'expose à être convaincu de mensonge ou d'erreur matérielle est un niais qui ne sait pas son métier—et ce n'est pas le cas—ou un subalterne qui travaille pour un public et de pareils suffrages peuvent convenir à d'autres, mais Voltaire était trop aristocrate pour s'en contenter. Il a voulu se venger du roi de Prusse, c'est entendu, mais la vengeance est un plat qu'il faut cuisiner avec art, c'est-à-dire, en l'espèce, avec exactitude.[1]

Souday a raison, bien que son argumentation soit peu convaincante; il parle en journaliste plus qu'en historien et les clichés dont sa prose est remplie n'inspirent pas confiance. Mais si on procède de manière plus scientifique, si, par exemple, on compare les *Mémoires* aux innombrables lettres de Voltaire écrites pendant cette période de vingt-cinq ans environ, on s'aperçoit qu'il déforme assez peu, sinon pour se donner quelquefois le beau rôle, ce qui est assez facile à déceler. Il lui arrive aussi d'exagérer une situation afin de faire rire, car on ne peut pas attendre de Voltaire qu'il soit aussi ennuyeux que Dangeau. Les journaux et les lettres des contemporains confirment également le bien-fondé des assertions de Voltaire. Et lorsque parfois un témoin vient le contredire, j'ai pu constater que bien souvent c'est Voltaire qui a raison, d'abord parce qu'il était admirablement bien placé pour savoir la vérité, ensuite parce que, généralement, dans les faits qu'il rapporte, il n'a pas intérêt à mentir. Enfin son sens de l'histoire et plus largement son intelligence lui ont permis de nous donner parfois la meilleure explication des événements auxquels il a pris part. C'est pourquoi je n'ai jamais hésité à utiliser les *Mémoires*, en prenant bien entendu certaines précautions à leur égard. Et, chaque fois que j'ai eu l'occasion de le vérifier, j'ai constaté que Voltaire avait été un chroniqueur fidèle.[2]

On ignore les raisons qui l'ont déterminé à entreprendre la rédaction de ses *Mémoires*. On ne trouve rien dans la *Correspondance* qui explique ce qui l'a poussé à écrire cette curieuse apologie. S'est-il senti soudain menacé? y a-t-il eu un événement qui l'a incité à vouloir se justifier aux yeux du public? On ne sait et je crois que, dans l'état actuel de nos connaissances, il serait vain de chercher ce qui a poussé Voltaire à se lancer dans ces confidences contrôlées.

S'il est impossible de savoir ce qui fut à l'origine du livre, il est par contre facile de comprendre les motifs qui ont amené sa composition. Et pourtant là une grave erreur a été commise que je crois devoir réfuter en détail. Ce n'est pas, comme l'ont cru la plupart des contemporains, suivis par un grand nombre de critiques, un désir de vengeance qui animait Voltaire contre le roi de Prusse. Il est facile de voir comment les témoins, qui ignoraient tout de la situation, se sont trompés en voulant expliquer logiquement les faits: Voltaire avait longtemps et fortement protesté contre le traitement que lui et sa nièce avaient subi à Francfort au mépris du droit des gens. Un homme aussi emporté que lui ne pouvait pas ne pas avoir songé à prendre sa revanche. Mais comment un écrivain pouvait-il s'attaquer à un souverain tout-puissant sans avoir à payer le prix de son audace? Il avait alors reporté son projet pour après sa mort et avait préparé de longue main un livre satirique où serait exposée la vie privée du roi de Prusse, puisque l'homme d'état était impossible à ridiculiser.

La moindre réflexion suffit à démontrer l'inanité d'un tel machiavélisme. L'hypothèse ne tient pas compte du caractère de Voltaire, incapable de dissimuler ses sentiments pendant des années. Elle n'explique pas le long délai entre la mort de l'écrivain et la parution des *Mémoires*, délai qui risquait de lui faire perdre le bénéfice de sa vengeance si Frédéric venait à mourir dans l'intervalle. Elle ne prend pas en considération la réconciliation intervenue entre ces deux esprits

130

supérieurs, trop intelligents pour ne pas se rendre mutuelle-
ment hommage. En prononçant l'éloge funèbre de Voltaire,
Frédéric avait montré qu'il ne subsistait plus rien des ressen-
timents d'autrefois. Comment un homme aussi méfiant que lui
aurait-il pu se laisser abuser par les sentiments réels de son
ancien ami? Enfin et surtout cette déplaisante explication n'est
justifiée en rien par le contenu des *Mémoires*, qui attaquent
trop de gens sur le même ton pour que Frédéric ait été la victime choisie de Voltaire. Il est bien certain que le roi de Prusse est passablement malmené dans l'ouvrage, et que ce n'était
pas ainsi qu'on traitait d'ordinaire les souverains régnants et
victorieux, mais ces piques n'étaient pas grand'chose pour qui
connaît les procédés diffamatoires que Voltaire n'hésitait pas
à employer quand il était en colère et voulait perdre un ennemi. Bien entendu un Frédéric est d'une autre stature qu'un
Fréron ou un Le Franc de Pompignan, mais il suffit de se rappeler de quelle manière abusive Voltaire a traité Jean-Jacques
Rousseau pour se rendre compte que le portrait de Frédéric
ne ressemble en rien à pareille charge. Il est sans aucun doute
très sarcastique, il est tout à fait irrespectueux, ce qui consti-
tue déjà une belle audace pour l'époque, mais il ne cherche
pas à détruire absolument une personne haïe. Et c'est justement parce que Voltaire opère avec un certain détachement,
parce qu'il procède plus par allusions que par invectives que
son comique devient si efficace. Je n'aime pas Voltaire lorsqu'il rivalise d'insultes avec Jean-Baptiste Rousseau ou avec
Desfontaines, les références continuelles à Nonotte ou à Chau-
meix deviennent lassantes dans les derniers ouvrages. Jamais
il n'est plus drôle que quand il est malicieux, lorsque son in-
dignation, toujours présente, est assez contrôlée pour s'aiguiser
en pointes ironiques, dures et spirituelles, comme c'est le cas
dans les *Mémoires*. La pseudo-impartialité de Voltaire est telle que je crois pouvoir dire que, par certains côtés, l'image de
Frédéric est flattée. Celui qu'il a peint a certainement d'in-
croyables petitesses, son caractère est laid, ses mœurs répré-
hensibles, ce n'en est pas moins une personnalité remar-

quable, un des grands hommes du siècle et certainement sa figure la plus originale. On comprend dès lors pourquoi le roi de Prusse, en dehors de son désir de ne pas attirer l'attention par ses protestations, n'a pas réagi à la parution du livre: il savait que son ancien chambellan ne lui faisait pas de tort.

Cette modération de Voltaire me paraît même, en un sens, assez remarquable si l'on songe que le livre a été écrit en 1759-60, c'est-à-dire à une époque encore assez proche des événements de Francfort. Ces sept ans environ n'ont pas fait oublier l'incident à Voltaire, ni fait disparaître son ressentiment, mais ils ont calmé sa colère. Son heureuse installation en Suisse a aussi contribué à rendre moins vifs les souvenirs des années en Allemagne. Voltaire n'est plus dans une position humiliée, où la vengeance est une compensation nécessaire, il peut se permettre d'être généreux. Je ne serais pas surpris qu'il ait eu le sentiment de ménager Frédéric et non de le charger. Ce n'est d'ailleurs ni par un souci d'équité ni en considération de son ancienne amitié pour le roi de Prusse. Simplement il a cru indispensable de parer Frédéric de mille prestiges afin de justifier sa conduite envers ce souverain, lui qui faisait profession de mépriser les grands.

Car, à mon avis, Voltaire n'a pas eu d'autre but, en écrivant ses *Mémoires*, que de justifier sa conduite pendant les vingt-cinq années qui séparent sa rencontre avec madame du Châtelet du moment où il rédige son livre. On remarquera tout d'abord qu'il ne dit pas un mot de ses quarante premières années, ce qui est assez exceptionnel pour qui raconte sa vie. D'autre part, une fois parvenu à un certain point de son existence il ne voit plus la nécessité de poursuivre plus avant son récit. On notera encore avec quelle brièveté et quelle froideur il parle de sa liaison avec madame du Châtelet. Pourquoi la rappeler si elle ne lui tient plus à cœur? C'est qu'elle est nécessaire pour expliquer la situation dans laquelle se trouve Voltaire au moment où il entre en relation avec Frédéric, alors prince royal de Prusse; elle sert ensuite à expliquer pourquoi il ne s'est pas installé plus tôt à Berlin, et pourquoi, après sa

mort, il n'avait plus de raison de ne pas s'y rendre. Ainsi, ce
que Voltaire entend nous raconter, ce sont ses relations avec
Frédéric, basées sur une amitié littéraire, et comment le fait
que Frédéric était roi de Prusse a fait que Voltaire, sans
l'avoir sollicité, s'est trouvé devenir homme politique. En somme Voltaire estime utile de relater les événements de sa vie
publique (et les événements de sa vie privée qui servent à les
expliquer). Si cette hypothèse est exacte, elle justifie son silence sur ses années de formation, sur son voyage en Angleterre, sur sa carrière de poète. On comprend aussi pourquoi,
après l'échec de ses projets de médiation pour amener la paix
entre la France et la Prusse, il a aussitôt interrompu un livre
qui n'avait plus de raison d'être. (Mais il était trop écrivain
pour détruire une œuvre dont il savait la valeur.) Désormais,
malgré l'éclat que va prendre son existence en Suisse, puis
à Ferney, c'est celle d'un citoyen, celle d'un homme de lettres qui ne doit compte au public que de sa production littéraire.

Ainsi s'explique le caractère unique de ces *Mémoires*. Rien
ne serait plus facile—et probablement plus vain—que de les
opposer aux *Confessions* de Jean-Jacques Rousseau. Voltaire
parle volontiers de lui-même; très souvent il cite son propre
exemple pour illustrer un point d'ordre général; très souvent,
et surtout dans ses dernières années, il amène à tout propos
ses ennemis sur la scène, leur attribuant ainsi une importance
exagérée, mais il n'éprouve aucun plaisir à se raconter. Une
histoire ne lui semble pas privilégiée parce que c'est à lui
qu'elle est arrivée. Il n'éprouve à aucun moment le désir de
recapturer le passé, il ne s'attendrit pas sur sa jeunesse. Voltaire vit trop dans le présent pour incliner à la nostalgie. Sa
confession est dirigée et tend vers un but. Aucune effusion
dans ces *Mémoires*, aucun lyrisme. L'œuvre est engagée, les
armes utilisées ici sont celles qui lui ont toujours réussi, l'ironie,
l'irrespect, le rire. En étudiant le manuscrit conservé à la Bibliothèque Nationale, qui est de la main de Wagnière, le secrétaire, et de Voltaire pour les dernières pages, j'ai été frappé

133

de constater que, parmi les rares corrections qui figurent dans le manuscrit, certaines sont dues à une confusion entre la première et la troisième personne du singulier, entre le "je" et le "il." Rien ne saurait mieux prouver le détachement avec lequel ces confessions sont écrites. Dans un récit d'aventures si personnelles, et dont certaines ont eu les plus grandes répercussions sur sa vie, Voltaire parle de lui-même comme d'un tiers, comme s'il s'agissait de quelqu'un d'autre. Il se regarde agir, de la même façon qu'un Zadig ou une Cunégonde ont le détachement nécessaire pour être les témoins objectifs de leurs propres malheurs.

Et peut-être le point le plus curieux du livre est de voir Voltaire se traiter et traiter ses contemporains comme s'ils étaient les héros de ses romans. Lui-même ici n'est pas tellement loin de ressembler quelquefois à Candide. Ce n'est pas que les histoires qu'il raconte aient le moindre rapport avec celles de son personnage, mais la manière de raconter produit le rapprochement.

Loin de donner aux personnages l'éclat et l'ampleur qu'exige leur rôle de premier plan, il les réduit à l'état de marionnettes, parce que la comédie voltairienne exige au départ des êtres unidimensionnels. Le réel, par une première manipulation, va être ainsi ramené à l'artificiel. C'est là une forme grave d'irrespect. L'histoire qui nous est racontée n'est plus considérée d'en haut, dans son déroulement fatal, imposé par le conflit des forces en présence ou par la volonté supérieure d'un individu d'exception, militaire ou diplomate. Non, l'histoire se fragmente en une série de petits faits, reliés par une causalité immédiate, qui est d'autant plus marquée qu'elle est souvent incongrue et entachée de comique.

En un sens, Voltaire applique ici sa théorie des petites causes pour expliquer les grands événements, et qui n'est jamais que le nez de Cléopâtre, dont parlait Pascal. Les *Mémoires*, plus encore que les œuvres historiques, semblent la mise en pratique des remarques qu'en 1738 Voltaire faisait déjà à Frédéric:

134

Si la duchesse de Marlborough n'avait pas jeté l'eau d'une jatte au nez de milady Masham et quelques gouttes sur la reine Anne, la reine Anne ne se fût point jetée entre les bras des torys et n'eût point donné à la France une paix sans laquelle la France ne pouvait plus se soutenir.[3]

La guerre de Succession d'Autriche, puis la guerre de Sept Ans, avec son spectaculaire renversement des alliances, n'ont produit aucun résultat décisif; des pays ont été ruinés, des milliers d'hommes tués pour rien. La marche des événements a échappé à ceux qui croyaient les mener. Les efforts des militaires, des diplomates n'ont abouti à rien ou à des effets que personne n'avait prévu, et les *Mémoires* reflètent cette impression de chaos, dont la lettre de Voltaire écrite en 1748 au comte d'Argenson donne une bonne idée:

Il me paraît par tous les mémoires qui me sont passés par les mains que M. le maréchal de Maillebois s'est toujours très bien conduit quoiqu'il n'ait pas été heureux. Je crois que le premier devoir d'un historien est de faire voir combien la fortune a souvent tort, combien les mesures les plus justes, les meilleures intentions, les services les plus réels ont souvent une destinée désagréable. Bien des honnêtes gens sont traités par la fortune comme je le suis par la nature.[4]

La fortune est donc aveugle, imprévisible, et les *Mémoires* ne manquent pas d'illustrer abondamment ce point. Lui-même, marionnette parmi les marionnettes, car il a l'habileté de ne pas s'excepter de la loi générale, fait fausse route comme les autres. Mais pour donner à sa démonstration un tour plus vivant et en accentuer le caractère comique, le satirique qu'il est n'hésite pas à aggraver la situation par l'introduction de causalités imaginaires. De même qu'un romancier dramatisera une scène potentiellement pathétique, de même Voltaire glisse des incongruités qui feront rire dans sa présentation des événements. Voilà pourquoi il invente de faux rapports entre des faits exacts et dont personne ne saurait douter. Le lecteur accepte d'autant plus volontiers l'explication qui

135

lui est offerte sur un ton de badinage que, sur le moment, l'invention comique l'emporte dans son esprit sur la vérité historique. Voici, par exemple, comment Voltaire termine le récit de sa mission diplomatique auprès de Frédéric II en 1743, et comment il explique que cette négociation heureuse ne lui a valu aucune récompense:

> La duchesse de Châteauroux fut fâchée que la négociation n'eût pas passé immédiatement par elle; il lui avait pris envie de chasser M. Amelot, parce qu'il était bègue et que ce petit défaut lui déplaisait; elle haïssait de plus cet Amelot, parce qu'il était gouverné par M. de Maurepas; il fut renvoyé au bout de huit jours, et je fus enveloppé dans sa disgrâce.[5]

Si l'on examine de près ce paragraphe, si innocent d'apparence, on constate que tous les faits mentionnés sont exacts: (1) madame de Châteauroux fut fâchée de voir que Voltaire négociait pour le compte des Secrétaires d'Etat au lieu de passer par son ami Richelieu et par elle; (2) Amelot était bègue; (3) il était gouverné par son collègue Maurepas; (4) elle le haïssait; (5) elle le fit renvoyer; (6) le renvoi se fit brutalement. Tout est donc vrai dans ce résumé, excepté le rapport supposé entre le bégaiement d'Amelot et sa disgrâce; aucun historien ne mentionne cette relation de cause à effet; j'ai entre les mains les lettres manuscrites de madame de Châteauroux au duc de Richelieu, elles ne parlent guère de cette infirmité du ministre des Affaires Etragères; c'est donc une invention de Voltaire pour rendre l'histoire plus incongrue, plus mécaniquement grotesque. En somme si Amelot n'avait pas été bègue, Voltaire aurait pu faire carrière à Versailles et la face du monde eût été changée!

Tout le livre est écrit dans ce style, ce qui rend sa lecture fort divertissante. Fort instructive aussi, car ce parti pris d'exactitude dans l'énoncé des faits donne à ces *Mémoires* une grande valeur d'information, mais on comprend qu'une vérité aussi allègrement manipulée ait pu inspirer des inquiétudes à ceux qui voulaient y chercher des matériaux historiques.

136

Cette création de faux rapports entre deux séries de faits est un des procédés les plus savoureux du comique voltairien, un de ceux que l'on remarque le plus fréquemment. Seulement, à la différence de ce qui se passe dans les *Contes* par exemple, comme ici les personnages sont réels, le persiflage prend aussitôt l'allure d'une médisance. Ainsi lorsque Voltaire déclare que Zadig "savait de métaphysique ce qu'on en a su dans tous les âges, c'est-à-dire fort peu de chose,"[6] ou encore quand il fait dire au frère de Cunégonde: "vous savez, mon cher Candide, que j'étais fort joli; je le devins encore davantage; aussi le révérend père Croust, supérieur de la maison, prit pour moi une tendre amitié,"[7] ces traits d'esprit ne passent pas pour des méchancetés. On admire en passant l'emploi de "c'est-à-dire" pour introduire une contradiction; on se rend compte que toute l'accusation d'homosexualité contre le jésuite repose sur l'heureuse utilisation de l'adverbe "aussi" soutenu par les deux adjectifs ambigus "joli" et "tendre." Mais quand, dans les *Mémoires*, il nous dit, reprenant les mêmes procédés:

> Un jeune courlandais, nommé Keyserling, qui faisait aussi des vers français tant bien que mal, et qui en conséquence était son favori, nous fut dépêché à Cirey des frontières de la Poméranie,[8]

on ne peut pas ne pas noter l'attaque perfide et enjouée sur les goûts littéraires du roi de Prusse (un des sujets de plaisanterie les plus fréquents du volume), attaque constituée autour des mots "aussi" et "en conséquence," qui encadrent autant "vers français" que "tant bien que mal."

Voltaire se sert de la fausse relation de temporalité aussi heureusement que de la fausse causalité. A propos de George Fox dans les *Lettres philosophiques*, il dit: "S'il n'avait prêché que contre les gens de guerre, il n'avait rien à craindre, mais il attaquait les gens d'Eglise: il fut bientôt mis en prison."[9] La répétition du mot "gens" suffit à créer le parallélisme des deux groupes et l'opposition des résultats, soulignée par

137

"mais." Par contre aucun terme grammatical n'exprime la conséquence de cette opposition tant la suite des événements est prévisible, de telle sorte que "bientôt," loin de porter le poids de la satire n'a qu'une valeur de renforcement. L'effet comique de manipulation du temps est beaucoup plus marqué dans le compte rendu que donne Voltaire de la première grande victoire remportée par Frédéric à Mollwitz. Le roi avait dû s'enfuir avec sa cavalerie, mais l'infanterie avait gagné la bataille. Voici comment l'écrivain rassemble ces données contradictoires, je ne donne que la fin de ce passage où l'ironie est constante et très appuyée:

> Si la cavalerie prussienne était mauvaise, l'infanterie était la meilleure de l'Europe. Elle avait été disciplinée pendant trente ans par le vieux prince d'Anhalt. Le maréchal de Schwerin, qui la commandait, était un élève de Charles XII; il gagna la bataille aussitôt que le roi de Prusse se fut enfui. Le monarque revint le lendemain, et le général vainqueur fut à peu près disgrâcié.[10]

A lire ce texte, non seulement Frédéric n'a pris aucune part à la bataille, mais encore les véritables vainqueurs ne lui doivent rien. Voltaire prend soin de spécifier que d'Anhalt est très vieux, que Schwerin a été formé par Charles XII. Bien plus il a suffi que le roi de Prusse s'enfuie pour que la chance tourne, comme s'il avait constitué l'unique obstacle à la victoire. L'effet de manipulation est obtenu en rapprochant "gagna" et "enfui" en les liant par "aussitôt que." Stylistiquement l'économie des moyens est remarquable. Enfin le passage se termine par un trait d'ingratitude, ce qui lui donne une importance particulière. Impossible d'imaginer une charge plus forte contre un roi victorieux, qui se révèlera comme le plus grand général de son temps.

Cette causalité supposée peut prendre une tournure particulière tant l'esprit de Voltaire est ingénieux. En 1758, il a sollicité l'aide du cardinal de Tencin pour essayer de négocier des pourparlers de paix entre la France et la Prusse. La médiation fut désavouée et quelques mois plus tard, Tencin mourut. Il avait soixante-dix-huit ans et était, depuis un certain temps déjà, malade. Sa mort n'était donc pas tellement étonnante, mais en modifiant les dates, Voltaire veut établir un rapport entre cette mort et le chagrin qu'il suppose que le cardinal a dû éprouver. Ensuite il réfléchit sur cette histoire et s'étonne d'une douleur dont personne d'autre que lui n'a jamais parlé:

> . . . L'abbé de Bernis dicta au cardinal la réponse qu'il devait faire: cette réponse était un refus net d'entrer en négociation. Il fut obligé de signer le modèle de la lettre que lui envoyait l'abbé de Bernis; il m'envoya cette triste lettre qui finissait tout, et il en mourut de chagrin au bout de quinze jours.
> Je n'ai jamais trop conçu comment on meurt de chagrin, et comment des ministres, et de vieux cardinaux, qui ont l'âme si dure, ont pourtant assez de sensibilité pour être frappés à mort par un petit dégoût: mon dessein avait été de me moquer de lui, de le mortifier, et non pas de le faire mourir.[11]

Ces réflexions sur le cardinal de Tencin ne sont pas isolées dans le volume. Au contraire elles en sont un des traits caractéristiques. Le récit est accompagné d'un commentaire continuel, soit sous la forme d'interventions directes à la première personne, soit sous forme de commentaires moraux ou ironiques. C'est là un procédé que Voltaire affectionne, jusque dans ses contes, et permet de donner l'impression que le récit, quelle que soit son extravagance, est sous le contrôle de la raison, puisque toujours un raisonneur commente l'action. Seulement ici la situation est assez différente parce qu'il présente des personnages réels, et lui tout le premier, ce qui implique une grande subjectivité. Mais, nous avons vu que, par un artifice essentiel, l'auteur a transformé ses contemporains en marionnettes. Or, des marionnettes supposent un montreur de marionnettes. Voltaire va donc assumer désormais un double rôle: acteur principal et marionnette d'une part, entraîné dans une série d'événements plus étonnants les uns que les autres et, d'autre part, narrateur et commentateur objectif de cette même histoire, dont il dégage certaines leçons pour le lecteur.

C'est par une alternance de ce jeu double que Voltaire prétend justifier sa conduite: sa position n'est pas tellement facile à défendre, les résultats de toutes ces années si remplies ne sont pas trop brillants. Il lui faut expliquer pourquoi il n'a jamais pu s'imposer à Versailles, pourquoi il a dû quitter la Prusse et chercher refuge en Suisse, poursuivi par les sarcasmes des petits auteurs et des dévots. C'est seulement au moment où il entreprend la rédaction de ses *Mémoires* qu'il va prendre sa revanche, devenir le roi Voltaire, le patriarche des lettres françaises. Mais, ne pouvant prévoir l'avenir, il voudrait pour le moment prouver à ses lecteurs qu'il n'a été ni joué ni mystifié. Il arrive plusieurs fois à Voltaire dans la discussion avec un interlocuteur de se faire la part plus belle qu'elle n'a dû être dans la réalité, mais, dans l'ensemble, cette attitude est assez rare, malgré la tentation qu'il pourrait avoir de se justifier ainsi sans peine par un dialogue spirituel. Dans l'ensemble, il prend plus volontiers l'aspect d'un naïf, il confesse volontiers ses erreurs, ses illusions. L'aveu est sans importance, chacun sait bien que la bêtise n'est pas son fort. Et ainsi il ne se dissocie pas des autres protagonistes du livre; en même temps il laisse entendre qu'il n'a pas cherché la gloire et que ce sont les occasions qui se sont présentées à lui. Ainsi, parlant de son installation en Prusse, installation que presque tous ses amis lui avaient déconseillée et que ses ennemis lui reprochaient, il déclare:

> Il n'y eut point de séduction flatteuse qu'il n'employât pour me faire venir.
> Le moyen de résister à un roi victorieux, poète, musicien et philosophe, et qui faisait semblant de m'aimer! Je crus que je l'aimais.[12]

Il suffit de regarder de près ce passage pour se rendre compte à quelle point la naïveté y est habile. Ce n'est pas celle de Candide, masque commode pour pousser l'adversaire et le

forcer à étaler sa sottise. Ici les mots sont calculés. Il faut justifier le départ en Prusse, le roi est un charmeur, il a toutes
les qualités qui pouvaient séduire un Voltaire; aucune de celles qui auraient tenté un courtisan n'est mentionnée. Mais Voltaire n'a pu rester à Berlin: Frédéric était une coquette qui a
joué une comédie pour s'attirer un poète en renom. Il a été
dupe, mais en partie seulement: "Je crus que je l'aimais." Et,
à ceux qui pourraient alors lui reprocher un manque de sin-
cérité, il oppose d'avance le fait que Frédéric, lui, "faisait
semblant" de l'aimer, ce qui est pure hypocrisie de sa part,
puisqu'il ne se trompait pas sur ses propres sentiments.

Voltaire ne joue pas tout le temps ce personnage de naïf,
ce serait un masque trop visible. Après tout, un homme comme lui ne fréquente pas les rois et les ministres de deux pays
par hasard; il est le plus grand poète de son temps et ne cherche à minimiser ni la valeur de son talent ni la qualité de ses
accomplissements, mais, même alors, il bannit toute vanité de
ses propos et est le premier à se moquer des lauriers qu'en
réalité il a tout fait pour obtenir. Et ainsi sa réussite fait partie
de la folie universelle. Parlant de ses relations avec madame
de Pompadour:

> Je passai quelques mois avec elle à Etiole, pendant que le roi
> faisait la campagne de 1746.
> Cela me valut des récompenses qu'on n'avait jamais don-
> nées ni à mes ouvrages ni à mes services. Je fus jugé digne
> d'être l'un des quarante membres inutiles de l'Académie. Je
> fus nommé historiographe de France; et le roi me fit présent
> d'une charge de gentilhomme ordinaire de sa chambre. Je con-
> clus que, pour faire la plus petite fortune, il valait mieux dire
> quatre mots à la maîtresse d'un roi que d'écrire cent volumes.[13]

Cette conscience de son talent, cette modestie et cette moquerie de soi qui coexistent en lui se retrouvent à chaque page
de la correspondance, c'est un trait de son caractère. Nulle
part il ne lui a été plus utile que dans ce livre. Se jugeant sans
indulgence apparente, il peut se permettre des portraits nu-

ancés, où le compliment est atténué par une critique, même quand il s'agit d'une personne chère: "Enfin notre jésuite ayant entendu parler de Mme du Châtelet, qui était *très bien faite* et *encore assez belle,* imagina de la substituer à Mme de Boufflers."[14]

Une des raisons pour lesquelles il est interdit à Voltaire de se traiter avec complaisance, s'il en avait eu l'envie, c'est le dénigrement systématique que subissent tous ceux qui se trouvent évoqués dans ce livre. Le vent de colère ironique, qui soufflait sur *Candide,* ne s'est pas apaisé dans les *Mémoires.* Mais, comme il s'agit de personnages réels, ce n'est plus le monde qui est fou, ce sont les gens qui y sont vils et méchants. Personne n'échappe ici à la griffe de l'auteur et, à ce point de vue, dans une atmosphère enjouée, dans un récit enlevé, les *Mémoires* constituent un vrai jeu de massacre. En voici quelques exemples:

"Mlle Poisson, dame Le Normand, marquise de Pompadour, était réellement premier ministre d'Etat."[15] Cette moquerie des origines de madame de Pompadour n'est pas du meilleur goût, d'autant qu'il aime assez la marquise, et l'opposition avec premier ministre n'est pas assez forte pour justifier cette sortie, qui ne peut s'expliquer que par cette mauvaise humeur généralisée. Il est naturellement beaucoup plus dur pour son vieil ennemi, l'ancien évêque de Mirepoix: "Un vieil imbécile, précepteur du dauphin, autrefois théatin, et depuis évêque de Mirepoix, nommé Boyer. . . ."[16] Cette médisance ne se limite pas aux grands, elle atteint de petits personnages, auxquels probablement Voltaire n'avait sans doute rien à reprocher: "d'Argens n'avait pour tout bien dans le monde que ses *Lettres juives* et sa femme, nommée Cochois, mauvaise comédienne de province, si laide qu'elle ne pouvait rien gagner à aucun métier, quoiqu'elle en fît plusieurs."[17] C'est là ce qui s'appelle une exécution en règle, fort spirituelle dans sa méchanceté. Voltaire introduit une double perspective à propos de d'Argens: les *Lettres juives,* son titre de gloire, dont il ne parle pas et sa femme, sur laquelle il s'acharne,

142

finissant par une accusation contournée et pourtant impossible
à ne pas comprendre.

Naturellement Frédéric est ici la cible favorite de Voltaire.
Il l'attaque sur ses vers, ses mœurs et son caractère. Pour se
moquer des prétentions littéraires du roi, il utilise le procédé
fort simple qui consiste à citer des poésies du roi, suivies ou
précédées d'un commentaire ironique, le jeu consistant à ne
jamais trouver absolument bons ou mauvais les passages qu'il
reproduit:

> Le roi m'envoya à Bruxelles une relation de son voyage, moi-
> tié prose et moitié vers, dans un goût approchant de Bachau-
> mont et de Chapelle, c'est-à-dire autant qu'un roi de Prusse
> peut en approcher.[18]

> Il m'envoya cette épître écrite de sa main. Il y a plusieurs
> hémistiches pillés de l'abbé de Chaulieu et de moi. Les idées
> sont incohérentes, les vers en général mal faits, mais il y en a
> de bons; et c'est beaucoup pour un roi de faire une épître de
> deux cents mauvais vers dans l'état où il était.[19]

En ce qui concerne l'homosexualité de Frédéric, la dénoncia-
tion est sans équivoque:

> Quand Sa Majesté était habillée et bottée, le stoïque donnait
> quelques moments à la secte d'Epicure: il faisait venir deux
> ou trois favoris, soit lieutenants de son régiment, soit pages, soit
> heiduques ou jeunes cadets. On prenait du café. Celui à qui on
> jetait le mouchoir restait demi quart d'heure tête à tête. Les
> choses n'allaient pas jusqu'aux dernières extrémités, attendu
> que le prince, du vivant de son père, avait été fort maltraité
> dans ses amours de passade, et non moins mal guéri. Il ne pou-
> vait jouer les premiers rôles; il fallait se contenter des seconds.[20]

Ensuite Voltaire ne fait plus allusion aux mœurs du prince
que par des remarques rapides et amusées, afin de rappeler
la chose sans y insister: "Le roi avait fait enlever à Venise
cette danseuse par des soldats qui l'emmenèrent par Vienne
même jusqu'à Berlin. Il en était un peu amoureux, parce qu'elle avait les jambes d'un homme."[21]

143

Quant aux critiques du caractère, elles portent essentiellement sur la duplicité du roi et sur son avarice. Or, chose amusante, ce sont là également les deux traits de caractère que Frédéric reproche à Voltaire.

Jusqu'à présent j'ai montré l'acteur Voltaire aux prises avec les autres interprètes de la pièce dont Frédéric est la vedette. Je n'ai fait que mentionner le narrateur, c'est-à-dire le personnage qui se mêle à l'action pour la commenter. Il est toujours très instructif de voir comment dans un Journal ou dans un roman à tendances fortement autobiographiques l'auteur se sauve des accusations qu'il a portées contre lui-même, justement par le moyen des faiblesses qu'il a eu le courage de confesser. Voltaire n'agit pas autrement dans ses *Mémoires*, qui ne sont pas autre chose qu'une apologie comique. Tout d'abord il se présente avec les autres, insecte comme eux, et, à ce titre, il participe aux folies du monde. Mais, promu soudain narrateur par la grâce de la fiction littéraire, il prend une position d'entomologiste. Du coup le voilà juge et partie, il a retrouvé le sentiment de sa supériorité, sans que le personnage qu'il joue ait cessé d'être humble. Et à la fin du livre, quand il se remet à l'œuvre il a pratiquement disparu de la scène. Ce sont maintenant les autres, et les autres seuls qui le font rire. Il regarde de haut Frédéric qui croyait entrer en vainqueur à Dresde et s'est fait battre par les Autrichiens, rappelant ainsi à l'auteur la fable du *Pot au lait* de La Fontaine; il se moque de l'ex-lieutenant de police, Berryer, devenu ministre de la marine, et dont la flotte vient d'être détruite par les Anglais; il se moque tout autant de Silhouette, connu jusqu'alors "pour avoir traduit en prose quelques vers de Pope,"[22] (on notera le mépris dans les mots "en prose" et "quelques") et qui, devenu contrôleur général des finances, a ruiné son pays en quatre mois. Voltaire acteur a disparu, il ne reste plus que l'observateur amusé de ce grand carnaval qu'est le monde des hommes. Et ce n'est pas pour rien que le livre s'achève en pirouette, un peu comme s'achève le *Siècle de Louis XIV* par les cérémonies chinoises:

144

Comme cette grande et horrible tragédie est toujours mêlée
de comique, on vient d'imprimer à Paris *les Poëshies du roi
mon maître*, comme disait Freytag; il y a une épître au maréchal Keith, dans laquelle il se moque beaucoup de l'immortalité
de l'âme et des chrétiens. Les dévots n'en sont pas contents, les
prêtres calvinistes murmurent; ces pédants le regardaient comme le soutien de la bonne cause, ils l'admiraient quand il je-
tait dans des cachots les magistrats de Leipzig, et qu'il vendait
leurs lits pour avoir leur argent. Mais depuis qu'il s'est avisé
de traduire quelques passages de Sénèque, de Lucrèce et de
Cicéron, ils le regardent comme un monstre. Les prêtres ca-
noniseraient Cartouche dévot.[23]

C'est donc un monde définitivement dépourvu de sens que
celui où le général vainqueur se fait battre, où le chef de la
police est mis à la tête de la marine, où un traducteur passe
à celle des finances, où les prêtres applaudissent aux plus
grandes injustices et ne tolèrent pas qu'on reproduise les maximes des Anciens. Mais cet univers ridicule est en même
temps tragique parce que les gens s'y prennent au sérieux.
En face de cette contradiction, il n'y a qu'une attitude possible, lorsqu'on a la chance de ne pas être dans la mêlée: rapporter ce qu'on a vu en riant.

L'on comprend pourquoi Voltaire n'a pas tenté de plaider
sa cause par une défense en règle. Il a préféré se moquer de
lui-même et des autres, et le comique, ainsi répandu sur
l'œuvre, est venu lui apporter son unité, sa raison d'être et sa
force de conviction. Du point de vue de l'esprit, les *Mémoires*
valent les meilleurs contes, quoiqu'il faille parfois connaître
le dessous des choses pour en apprécier pleinement le sel. Je
dirai même que la ressemblance est parfois si grande avec les
Contes qu'on a quelquefois l'impression de retrouver une
phrase connue. Ainsi Voltaire écrit dans *Candide*, lors de la
leçon de physique expérimentale: "Comme mademoiselle
Cunégonde avait beaucoup de dispositions pour les sciences
. . . ,"[24] et dans les *Mémoires*: "C'était Mme la marquise du
Châtelet, la femme de France qui avait le plus de dispositions
pour toutes les sciences."[25] Et je ne crois pas qu'il y ait là la

145

moindre intention parodique. Dans *Zadig* on lit: "Zadig disait: Je suis donc enfin heureux! Mais il se trompait."[26] La même construction se trouve dans les *Mémoires*: "Il crut être amoureux d'elle, mais il se trompait: sa vocation n'était pas dans le sexe."[27] Et comment la phrase suivante ne ferait-elle pas songer à *Micromégas*: "J'aime à me rappeler cette aventure qui fait voir les petitesses de ceux qu'on appelle grands."[28] Dans *Candide* il y a le fameux passage dans le récit de Cunégonde: "Le brutal me donna un coup de couteau dans le flanc gauche dont je porte encore la marque.—Hélas! j'espère bien la voir, dit le naïf Candide.—Vous la verrez, dit Cunégonde. . . . "[29] J'ai cru qu'une situation semblable se trouvait dans les *Mémoires*; on peut lire dans toutes les éditions à propos de la margrave de Bareith: "Il en resta à la princesse une contusion au-dessous du téton gauche qu'elle a conservée toute sa vie comme une marque des sentiments paternels et qu'elle m'a fait l'honneur de me montrer."[30] Malheureusement la ressemblance est due à une erreur de lecture, le manuscrit porte au-dessus et non au-dessous du téton gauche, ce qui a pour effet de faire disparaître et la plaisanterie et l'inconvenance.

Il ne saurait être question d'étudier le comique de Voltaire dans les *Mémoires*, alors qu'il a à peine été examiné dans le reste de son œuvre. Ce que l'on peut dire toutefois c'est que les qualités majeures, la rapidité du rythme et la légèreté du ton, s'y retrouvent. Cette revue des événements se déroule sur un tempo extrêmement vif, avec, comme toujours chez Voltaire, des accélérations et des ralentissements pour donner l'impression de mouvement. Voici par exemple le récit de la célèbre maladie de Louis XV à Metz; on remarquera comment elle se déroule sous la forme d'une succession de faits, les uns importants, les autres moins, mais tous traités de la même façon, et l'on notera l'accélération soudaine à la fin de la citation:

Il arriva quelque temps après que Louis XV fut malade à l'extrémité dans la ville de Metz; M. de Maurepas et sa cabale prirent ce temps pour perdre Mme de Châteauroux. L'évêque de Soissons, Fitz-James, fils du bâtard de Jacques II, regardé comme un saint, voulut, en sa qualité de premier aumônier, convertir le roi, et lui déclara qu'il ne lui donnerait ni absolution ni communion, s'il ne chassait sa maîtresse et sa sœur, la duchesse de Lauraguais, et leurs amis. Les deux sœurs partirent, chargées de l'exécration du peuple de Metz. Ce fut pour cette action que le peuple de Paris, aussi sot que celui de Metz, donna à Louis XV le surnom de *Bien-Aimé*. Un polisson, nommé Vadé, imagina ce titre que les almanachs prodiguèrent. Quand ce prince se porta bien, il ne voulut être que le bien-aimé de sa maîtresse. Ils s'aimèrent plus qu'auparavant. Elle devait rentrer dans son ministère; elle allait partir de Paris pour Versailles, quand elle mourut subitement des suites de la rage que sa démission lui avait causée. Elle fut bientôt oubliée.

Il fallait une maîtresse. Le choix tomba sur une demoiselle Poisson, fille d'une femme entretenue et d'un paysan de La Ferté-sous-Jouarre, qui avait amassé quelque chose à vendre du blé aux entrepreneurs des vivres.[31]

Cette impression de vitesse est encore accrue par les confusions, par les généralisations. Ainsi, parlant du comte de Maurepas, qui faillit perdre sa place à cause de madame de Châteauroux et fut finalement chassé à la demande de madame de Pompadour: "Il avait la manie de se brouiller avec toutes les maîtresses de son maître, et il s'en est trouvé mal."[32]

Le badinage du ton favorise cette impression de vivacité et ce rythme soutenu vient tout autant ôter au récit toute possibilité d'attendrissement, voire d'émotion. Voici de quelle manière Voltaire rend compte de la mort de La Mettrie, qui avait été le premier à lui signaler la duplicité de Frédéric:

La Mettrie mourut après avoir mangé chez milord Tyrconnel, envoyé de France, tout un pâté farci de truffes, après un très long dîner. On prétendit qu'il s'était confessé avant de mourir; le roi en fut indigné: il s'informa exactement si la chose était vraie; on l'assura que c'était une calomnie atroce, et que La Mettrie était mort comme il avait vécu, en reniant Dieu et les médecins. Sa Majesté, satisfaite, composa sur-le-champ son oraison funèbre. . . . [33]

147

Cependant, qu'on ne s'y trompe pas, il n'y a pas d'opposition entre le fond et la forme; l'unité des *Mémoires* vaut celle des *Contes* ou des meilleures facéties. Cette gaîté si naturelle, qui imprègne toute l'histoire, n'est pas l'artifice heureux d'un écrivain qui connaît son métier. Elle correspond à la pensée de l'auteur qui a voulu, au milieu d'événements incohérents, mettre sous les yeux du lecteur un groupe de personnages originaux, qui se sont trouvés amenés par la singularité de leurs caractères à traiter en se jouant des sujets les plus graves, sans que cette fantaisie ait nui à leurs négociations. Il faut voir avec quelle délectation Voltaire transcrit les petits vers par lesquels Frédéric répond à ses graves questions politiques. Les historiens ont cru voir dans ce divertissement la preuve que Frédéric se moquait de ce poète-diplomate amateur. Cela m'étonnerait. Car, à supposer que Voltaire ait été abusé sur le moment, il était trop fin pour ne pas rétablir la vérité et il ne serait pas mis dans le cas de révéler les circonstances d'une négociation, dont personne d'autre n'avait parlé, et dans laquelle il aurait tenu un rôle ridicule. Il soutient d'ailleurs aussitôt après que la négociation s'est heureusement terminé et il semble bien que les faits confirment l'opinion de Voltaire. Voici comment il rapporte le détail de cette négociation:

> Je lui envoyais de ma chambre à son appartement mes réflexions sur un papier à mi-marge. Il répondait sur une colonne à mes hardiesses. J'ai encore ce papier où je lui disais: Doutez-vous que la maison d'Autriche ne vous redemande la Silésie à la première occasion? Voice sa répose en marge:
>
> Ils seront reçus, biribi,
> A la façon de barbari,
> Mon ami.[33]

La leçon qu'on peut tirer des *Mémoires* est implicite; Voltaire ne croit pas aux messages didactiques, il demande un effort de son lecteur pour compléter la démonstration et la formuler selon ses propres besoins. Que nous dit-il? Sans

148

l'avoir cherché, il s'est trouvé mêlé aux négociations politiques de son temps, elles ne lui ont valu aucun avantage, ni à lui ni à tous ceux qui se croyaient de fins politiques et ont été trompés dans leurs prévisions. Toutes les faveurs lui ont attiré une foule d'ennemis jusqu'au moment où il a pu s'éloigner de cette farce tragique et se trouver une retraite à son goût. Les misères du monde ne méritent que le rire des spectateurs. Que faire alors sinon ce que l'on aime? Arrivé enfin au port après de longues péripéties, bien installé dans sa maison des Délices, Voltaire répète sous une forme personnelle l'apologue de *Candide*: "Tout ceci est bien dit, mais il faut cultiver son jardin."

1. Paul Souday, *Voltaire démiurge* (Paris: Emile Hazan, 1927), p. vii.

2. J'ai utilisé les *Mémoires* notamment dans mon livre, *Les Tencin* (Genève: Droz, 1970) et dans mes articles, "Voltaire et le cardinal de Fleury," *Revue du dix-huitième siècle*, No. 2 (1970), et "La mission diplomatique de Voltaire en 1743," ibid., No. 3 (1971).

3. Voltaire à Frédéric, 5 août 1738. Cité par René Pomeau dans son Introduction aux *Œuvres historiques* (Paris: Pléiade, 1957), p. 18.

4. Voltaire à d'Argenson, *Voltaire's Correspondence*, D 3723, 19 juillet 1748, 10: 282.

5. *Mémoires pour servir à la vie de M. de Voltaire, écrits par lui-même* (Paris: Louis Conard, 1914), p. 59.

6. Les citations des *Contes* sont prises dans l'édition *Romans et contes* (Paris: Garnier-Flammarion, 1966), p. 30.

7. *Candide*, p. 209.

8. *Mémoires*, p. 17.

9. *Lettres philosophiques* (Paris: Garnier, 1962), p. 11.

10. *Mémoires*, p. 31.

11. Ibid., p. 103.

12. Ibid., p. 67.

13. Ibid., p. 62.

14. Ibid., p. 64. Les italiques ne sont pas dans le texte.

15. Ibid., p. 92.

16. Ibid., p. 40.

17. Ibid., p. 78.

18. Ibid., p. 19.

19. Ibid., p. 98.

20. Ibid., p. 46.

21. Ibid., p. 54.

22. Ibid., p. 125.
23. Ibid., p. 126.
24. *Candide*, p. 180.
25. *Mémoires*, p. 2.
26. *Zadig*, p. 42.
27. *Mémoires*, p. 13.
28. Ibid., p. 41.
29. *Candide*, p. 193.
30. *Mémoires*, p. 12.
31. Ibid., p. 59.
32. Ibid., p. 40.
33. Ibid., p. 72.
34. Ibid., p. 58. Il s'agit là du refrain d'une chanson en vogue.

Voltaire's Debt to the *Encyclopédie*
In the *Opinion en alphabet*

JEANNE R. MONTY

In his now standard work *Voltaire et l'Encyclopédie* Raymond Naves asserted that although "on trouve dans les pages de Voltaire soit des souvenirs du texte encyclopédique, soit des réfutations, soit des arguments précis qu'il s'approprie, soit même des passages qu'il recopie sans toujours le signaler," the *Encyclopédie*'s major influence on Voltaire was an "influence par contradiction."[1] This conclusion, although valid for the bulk of Voltaire's later works, especially the alphabetical articles known since the Kehl edition as the *Dictionnaire philosophique*, cannot, however, be applied to the *Opinion en alphabet*, which is directly related to the *Encyclopédie*. Indeed, the recognition of such a relationship is basic to an understanding of the latter Voltairean work. This paper therefore has a dual aim: to demonstrate the extent and character of the *Encyclopédie*'s influence on the *Opinion en alphabet*, as well as to define the *Opinion en alphabet*'s nature and purposes and suggest a probable history of its composition.

The Kehl editors, who first published the *Opinion en alphabet* in their *Dictionnaire philosophique*, provided few facts concerning its origin or nature. They stated that it consisted of manuscript articles in Wagnière's hand, but they failed to establish a list of the texts found therein and later identified, in a footnote, only one article: "Moïse III." The "Avertissement de la collection intitulée *l'Opinion en alphabet*," presumably by Voltaire himself, refers only vaguely to the nature

153

of that work: "Cet alphabet est extrait des ouvrages les plus estimés qui ne sont pas communément à la portée du grand nombre."

For lack of more precise information, and in the absence of the original manuscript, it has been assumed that all previously unpublished material that first appeared in the Kehl *Dictionnaire philosophique* was in fact part of the *Opinion en alphabet*. This includes the articles "Abbaye I," "Abraham III," "Adam III," "Ange II," "Athée I, II," "Banque," "Bien (Du bien et du mal, physique et moral)," "Conciles I," "Conquête," "Décrétales," "Dieu I," "Eclipse," "Fanatisme I," "Foi II," "Franc-arbitre," "Généalogie I," "Hérésie III," "Inquisition I," "Juifs II, III," "Kalendes," "Livres III," "Locke II," "Messe," "Moïse III," "Noël," "Oracles II," "Pierre le Grand et Jean-Jacques Rousseau II," "Prétentions de l'empire," "Prophéties I," "Quête," "Reliques," "Sibylle," "Suicide," "Théologie," "Université," "Vision de Constantin," "Xavier," "Yvetot," "Zèle."[2]

Whether all these articles are indeed part of an alphabetical work conceived by Voltaire as a unit is yet open to question. At least one article, "Prétentions de l'empire," consisting of bare reading notes, would seem to belong more properly to the *Notebooks* than to the *Opinion en alphabet*: Voltaire has done no more than copy the table of contents of Jean Rousset de Missy's *Les Intérêts présents et les prétentions des puissances de l'Europe* (La Haye, 1741), merely adding to each chapter heading a one- or two-sentence summary of Rousset de Missy's discussion (1:114–260) of the Empire's claim to the territories listed. Voltaire's subtitle, "tirées de Glafey et Schweder," also leads back to Rousset de Missy, who acknowledges (1:vii) that his section on the "Prétentions de l'Empire" is derived from Adam Glafey and Christoph Schweder's *Theatrum historicum praetensionum et controversiarum illustrium in Europa* (Leipzig, 1727).

These reading notes are found almost verbatim in the Piccini *Notebooks*,[3] dating on the whole from 1750 to 1755.[4] Variants include two probable typographical errors, the added information, in the *Notebooks*, that the notes taken from Glafey and Schweder were "traduites par Rousset," and the statement, omitted from the *Notebooks*, that "presque tous les états d'Italie sont ou ont été vassaux de l'empire." It seems unlikely that Voltaire would have transferred a long passage from the *Notebooks* to a projected *Opinion en alphabet* with so little revision. Such was not his habit, as can be seen from the many texts in the *Essai sur les mœurs*, the *Dictionnaire philosophique*, the *Questions sur l'Encyclopédie*, which have been traced back to earlier jottings in the *Notebooks*. On the other hand, there is no logical reason for Piccini to have lifted the article "Prétentions de l'empire" from the Kehl *Dictionnaire philosophique* to add to the *Notebooks*. It would be the only case on record. That there were two manuscripts of that article, now both lost, is almost certain. I am inclined to believe that at some time the passage in the *Notebooks* was copied by Wagnière and filed with the other texts that became the *Opinion en alphabet*. But it was not originally written for that purpose.

There remains, however, a core of articles that are linked internally through many cross-references, and that were undoubtedly conceived as a unit. They are: "Conciles I," "Eclipse," "Généalogie I," "Hérésie III," "Inquisition I," "Kalendes," "Livres III," "Messe," "Prophéties I," "Reliques," "Sibylle," "Université," "Vision de Constantin," "Xavier," "Yvetot," "Zèle." Without excluding other articles that, by their nature, may not lend themselves to cross-references,[5] we can identify these "core" articles as originally intended for an alphabetical work that Voltaire, for some reason, did not see fit to publish, and that later became the *Opinion en alphabet*.

The majority of these "core" articles (twelve out of sixteen) are also linked externally through a common source: Diderot's *Encyclopédie*, one of the "ouvrages les plus estimés" to which the "Avertissement" refers. In turn, twenty-one of the thirty-eight articles presumed to belong to the *Opinion en alphabet* (excluding "Prétentions de l'empire") are related to the *Encyclopédie*.[6] And contrary to Raymond Naves's general conclusion, in only four of those twenty-one articles, "Adam III," "Foi II," "Locke II," and "Théologie," does Voltaire refute statements made in the *Encyclopédie* or condemn them as being irrelevant. The other seventeen articles evince a positive influence of the *Encyclopédie* in the form of direct and extensive copying. These are (followed by their source[s] in the *Encyclopédie*):

> Abbaye I—Ab, by Mallet.[7]
> Décrétales—Décrétales (fausses), by Bouchaud.[7]
> Fanatisme I—Fanatisme, by Deleyre.
> Hérésie III—Hérétique, by Jaucourt.[7]
> Inquisition I—Inquisition, by Jaucourt.
> Juifs III—Juif, by Jaucourt.
> Kalendes—Fête des ânes, by Mallet; Fête des fous, by Jaucourt.[7]
> Livres III—Livre, probably by Diderot.[8]
> Messe—Danse sacrée, by Cahusac;[7] Messe, by Jaucourt; Agapes, by Mallet.
> Oracles II—Oracles, by Jaucourt; Eloge de M. Du Marsais, by d'Alembert.[7]
> Reliques—Relique, by Jaucourt.
> Sibylle—Sibylle, by Jaucourt; Sibyllins (livres), by Jaucourt.
> Université—Université, by Jaucourt.
> Vision de Constantin—Vision céleste de Constantin, by Jaucourt.
> Xavier—Xavier, by Jaucourt.
> Yvetot—Yvetot, by Jaucourt.
> Zèle—Zèle, by Jaucourt.

At times the borrowing may be brief: four or fewer paragraphs of Voltaire's text. Such is the case in "Abbaye I," "Hérésie III," "Inquisition I," "Livres III," "Université," "Xavier," "Yvetot," "Zèle." Generally the copied passage forms the

156

opening paragraphs of Voltaire's article, which then proceeds in a direction other than that of the *Encyclopédie*. "Livres III," for example, begins with two paragraphs copied from the *Encyclopédie* decrying the multiplication of books and the impossibility for one to read even a fraction of them; it then continues with considerations on the reading of the Bible. In "Yvetot" a four-paragraph discussion on the origins of that alleged kingdom, copied from Jaucourt, leads, somewhat surprisingly, to a lengthy denunciation of papal excommunications throughout the ages.

It would be rash to conclude, however, that Voltaire's procedure here necessarily indicates dissatisfaction with the ideas expressed in the *Encyclopédie*. He could hardly have objected very strenuously to Jaucourt's "Inquisition": that article was borrowed in large part from chapter 140 of his own *Essai sur les mœurs!*[9] It may be that some of the added paragraphs are indeed Voltaire's own. Or it may be that some have been copied from other, as yet unidentified, articles of the *Encyclopédie*: "Messe" has been traced back to three different articles by three different authors! In other cases, as in "Inquisition I" and "Zèle," passages from the *Encyclopédie* are simply joined to excerpts from other published or unpublished works.

"Inquisition I" opens with several introductory sentences from Jaucourt's article "Inquisition" in volume 8 (1765) of the *Encyclopédie*. The following forty-one paragraphs, which complete Voltaire's text, are either verbatim copies or summaries of abbé Morellet's *Manuel des inquisiteurs, à l'usage des inquisitions d'Espagne et de Portugal, ou Abrégé de l'ouvrage intitulé Directorium Inquisitorum composé vers 1358 par Nicolas Eymeric, grand inquisiteur dans le royaume d'Aragon* (Lisbon [Paris], 1762), although the debt is never acknowledged. Voltaire's only contribution consists of correcting one of Morellet's errors (p. 170) and substituting "Innocent VII" for "Clément VII" as pope at the time of King John I of Portugal. The larger part of "Inquisition I" thus reproduces Voltaire's own reading notes, a fact that emerges clearly when one compares it with the articles "Inquisition" in the 1769 *Raison par alphabet* and "Aranda" in the 1770 *Questions sur l'Encyclopédie*, which are based on those notes.[10]

The article "Zèle" proceeds in similar fashion: the first few sentences, copied from the *Encyclopédie*, are followed first by a long quotation from Julian the Apostate's Epistle LII, already cited in the articles "Julien" of the *Dictionnaire philosophique* and "Apostat" of the *Questions sur l'Encyclopédie*, and then by twenty-two paragraphs taken from Isaac de Beausobre's *Histoire critique de Manichée et du manichéisme*, 2 (Amsterdam, 1739): 726-56, although in this case the debt is partially acknowledged. "Zèle" is also different from "Inquisition I" in that Voltaire has omitted the major part of Beausobre's commentary and copied mainly that author's quotations and references: the *Opinion en alphabet* article is composed almost entirely of quotations linked by a minimum of discussion.

When Voltaire copies from the *Encyclopédie*, his method varies. In "Yvetot," he follows Jaucourt's text quite closely:[11]

Voltaire	Jaucourt
C'est le nom d'un bourg de France,	Bourg de France en Normandie, au pays de Caux, à deux lieues de
à six lieues de Rouen en Normandie,	Caudebec, et à six de Rouen. . . .
	On a raconté bien des fables au
qu'on a qualifié	sujet de ce bourg qu'on s'est avisé
de royaume pendant longtemps,	pendant longtemps de qualifier de
d'après Robert Gaguin, historien	royaume, d'après Robert Gaguin, his-
du seizième siècle. Cet	torien du seizième siècle. Cet his-
écrivain rapporte	torien, liv. II, fol. 17, rapporte
que Gautier ou Vautier, seigneur	que Gautier ou Vautier, seigneur
d'Yvetot, chambrier du roi Clotaire	d'Yvetot, chambrier du roi Clotaire
I, ayant perdu les bonnes grâces de	I, ayant perdu les bonnes grâces de
son maître par des calomnies	son maître par des charités qu'on
dont on n'est pas	lui prêta, et dont on n'est pas
avare à la cour, s'en bannit de son	avare à la cour, s'en bannit de son
propre mouvement, passa dans les	propre mouvement, passa dans les
climats étrangers, où pendant dix	climats étrangers, où pendant dix
ans il fit la guerre aux ennemis de	ans il fit la guerre aux ennemis de
la foi; qu'au bout de ce terme, se	la foi; qu'au bout de ce terme, se

158

flattant que la colère du roi serait apaisée, il reprit le chemin de la France; qu'il passa par Rome où il vit le pape Agapet, dont il obtint des lettres de recommendation pour le roi qui était alors à Soissons, capitale de ses états. Le seigneur d'Yvetot s'y rendit un jour de vendredi saint et prit le temps que Clotaire était à l'église pour se jeter à ses pieds en le conjurant de lui faire grâce par le mérite de Celui qui en pareil jour avait répandu son sang pour le salut des hommes; mais Clotaire, prince farouche et cruel, l'ayant reconnu, lui passa son épée au travers du corps. Gaguin ajoute que le pape Agapet, ayant appris une action si indigne, menaça le roi des foudres de l'Eglise s'il ne réparait sa faute; et que Clotaire, justement intimidé, et pour satisfaction du meurtre de son sujet, érigea la seigneurerie d'Yvetot en royaume, en faveur des héritiers et des successeurs de Gautier; qu'il en fit expédier des lettres signées par lui et scellées de son sceau; que c'est depuis ce temps-là que les seigneurs d'Yvetot portent le titre de rois; et je trouve, par une autorité constante et indubitable, continue Gaguin, qu'un événement aussi extraordinaire s'est passé en l'an de grâce 536. . . .

flattant que la colère du roi serait adoucie, il reprit le chemin de la France; qu'il passa par Rome où il vit le pape Agapet, dont il obtint des lettres de recommendation pour le roi, qui était alors à Soissons, capitale de ses états. Le seigneur d'Yvetot s'y rendit un jour de vendredi saint de l'année 536; et ayant appris que Clotaire était à l'église, il fut l'y trouver, se jeta à ses pieds, et le conjura de lui accorder sa grâce par le mérite de Celui qui en pareil jour avait répandu son sang pour le salut des hommes; mais Clotaire, prince farouche et cruel, l'ayant reconnu, lui passa son épée au travers du corps. Gaguin ajoute que le pape Agapet, ayant appris une action si indigne, menaça le roi des foudres de l'Eglise s'il ne réparait sa faute, et que Clotaire, justement intimidé, et pour satisfaction du meurtre de son sujet, érigea la seigneurerie d'Yvetot en royaume, en faveur des héritiers et des successeurs du seigneur d'Yvetot; qu'il en fit expédier des lettres signées par lui et scellées de son sceau; que c'est depuis ce temps-là que les seigneurs d'Yvetot portent le titre de rois; et je trouve, par une autorité constante et indubitable, continue Gaguin, qu'un événement aussi extraordinaire s'est passé en l'an de grâce 536. . . .

In "Université," on the other hand, Voltaire has assembled in his own first two paragraphs material contained in the first eight paragraphs of Jaucourt's article.[12] Nor are the passages copied in the order in which they appear in the *Encyclopédie*. There are several cuts, reordering of material, and stylistic variants. Numbers in parentheses before each fragment of Jaucourt's text will identify the paragraph in the *Encyclopédie*.

159

Voltaire	Jaucourt
Du Boulay, dans son histoire de l'université de Paris, adopte les vieilles traditions incertaines, pour ne pas dire fabuleuses, qui en font remonter l'origine jusqu'au temps de Charlemagne. Il est vrai que telle est l'opinion de Gaguin et de Gilles de Beauvais; mais outre que les auteurs contemporains comme Eginhard, Almon, Reginon et Sigebert ne font aucune mention de cet établissement, Pasquier et du Tillet assurent expressément qu'il commença dans le douzième siècle, sous les règnes de Louis le Jeune et de Philippe Auguste.	(7) Du Boulay, qui a écrit une histoire très ample de l'université de Paris, a adopté de vieilles traditions incertaines, pour ne pas dire fabuleuses, qui en font remonter l'origine jusqu'au temps de Charlemagne. . . . (6) Telle est l'opinion de Gaguin, de Gilles de Beauvais, etc., mais les auteurs contemporains comme Eginhard, Almon, Reginon, Sigebert, etc. ne font pas la moindre mention de ce fait. Au contraire, Pasquier, du Tillet, etc. assurent expressément que les fondements de cette université ne furent jetés que sous les règnes de Louis le Jeune et de Philippe Auguste, dans le douzième siècle. . . .
D'ailleurs les premiers statuts de l'université ne furent dressés par Robert de Corcéon, légat du Saint-Siège, que l'an 1215; et ce qui prouve qu'elle eut abord la même forme qu'aujourd'hui, c'est qu'une bulle de Grégoire IX, de l'an 1231, fait mention des maîtres en théologie, des maîtres en droit, des physiciens (on appelait alors ainsi les médecins), et enfin des artistes. Le nom d'université vient de la supposition que ces quatre corps que l'on nomme facultés faisaient l'université des études, c'est-à-dire comprenaient toutes celles que l'on peut faire.	(7) Ses premiers statuts furent dressés par Robert de Corcéon, légat du Saint-Siège, en 1215. . . . (7) Grégoire IX, par sa bulle de l'an 1231, fait mention des maîtres en théologie, en droit, des physiciens (c'est ainsi qu'on appelait alors les médecins), et des artistes. . . . (3) On les appelle université ou écoles universelles parce qu'on suppose que les quatre facultés sont l'université des études, ou comprennent toutes celles que l'on peut faire.

When the passage to be copied is more extensive, or when it forms the greater part or even totality of Voltaire's article, as in "Décrétales," "Fanatisme I," "Juifs III," "Kalendes," "Messe," "Oracles II," "Reliques," "Sibylle," "Vision de Constantin," there is relatively little rewriting of the text. Instead, Voltaire reorganizes and shortens the original article by rearranging the order of presentation, by eliminating long quotations and discussions of proofs, and by omitting entire paragraphs or blocks of paragraphs. An extreme example of this would be the article "Vision de Constantin," where the seventy-three paragraphs of Jaucourt's "Vision céleste de Constantin" are reduced to eighteen, and given in the order: 2, 15–19, 4–5, 19, 21–25, 27–28, 33, 28, 37, 35.

In "Décrétales," on the other hand, the order of presentation remains the same in both articles, although Voltaire reinforces the impact of his, or rather Bouchaud's, argument by making numerous cuts in the latter's rather verbose text. The passage below illustrates Voltaire's various "editorial methods":

Voltaire	Bouchaud
Outre les véritables, recueillies par Denis le Petit, il y en a une collection de fausses, dont l'auteur est inconnu, de même que l'époque. Ce fut un archevêque de Mayence, nommé Riculphe, qui la répandit en France, vers la fin du VIIIe siècle;	Ce fut Riculphe, archevêque de Mayence, qui la répandit en France, comme nous l'apprenons d'Hincmar de Reims dans son opuscule des 55 chapitres contre Hincmar de Laon, chap. iv. . . . On voit au livre VII des capitulaires, cap. ccv,
il avait aussi apporté à Worms une épître du pape Grégoire de laquelle on n'avait point entendu parler auparavant; mais il n'en est resté aucun vestige, tandis que les fausses décrétales ont eu, comme nous l'allons voir, le plus grand succès pendant huit siècles.	qu'il avait apporté à Worms une épître du pape Grégoire dont on n'avait point entendu parler jusqu'alors, et dont par la suite il n'est resté aucun vestige. Au reste, quoiqu'il soit assez constant que la compilation des fausses décrétales n'appartient à aucun Isidore,
Ce recueil porte le nom d'Isidore Mercator, et referme un nombre infini de décrétales	comme cependant elle est connue sous le nom d'Isidore Mercator, nous continuerons de l'appeler ainsi.
	. . . . . . °
faussement attribuées aux papes depuis Clément Ier jusqu'à Sirice;	Il rapporte sous le nom des papes des premiers siècles, depuis Clément Ier jusqu'à Sirice, un nombre infini de décrétales inconnues jusqu'alors et avec la même confiance que si elles contenaient

161

la fausse donation de Constantin;
le concile de Rome sous
Sylvestre; la lettre d'Athanase à
Marc;

celle d'Athanase
aux évêques de
Germanie et de Bourgogne; celle de
Sixte III aux Orientaux;
celle de Léon Ier

touchant les
privilèges des chorévêques;

celle de Jean Ier à
l'archevêque Zacharie; une de
Boniface II à Eulalie d'Alexandrie,
une de Jean III aux
évêques de France et de Bourgogne,
une de Grégoire, contenant
un privilège du monastère de Saint-
Médard; une du même à Félix,
évêque
de Messine, et plusieurs autres.

L'objet de
l'auteur a été d'étendre
l'autorité du pape et des
évêques. Dans cette vue il établit
que les évêques ne peuvent être
jugés définitivement que par le pape
seul; et il répète souvent cette
maxime,

que non seulement tout évêque, mais
tout prêtre, et en
général toute personne opprimée
peut en tout état de cause appeler
directement au pape.

162

la vraie discipline de l'Eglise des
premiers temps. Il ne s'arrête point
là; il y joint plusieurs autres
monuments apocryphes: tels sont
la fausse donation de Constantin;
le prétendu concile de Rome sous
Sylvestre; la lettre d'Athanase à
Marc, dont une partie est citée dans
Gratien, distinct. xvi, can. 12;
celle d'Athanase, successeur de
Sirice, adressée aux évêques de
Germanie et de Bourgogne; celle de
Sixte III aux Orientaux. Le grand
saint Léon lui-même n'a point été
à l'abri de ses téméraires entreprises; l'imposteur lui attribue
faussement une lettre touchant les
privilèges des chorévêques. Le p.
Labbé avait conjecturé la fausseté
de cette pièce, mais elle est dé-
montrée dans la onzième dissertation
du p. Quesnel. Il suppose pareille-
ment une lettre de Jean Ier à
l'archevêque Zacharie, une de
Boniface II à Eulalie d'Alexandrie,
une de Jean III adressée aux
évêques de France et de Bourgogne,
une de Grégoire le Grand contenant
un privilège du monastère de Saint-
Médard; une du même à Félix,
évêque
de Messine, et plusieurs autres.

.   .   .   .   .   .

D'ailleurs l'objet principal de
l'imposteur avait été d'étendre
l'autorité du Saint-Siège et des
évêques. Dans cette vue il établit
que les évêques ne peuvent être
jugés définitivement que par le pape
seul, et il répète souvent cette
maxime.

.   .   .   .   .   .

Il paraît qu'il avait fort à cœur
cet article, par le soin qu'il
prend de répandre dans tout son
ouvrage, que non seulement tout
évêque, mais tout prêtre, et en
général toute personne opprimée,
peut en tout état de cause appeler
directement au pape.

It is clear that when Voltaire transferred to his *Opinion en alphabet* large segments from the *Encyclopédie*, he did so with very little revision. It is also clear that more is involved here than the negative influence that Raymond Naves discerned in the *Questions sur l'Encyclopédie* and even the *Dictionnaire philosophique*. We can easily dismiss the possibility that it is the encyclopedists themselves who borrowed from Voltaire without acknowledgement—as they undoubtedly did in many other instances. For they always copied from published sources; and there is no evidence that Voltaire ever transmitted to Bouchaud, Deleyre, Cahusac, or others, any of his unpublished writings or reading notes. But more than that, we have the statement of the "Avertissement de la collection intitulée l'*Opinion en alphabet*," that the collected articles are indeed excerpts from other works. We have the fact that although the *Encyclopédie* is the main source for the *Opinion en alphabet*, other texts—for example, those of the abbé Morellet and of Beausobre—are also involved. Finally, we have stylistic proof: whenever there has been found an original source on which both the *Encyclopédie* and the *Opinion en alphabet* articles are based, as in "Yvetot" and "Université," stylistic comparison reveals that Jaucourt's text is much closer to the original than Voltaire's. Each subsequent author provides a few variants; but all Jaucourt variants are reproduced by Voltaire, whereas no Voltairean variant is found in the *Encyclopédie*.

It can be stated that the *Opinion en alphabet* is derived, to a great extent, from the *Encyclopédie*, and that it cannot, as a whole, antedate 1765, when the last volumes of that work appeared. A few large segments, however, may date back to 1762 ("Inquisition I") or even to 1750–55 (if "Prétentions de l'empire" is to be considered a legitimate part of the *Opinion en alphabet*).

Several questions remain: Why did Voltaire write, or edit, these articles? Why did he refrain from publishing them? Where did the Kehl editors find the manuscript? I would hypothesize that the major part of the *Opinion en alphabet* consists of articles written or edited by Voltaire in 1768–69 as part of his intended contribution to Panckoucke's proposed *Encyclopédie*. Panckoucke's aim was to improve the existing work by revising some of the original articles, by substituting new articles for the weaker ones, and by adding others on topics not discussed earlier. Voltaire even advised the publisher, in October/November 1768, on the procedures to be followed: "Gardez-vous bien encore une fois de retrancher tous les articles de m. le chevalier de Jaucourt. . . . Songez surtout qu'il faut plutôt retrancher qu' ajouter à cette encyclopédie. Il y a des articles qui ne sont qu'une déclamation insupportable" (Best. 14320). A year later, Voltaire explained to Madame Denis his working method: "Ce sera pour moi un grand amusement pour l'hiver, il ne m'en coûtera que la peine de dicter. Ce serait pour moi un fardeau insupportable de feuilleter et d'écrire. Cette petite occupation me consolera" (Best. 14956). Voltaire does not then intend to create an original work: he will simply improve the quality of the articles meant for Panckoucke by omitting the lengthy discussions and unnecessary details that mar the *Encyclopédie*, and by dictating from existing texts, either published or unpublished. Such is the method followed in the *Opinion en alphabet*.

Voltaire could not, however, remain satisfied with mere revision and compilation. We know that by December 1769 he had more than 100 articles ready for Panckoucke (Best. 15034). Shortly after, the collaboration ceased: Voltaire had decided to publish his own *Questions sur l'Encyclopédie*, in which are undoubtedly incorporated many of the articles originally intended for Panckoucke. But perhaps not all: in particular, the articles "Fanatisme" and "Juifs" mentioned by Voltaire in his letter to Panckoucke of 29 September 1769 (Best. 14944) correspond much more to the present *Opinion en alphabet* articles than to those of the *Questions sur l'Encyclopédie*. It would seem that the articles written by Voltaire to supplement the deficiencies (as he saw them) of the *Encyclopédie*, or to refute views that were unacceptable to him, took their place in the *Questions sur l'Encyclopédie*. Others, which were mere revisions of existing articles or which followed too closely the text of the *Encyclopédie* or of some other work, were kept, for the time being, in manuscript form.

The existence of the "Avertissement" would indicate, however, that Voltaire's interest in the discarded articles was later revived, and that he then intended to publish them with the warning that this was a compilation and not an original work. I believe this renewal of interest came in 1777–78 when Voltaire began to revise his complete works for publication by Panckoucke. He indicated at the time that some "pièces nouvelles" would be included (Best. 19756). It is therefore not improbable that, when Panckoucke acquired from Madame Denis, in September 1778, some thirty revised volumes of the 1775 "édition encadrée" along with "le reste des manuscrits," the *Opinion en alphabet* was included in the transaction, and later sold to Beaumarchais,[13] to be finally incorporated into the Kehl edition of Voltaire's *Œuvres complètes*.

One could conclude that the *Opinion en alphabet* belongs more properly among the works edited by Voltaire than among his original writings, although the multiplicity of texts edited, implying a choice of material and ideas as well as of style, would lead me to retain the *Opinion en alphabet* among Voltaire's alphabetical works. In that case, however, the current notions of Voltaire's limited debt to the *Encyclopédie* must be seriously revised.

1. *Voltaire et l'Encyclopédie* (Paris: Les Presses Modernes, 1938), pp. 105 n. 29, 157, 160. The later studies of René Pintard, "Voltaire et l'Encyclopédie," *Annales de l'Université de Paris*, No. 22 (October 1952), pp. 39–56; Jean Fabre, "Deux Définitions du philosophe: Voltaire et Diderot," *La Table Ronde*, No. 122 (February 1958), p. 140 n; Jacques Proust, *Diderot et l'Encyclopédie* (Paris: Colin, 1962), p. 528 n; Marta Rezler, "Voltaire and the *Encyclopédie*: A Re-examination," *SVEC* 30 (1964): 147–87, have not substantially altered this conception of Voltaire's debt to the *Encyclopédie*.
2. This list is based on Bengesco, *Voltaire: bibliographie de ses œuvres* (Paris, 1882–90), 1:425–26. It excludes, however, the generally short "addi-

tions" to previously published articles, with the exception of "Prétentions de l'empire," which is in fact a separate section of the article "Prétentions." Four articles or sections have been deleted: "Euphémie" and "Somnambules," which belong to the *Questions sur l'Encyclopédie*; "Philosophe I," which appeared in the 1765 *Dictionnaire philosophique*; and "Inquisition II," which first appeared in the 1769 *Raison par alphabet*. Professor J. Vercruysse has recently indicated that further revisions to Bengesco's list will be made in the edition now in progress of Voltaire's *Complete Works* ("Les Œuvres alphabétiques de Voltaire," *Revue de l'Université de Bruxelles*, 22 [1969–70]: 96).

3. *Voltaire's Complete Works*, ed. Theodore Besterman, 82 (Geneva, 1968): 542–44.

4. Besterman, ed., *Voltaire's Notebooks*, in *Complete Works*, 81 (Geneva, 1968): 33.

5. Such as "Moïse III," which we know to belong to the *Opinion en alphabet*. Yet it, as well as "Abraham III" and "Athée I" may have been written as early as 1752. See R. Pomeau, *La Religion de Voltaire* (Paris, 1956), pp. 174, 279.

6. Given the nature of that work and of Voltaire's "borrowings," as described below, it is probable that not all cases have been found. More will undoubtedly come to light as a result of the new edition of Voltaire's works.

7. Information supplied by Mr. Ross Donnelly of New Orleans, La.

8. John Lough, "The Problem of the Unsigned Articles in the *Encyclopédie*," *SVEC* 32 (1965): 373; *The Encyclopédie in 18th-Century England and Other Studies* (Newcastle upon Tyne, 1970), p. 213.

9. Naves, *Voltaire et l'Encyclopédie*, p. 150.

10. Voltaire read Morellet's work in January/February 1762 (Best. 9488, 9494, 9495, 9509), and presumably took notes at that time. The later texts are much more concise, and much more pointed, than the original one, but the order of presentation and the examples given remain identical. For example, a single sentence in the *Raison par alphabet*: "Jésus-Christ est le premier inquisiteur de la nouvelle loi, les papes furent inquisiteurs de droit divin, et enfin ils communiquèrent leur puissance à saint Dominique," summarizes the longer text in the *Opinion en alphabet*, copied verbatim from Morellet, p. 190: " . . . bornons-nous à la nouvelle loi dont Jésus-Christ, selon lui [Luis de Páramo], fut le premier inquisiteur. Il en exerça les fonctions dès le treizième jour de sa naissance, en faisant annoncer à la ville de Jérusalem par les trois rois mages qu'il était venu au monde, et depuis en faisant mourir Hérode rongé de vers, en chassant les vendeurs du temple, et enfin en livrant la Judée à des tyrans qui la pillèrent en punition de son infidélité. Après Jésus-Christ, saint Pierre, saint Paul et les autres apôtres ont exercé l'office d'inquisiteur qu'ils ont transmis aux papes et aux évêques leurs successeurs. Saint Dominique, étant venu en France avec l'évêque d'Osma dont il était archidiacre, s'éleva avec zèle contre les Albigeois et se fit aimer de Simon, comte de Montfort. Ayant été nommé par le pape inquisiteur en Languedoc, il y fonda son ordre qui fut approuvé en 1216 par Honorius III."

11. Jaucourt himself is copying here, with slight stylistic variants, which in turn are copied by Voltaire, abbé de Vertot's "Dissertation sur l'origine

du royaume d'Yvetot," *Mémoires de l'Académie des inscriptions et belles-lettres*, 4 (1723): 728–31.

12. In turn a summary of Etienne Pasquier, *Recherches de la France*, in *Œuvres* (Paris, 1723), 1:273–74.

13. The Voltaire-Panckoucke-Beaumarchais relationship has been well studied by George B. Watts in his "Voltaire and Charles Joseph Panckoucke," *KFLQ* 1 (1954): 179–97; "Panckoucke, Beaumarchais, and Voltaire's First Complete Edition," *Tennessee Studies in Literature* 4 (1959): 91–97; "Catherine II, Charles-Joseph Panckoucke, and the Kehl Edition of Voltaire's *Œuvres*," *Modern Language Quarterly* 18 (1957): 59–62.

Ulcerated Hearts: Love in Voltaire's *La Mort de César*

Crains des cœurs ulcérés, nourris de désespoir (I,4)

One of Voltaire's objectives in his early plays was to reduce the importance of love and to eliminate gallantry from tragedy. Believing with such critics as Rapin, Le Bossu, and Dacier that Racine's emphasis on love had caused a general decadence in French tragedy—a decadence that had become more pronounced in the plays of Racine's eighteenth-century imitators—Voltaire strove to invest tragedy with a dignity it had lost through excessive preoccupation with *amour galant*. Indeed, in his preface to *Mariamne* (1725) he argues fervently that the proper subject of a tragedy is "les intérêts de toute une nation." Criticizing Racine, Voltaire notes that even though the protagonists in *Britannicus*, *Phèdre*, and *Mithridate* are princes, "tout l'intérêt [de ces trois pièces] est renfermé dans la famille du héros de la pièce; tout roule sur des passions que des bourgeois ressentent comme les princes; et l'intrigue de ces ouvrages est aussi propre à la comédie qu'à la tragédie."[1]

One year after the publication of *Mariamne* Voltaire fled to England. During his three years in exile, he assiduously attended performances at the Drury Lane Theatre. He soon realized that the famous tragedies of the English stage, especially Shakespeare's, treated a considerably broader range of subjects than did contemporary French tragedies, with their emphasis on amatory intrigue. Particularly impressed by Shakespeare's *Julius Caesar* and Addison's *Cato*, Voltaire wrote one play, *Brutus*, and started another, *La Mort de Cé-*

sar, while in England; in both he attempted to adapt the didactic tradition of the English Augustan theater to contemporary French theater.[2]

La Mort de César was not completed until June 1731, several months after Voltaire's return to France. It was published in 1736 with a preface that Voltaire himself had written and that opens with the resounding sentence: "Nous donnons cette édition de la tragédie de la *Mort de César* de M. de Voltaire, et nous pouvons dire qu'il est le premier qui ait fait connaître les muses anglaises en France." In a letter to abbé Asselin written a year before the publication of his tragedy, Voltaire clearly indicated what he considered to be the two principal originalities of his play: "Cette pièce [*La Mort de César*] n'a d'autre mérite que celui de faire voir le génie des Romains, et celui du théâtre d'Angleterre."[3]

However innovative Voltaire may have wished to be, he was nevertheless acutely aware of the peculiar demands of the French public, which remained hostile to changes in the classical form of tragedy, but which expected ever larger doses of pathos in the plays it attended. Despite his protests against *amour galant,* he knew that tenderness, compassion, and abundant tears were essential ingredients in a successful tragedy. Years later, and with amused condescension, the aging Voltaire would even speak of the "Quinauderie" he had introduced in his plays to satisfy the public's insatiable appetite for tales of unhappy love: "Le parterre de Paris et les loges sont plus galants que moi: ils donnent la préférence à ma *Quinauderie.*"[4] Despite this patronizing attitude, Voltaire had, as Ridgway and Vrooman, two of the most astute students of Voltaire's theater, have pointed out, a marked talent for creating pathetic situations. "J'ai une envie démesurée de vous faire pleurer," wrote Voltaire to a correspondent in 1739 (Best. D1746), thereby suggesting an important characteristic of his tragedies. Quoting the phrases "adoucir les caractères désagréables" and "émouvoir la pitié" that Voltaire used in his preface to *Mariamne,* Ridgway defines Voltairean trag-

170

edy in the following terms: " 'Adoucir les caractères désagréables', n'oublier jamais le public pour qui l'on écrit, 'émouvoir la pitié', peindre un amour qui inspire le repentir: voilà la clef de la tragédie voltairienne."[5] Dealing with a subject as austerely political as the assassination of Caesar, Voltaire strove to "émouvoir la pitié" by developing Plutarch's suggestion that Brutus was Caesar's son and by shifting the interest of the tragedy away from the political intrigue to the pathetic love between a father and a son who are publicly committed to positions that pit them against each other.

Since there are no women in *La Mort de César*, several critics have stated flatly that there is no love interest in the play. Others have noted, without however pursuing the idea, that the tender but anguished relationship between César and Brutus replaces the more traditional love intrigue in contemporary tragedies. Indeed, one of the most striking features of *La Mort de César* is the way in which Voltaire introduces situations and language appropriate to a love story into the economy of his tragedy. "Personne," wrote Voltaire in his preface to the play, "n'ose guérir le théâtre français de cette contagion [amour]"; nor did he. By eliminating women from *La Mort de César* he did not rid his tragedy of the contagion of love. The manner in which love, shooed out one door, slips back in through another deserves, I believe, a closer examination.

As the play opens, César is the undisputed ruler of the greater part of the world. For forty years he has fought, conquered, and governed. Now at the zenith of his power, he is about to be crowned king before embarking on his last and most ambitious expedition. The first speaker in the play is Antoine, whose words celebrate César's present grandeur and evoke the emperor's even more glorious future: "César, tu vas régner; voici le jour auguste . . . " (I, 1). Impatiently, César's soldiers wait for their commander, who will join them immediately after his coronation. Soon the invincible legions will be on their way to the Orient, where they will vanquish the few remaining peoples not yet subjected to Roman rule. The banners are unfurled, the ships are ready. The mood is ebullient and triumphant.

Suddenly, however, Antoine realizes that César does not share his own enthusiasm. Somber and despondent, César grieves over a pain so private that even Antoine, his closest adviser, cannot guess its cause. Interrupting his paeon of praise, Antoine anxiously interrogates the emperor:

> Quoi! tu ne me réponds que par de longs soupirs!
> Ta grandeur fait ma joie et fait tes déplaisirs!
> Roi de Rome et du monde, est-ce à toi de te plaindre?
> César peut-il gémir, ou César peut-il craindre?
> Qui peut à ta grande âme inspirer la terreur?

To which César answers:

> L'amitié, cher Antoine: il faut t'ouvrir mon cœur.

(I,i)

Indeed, he proceeds to open his heart, revealing his love for a son whose identity has been kept a secret even from the young man himself. As Antoine listens in horror, César confesses that Brutus, one of the most violent of the emperor's political opponents, is in fact the son he loves and admires. Brutus, too, once he learns that César is his father, is torn by inner conflict, for he has solemnly vowed to kill the tyrant César. Interwoven into the play's political texture (liberty versus tyranny, Jacobinism versus monarchy) is then the plaintive theme of two ulcerated hearts.

The elegiac music of César's love for Brutus significantly alters the martial melodies that open the play. The tenderness of paternal love overshadows the theme of political ambition that Antoine clearly enunciates in his first speech. Voltaire's César is essentially a troubled father, not an intrepid conqueror. Although he is about to engage in a grandiose en-

172

terprise designed to crown his long career, César is strangely passive and immobile throughout the entire tragedy. His overwhelming desire to win his son's love impairs his political judgment and prevents him from punishing the conspirators. Preoccupied with his love, he seeks, unwisely, to win the affection rather than the fearful respect of his subjects. Thus love corrupts César's sense of the political reality on which his authority rests, i.e., fear, and assures his ruin.

From the first scene of the play César the public man who wishes to conquer the world is thwarted by César the private man whose heart is full of *amitié* or *amour*—the words are used interchangeably throughout the play. Antoine's opening speech, which evokes the emperor's imperial persona, is counterbalanced by César's first line, which suggests the emotional climate of his private world. The key words *amitié, cher,* and *cœur,* which appear repeatedly whenever César talks about Brutus or finds himself face to face with his son, circumscribe the emperor's private world from which waft the "longs soupirs" that startle and dismay Antoine. Although he has subdued innumerable warring tribes, he cannot quell the bitter turmoil that rages in his heart. Speaking to Antoine, César declares: "Il n'est plus temps, ami, de cacher l'amertume / Dont mon cœur paternel en secret se consume" (I, 1). Antoine listens in astonishment as the emperor, weary, languid, and melancholic, reveals his secret. César's confession of his love for Brutus is curiously reminiscent in tone, structure, and even vocabulary of Phèdre's confession of her love for Hippolyte. With Antoine playing a role similar to that of Oenone, César finally discloses his "tendre amitié" for a son who was brought up by his enemies.

When Antoine remarks that Brutus does not resemble his father, César answers with an impassioned account of his love for his son. A secret bond, a "charme séducteur," attracts the tender César to Brutus, who, like Hippolyte, is young, proud, and *farouche.* Indeed, *farouche* is the word most frequently used to describe Brutus.

173

César

Il a d'autres vertus: son superbe courage
Flatte en secret le mien, même alors qu'il l'outrage.
Il m'irrite, il me plaît; son cœur indépendant
Sur mes sens étonnés prend un fier ascendant.
Sa fermeté m'impose, et je l'excuse même
De condamner en moi l'autorité suprême:
Soit qu'étant homme et père, un charme séducteur,
L'excusant à mes yeux, me trompe en sa faveur;
Soit qu'étant né Romain, la voix de ma patrie
Me parle malgré moi contre ma tyrannie,
Et que la liberté que je viens d'opprimer,
Plus forte encor que moi, me condamne à l'aimer.

(I,1)

Although Voltaire is here describing paternal love, he has
couched it in the traditional language of erotic affection, the
language his public expected to hear in a tragedy. Beginning
quietly, César describes how his love for Brutus grew. Both
irritated and pleased by his son's "superbe courage," César
quickly succumbed to Brutus's seductive and irresistible
charm. As he speaks, César becomes increasingly engrossed
in his consuming passion for his son.

Te dirai-je encor plus? Si Brutus me doit l'être,
S'il est fils de César, il doit haïr un maître.
J'ai pensé comme lui dès mes plus jeunes ans;
J'ai détesté Sylla, j'ai haï les tyrans.
J'eusse été citoyen si l'orgueilleux Pompée
N'eût voulu m'opprimer sous sa gloire usurpée.
Né fier, ambitieux, mais né pour les vertus,
Si je n'étais César, j'aurais été Brutus.

(I,1)

The technique Voltaire here uses is similar in intent and dramatic purpose (if not in poetic power) to that used so cun-
ningly by Racine in act II, scene 5 of *Phèdre*. Unable to contain her desire to establish a bond between herself and
Hippolyte, Phèdre slips into the conditional perfect verb tense
and imagines a hypothetical past in which she and Hippolyte

174

were once joined. Similarly, César identifies himself with Brutus by affirming that when young he, too, thought and acted as Brutus now thinks and acts. For a fleeting moment he slips from behind his public image as emperor and tyrant; he joins Brutus in an imaginary world where liberty reigns and tyrants are stifled. Strangely divided against himself, César momentarily agrees with the political views of the conspirators and with their demand for liberty. His love for Brutus has so sensitized him to the ideal for which the conspirators are struggling that he wishes to deserve their admiration by an act of *bonté*. But, as Antoine tells him, "la bonté . . . détruit l'ouvrage de ta grandeur" (I, 4). Long before the conspirators put an end to César's dazzling career, love has already undermined the emperor's greatness, for it has eroded the political principles on which his authority rests. Even more than the conspirators, it is César's love for Brutus that conspires against the emperor's tyrannical rule. The conspirators administer the *coup de grâce*, but it is love that topples César from his seat of power.

In his intense desire to be loved by a son he loves, César entertains the false hope that Brutus will be tempted by "l'éclat du diadème" (I, 4). Like Phèdre, who believes that she can tempt Hippolyte by holding before him the crown, César believes that Brutus, for personal advantage and gain, can be enticed into abandoning his fervent wish to restore republican rule at the expense of César's life. Both Phèdre and César are deceived by their own desires.

If César secretly admires Brutus's *fermeté farouche* and his implacable thirst for liberty, Brutus on the other hand admires and even loves César, although he hates and indeed has vowed to kill the tyrant. At the end of act I Brutus does not yet know that he is César's son. When the emperor confronts the conspirators and accuses them of plotting his destruction, Brutus tells him not only that the accusation is true but that the conspirators prefer death to life under a tyrant. Awaiting César's anger, he expects to be struck a mortal blow. "César,

175

qu'à ta colère aucun de nous n'échappe; / Commence ici par
moi: si tu veux régner, frappe" (I, 3). But César cannot strike
his son.

After learning the identity of his father, the unhappy Brutus ("malheureux" is used to describe Brutus almost as frequently as is "farouche") confesses to his fellow conspirators
that although he deplores César's tyranny he esteems César
the man:

> Je vous dirai bien plus; sachez que je l'estime:
> Son grand cœur me séduit, au sein même du crime;
> Et si sur les Romains quelqu'un pouvait régner,
> Il est le seul tyran que l'on dût épargner.

When in the following scene Brutus is alone with César, he
uses even stronger language, and confesses to the emperor his
deep affection for him:

> *César*
>
> Mais peux-tu me haïr?
>
> *Brutus*
>   Non, César, et je t'aime.
> Mon cœur par tes exploits fut pour toi prévenu,
> Avant que pour ton sang tu m'eusses reconnu.
> Je me suis plaint aux dieux de voir qu'un si grand homme
> Fût à la fois la gloire et le fléau de Rome.
> Je déteste César avec le nom de roi;
> Mais César citoyen serait un dieu pour moi;
> Je lui sacrifierais ma fortune et ma vie.
>
> (III,4)

Once again the verbs are in the conditional tense, suggesting
a wish that will not be realized, for an impossible condition
(the elimination of César's tyranny) would have to be fulfilled
before the desire could become a reality. In an empyrean of
impassioned rhetoric, both César and Brutus affirm their devotion to each other. Each then pleads with the other, urging
him to abandon his most cherished political views. In a tab-

leau worthy of Greuze, the weeping Brutus throws himself at his father's feet; calling himself "un fils qui frémit et qui t'aime," he urges César for the last time to renounce the royal crown in the name of republican liberty. When César rejects his son's entreaty, the two men part, sorrowfully. Brutus does not reappear in the play; César meets his death at the hands of the conspirators.

From the standpoint of political ideology, *La Mort de César* contains a discussion of two forms of government. Several competent critics have studied in detail the play's political content. But Voltaire, eager to satisfy his public's taste for "le pathétique," charged the play with an affective as well as an intellectual content. The dramatic quality of the play is ultimately derived not from the confrontation of two opposing political ideologies but rather from the hopeless love of a father and a son who, because of circumstances and public commitments, must needs be adversaries. Voltaire's critical statement concerning Racine's *Britannicus*, *Phèdre*, and *Mithridate* could well apply to *La Mort de César*. Although César and Brutus are glorious political figures, "tout l'intérêt est refermé dans la famille du héros de la pièce. . . . "[6]

1. Voltaire, *Œuvres*, ed. Moland (Paris, 1877-85), 2:167.

2. For a discussion of the relationship between Voltaire's theater and English theater, see T. W. Russell, *Voltaire, Dryden, and Heroic Tragedy* (New York: Columbia University Press, 1946). Other useful studies that deal more specifically with *La Mort de César* are Voltaire, *La Mort de César*, ed. André-M. Rousseau (Paris: Société d'édition d'enseignement supérieur, 1964); Ronald S. Ridgway, *La Propagande philosophique dans les tragédies de Voltaire*, SVEC 15 (1961); Jack R. Vrooman, *Voltaire's Theatre: The Cycle from Oedipe to Mérope*, SVEC 75 (1970); G. Defaux, "L'idéal politique de Voltaire dans la *Mort de César*," *Revue de l'Université d'Ottawa* 40 (1970): 418-40.

3. Best. 90.

4. Best. 13562.

5. Ridgway, *La Propagande philosophique*, p. 67.

6. See note 1.

A Reevaluation of
Rousseau's Political Doctrine

VIRGIL W. TOPAZIO

In spite of the contradictory interpretations to which the political works of Jean-Jacques Rousseau lend themselves, "among friends and enemies alike [he] is taken by general agreement as the true prophet if not the very source and fountainhead of the modern democratic state."[1] Some critics do, of course, occasionally question Rousseau's pervasive influence as a political thinker, for instance, Paul Spurlin in his recent book, *Rousseau in America*.[2] Generally speaking, however, most contemporary critics accept the preeminence and originality of Rousseau's political ideas, regardless of the numerous sources and influences their research reveals. Jean Starobinski, for example, after mentioning works that might have served as source materials for the *Second Discours* categorically proclaimed it "une œuvre-source, à partir de laquelle on peut faire commencer toute la réflexion moderne sur la nature de la société."[3]

In this examination of the political works of Rousseau, in particular the *Contrat social*, we shall be concerned primarily with the originality of the two basic concepts of "la volonté générale" and "la souveraineté." As implied above, most critics, even the most unabashed Rousseau apologists, readily admit that countless writers undoubtedly influenced the formulation of Rousseau's political philosophy. We personally find that the extensive and exhaustive notes of Robert Derathé in the Pléiade edition of the *Contrat social* make it abundantly clear that almost any idea commonly associated with Rousseau was similar to, if not a repetition of, ideas previously presented by Aristotle, Plato, Machiavelli, Grotius, Hobbes, Locke, Burlamaqui, and Montesquieu, to mention only those frequently alluded to or quoted by Rousseau himself. In this study we shall limit ourselves to Adémar Fabri, abbé de Saint-Pierre, and Diderot.

Jules Vuy, a distinguished nineteenth-century jurisconsult, historian, and archaeologist, was the first to reveal Rousseau's indebtedness to Adémar Fabri's *Coutumes, ordonnances, franchises & libertés de la ville de Genève*, first published in 1387. The idea unmistakably established in the work of this fourteenth-century prince-bishop ruler of Geneva became one of the two cardinal tenets of the *Contrat social*, namely, the idea of permanent sovereignty of the people who are endowed with inalienable, indivisible, and imprescriptible rights. Jules Vuy, in his *Origines des idées politiques de Rousseau* (1889), carefully substantiated his claim through a methodical study of the *Franchises* and the *Contrat social*, and it should be pointed out that the critics of the day fully supported his position.

Rousseau's familiarity with the "franchises" was understandable, given his intention at one point of writing a history of Geneva. In addition, during the controversy that raged over the Petit Conseil's having levied a tax on the "bancs d'église" in 1757 without the advice and consent of the Conseil Général, Deluc, a very close friend of Rousseau, used Fabri's "franchises" to support the sovereignty of the Conseil Général. Later, in the *Lettres écrites de la Montagne*, a rebuttal to Jean-Robert Tronchin's *Lettres écrites de la Campagne*, Rousseau also relied upon these same "franchises" to support the Représentants' protest that a citizen had been denied his rights: "Ces droits réclamés par les Réprésentans en vertu des Edits," Rousseau insisted, "vous en jouissiez sous la souveraineté des Evêques, Neufchâtel en jouit sous ses Princes, et à vous Républicains on veut les ôter! Voyez les Articles 10, 11, et plusieurs autres des franchises de Genève dans l'acte d'Ademarus Fabri."[4]

180

In what way did the "franchises" establish the sovereignty of the people of Geneva in the fourteenth and fifteenth centuries well enough to justify Rousseau's reference to it as "plus libre que s'il eût été entièrement républicain"? Their importance stemmed from the fact that they set down in writing the "coutumes, ordonnances, franchises & libertés" consecrated by time and accepted by the people. In effect, this created a constitution or a set of codified statutes that guaranteed equality and liberty under laws uniformly applicable to everyone in the state, from the prince-bishop to the lowest Genevan.[5] In addition, the people were given the right to participate actively in governing the city: "Les dits Citoyens, Bourgeois & Jurés de la dite Cité, puissent chaque année établir, créer, faire & ordonner quatre d'entr'eux pour Procureurs & Syndics de la dite Cité, & à ces quatre accorder leur plein & entier pouvoir; lesquels quatre élus, ou à élire, puissent faire & gérer les affaires utiles & nécessaires de la dite Cité & des Citoyens" (*Coutumes*, p. 43). Broad powers were likewise granted to the citizens in the field of justice, for it was henceforth agreed that no one "puisse être jugé ou condamné, ni même absous, que par les Citoyens" (p. 33).

The crucial test of the citizens' sovereignty came thirty-three years after the initiation of the "franchises," when the neighboring state of Savoie attempted to annex Geneva. "Le Conseil Général fut immédiatement convoqué . . . ecclésiastiques et laïques, nobles et roturiers (*nobiles et ignobiles*), marchands, manœuvriers, propriétaires, toutes les classes, en un mot, tous égaux en droit, se prononcèrent également à l'unanimité, après une délibération longue et solennelle . . . contre les prétentions d'Amédée VIII."[6] What a marvelous example of "volonté générale" and "souveraineté" for the future author of the *Contrat social*! Jules Vuy stated that Rousseau "citait toujours avec admiration" this great day in the self-government of Geneva, the city-state he had used as a model for his ideal state.[7] His fondness for his "patrie," especially before disillusionment set in after *Emile* and the *Contrat social* were publicly burned, was obvious in the excessive praise of the "dédicace" to the *Second Discours* and his reference in the article "Economie politique" to Geneva as "l'exemple de la sagesse et du bonheur que je voudrois voir regner dans tous les pays" (3:267). How, he asked Tronchin in the *Lettres écrites de la Montagne*, could Geneva condemn his *Contrat social*, since what he had presented was "trait pour trait l'image de votre République, depuis sa naissance jusqu'à ce jour" (3:809)?

In keeping with his typically contradictory and paradoxical nature, Rousseau was "démocrate par principe, aristocrate par naissance."[8] He was a proud "citoyen" of Geneva, where only the "citoyens" and "bourgeois" participated in the governmental and legislative processes; the "habitans," "natifs," and "sujets" were disfranchised. Even Rome, which he unqualifiedly called "le meilleur Gouvernement qui ait existé" (3:809), had a somewhat similar division of classes. There is justification for Starobinski's observation that "Rousseau est prêt à accepter un monde où n'existe qu'une pseudo-égalité sociale, à condition qu'il soit possible *quelquefois* de faire en sorte que tous se sentent égaux. Tout se passe comme si l'essence de l'égalité consistait dans le sentiment d'être égal."[9]

Now, the ideal state or social structure for Rousseau was one in which every person always participated in the "souveraineté," an arrangement admittedly possible only in a small community whose inhabitants were devoid of, or above, human passions, for "un gouvernement si parfait ne convient pas à des hommes" (*Contrat social*, 3:406). With the ideal impossible of attainment, he settled for the aristocratic form of government, resembling his beloved class-structured Geneva, as "le meilleur des Gouvernemens" fully aware that it was also "la pire des souverainetés" (3:809). It was precisely this lack of class distinction in the franchises-governed Geneva that annoyed Tronchin, who in his *Lettres de la Campagne* indignantly asked the Représentants, "Y a-t-il de la prudence à citer cet Acte de 1420 où les Citoyens & Bourgeois sont confondus avec les Natifs & Habitans?"[10]

Jules Vuy's position, fully warranted by an examination of Adémar Fabri's "franchises," is that "la maîtresse colonne de son système" was introduced by Fabri and placed into operation four hundred years before the *Contrat social*. "Sans doute," Vuy pointed out, "la souveraineté dont parle Rousseau, dans le *Contrat social*, n'est exactement ni ce qu'elle était à Genève dans les quatorzième et quinzième siècles, ni ce qu'elle était dans le dix-huitième, au moment où parut ce livre fameux, mais l'idée-mère, qu'il applique à cette souveraineté, est bien celle qu'il a puisée dans les franchises de 1387, celle que mit en avant Deluc père dans la controverse de 1757, celle que defendirent les représentants, ses contemporains, à propos de la charte d'Adémar fabri."[11]

A close study of the "franchises" and of Jules Vuy's arguments should dissuade even the most skeptical from lightly dismissing Fabri's influence, as scholars tend to do, following the example of Charles E. Vaughan in his scholarly two-volume study of the political writings of Rousseau. Vaughan did admit that "nothing could be more trenchant than M. Vuy's assertions of his claims," but inexplicably minimized these claims on the grounds that Fabri had not developed a political philosophy.[12] He did agree that the idea of sovereignty was advocated by the "franchises," along with many other ideas that form an integral part of Rousseau's political doctrine. One thing seems indisputable: they were better suited to produce the results and achieve the goals Rousseau sought through his *Contrat social*. Certainly, the *Projet de constitution pour la Corse* and *Considérations sur le gouvernement de Pologne*, Rousseau's two attempts to implement the abstract ideals of his *Contrat social*, would scarcely qualify in the minds of many political scientists as the "very wise and practical treatises" a recent critic found them to be.[13]

About the influence of the abbé de Saint-Pierre there can be little doubt in view of the two years, from 1754 to 1756, Rousseau spent editing the abbé's voluminous works, *La Paix perpétuelle* and *La Polysynodie*. At the time he started this task, he had probably just finished the *Second Discours*. On the other hand, in 1755, while immersed in the abbé's writings and therefore most likely influenced by his ideas, he wrote the article "Economie politique" for the fifth volume of the *Encyclopédie*. Indeed, it is quite likely that Diderot asked Rousseau to write this article precisely because he knew Rousseau was deeply involved in the editing of Saint-Pierre. Rousseau's *L'Etat de guerre* was also written around this same period; Vaughan judges between 1753 and 1755.[14] And, of course, he was soon to settle down to the writing of the *Contrat social*. One has to wonder at this tremendous output of political works dating from the time the lengthy volumes by Saint-Pierre were placed in his care.

To be sure, Rousseau, as a result of his Venetian experiences, had thirteen or fourteen years before decided to write a major work, tentatively entitled the *Institutions politiques*, and apparently around 1751 had started some work on this project (*Confessions*, 1:404–5). It is doubtful, however, that he ever seriously felt he could complete this "entreprise . . . certainement au-dessus de mes forces,"[15] with which he had hoped to "mettre le sceau à ma réputation" (1:404). As late as 1756, he was encouraging Voltaire to write this much-needed "catéchisme du citoyen" and assuring him it would be a fitting climax to his brilliant career.[16]

When Rousseau undertook the editing of the work of Saint-Pierre, "whom as an old man, he had slightly known," he originally had planned to publish two volumes, "l'un desquels eût contenu les extraits des Ouvrages, et l'autre un jugement raisonné sur chaque projet." These works had been previously published by Saint-Pierre: the first in two volumes in 1713, with a third volume in 1717; the second had appeared in 1719. In the *Confessions* Rousseau explained that the understanding was he could "penser quelquefois par moi-même" (1:408). He did complete an *Extrait* of the *Paix perpétuelle* and the *Polysynodie*, both accompanied by a *Jugement* of Rousseau. These were completed in 1756. Yet, only the *Extrait du Projet de Paix perpétuelle* was published during his lifetime, in

1760; the others appeared for the first time in the 1782 edition of Rousseau's *Œuvres*.

The *Projet de Paix perpétuelle* contained more of Rousseau than Saint-Pierre, Vaughan maintained, whereas the *Polysynodie* was faithful to Saint-Pierre's text. Merle L. Perkins, in his *The Moral and Political Philosophy of the Abbé de Saint-Pierre*, found that Rousseau had skillfully condensed the three-volume original to a few pages, but insisted that "the view that in these works Rousseau is often on essential points in opposition to Saint-Pierre and even the originator of many ideas does not withstand scrutiny."[17] What is more, after making a detailed study of the recommendations and criticism listed in the *jugements*, Perkins argued that Rousseau's objections had been already answered or foreseen, and the supposed innovations had actually been developed in the abbé's works. In fact, Perkins continued, "many of the basic principles of the *Contrat social* were already present in Saint-Pierre's writings."[18]

The abbé de Saint-Pierre may not have been a captivating writer à la Jean-Jacques; he was, however, an advanced political thinker, who accepted "[le] Peuple, souverain par nature" (*Paix perpétuelle*, 3:565), endowed with "le pouvoir souverain," bedrock of Rousseau's *Contrat social*. The originality of his mind was demonstrated in his conception of a confederation of states, presented in the *Projet de Paix perpétuelle*, which he terminated with this somber warning: "Si . . . ce Projet demeure sans exécution, ce n'est donc pas qu'il soit chimérique; c'est que les hommes sont insensés, et que c'est une sorte de folie d'être sage au milieu des fous" (3:589). It is interesting to note that the twentieth century has been more receptive to the abbé's idea than was Rousseau, who pronounced Saint-Pierre's association of states too idealistic and impracticable. What Rousseau feared were the drastic changes such a plan entailed. The conclusion of his *Jugement sur le Projet de Paix perpétuelle*" reads: "Admirons un si beau plan, mais consolons-nous de ne pas le voir exécuter; car cela ne peut se faire que par des moyens violens et redoutables à l'humanité" (3:600). This same fear was expressed in his *Jugement sur la Polysynodie*: "Nul n'ignore combien est dangereux dans un grand Etat le moment d'anarchie et de crise qui précède nécessairement un établissement nouveau. . . . Quand tous les avantages du nouveau plan seroient incontestables quel homme de sens oseroit entreprendre d'abolir les vieilles coutumes, de changer les vieilles maximes et de donner une autre forme à l'Etat que celle où l'a successivement amené une durée de treize cens ans?" (3:637–38).

Later, in *Emile*, where he credited Saint-Pierre with having proposed the idea of "une association de tous les Etats de l'Europe" (4:848), Rousseau found this concept more acceptable as a solution to the problem constantly plaguing a small state—how to prevent its being subjugated by a large, powerful state. In the *Contrat social* he indicated that he had planned to resolve this problem "lorsqu'en traitant des rélations externes j'en serois venu aux confédérations. Matiere toute neuve et où les principes sont encore à établir" (3:431).

Perkins's specific list of the ideas of Saint-Pierre emphasized in the *Contrat social* further substantiates Rousseau's debt to Saint-Pierre. They are:

> (1) the part ego and self-preservation play in the origin of society; (2) the concept of society as artificial, yet closely linked to nature or necessity; (3) the preference given to practical democratic procedures, unanimity and majority; (4) the contrast of private will, including government and church, with sovereignty, which is conceived as the ideal interest or will of the nation; (5) the definition of liberty; and (6) the ascendant role given to positive law over universal justice. Treating those matters, Saint-Pierre argues convincingly and originally about major political problems which engross Hobbes, Rousseau, and more recent writers on national and international government.[19]

In the article "Ce que Jean-Jacques Rousseau doit à l'abbé de Saint-Pierre," S. Stelling Michaud once again underscored Rousseau's indebtedness:

C'est le mérite de Ch.W. Hendel et de Merle L. Perkins, d'avoir montré à quel point l'abbé de Saint-Pierre avait anticipé sur certaines idées de Jean-Jacques. Tout ce que Rousseau a écrit sur les fondements de l'ordre social, sur la souveraineté politique et la nature du gouvernement, sur les relations entre Etats, sur le problème de la guerre et de la paix doit être rattaché plus ou moins directement à ce dialogue à cœur ouvert et par delà le tombeau avec l'auteur du Projet de paix perpétuelle.[20]

We have noted that Fabri and Saint-Pierre had already advocated Rousseau's seminal doctrine of sovereignty. If Diderot was presenting his own idea of "volonté générale" in "Droit naturel," the article that appeared in the fifth volume of the *Encyclopédie* (1755), along with Rousseau's "Sur l'Economie politique," then Diderot unquestionably supplied Rousseau with this principle. With sovereignty, it lies at the very root of Rousseau's theory of state; and according to Vaughan, this was the first mention of the general will in political speculation.[21] Unlike Vaughan we find it perfectly reasonable to credit Diderot with its originality.

To begin with, after his first mention of "volonté générale" in "Sur l'Economie politique," Rousseau referred his readers to Diderot's article as "la source de ce grand et lumineux principe, dont cet article est le développement" (3:245). And, in fact, Diderot did present an intelligible and precise concept of "volonté générale" in the article "Droit naturel." For example, in attempting to determine the source of equity and justice that was to serve as the base for general will, Diderot answered: "Où? Devant le genre humain; c'est à lui seul qu'il appartient de la décider, parce que le bien de tous est la seule passion qu'il ait. Les volontés particulières sont suspectes; elles peuvent être bonnes ou méchantes, mais la volonté générale est toujours bonne; elle n'a jamais trompé, elle ne trompera jamais." In the next paragraph Diderot continued: "C'est à la volonté générale que l'individu doit s'adresser pour savoir jusqu'où il doit être homme, citoyen, sujet, père, enfant,

187

et quand il lui convient de vivre ou de mourir." And in answer to "Où est le dépot de cette volonté générale; où pour-
rai-je la consulter?", Diderot realistically replied: "Dans les
principes du droit écrit de toutes les nations policées; dans les
actions sociales des peuples sauvages et barbares."[22]

More significant, in our estimation, is the fact that in the
first draft of the *Contrat social*, Rousseau devoted most of the
second chapter, later canceled in the final version, to a refuta-
tion of Diderot's conception of the "volonté générale." He
objected to Diderot's description of general will in each individual as "un acte pur de l'entendement qui raisonne dans
le silence des passions sur ce que l'homme peut exiger de son
semblable, et sur ce que son semblable est en droit d'exiger de
lui."[23] Rousseau protested: "Mais où est l'homme qui puisse
ainsi se séparer de lui même et si le soin de sa propre conser-
vation est le premier précepte de la nature, peut on le forcer
de regarder ainsi l'espéce en général pour s'imposer, à lui, des
devoirs dont il ne voit point la liaison avec sa constitution
particulière? Les objections precedentes ne subsistent-elles
pas toujours, et ne reste-t-il pas encore à voir comment son
intérest personnel exige qu'il se soumette à la volonté générale?" (3:286). Ironically, Rousseau's final position in the
Contrat social is virtually identical with that of Diderot in the
"Droit naturel," and these objections of Rousseau have since
occurred to many readers of the final draft of the *Contrat
social*.

Quite obviously, at the time he wrote this first draft the two
had already quarreled, and Rousseau was really objecting to
Diderot's insistence upon reason, the handmaiden of the *philosophes*, for whom Rousseau had developed a blinding animosity. What aggravated Rousseau's bitterness was his conviction that Diderot had him in mind in the article "Droit
naturel" when he declared that a person who refused to reason was "une bête farouche" who should be stifled. Nor was
he pleased by Diderot's pronouncement, "L'homme qui n'é-
coute que sa volonté particulière est l'ennemi du genre hu-

188

main."[24] Rousseau's resentment would be difficult to understand without the drastic transformation that took place in the mid-fifties. In the *Premier Discours* he had, after all, shown himself to be in perfect agreement with Diderot's position, when he stated: "En politique, comme en morale, c'est un grand mal que de ne point faire de bien; et tout citoyen inutile peut être regardé comme un homme pernicieux" (3:18).

Vaughan rejected Diderot's originality with regard to "volonté générale" on the same grounds he denied Fabri's originality in "souveraineté," that is, "The author of 'Droit naturel' had not taken the pains to weave a consistent theory, . . . he had never thought out the question as a whole."[25] Furthermore, Diderot's originality was questioned by Vaughan because he had not taken credit for this "when, in after years, he went about picking up every missile, fair or foul, deadly or frivolous, which might serve to belittle the genius, and blacken the character of Rousseau."[26] As for the first argument, no one denies that Rousseau developed more fully the doctrine of general will, though one may question whether it was more lucid. The pertinent question is: Who originated the idea? The weight of the evidence unmistakably points to Diderot. The second argument might be acceptable to Rousseauistes; others would certainly challenge it.

From what we have said, what should one conclude about the originality of Rousseau's political theories? Let us turn to Rousseau himself for guidance; he seemed to recognize his limitations better than most scholars. In the *Confessions* he told us why Mme Dupin and the abbé de Mably had selected him to edit the works of Saint-Pierre. It was the kind of work, Rousseau confessed, "très convenable à un homme laborieux en manœuvre, mais paresseux comme auteur, qui trouvant la peine de penser très fatigante [*sic*], aimoit mieux en choses de son goût, éclaircir et pousser les idées d'un autre que d'en créer" (1:407–8). And many years before, in the first draft of the *Contrat social*, he stressed this point at the outset: "Tant d'Auteurs célébres ont traitté des maximes du Gouvernement

189

et des régles du droit civil, qu'il n'y a rien d'utile à dire sur ce sujet qui n'ait été déja dit. Mais peut-être seroit-on mieux d'accord, peut-être les meilleurs rapports du corps social auroient-ils été plus clairement établis, si l'on eut commencé par mieux déterminer sa nature. C'est ce que j'ai tenté de faire dans cet écrit" (3:281).

We are convinced that most, if not all, of Rousseau's political ideas were the common property of innumerable writers, and more specifically that general will and sovereignty had already been espoused by a smaller group well known to Rousseau. This supposition does not prevent us from concurring with Furio Diaz, who maintains: "Rousseau viene a coronare, con formulazione nettamente democratica, lo sviluppo del pensiero politico moderno."[27] The contribution of the stimulating and controversial Rousseau was not, however, as one scholar has alleged, due to his "power of clear and vivid writing."[28] We agree, instead, with Albert Schinz's view that the confusion produced by the *Contrat social* made Rousseau "le père illégitime" rather than "le père de la Révolution."[29] Yet, however obscure his reasoning became, his intentions were generally clear, and his unquestionable literary talents enabled him to infuse an otherwise prosaic subject with a psychological rather than logical unity that succeeded in inflaming the minds of his readers. Thus, ironically, more than with any other author of the eighteenth century, they identified with Rousseau, "qui ne fut occupé que des problèmes de son existence personnelle."[30]

The totalitarian nature of Rousseau's social contract, especially evident to the literal reader who insists upon a logical unity, can be attributed in part to his subconscious Calvinism that transmuted individualism into intense moral commitment. Although Rousseau rejected the doctrine of original sin, he felt that man could achieve personal redemption through the active struggle against selfish impulses and passions, exemplified in the social arena by the subjugation of one's "volonté particulière" to the "volonté générale." This explains the superiority for Rousseau of the moral freedom gained only in society over the physical liberty of "l'homme sauvage" and even "l'homme naturel."

Another basis for the totalitarian aspect of Rousseau's political doctrine—a doctrine that we feel is essentially a potpourri of others' ideas—was his profoundly pessimistic view of human nature. Confronted with what he considered inevitably deteriorating social and political conditions that threatened to engulf man and strip him of his individuality, freedom, and equality, Rousseau fanatically overstated the restraints designed to counteract those inexorable forces at work against the individual. As a result, his "principe romantique d'affranchissement social"[31] evolved as a useful instrument for tyranny, as many distinguished scholars, including Albert Schinz and Lester Crocker, have pointed out, and as the French Revolution tragically demonstrated.

Notwithstanding the diametrically opposed interpretations to which Rousseau's political doctrine lends itself, one fact remains constant: "Chez lui et avec lui, le concept de loi, et de loi à la fois morale et politique, après avoir habité pendant longtemps avec les spécialistes, entre dans la demeure de la philosophie qu'il ne quittera pas."[32]

1. Alfred Cobban, *Rousseau and the Modern State* (London: Allen and Unwin, 1934), p. 34.

2. Paul Spurlin, *Rousseau in America, 1760–1809* (University of Alabama Press, 1969), pp. 105–6.

3. Jean Starobinski, *Jean-Jacques Rousseau, la transparence et l'obstacle* (Paris: Gallimard, 1971), p. 338.

4. Rousseau, "Huitième Lettre," *Œuvres complètes*, ed. Bernard Gagnebin and Marcel Raymond, 4 vols. (Paris: Gallimard, 1959–69), 3:866. All references to Rousseau's works will be to this Pléiade edition.

5. Adémar Fabri, *Coutumes, ordonnances, franchises & libertés de la ville de Genéve, recueillies & publiées en l'année 1387* (n.p., 1767). See pp. 88–89.

6. Jules Vuy, *Origines des idées politiques de Rousseau* (Geneva: Slatkine, 1970), p. 128.

7. Vuy, *Origines*, p. 129.

8. Ibid., p. 139.

9. Starobinski, *Jean-Jacques Rousseau*, p. 125.

10. Jean-Robert Tronchin, *Lettres de la Compagne* (Geneva: Proche, 1965), p. 69.

11. Vuy, *Origines*, pp. 11, 189.

12. C. E. Vaughan, *The Political Writings of Jean-Jacques Rousseau*, 2 vols. (London: Cambridge University Press, 1915), 2:4–5.

13. Henri Peyre, Introduction to E. Durkheim, *Montesquieu and Rousseau: Forerunners of Sociology* (Ann Arbor: University of Michigan Press, 1960), p. xv. See the *Projet de constitution* (3:943) for the oath of total and irrevocable alienation Rousseau would have each Corsican take.

14. Vaughan, *The Political Writings*, 1:284.

15. Rousseau, *Correspondance générale*, ed. Théophile Dufour (Paris: Colin, 1924–33), 7:64.

16. Letter of 18 August 1756, *Correspondance générale*, 2:323.

17. M. L. Perkins, *The Moral and Political Philosophy of the Abbé de Saint-Pierre* (Paris: Minard, 1959), p. 131.

18. Ibid., p. 98.

19. Ibid., p. 141.

20. S. Stelling Michaud, *Etudes sur le Contrat social de Jean-Jacques Rousseau* (Paris: Société les Belles Lettres, 1964), p. 38.

21. Vaughan, *The Political Writings*, 1:424.

22. Diderot, *Œuvres complètes*, ed. Assézat (Paris: Garnier, 1875–77), 14:299–300.

23. Ibid., p. 300.

24. Ibid.

25. Vaughan, *The Political Writings*, 1:426.

26. Ibid., 1:425.

27. Furio Diaz, *Filosofia e politica nel Settecento francese* (Torino: Einaudi, 1962), p. 352.

28. See above, note 13.

29. A. Schinz, *La Pensée de Jean-Jacques Rousseau* (Paris: Alcan, 1929), p. 519.

30. Eric Weil, "J.-J. Rousseau et sa politique," *Critique* 8 (January 1952): 7.

31. A. Schinz, *La Pensée de Jean-Jacques Rousseau*, p. 519.

32. E. Weil, "J.-J. Rousseau et sa politique," p. 14.

Literature and the "Natural Man"
In Rousseau's *Emile*

*La littérature et le savoir de notre
siècle tendent beaucoup plus à
détruire qu'à édifier.*—Preface to *Emile*

JAMES F. HAMILTON

Rousseau's concept of art has been obscured by its more striking counterpart—nature. Idealized as the absolute measure of man and society, it is related in the history of ideas to eighteenth-century utopianism and is interpreted autobiographically as the subconscious attempt by Rousseau to justify his own maladjustment and initial lack of success in Paris.[1] Despite the disproportionate significance attributed to nature and art in Rousseau's thought, they constitute, in my opinion, two cutting edges of the same sword raised against established authority and tradition. This view is based upon the contention that Rousseau conceives of art in a systematic way. I propose, first, to elucidate his theory of art and, then, to examine it for consistency in *Emile*, where literature is utilized in educating the "natural man."

Rousseau's theory of literature, as introduced in the *Discours sur les sciences et les arts* (1750), issues from a broad sociological perspective that identifies government and art as the two main forces in society. Compared by Rousseau to the body and the soul, they are meant to complement one another in rendering man a well-integrated, happy being. Their balance in power results in liberty. However, instead of offering moral examples worthy of art's originally benevolent function of promoting mutual respect and understanding, Rousseau feels that art has traditionally collaborated with the government in ruling the majority (3:6).[2] Supposedly, the artist forfeits his independence for the comfort, leisure, and

195

luxury necessary to the cult of art. In exchange for royal patronage, he not only turns his back on the general interest but blinds man to the reality of an eroded freedom by preoccupying his mind with aesthetic illusions. Elegant architecture justifies tyranny, and heroic paintings give the impression that virtue still endures (3:12, 22). Tragedy glorifies aristocracy and teaches man that he is not free; the clowns of comedy make the people forget its misery and leaders (pp. 174, 140). In short, the arts "étendent des guirlandes de fleurs sur les chaînes de fer" (3:7). Royal authority is rendered absolute when art establishes its own value system based upon the socioaesthetic "virtues" or *politesse, bienséance, goût.* Enforced through the king's arm in society, the salon, they prevent any united resistance to his will by controlling social conduct, segregating citizens along sociocultural lines, and by effacing the general moral system of values.[3]

Rousseau's conspiratorial theory of literature continues its radical course in the *Discours sur l'origine de l'inégalité* (1755) where the origins of art are put on trial. Rousseau frees mankind from the demoralizing guilt of a crime committed against God through the implied concept of a founding "political sin." He accuses the original founders of the "social state"—"les plus capables" and "quelques ambitieux"—of forcing the innocent majority out of nature's paradise, "la société naissante," and into the political state, which is corrupted on purpose through a false pact, one calculated to perpetuate and magnify the initial advantage of those emerging from nature first (3:178). As their supposed spiritual descendants, the *philosophes* are enjoined to atone for their part in the "political sin" by renouncing patronage ("pour le poète, c'est l'or et l'argent") in order to represent the best interests of humanity (3:171). Primary condemnation falls implicitly on royalty and salon society as the major inheritors of the first elite who institutionalized their privileges in the "social state" as "les riches."[4]

Of the three powers in collaboration against the general

196

good, the salon is regarded evidently by Rousseau as being the most vulnerable to attack and most offends his principle of nature and personal sensitivities. Rousseau's campaign against the salon is unleashed in the *Premier Discours,* where he openly denounces the excessive, unnatural power of "une jeunesse frivole," the salon, to decide the fate of literary works (3:21). His recommendations to institute independent academies or restrict creativity to the genius aim at neutralizing its influence. The thrust continues in the *Second Discours,* in which such rustic ideals as family love, patriarchal authority, and simplicity are presented as conforming to man's natural goodness; and, by implication, the salon values of *goût, bienséance,* and *politesse* become corrupt deviations. So too the salon's interpretation of *sociabilité* is challenged by Rousseau in the *Notes,* where he supports as a viable option the abandonment of society and return to nature in the form of an agricultural community (3:207).

Rousseau's revolt against tradition both in politics and aesthetics, as embodied in the salon, reaches its violent climax in his third major work—the *Lettre à d'Alembert sur les spectacles* (1758). Rousseau censures the French classical theater for its monarchical, salon ethic that undermines the values of a republic as perceived by legitimate authority—the *philosophe* and the legislator. The salon assures its leadership in society, according to Rousseau, by demanding plays about love, the realm in which it legislates appropriate conduct. Racine's *Bérénice* and Voltaire's *Zaïre* are blamed by Rousseau for exaggerating the love interest to the detriment of "des intérêts d'Etat" (p. 159). Seeking only to please by mirroring polite society, the theater fails to awaken, in his opinion, the spectator's conscience. As his prime example of the salon ethic dramatized on stage, Rousseau criticizes Molière's *Le Misanthrope* by contrasting the deceit, slander, self-interest, corruption, and affectation found in Célimène's salon with Alceste's relative measure of virtue.

Although Rousseau concedes that the ideal of passionate

love is capable of elevating standards of conduct in a monarchy, its acceptance by Geneva would constitute a retreat from the higher ideals of love in a republic—*la patrie* and *l'humanité* (p. 218). Because dramatic art is bound to the traditions of a monarchical, salon society, Rousseau points to the necessity for a philosophic literature that would shun pure diversion, expose corruption, illustrate republican ideals, and disappear in a just society through lack of *raison d'être*. The dramatic spectacle would be replaced, as seen in the conclusion to the *Lettre à d'Alembert*, by popular festivals, and athletic associations would take the place of literary salons.

Although Rousseau's sociopolitical theory of art proceeds to its logical consequences, he is capable of altering his position on basic issues. For example, he denounces private property in the *Second Discours* as the source of crimes, wars, murders, troubles, and atrocities (3:164); yet, it is rehabilitated in *Emile* as the logical link between the material and intellectual spheres whose character enables the pupil to grasp his first concept (4:330). Literature performs a similar function in Emile's education. Because Rousseau proposes to form both "l'homme naturel" and "l'homme civil," a contradiction, literature proves to be indispensable in bridging the gap between natural virtue and moral conduct, sensation and sentiment, and independence and the demands of citizenship (4:29). Thus it would appear that nature and art are finally reconciled within the framework of Rousseau's pedagogical program.

The initial phase of Emile's education adheres strictly to the principle of nature. It aims at preserving man's innate goodness as seen in the "negative virtues" of happy ignorance and indifference to others, and it does not attempt to teach the child morality and truth but to protect his heart from vice and his mind from error (4:323). Because literature reflects the prejudices of society and deals with moral questions beyond the child's comprehension, it is prohibited from his learning experience. The method of "l'éducation négative" requires, therefore, that Emile be separated from society and its art. To illustrate the inappropriateness of literature in elementary education, Rousseau evaluates the *Fables* of La Fontaine.

Consistent with his criticism of the theater, Rousseau reproaches the *Fables* for an art of imitation that reinforces unjust values. They fail to offer an elevating ideal of conduct and alternatives to the corrupt social code. Their wisdom is founded on conformity as manifested by cleverness and deception. In defense of his thesis, Rousseau analyzes the celebrated fable *Le Corbeau et le Renard*. His criticism of the fox resembles that of Philinte in his attack on *Le Misanthrope*. He is the *raisonneur*, the self-interested *philosophe*, the false friend, and the flatterer. He practices a double morality by saying one thing and doing the opposite. Just as Philinte represents the ideal of moderation, Rousseau believes that the fox becomes the hero of the little drama. Consequently, the child identifies with him—the charlatan (4:356).

Rousseau's exclusion of La Fontaine from Emile's education is only a provisional one. Just as the utility of the theater depends upon its sociopolitical context, the age of Emile determines the value of the *Fables* in his learning program. Unsuitable in his childhood, they play a crucial role in the development of Emile's judgment in early manhood. Before considering the problems arising from social relations, as dramatized in the *Fables*, Emile must first complete his apprenticeship in the rapports between man and things. From age twelve to fifteen, he moves from the level of sensations to basic ideas. This development requires a learning experience that will act as a transition between Emile's physical skills in nature and the material truths of society without arousing his passion or posing the complexity of moral decisions. The need is satisfied by Daniel Defoe's *Robinson Crusoe*. However, its choice and use do not reflect necessarily an acceptance of literature. They are governed by ideological rather than literary criteria.

199

In order to circumvent the problems of social man and protect Emile from false values, Rousseau proposes to teach only that part of the novel which deals with Crusoe's life on the island: "Ce roman débarrassé de tout son fatras, commençant au naufrage de Robinson près de son Isle, et finissant à l'arrivée du vaisseau qui vient l'en tirer sera tout à la fois l'amusement et l'instruction d'Emile durant l'époque dont il est ici question" (4:455). The novel is praised neither for its aesthetic beauty nor for its portrayal of tragic emotions but as an effective means to teach Emile "les vrais rapports des choses" (4:455). Rousseau uses Robinson Crusoe as a case history of Man without moral relations, freed through necessity from the habits, conventions and prejudices of society.

Crusoe's island functions as a laboratory, purified of influences alien to nature, where Emile experiences "les rapports réels et matériels" and invents the values needed to judge man in relation to objects. He holds an instrument in higher esteem than an art object and learns to measure a man's worth by the utility of his material contribution. Consequently, the artisan wins his admiration, and the artist incurs his scorn. This view, although acquired before the completion of his education, remains a permanent attitude on the part of Emile. Motivated probably by Rousseau's petty bourgeois resentment of the rich, its weight falls heavily on the artist and, by implication, heavier still on his patrons.

The tempo and difficulty of Emile's education increase dramatically after the Crusoe adventure. He must progress from the study of "objets sensibles aux objets intellectuels." But they involve the passions (4:524). At this point, Rousseau encounters a dilemma, for his method requires that all learning be based on experience. For example, Emile identified with the hero of *Robinson Crusoe* by living and dressing like him. Consistency would seem to require that Emile adopt now the habits and costume of a libertine. Again, Rousseau resolves the contradiction through literature. The student reads Plutarch's *Lives*. Unlike modern history, it reveals the man behind the public figure and allows Emile to understand the often dishonest, vicious motives of conduct in society from a safe, objective distance (4:530). The *Lives* offer another advantage. Its individual histories lend themselves to the justification of Rousseau's view of man as being "naturally good" but corrupted by society (4:525). Evidently, Rousseau will discuss with Emile only those great men who illustrate his doctrine.

Emile's instruction in moral relations is complicated further by the appearance of *l'amour-propre* (4:536). At eighteen years of age, Emile can no longer be warned or corrected directly without challenging his self-esteem and, thus, provoking rebellion. Rousseau avoids the danger by using La Fontaine's *Fables*. Just as the *Lives* assure Emile an objective distance from which to judge vice, the *Fables* enable him to evaluate his own mistakes in a disinterested manner by seeing them enacted "sous un masque étranger" (4:540). Through the presentation of selected *Fables* that correspond to Emile's personal experiences, the teacher helps the adolescent to understand his errors of judgment without offending him. Hence, experience and literature work in concert. The utility of the *Fables* derives not from their preventive capacity but from the art of generalizing on a personal experience. They engrave its lesson on Emile's memory and transform it into a moral principle (4:541).

Rousseau's use of the *Fables* is contingent, however, upon two changes in their organization. He contends, first of all, that the moral attached to the *Fables* distracts from Emile's freedom to reason and his pleasure of self-discovery (4:541). In order to rectify this supposedly philosophic weakness, Rousseau proposes to discard the *Fables'* aphorisms just as he dismissed the beginning and end of *Robinson Crusoe*. Secondly, Rousseau rearranges the *Fables* into "un ordre plus didactique" so as to relate them better to the moral and intellectual needs of his student's development (4:542).

The rise of Emile's *amour-propre*, which necessitates indirect analysis of his faults through La Fontaine's *Fables*, introduces the general subject of love. Emile will search soon for a mate, and his adolescent self-love must be extended to others as a mutual sentiment in "le véritable amour" (4:493). Emile has an advantage over the traditionally educated student because he has not been conditioned by literature's stylized portrayal of love. His "negative education" safeguarded him from the literary game of love with all its conventions. He has not mimicked emotions beyond his comprehension. Consequently, his feelings retain their natural, true character (4:505).

Although at a theoretical advantage in attaining "real love," Emile runs the risk of corruption if he is instructed through direct experimentation. Once more, Rousseau solves the inherent contradiction of his method through art. Emile's emotions and understanding of love are refined in Paris by attending the theater. This expedient makes Rousseau vulnerable, in view of his *Lettre à d'Alembert sur les spectacles*, to the charges of inconsistency and hypocrisy. However, in his dramatic criticism, Rousseau conceded the theater's ideal of love as an uplifting force in a monarchy, and Emile is not destined to live in a republic (pp. 174, 218). His Mentor will select no doubt the plays most appropriate to Emile's emotional development. The violent passions of the theater are mollified by Emile's reading of poetry, especially Italian poetry. It is meant not to embellish his mind for polite conversation but to render him capable of deep sentiments. Once imbued with the ideal of a complete relationship with a woman, he becomes immune to the illusory happiness of a love based upon self-interest (4:677).

The role of literature in preparing sexual roles is best defined in the education of Sophie, the future wife of Emile. Her ideal of the perfect man is derived from reading Fénelon's *Télémaque*. The hero constitutes an image of perfection that enables her to surmount temptation. Sophie's courtship by Emile is accompanied by reappearing analogies with *Té-*

lémaque. For example, he and his tutor seek shelter from a storm at the home of Sophie. Their arrival is compared by her father to that of Télémaque and Mentor on the island of Calypso (4:775). Similarly, after falling in love, Emile must leave (but only temporarily) because passion places the couple outside of nature, society, and philosophic moderation. Emile and Sophie err by giving no thought to their future responsibilities as parents and citizens.

It is concluded that Emile and Sophie are too young and immature for marriage; he is twenty-two and she, eighteen. By traveling for two years with his Mentor, Emile is to learn "les rapports nécessaires des mœurs au gouvernement" through direct observation and discussion of Montesquieu's *De l'esprit des lois* (4:850). Paradoxically, Emile must leave Sophie in order to love her completely. By finishing his education through the study of governments, it is implied that their marriage will be based on reason, social consciousness, and moral commitment. Emile postpones his natural inclination and, in doing so, elevates his love from the fiction of an illusory passion to a social act. Upon his departure, he and Sophie give each other symbolic gifts from among their favorite readings. Emile will study *Télémaque*, and Sophie, Addison's *Spectateur* (4:825). The exchange acts not only as an engagement; it signifies that Emile has yet to become a mature man and that Sophie must expand her view of the world beyond the desire for a personal, domestic bliss.

To summarize, the task of this study is to evaluate Rousseau's use of literature in educating the "natural man." Is it consistent with his conspiratorial theory of art? I maintain that Rousseau does not retreat from his basic position as introduced in the *Premier Discours*. His suspicion of collaboration between the artist, the throne, and the salon against the general good continues below the surface of *Emile* and erupts on occasion: "C'est le peuple qui compose le genre humain; ce qui n'est pas peuple est si peu de chose que ce n'est pas la peine de le compter. . . . Respectez donc votre espece; songez qu'elle est composée essenciellement de la collection des peuples; que quand tous les Rois et tous les Philosophes en seroient ôtés, il n'y paraîtroit gueres, et les choses n'en iroient pas plus mal" (4:509–10). Rousseau is confident that Emile will never become a writer. It would necessitate his courting of influential, wealthy patrons; and literary honors have little merit in his eyes, since "le peuple ne donne ni chaires ni pensions ni places d'Academies . . . " (4:837). In fact, Emile's knowledge of literature is extremely superficial, but his mastery of a trade is complete. As an artisan, he identifies with the general interest and assures his personal dignity through economic independence.

Paradoxically, literature poses a major threat to Emile's education as a child but plays an indispensable role in forming his character and developing his sensitivity as a young adult. In Emile's development, art bridges the gap between nature and society. However, he is not exposed to literary works until his reason has been grounded on rational, material truths. Hence, the salon's socioaesthetic principles have no hold upon him. When Emile cultivates taste, it is merely for the purpose of acquiring another tool, l'instrument with which to expand his judgment and facilitate his adjustment to society (4:671). His appreciation of artistic beauty compensates, in part, for the loss of his rustic delights, but he negates the pretensions of taste to either a rational or moral foundation (4:677). Thus, Rousseau continues to undermine the authority of the salon "savantes, les arbitres de la littérature," in order to purge the enlightenment of its discriminatory social prejudices (4:673).

In conclusion, I maintain that Rousseau accepts literature and private property in his pedagogical program only in the sense of their originally benevolent functions as stipulated in the principles of se plaire and la main d'œuvre (3:6, 173). Through the study of selected works, Emile adds a social, moral dimension to his behavior that enables him to live in close approximity with his fellow man. However, Rousseau's manipulation of literature in his "programmed" education poses another, broader problem especially when considering his definition of authority: "Qu'il croye toujours être le maître et que ce soit toujours vous qui le soyez. Il n'y a point d'assujetissement si parfait que celui qui garde l'apparence de la liberté; on captive ainsi la volonté même" (4:362). The recommendation of total control through deception together with Rousseau's recriminations against the rich and powerful make him vulnerable to the charge of preparing twentieth-century totalitarianism. However, such an interpretation of *Emile* would grant precedence to the novel's hypothetical implications without regard for its actual influences. The history of pedagogy verifies the positive, enduring impact of *Emile*. Rousseau's defense of individual differences and affirmation of a social mission in education have been respected as basic ideals in progressive teaching for two centuries.[5]

The severe restrictions imposed upon literature in Emile's education pay a negative tribute to its influence in the formation of social, political, and moral values. Despite its excesses, Rousseau's theory of art makes a contribution analogous to Montesquieu's *De l'esprit des lois*. He reveals the "spirit" of literatures that functions both as the effect and cause of customs and mores. Social progress, within his primary context of French absolute monarchy and its salon society, requires that the writer renounce patronage, align himself with the general interest, expose injustice, and offer constructive alternatives. As a vehicle of change, Rousseau composes the pedagogical novel, *Emile*, where the cultural attitudes of French classicism and its sociopolitical implications are laid bare. By increasing our awareness as to the rapports between literature and such determining factors as type of government, class structure, institutions, and economic conditions, Rousseau ranks with Montesquieu as one of the two foremost *philosophes* in the Age of Ideas who prepare the modern social sciences. It is a debt recognized by Auguste Comte, Emile Durkheim, and Claude Lévi-Strauss.[6]

1. See Arthur O. Lovejoy, "The Supposed Primitivism of Rousseau's *Discourse on Inequality*," *Modern Philology* 21 (1923): 165, and George Havens, "The Road to Rousseau's *Discours sur l'inégalité*," *Yale French Studies* 40 (1968): 31.

2. References to the Pléiade edition of Rousseau's *Œuvres complètes* are indicated by volume and page number. Those to the *Lettre à d'Alembert sur les spectacles* refer to *Du contrat social* (Paris: Garnier, 1962) and are indicated by page number.

3. For a discussion, see my article, "A Theory of Art in Rousseau's First Discourse," *SVEC* 94 (1972): 73–87.

4. See my article, "Parallel Interpretations, Religious and Political, of Rousseau's *Discours sur l'inégalité*," *SVEC* 94 (1972): 7–16.

5. See Maurice Debesse, "L'Influence pédagogique de l'*Emile* depuis deux siècles," *Jean-Jacques Rousseau et son œuvre: Problèmes et recherches* (Paris: Klincksieck, 1962), p. 217.

6. Auguste Comte, *Cours de philosophie positive* (Paris: Scheicher, 1908), 4:127–32; Emile Durkheim, *Montesquieu and Rousseau, Forerunners of Sociology*, tr. Ralph Manheim (Ann Arbor: University of Michigan, 1960); Claude Lévi-Strauss, "Jean-Jacques Rousseau, fondateur des sciences de l'homme," *Jean-Jacques Rousseau* (Neuchâtel: La Baconnière, 1962), pp. 239–48.

Rousseau's Antifeminism in the
Lettre à d'Alembert and *Emile*

In 1949, long before the current movement for women's rights brought the issue of feminism to the forefront of the American social and political consciousness, Simone de Beauvoir had published her now classical analysis of woman's role in human society in a two-volume work entitled *Le Deuxième Sexe*. A basic premise of that work is that, as far back as history records, women have always had a subordinate role to men and that insofar as this relationship to men seems to escape the accidental character of historical events, the separate status of women, or their "otherness," as Mme de Beauvoir calls it, takes on the quality of an absolute. The author of *Le Deuxième Sexe* devotes a good part of the first volume of her work to demonstrating how, through various historical periods, woman has been man's vassal if not his slave, how the two sexes have always been unequal, and how, despite the evolution of woman's status in the post–World War II period, she still remains seriously disadvantaged. Mme de Beauvoir provides the details to show that the legal status of woman has almost never been identical to that of man and that even when rights have been granted to her in principle and by law, long tradition and habit have prevented these rights from assuming concrete significance.

According to Mme de Beauvoir, men have always displayed satisfaction in believing themselves to be the divine objects of creation; and to illustrate this characteristic male attitude, she uses the Hebrew morning prayer in which the Orthodox

Jew chants: "Blessed be our Lord and the Lord of all the universe for not having made me a woman."

Literature provides Simone de Beauvoir with a convenient source to prove her case.[1] She calls her reader's attention to the antifeminine stance of writers throughout French literature and considers this part of a well-defined tradition going back to Jean de Meung in medieval literature and continuing to our day in the writings of Henry de Montherlant. It is in the eighteenth century, however, that she notes the development of a new democratic spirit among certain writers who approached the question of the status of women in an objective manner. She particularly singles out the utterances of Diderot in praising some of these unusually impartial *philosophes*. It is likely that she had in mind Diderot's presentation of the condition of women in the eighteenth century in his novel *La Religieuse* and some of his *contes* as well as his plea on behalf of women in the *Essai sur les femmes*. Among other examples of an enlightened attitude toward women in the eighteenth century, she notes Voltaire's denunciation of the injustice of their condition, Montesquieu's paradoxical statement that women ought to be subordinate to men in the home but play an important role in the outside world of politics, Helvétius's and d'Alembert's criticism of the absurd education to which women in their time were subjected and which these *philosophes* saw as a principal cause of their inferior status, and Condorcet's egalitarian position on women's rights.[2] But perhaps, curiously, a more typical reflection of the prevailing attitude toward women in eighteenth-century France is to be found in the works of another contemporary author—himself an "outsider"—whose writings on education, society, and politics were innovative and radical, yet whose attitude toward women would seem to illustrate rather well the traditional antifeminine literary bias noted by Mme de Beauvoir. That writer is Jean-Jacques Rousseau, and in light of Simone de Beauvoir's thesis, I should like to examine Rousseau's attitude toward women in two of his major theoretical writings, the *Lettre à d'Alembert* and *Emile*.[3]

Rousseau's commentary on women and their status in society is broached in his *Lettre à d'Alembert* (1758) in the context of a broad critique of the social role of the theater. The general subject of the relationship of the arts and sciences to society had attracted the author's attention in two earlier works, the *Discours sur les sciences et les arts* (1750) and the *Discours sur l'origine de l'inégalité* (1755), two pioneering and heterodox treatises that shocked the eighteenth-century literary world. In all three of these works Rousseau adopted a position that seems paradoxical for a writer in the Age of Enlightenment, since the general line of his argument was that the evolution of the arts and sciences had been to the detriment and corruption of humanity and that if it was not practical for man to return to the ideal of a state of nature, at least the arts and sciences should be discouraged—especially those that were related to a spirit of luxury and were therefore a reflection of the unacceptable social conditions of the eighteenth century. In this connection, Rousseau took particular umbrage at d'Alembert's article "Genève" in the *Encyclopédie*, in which the Parisian mathematician recommended the establishment of a permanent theater in Rousseau's home town, the Calvinist city of Geneva.

In his lengthy public letter to d'Alembert, Rousseau offers an analysis of the French theater of the seventeenth and eighteenth centuries and thoroughly condemns it as an instrument of immorality. The Calvinism of Rousseau's birthplace, Rousseau's difficult Parisian experience, and his own dissatisfaction with the intellectual spirit of the Enlightenment were the principal factors that influenced his conclusions. Among other reasons for Rousseau's discontent with the theater was what he judged to be the excessive role of women in theatrical life. Rousseau particularly pointed to the vital importance of love as a dramatic theme, especially in French classical tragedy; the manner in which the theme was generally treated seemed to show that women exercised great influence and power over men, much to the annoyance of Rousseau. It is in his analysis of the role of women in the theater that Rousseau's antifeminist bias emerges rather sharply. This analysis brings Rousseau to a more general consideration of the role of women in society in the course of which he argues seriously that decision-making is a masculine prerogative with which women should not interfere. As a matter of fact, Rousseau was quite disturbed by what he considered to be the over-influential role of women in contemporary French society. In the *Lettre à d'Alembert*, a description of the type of woman he particularly found objectionable emerges: she was socially active, she determined new style trends, she articulated definite opinions about cultural and moral values, and, in general, she was sought after because of her socially influential position. As a model for this antipathetic type, Rousseau no doubt had in mind some of the women prominent in the eighteenth-century French literary salons.[4] That was an institution with which he had been acquainted at first hand, of course, in his early years in the French capital as an aspiring writer who had tried Father Castel's advice of making his way in Paris through the influence of women and later as a lionized figure of the literary and musical world of the French capital.[5] It was also an institution he was now rejecting and castigating as typical of the hypocrisy and artificiality of eighteenth-century French culture.

Underlying Rousseau's thesis condemning the theater was his conviction that it was a literary genre that reflected and restated social mores and not an instrument that would change them. He was particularly incensed at the image of woman he found reflected in the theater. If it was true, he proclaimed, that in contemporary society women really were quite ignorant but foisted themselves on men as arbiters of everything, the situation was even worse in the theater: "Au théâtre, savantes du savoir des hommes, philosophes grâce aux auteurs, elles écrasent notre sexe de ses propres talents. . . . Parcourez la plupart des pièces modernes; c'est toujours une femme qui sait tout, qui apprend tout aux hommes. . . ."[6] Not only are dramatic authors chastised for present-

212

ing this assertive image of women to the theater-going public, but one has the sense that Rousseau felt that women themselves, if left unbridled, represented a serious danger to male authority and prerogative.

In attacking the theater, Rousseau was comfortably subscribing to the status quo of his native Geneva, where the institution was officially proscribed. He harshly criticized the acting profession on the traditional grounds of being licentious, disorderly, and dishonorable. The actor typified for him essentially a person whose existence was predicated on an enterprise that was counterfeit and artificial; and to succeed in this profession, one had to mask one's true thoughts and feelings. Although any actor was considered a morally suspicious person in Rousseau's treatise, his censure of the profession was even more stringent as he focused on its female members. Clearly Rousseau thought it necessary to use different moral standards in judging men and women. In general, it was appropriate for men to occupy the center of the social and political arena, and inappropriate for women to do so. To Rousseau's way of thinking, a woman of good morals had to lead a secluded and domestic life; her principal concern had to be for the care of her family and household; and the dignity of her sex necessarily resided in her humility.

In the portrait of the actress that Rousseau conjured up in his imagination, she was aggressive, was knowledgeable only in the ways of coquetry and love, dressed immodestly, was constantly surrounded by sensual and unbridled youth, and frequented an atmosphere where she was habitually subjected to the mellifluous voice of love and pleasure. Could one be so naïve as to believe that an innocent girl would be able to preserve her moral integrity in such an environment? On the contrary, for any woman who decided to become an actress thereby attracted the attention of men and corrupted herself. Any woman who exhibited her person brought herself dishonor; and indeed, as Rousseau extends the argument, a woman who performed in public for compensation would also

213

not be reluctant to offer her own person up for sale for a price. Being an actress was really only one step away from prostitution.

In the course of these ruminations, Rousseau brings himself to reflect briefly on the general problem of sexual ethics, and here again his views are decidedly conservative and traditional. Arguing on behalf of female sexual decency, Rousseau maintains that the principle of sexual modesty for women is not merely a social invention designed to protect the rights of fathers and husbands and to preserve the integrity of the family structure. He rejects any notion of sexuality as an inherently amoral natural phenomenon, and holds that a distinction must be made between the propriety of male and female sexual conduct even though both sexes may be driven by similar instincts. Rousseau attempts to remove the entire question of sexual ethics from the context of social philosophy by asserting that the dictates of sexual propriety are determined by nature and not by society. He specifically maintains that nature requires that the needs of human sexuality be fulfilled with an inherent feeling of shame. However, he backs away from explaining why nature would particularly endow human beings with such feelings: "Est-ce à moi de rendre compte de ce qu'a fait la nature?" (p. 190). Yet, Rousseau does suggest that a feeling of shame associated with the sexual act is nature's way of protecting human beings from their own weakness. All the same, Rousseau attempts to justify a more rigorous code of sexual conduct for women by asserting the importance of guaranteeing to the child the authenticity of his father. Men may be assertive and audacious; indeed, that is their destiny, says Rousseau, since one of the two sexes must make the overtures. The same standard applied to women would be odious: "Toute femme sans pudeur est coupable et dépravée, parce qu'elle foule aux pieds un sentiment naturel à son sexe" (p. 191).

In Rousseau's portrait of the ideal woman, she is a mother surrounded by her children, instructing the servants in the administration of the household, assuring her husband a happy life, and wisely governing her home. A woman outside her home loses her greatest splendor, and her place cannot be in public life. Of this, Rousseau is firmly convinced: "Partout on considère les femmes à proportion de leur modestie . . . partout on voit qu'alors, tournant en effronterie la mâle et ferme assurance de l'homme, elles s'avilissent par cette odieuse imitation, et déshonorent à la fois leur sexe et le nôtre" (pp. 193-94).

Typically, Rousseau reverted to antiquity to find a reaffirmation of his ideal models, and one of these models to which he consistently referred was the city of Sparta.[7] Rousseau evoked for his contemporaries the image of the idealized woman of Sparta. She conducted herself virtuously by living a very circumscribed existence, rarely displaying herself in public and never with men. Significantly, in the context of the *Lettre à d'Alembert,* the virtuous woman of Sparta attended the theater only on rare occasions. If she ever exceeded the bounds of female modesty, her conduct was usually met with public censure, Rousseau notes. As he moved on from this model of antiquity to consider the evolution of mores in modern Europe, he was saddened to see in them a demonstration of how thoroughly women's morals had declined. The origin of this change is ascribed by Rousseau, in his rapid historical reconstruction, to the invasion of Europe by barbarian hordes accompanied in their military camps by their women. He traces another source of corruption of European mores to the literature of chivalry in which beautiful ladies spent their lives being carried off by men with no evident harm to their well-being or honor. The freedom that this literature inspired spread to the royal courts and to large cities, where chivalry degenerated into a cruder way of life. The end result of this historical deterioration was that "la modestie naturelle au sexe est peu à peu disparue et . . . les mœurs des vivandières se sont transmises aux femmes de qualité" (p. 195). That Rousseau's evocation of the virtues of Sparta and his imaginative

215

rewriting of history had their source more in his need to provide a corrective to the decadence of modern culture than in actual history did not seem to have as much importance as their usefulness in highlighting the corruption of contemporary Paris. How good it was to have an ideal moral model with which to confound modern vice and to prove such personal and firmly held convictions.

D'Alembert replied to Rousseau's critique in a public letter that illustrates interestingly the more liberal eighteenth-century attitude toward women noted by Simone de Beauvoir.[8] In his reply, d'Alembert attempted first to undermine Rousseau's antifeminist position through an *ad hominem* argument, suggesting that his reaction might be ascribed to some personal problems he had had with the opposite sex—perhaps a twitting allusion to Rousseau's difficulties with Mme d'Epinay and her sister-in-law, Mme d'Houdetot. Then, coming to grips more fundamentally with the actual reasons for the sorry plight of women in eighteenth-century France, d'Alembert speaks eloquently and passionately against the disastrous and almost "murderous" education to which they were subjected. If these women were to be faulted on their morality, d'Alembert lays the blame squarely on an education that consciously taught them to conceal their true feelings, thoughts, and opinions in order to survive in a society dominated by men. Women had been consistently deprived of any training that could have enlightened them or elevated them from their inferior status, but with the advent of enlightenment the *philosophe* d'Alembert predicted a reformation of the condition of women and a more moral relationship between the sexes: "Nous cesserons de tenir les femmes sous le joug et dans l'ignorance, et elles de séduire, de tromper et gouverner leurs maîtres. L'amour sera pour lors entre les deux sexes ce que l'amitié la plus douce et la plus vraie est entre les hommes vertueux; ou plutôt ce sera un sentiment plus délicieux encore . . . sentiment qui dans l'intention de la nature, devait nous rendre heureux, et que pour notre malheur nous avons su altérer et corrompre."[9]

216

Rousseau paid no heed to d'Alembert's advice and certainly not to his remarks on the need to reform the education of women. This is a subject with which Rousseau dealt at length four years later in his educational treatise *Emile*, and though his analysis of the role of women and their familial and social relationship to men is elaborated upon in that work in greater detail, his premises remained essentially those already laid in the *Lettre à d'Alembert*.

Characteristically, the first four books of *Emile* are devoted to the education of the male child, and it is only in the final book that Rousseau is forced to broach the question of feminine education, since the capstone of the work is Emile's marriage and his future paternity. It is Emile's relationship to women and his new family life that bring Rousseau eventually to reflect on the education of his spouse. Every reader of *Emile* will recall that Rousseau had urged preceptors of male children not to be too severe and deprive them of the joys of their childhood; he had argued that childhood had its own status and rights and was not to be viewed as a mere preparation for adult life. Girls, however, were apparently not to enjoy the same privilege; according to Rousseau's scheme, their childhood *was* to be a preparation for their future adult position of subservience. Thus, Rousseau remarks with some consistency in the fifth book of *Emile*: "Ne souffrez pas qu'un seul instant dans leur vie elles ne connoissent plus de frein."[10] Accordingly, Rousseau offers two pedagogical models: a boy, Emile, who is to be raised in such a way that he will escape the prejudices of eighteenth-century society or at least be in a position to examine them critically, and a girl, Sophie, who is not to question but will simply reflect the *idées reçues* of a culture that Rousseau had repeatedly condemned as corrupt and fallen. Jean-Jacques apparently saw no contradiction in a marriage between an enlightened and free man and a socially conditioned woman who has all her life been taught not to doubt. In his view, the overriding principle was for the ideal wife not to usurp the male's prerogative by concerning herself with social or political matters. A woman's fulfillment of her familial role, and thus her role in life, could best be achieved by a preservation of, and a hearkening to, the innocence of her instinctive feelings rather than through the critical use of her intellectual faculties. How such good instinctual feelings were to survive an upbringing in a corrupt and despicable society Rousseau does not seem to make clear in *Emile*.

Rousseau's vantage point in considering the role of Sophie, Emile's future wife, is her function vis-à-vis Emile. Rousseau tells us in the opening lines of the last book of *Emile*: "Il n'est pas bon que l'homme soit seul; Emile est homme; nous lui avons promis une compagne, il faut la lui donner. Cette compagne est Sophie. En quels lieux est son azile? Où la trouverons-nous? Pour la trouver, il la faut connoitre" (p. 692). Thus, Sophie is of interest to Rousseau mainly in her capacity of completing Emile's life, since throughout his treatise there seems not to have been much consideration given to the nature, psychology or education of women per se.

As in the *Lettre à d'Alembert*, Rousseau's fundamental premise regarding the role of woman is based on her place in the natural order of things, an order not subject to social mutation. Once again, Rousseau attempts to eliminate any argument about modifying the social and intellectual position of women by insisting that their role is predetermined by nature and not subject to significant change. In *Emile*, Rousseau provides his reader with significant additional details regarding this ostensibly natural role. He informs us, for example, that by nature woman was created particularly to please man; man's virtue, on the other hand, lies in his strength, and if he should also happen to please woman, his need to do so is less direct. Since woman's role is to provide pleasure and to be subjugated to man, she must make herself agreeable to him. Any possible complaint about the inequality of the sexes is both wrong and futile since such inequality is not a product of human institutions or prejudice but of reason. Although disapproving of marital infidelity by either of the partners and

218

calling the man who deprives his wife of the "austere duties" of his sex unjust and barbaric, Rousseau clearly considers such activity on the part of women a much more serious matter: "La femme infidelle fait plus, elle dissout la famille, et brise tous les liens de la nature; en donnant à l'homme des enfans qui ne sont pas à lui elle trahit les uns et les autres, elle joint la perfidie à l'infidélité" (pp. 697-98). A wife must not only be faithful but must give others the impression of being so. Woman's natural destiny is also to produce children, and her ability to do so in abundance is socially important. For Rousseau, women who are diverted from this essential occupation become unworthy, and he particularly singles out for his contempt those who live "licentiously" in the larger cities and produce few children. That "civil promiscuity" which confuses the functions of the two sexes by advocating that they both may have the same jobs and do the same work can only lead to the most intolerable abuses. Having demonstrated to his satisfaction that men and women must have different functions in society, Rousseau concludes that their education must also be essentially different.

As a general principle discriminating the role of the two sexes, the author of *Emile* warns his reader that as soon as a woman attempts to usurp the rights of the male sex, she is condemned to a position of inferiority. At the same time, he assures us that the educational implication of his position is not that she must be kept in ignorance or reduced to the status of a household slave. Yet Rousseau quickly qualifies his recommendation for feminine education by asserting that though she must learn many things, these must include only that which it is appropriate for her to learn. Knowledge for the sake of knowledge is inadmissible as a principle, and a significant implication of Rousseau's position is that the acquisition of inappropriate knowledge can be harmful. As a guiding principle in the whole matter of feminine education, Rousseau believes that nature dictates that women are to be at the mercy of male judgment. A corollary of his position is

219

that her education must be the opposite of man's. If we may judge from his basic tenets regarding the social relationship of men and women, it is quite apparent that Rousseau's attitude toward the education of women is structured totally from the male point of view and that he is determined to preserve the superiority of male prerogatives. All of a woman's education must be conceived in terms of its relationship to man and its usefulness in serving man. Her pedagogical experience must have the following goals with respect to the masculine sex: "Leur plaire, leur être utiles, se faire aimer et honorer d'eux, les élever jeunes, les soigner grands, les conseiller, les consoler, leur rendre la vie agréable et douce, voilà les devoirs des femmes dans tous les tems, et ce qu'on doit leur apprendre dès leur enfance" (p. 703).

As in the case of Emile himself, Rousseau stresses the importance of not hurrying formal intellectual education for girls, particularly in the matter of reading and writing. Rousseau had postponed the process of active education for boys as late as possible so that the student would not be burdened with the prejudices of the educational system or of his teacher before he was rationally capable of judging their validity. Rousseau felt that it was even more desirable not to subject girls to compulsory learning or reading before they were really able to sense the value of their reading. He was convinced that more was to be lost than to be gained by teaching girls how to read and write too early, a feeling that was reinforced by his professed hostility to such intellectual disciplines. He wrote: "Il y en a bien peu qui ne fassent plus d'abus que d'usage de cette fatale science, et toutes sont un peu trop curieuses pour ne pas l'apprendre sans qu'on les y force quand elles en auront le loisir et l'occasion" (p. 708).

In Emile's education Rousseau had stressed the importance of not subjecting boys to a pedagogy predicated on authority or of forcing them to learn something whose utility they could not comprehend. This approach was basic to his liberal philosophy of education. However, in the matter of educating girls, Rousseau clearly and specifically prescribes the opposite course and turns to a program based on the principle of constraint. Logically, Rousseau reasoned, if the role of the female is to be subjugated to her male counterpart and to assume a position of obedience and servility, then a program of education allowing for personal development in an atmosphere of freedom would not only be out of order but also harmful, since it would not prepare a young woman for the realities of life but turn her into a misfit. Although he thought that a program of work and constraint for young ladies should be justified, Rousseau nevertheless insisted that it was fundamental to their education. Idleness and indocility are dangerous habits for a girl to assume and difficult to cure once acquired; girls must always be laborious and attentive, and they must feel subjugated at an early age. As with his general analysis of the role of women in society, Rousseau removes these pedagogical principles from the domain of the social sciences, insisting that they are derived from women's inherent and natural sexual role. Regardless of the social or historical context, Rousseau argues: "Elles seront toute leur vie asservies à la gêne la plus continuelle et la plus sévère. . . . Il faut les exercer d'abord à la contrainte, afin qu'elle ne leur coûte jamais rien à dompter toutes leurs fantaisies pour les soumettre aux volontés d'autrui" (p. 709).

Whereas in the case of Emile the development of understanding and judgment is fundamental to the educational enterprise and every aspect of his education must be justified in terms of its usefulness and applicability, the education of women is based on the principle of authority and specifically on the decisions of superior male judgment. The role of women throughout life is not merely to be physically subjugated to man but to his judgments as well. Therefore, they must not be allowed to think for themselves or substitute their judgments for those of men. Rousseau does not attempt to justify this position intellectually and even admits its possible injustice, but he does argue that this relationship is an immutable fact of human existence and that the education of women must prepare for it: "Faite pour obéir à un être aussi imparfait que l'homme, souvent si plein de vices, et toujours si plein de défauts, elle doit apprendre de bonne heure à souffrir même l'injustice, et à supporter les torts d'un mari sans se plaindre . . . " (pp. 710-11). Emile's education was constantly subjected to the question: "Of what use is that?" Sophie's must be based on a question no less difficult: "What effect will that have?" Consequently, in the early years of education when they can still not distinguish between good and evil or form judgments about other persons, girls must be inculcated with the rule of never uttering anything disagreeable whenever they speak. They must also be taught never to lie. Rousseau admits, however, that obedience to both of these principles may be quite difficult in practice.

In this system of ideal education, Rousseau was determined that Sophie would not be overburdened with excessive formal instruction nor did he find any reason for her to be. He had suggested, after all, at the beginning of Book IV that in many respects women would remain childlike all their lives. At the moment of marriage Sophie would be ready to be educated by her husband according to his desires and lights. She will not have acquired much formal knowledge, but her mind will have been nurtured so as to be receptive to learning. She will have never read a book except Barrême's *Livre des comptes faits* (1689), a work on home economics, and Fénelon's *Télémaque* (1699), a novel that had accidently fallen into her hands. Rousseau relishes over his "lovable ignoramus" ("ô l'aimable ignorante!"), is delighted that Emile will now assume the task of educating her and that he has not lost his masculine prerogative to do so: "Elle ne sera point le professeur de son mari mais son disciple; loin de vouloir l'assujetir à ses gouts elle prendra les siens. Elle vaudra mieux pour lui que si elle étoit savante: il aura le plaisir de lui tout enseigner" (pp. 769-70). More important than woman's erudition is the satisfaction of the male's ego in being able to impart to her all she need know. The completion of her education must remain his privilege.

As we have seen, Jean-Jacques's ideal of female domesticity was based on the principle that women confine their sphere of activity largely to the home and family and that they avoid mingling with, or becoming involved in, the community at large. In the opening pages of Book V, therefore, the author of *Emile* takes direct issue with Plato's views on the equality of the sexes and the desirability of eliminating the role of the family expressed in the *Republic.* In *his* fifth book Plato had argued that despite women's physical weakness, the natural capacities of both men and women were alike and women ought to share "naturally" in all of men's pursuits. Hence, the education of both sexes ought to be alike. Moreover, Plato had argued for dispensing with the family unit and for substituting a community where men and women cohabit collectively and "the children shall be common, and . . . no parent shall know its own offspring nor any child its parent."[11] Rousseau castigated Plato's notion of sexual equality in employment as a form of "civil promiscuity" and his dissolution of the family as a plan that would undermine civic duty because in his view the very foundation of civic-mindedness was in the family. Rousseau argued that it was the good son, the good husband, and the good father who ultimately became the good citizen. His circumscribed model of female activity would ensure that women concentrate on their essential duties as wives and mothers. Significantly, his model was also intended to promote their adherence to a life of virtue by reducing their opportunity for extramarital sexual activity, which Rousseau looked upon as a constant danger to their morality.

As an ideal woman, Sophie will personify perfect moral values. The practice of virtue is the *sine qua non* of her moral existence as well as an aesthetic attribute that transforms her from a state of human imperfection and endows her with quasi-angelic qualities. More concretely, the feminine prac-

223

tice of virtue implies not only honesty but a vow of extra-marital chastity that Sophie solemnly assumes although she is rather aware of the sacrifices that may be necessary to ful-fill it. Curiously, the institution of marriage is not questioned in this work, although Jean-Jacques himself avoided his own personal commitment to matrimony until quite late in life, at the age of fifty-six, and twenty-three years after the begin-ning of his liaison with Thérèse Levasseur. Nevertheless, Rousseau declares that Sophie must think about marriage in a positive way early in life because "du mariage dépend le sort de la vie" (p. 755). As part of the advice her parents pro-vide her in preparation for marriage, they warn Sophie of the dangers of the senses and of the misfortunes that will be-fall her if she succumbs to them. Sensual love is presented as a clearly insufficient criterion for choosing a partner, and in her quest for a husband Sophie's heart rejects those men to whom she is attracted by her senses. After it has been deter-mined that she will marry Emile, Rousseau does offer advice that will enable her to exercise some authority over him. The secret lies in her ability to control her love life with Emile, and this involves a rather delicate mastery of her will and her senses. She must make her physical favors to him rare and precious, but in such a way that Emile will also have no doubts about her love for him. Rousseau's prescription is expressed in the following terms: "Voulez-vous voir vôtre mari sans cesse à vos pieds? tenez-le toujours à quelque distance de vôtre per-sone. . . . Faites-vous cherir par vos faveurs et respecter par vos refus; qu'il honore la chasteté de sa femme sans avoir à se plaindre de sa froideur" (pp. 865-66).

Rousseau's analysis of the male-female relationship, as a number of critics have pointed out, is a dialectical one, and the whole question of which of the sexual partners ultimately predominates and which is reduced to subservience and obe-dience remains ambivalent in his presentation.[12] Rousseau's argument runs along the following lines: Man is the physi-cally stronger and woman the more passive partner whose

224

destiny is to be subordinate to the male and to provide him with pleasure. However, woman's frailty is only superficial since nature has imparted her with the ability to arouse the male's physical desires to a degree stronger than his capacity to gratify them; ultimately, therefore, the male is reduced to dependence. Hence, according to Rousseau, the artful woman will always keep her mate in a state of uncertainty, not letting him know finally whether she has yielded to him because of natural weakness or her own real desire to do so. In his dedication to the *Discours sur l'origine de l'inégalité*, Rousseau had addressed womankind in the following manner: "Aimables et vertueuses Citoyennes, le sort de vôtre sexe sera toujours de gouverner le nôtre. Heureux! quand vôtre chaste pouvoir exercé seulement dans l'union conjugale, ne se fait sentir que pour la gloire de l'Etat et le bonheur public. C'est ainsi que les femmes commandoient à Sparte, et c'est ainsi que vous méritez de commander à Genève."[13] And in a rather revealing passage of the *Lettre à d'Alembert*, Rousseau postulated that love is the dominion of women because nature had arranged things in such a way that the male can only subjugate her at the expense of his own freedom.[14] Thus, if man's happiness is dependent on his mate and his sexuality can prevail only with the sacrifice of his independence, the master-slave relationship becomes a seesaw situation in which the two partners remain interdependent. Nevertheless, Rousseau predicates the education of women on the principle of subjugation and constraint not only because this reflected the reality of her social and political condition in eighteenth-century Europe—and significantly, this was one aspect of the educational program in *Emile* where Rousseau was consistently determined to adhere to the status quo—but perhaps more fundamentally, as Pierre Burgelin has suggested,[15] because he considered women too dangerous to be free.

Rousseau's rather reactionary and repressive stance with reference to women's involvement in public affairs, to women's education, and to the general question of women's freedom and equality apparently belies the basically radical social and political ideas of such works as the *Discours sur l'origine de l'inégalité* and the *Contrat social*. This seeming contradiction in Rousseau's thought may be explained in a number of ways. The importance of the conjugal bond as the basis for the only "real" nucleus of the social structure may have loomed large in Rousseau's mind precisely because it was largely a notion foreign to his own unstable experience as a child deprived of a secure family relationship and as an adult whose experiences with women were largely outside the bonds of matrimony. Rousseau, then, perhaps understood the family unit to be the source of order and stability that he as an individual had lacked. On a more theoretical level, Rousseau may have wanted women to remain within a status quo sanctifying the marriage vow in order to guarantee the moral validity and viability of a "primitive social contract" that would be the foundation or nucleus of a larger social compact that would likewise be based on the principle of contractual responsibility and duty.

Significantly, in Rousseau's idea of the Social Contract, society assumes an existence of its own that is necessarily superior to the desires and freedom of the individual. Although Rousseau posited the need for new social institutions and was radical in envisaging a completely new political order, he may be seen as essentially conservative in limiting the freedom of the individual within the new society. Ultimately, the moral sanctity and order of the family—to be achieved by severely limiting the scope of women's activities to the sphere of the family nucleus and guaranteeing her integrity through the morality of female obedience and subservience—would contribute to the moral sanctity and order of the state. It is not surprising, then, that so many of the proponents of political authoritarianism in the nineteenth and twentieth centuries would look back to Rousseau as a spiritual ancestor. In this context Rousseau's attitudes on the relationship of the sexes expressed in the *Lettre à d'Alembert* and *Emile* may be seen as a rather cogent confirmation of Simone de Beauvoir's thesis in *Le Deuxième Sexe* regarding the historical status of women.

1. Simone de Beauvoir, *Le Deuxième Sexe* (Paris, 1949), 1:23.

2. Ibid., 1:23 and 1:181-82.

3. The subject of Rousseau and women is obviously a complex one, deserving of the extensive treatment of a monograph. In this essay, however, I should like to concentrate my discussion on these two significant and revealing Rousseau texts.

4. A primary example might have been his erstwhile friend Mme d'Epinay, a leader of an important salon at which such luminaries as Voltaire, Diderot, Grimm, and Rousseau himself had gathered. Mme d'Epinay was not only socially influential but an author in her own right. Coincidentally, Rousseau and Mme d'Epinay had quarreled and terminated their relationship in the year preceding the publication of the *Lettre à d'Alembert*.

5. See, e.g., Jean Guéhenno, *Jean-Jacques Rousseau* (Paris, 1948-52), 1: 272.

6. Jean-Jacques Rousseau, *Lettre à M. d'Alembert*, in *Du Contrat social* (Paris: Garnier, 1962), p. 161. All references to this work will be to this edition.

7. See, e.g., Judith N. Shklar, "Rousseau's Two Models: Sparta and the Age of Gold," *Political Science Quarterly* 81 (1966): 25-51.

8. Jean Le Rond d'Alembert, "Lettre à Jean-Jacques Rousseau, citoyen de Genève," in *Œuvres* (Paris, 1805), 5:309-67.

9. Ibid., p. 352.

10. Jean-Jacques Rousseau, *Emile*, in *Œuvres complètes*, ed. Bernard Gagnebin and Marcel Raymond, 4 vols. (Paris, 1959-69), 4:710. All references to *Emile* will be to the Pléiade edition.

11. Plato, *The Republic*, trans. Paul Shorey (Cambridge, Mass., and London, 1963), 1:455.

12. See, e.g., F. C. Green, *Jean-Jacques Rousseau* (Cambridge, 1955), pp. 260-61, and Pierre Burgelin, in Jean-Jacques Rousseau, *Œuvres complètes*, 4:1630.

13. *Œuvres complètes*, 3:119.

14. Garnier edition (Paris, 1962), p. 159.

15. *Œuvres complètes*, 4:1639. Cf. *Emile*, Livre V, 4:710.

Diderot's *Supplément* as
Pendant for *La Religieuse*

*I have multiplied visions and
used similitudes.*—Hosea 8:10

The often substantiated belief that Diderot's thoughts could be mercurial, his interests varied and mobile, and his convictions constantly at the mercy of his lively and far-roaming mind was already widely accepted in his day. In fact, he himself, in numerous instances, lent credence to such an opinion. In one of his more famous analogies, it will be recalled, he likened the Langrois to a weather vane. He hastened to add, however, that through years of enforced discipline and hard work in Paris he had succeeded in achieving a modicum of intellectual and emotional stability.

The echo of Diderot's intellectual and emotional inconstancy lingered on in his great posthumous writings. *Le Neveu de Rameau* drew both epigraph and inspiration from Horace's satire of a fellow who for inconsistency knew no peer. This fitted *Lui* admirably; and according to Daniel Mornet and countless readers both before and after him, *Lui* reflected one side of Diderot's essence. Moreover, both *Le Rêve de d'Alembert* and *Le Paradoxe sur le comédien* dwelt, among other things, on those individuals who—like the author himself—are viscerally vulnerable to their own sensitive natures and, because of their emotionalism, find themselves incapable of firmness in judgment and steadfastness in purpose. Diderot, in *Le Paradoxe*, said it with a decided economy of words: "L'homme sensible est trop abandonné à la merci de son diaphragme. . . . " To this he added forthwith: " . . . Si la Nature a pétri une âme sensible, c'est la mienne" (A.-T., 8:408).[1]

Le Rêve reiterated under various forms the conviction that in this great sea of matter that is the universe, there is not one molecule "qui ressemble à elle-même un instant" (A.-T., 2: 132).

It is hardly surprising, then, that such a mind should tend toward ideas, paradoxical and, at times, in confutation with one another. If we take the views of at least three or four present-day *dix-huitiémistes*, it becomes apparent that this part of Diderot's nature continues to be recognized at appropriate intervals. Georges May, for instance, referring to our *philosophe* and to one literary genre in particular, has this to say: "On pourrait, à propos des idées de Diderot sur le roman, s'amuser à découper et coller face à face des citations du philosophe contenant des déclarations contradictoires."[2] Robert Niklaus, from a different perspective, notes that "his approach in all his writings was undogmatic, empirical, and dialectical," but it also brought about "some of the real or apparent contradictions in his thought."[3] Perhaps still more arresting is the fact that Robert Mauzi, in *L'Idée du bonheur au XVIII*^e *siècle*, does not hesitate to devote an entire subchapter to "Les Contradictions de Diderot."[4]

Doubtless Diderot's fondness for engaging in the art of disputation and his choice of the dialogue as a favorite mode of literary expression have much to do with his apparent and, upon occasion, very real *volte-face*. Still, to counteract, at least partially, prejudice against this tendency on his part and that of the human race in general, he said something at once evident and wise. In his famous *Entretien* with d'Alembert, he suggested that in the final analysis we would find that in everything our true opinion is not the one about which we have never vacillated but the one to which we have most persistently returned (A.-T., 2:121). Effort will be made to adhere to this principle during the present inquiry.

Late in life Diderot had occasion to refer to *La Religieuse* as "la contre-partie de *Jacques le fataliste*."[5] Though his reasons for doing so were valid, he could—with equal and possibly greater justification—have said as much for *La Religieuse* and *Le Supplément au voyage de Bougainville*. The *Supplément*, conceived some ten years later, does—superficially at least—counterpoint *La Religieuse*. Primitive family life on this imagined Tahiti, where there is understanding, affection, and love of children, contrasts strongly with the middle-class, Parisian household of the Simonins, where inflexibility, bitterness, jealousy, and parsimony are the order of the day, and children but an added burden to the weight of existence. Tahiti is luminous and joyful; one senses the bright sunshine, the warm, soft nights, and the inviting cool of the cabins. The convents of Sœur Suzanne, with their heavy stone masonry, are cold, somber, and forbidding. Diderot's Tahiti represents the airiness of individual and even collective freedom, but the milieux into which Sœur Sainte-Suzanne is forced are encumbered with the fetters of moral, spiritual, and physical confinement. The one is marked by spontaneity and laughter, the other by frustrations and tears. The extreme consequences of island life are the enjoyment of it and the will to live; those of the convents are nothing but the ashes of death. The counterpoise could be continued at length. One could speak in terms of polarization. The present study, however, is not concerned with opposites and mutual exclusiveness. It is an inquiry into resemblances, parallelisms, and correspondences in style and themes between two of Diderot's writings that are not usually presented in such fashion.

The most obvious parallelism in *La Religieuse* and the *Supplément* is the method of over-all procedure basic to both. Although it is common enough in other writings of Diderot, it is particularly noticeable here. An event or a series of events in actual life serves as a springboard for his imagination, with the result that the finished product is an adroit blending of reality and myth.

Out of such very real persons as Marguerite Delamarre, the marquis de Croismare, and Denis Diderot with his little band of conspirators grows one of the great novels of the French eighteenth century.[6] And from two chapters of Bougainville's *Voyage autour du monde*[7] was fashioned one of the more ingenious, witty, and provocative dialogues of the Enlightenment. In both cases Diderot's fantasies played over certain *données*, and the result was, in each instance, a brilliant tour de force still as exemplary and as alive as it was some two centuries ago.

This approach where fact and invention are skillfully combined the better to create and even heighten credibility is a common-enough practice among writers, and Diderot was no exception. Less natural are those procedures that rely on certain formal stylistic patterns. Of considerable importance among these for Diderot is the use of the triadic division so prominent in various guises in a number of his writings. One of the most clear-cut examples is *Le Rêve de d'Alembert* which, with its three distinct yet closely related parts—the "Entretien," the "Rêve" proper, and the "Suite"—has been called a triptych. And the three "panels" are in fact a sort of altarpiece for Diderot's philosophical and scientific speculations as each section casts the light of understanding on the other two.

Both *La Religieuse* and *Le Supplément*, like *Le Rêve*, are based on this broad ternary device; but their structure is more complicated. For instance, the memoirs of Sœur Suzanne fall into three distinct parts with roughly the same allotted proportions as those in *Le Rêve*. The first part of *La Religieuse* is brief and chiefly concerned with Suzanne's place in the domestic life of the Simonins. The middle and, indeed, major subdivision of the memoirs gives an almost day-by-day account of Sœur Suzanne's existence as a nun. The concluding section, following her escape over the convent wall, deals rapidly and sketchily with her hand-to-mouth existence in Paris directly preceding her death.

But *La Religieuse* has a larger, an all-encompassing ternion. Herbert Dieckmann has convincingly shown that it was Diderot's intention to have those sections known as the *Préface-*

Annexe fused with the memoirs themselves, thus becoming an integral part of the novel in question.[8] We may then speak of a triadic structure—"Préface," "Religieuse," "Annexe"—embracing a smaller triadic structure, that which comprises the memoirs themselves.

The *Supplément* may be approached in much the same way, for it too follows the "rule of three" so far as the general structure is concerned. The work opens with a dialogue between A and B in which—like logicians from the Sorbonne—they introduce one another and the reader to Bougainville's recently published *Voyage*. The central part of the work directly pertains to what happens on the island: it includes both the old Tahitian's harangue and the intimacies under the roof of the younger Tahitian, Orou, all interspersed with passing comments between A and B. In the third and concluding section, A and B, seeing the Bougainville-Diderot Tahiti in retrospect, bring their disquisition to a close.

But as in the case of *La Religieuse*, one may consider *Le Supplément* also in relation to a superstructure. Here, though, we must go outside the work itself to find what might be called the two subsidiary sections forming the triad. They are, of course, the short stories *Ceci n'est pas un conte* and *Madame de La Carlière*, as Roger Lewinter and others have noted. M. Lewinter is quite explicit about this in his development of "Les Trois Codes" when he comments in detail that the two tales and *Le Supplément* "forment un tout," and, moreover, "constituent une œuvre à structure ternaire."[9]

The triadic division is a favorite form of presentation for Diderot when it is a question of details as well. In *La Religieuse* Suzanne's monastic experiences will take place in three convents; three mother superiors will have a strong impact on her life; and, as Pierre Sage notes, "Trois bons prêtres interviennent" on her behalf.[10] And Suzanne herself makes a point of the fact that three persons, extremely close to her, die one after the other.[11]

Among all these lesser triads there is one—perhaps more important than the others—that has its correspondence in the *Supplément*. As the heroine informs us at the beginning of *La Religieuse*, she is, in the familial order, the youngest of three sisters; she is, moreover, inexperienced in the facts of life, even innocent. If there is a heroine in the *Supplément*, it would have to be Thia, the youngest of the three daughters in Orou's family. Though she is far more aware of the forces of sexuality around her than is her counterpart, at the outset she too is unaware of the extent of their drive and evident fascination.

Finally, among the triadic devices is one that appears to be a favorite of Diderot's, stemming as it does from Greco-Latin turns of style.[12] It is the tricolon, with its arrangement of words or phrases in groups of three and, now and then, working up to a mild climax on the third. By way of illustration two or three examples drawn almost at random from each work should suffice. In *La Religieuse* we read: "Eh bien! maman, lui dis-je, rendez-moi vos bontés; rendez-moi votre presénce; rendez-moi la tendresse de celui qui se croit mon père" (A.-T., 5:29). And again: "Elle me plaignit, me consola, me fit espérer un avenir plus doux" (A.-T., 5:35–36). In the *Supplément* the "vieillard" shields the European intruder against the wrath of his people, and asks: "Eh! pourquoi les ai-je apaisés? pourquoi les ai-je contenus? pourquoi les contiens-je encore dans ce moment?" (A.-T., 2:217). A little further on, Thia, embracing the knees of the ship's chaplain, cries: "Etranger, n'afflige pas mon père, n'afflige pas ma mère, ne m'afflige pas!" (A.-T., 2:221). And one example among many is interesting; it is a tricolon composed of binary elements. Orou is questioning the right of church and state to call black white, and white black: "Tu ne saurais le penser, car, à ce compte, il n'y aurait ni vrai ni faux, ni bon ni mauvais, ni beau ni laid" (A.-T., 2:224).

Now for a semantic similarity. Since, in its various aspects, the father image plays a significant part throughout the writings of Diderot, it comes as no surprise that it reappears almost obsessively in the two works under consideration. Suzanne is surrounded by father images, but to little or no avail. Her legal father coldly rejects her filial love. Her biological father had been selfish and cruel, and her mother tells her: "Il n'est plus; il est mort sans se souvenir de vous; et c'est le moindre de ses forfaits" (A.-T., 5:29). And the three spiritual fathers—Père Séraphin, the *grand vicaire* M. Hébert, and Père Lemoine—are well-meaning but ineffectual. The marquis de Croismare will become the most authentic father image, embodying in her eyes all the idealized qualities of the male parent. His name is the first to be mentioned in the memoirs, and, in fact, the memoirs are addressed to him. In him she places all her hope.

In the *Supplément* the father image takes on new dimensions. The first one we meet in its pages is most impressive— an old man who bids a bitter farewell to Bougainville and his company in the name of all the Tahitians. The opening lines of "Les Adieux" partially reveal him for what he is: "C'est un vieillard qui parle. Il était père d'une nombreuse famille" (A.-T., 2:213). The "noble vieillard," silent and withdrawn, whom Bougainville mentions (*Voyage*, p. 192), as he speaks in the *Supplément* becomes an ancient Hebrew patriarch, perhaps another Ezekiel, whose prophecies of doom lament the loss of an Oceanic paradise. This venerable personage, more than ninety years old, in all his authority is speaking now wrathfully against the iniquities he has beheld, now pleased with the Tahitians who follow the dictate: "Be fruitful and multiply." We recognize him to be the God of Diderot's youth, more the Jehovah of the Old Testament than his unpredictable Christian God. He is the same father figure who appears in the parable of the young Mexican (A.-.T, 2:525-26), in one of the *philosophe*'s last *petits papiers*, the *Entretien d'un philosophe avec la maréchale de****, published in 1777. It is the God of Michelangelo Buonarroti, and the God of Genesis as the thundering voice becomes hushed: " . . . Un vaste silence régna dans toute l'étendue de l'île; et l'on n'entendit que le sifflement aigu des vents et le bruit sourd des eaux sur toute la longueur de la côte; on eût dit que l'air et la mer, sensibles à la voix du vieillard, se disposaient à lui obéir" (A.-T., 2:218).

Far different from this awesome father figure is the one provided by Orou, the model head of the wholesome, primitive "bourgeois" family of Tahiti. Orou, in his self-assured and extended argumentation, his ever-pressing concern for those close to him, his insistence on the rights of nature and those of man in society, is the reflection of the father image of Diderot's own father Didier. But it is also that of Denis, the son, when he becomes the understanding, gently indulgent paterfamilias, scrupulously solicitous of the welfare of his children. Orou is Diderot acting out a utopian fantasy, a persona some of whose principles run counter to his own eighteenth-century bourgeois interests and those of his beloved daughter, Angélique. Of the various father figures Diderot adopted in his writings and in his life, the one that concerned Angélique, both child and woman, was closest to his heart. Diderot's philosophic speculations were as subversive as those of any of his compeers; as the head of a middle-class family under the *ancien régime*, he became—like his father—a man of rational prudence keeping with some success the dress of the country where he was born.

What may be concluded from all this? Just as the father image—in terms of his father and in those of himself as father —dominates more of Diderot's thinking than is readily apparent, so the role it plays in *La Religieuse* and in the *Supplément* is more important than might at first be supposed. In the former the father figure is presented in terms that are multiple and complex. In the latter it is elemental and undeniably personal.

In an odd sort of way the *Supplément* once again appears, perhaps with intentional irony, as a pendant to *La Religieuse*. By pushing the symbolic value of the veils to its extreme consequence, Diderot develops another of his "similitudes." The distaff side of his Tahitians wears three sorts of veils, depend-

236

ing on the circumstances involved. A maiden wears the white veil of innocence; she is not yet ready to bear children. The mature woman wears a gray veil upon those occasions when she is indisposed and temporarily incapable of conceiving a child. And that woman who is barren and cannot bear children at all is forced to wear a black veil. If she continues to seek out members of the opposite sex—and it could be only for the purpose of self-indulgence—she is marked as wanton and becomes an outcast in Diderot's contrived little island paradise, and contrived it is since this formulation differs radically from the source text.

In *Le Voyage* Bougainville had spoken of the practice of wearing veils on Tahiti. But they were worn to designate mourning alone. They were, in consequence, convenient disguises for whoever wished to seek out trysting places. Since the privacy of a person in mourning was respected, a veil was often used to facilitate illicit love.

Both Bougainville and the native, Aotourou, who sailed with him back to France, insisted that love-making was the Tahitians' chief interest. Diderot, eighteenth-century *philosophe* that he was, seemed only too pleased to twist the facts in his campaign against celibacy and to promote an expanding population. He did so by stressing procreation itself as of foremost interest and importance among the natives of Oceania.

Poor Sœur Suzanne also wore a veil, but for none of the above reasons. Her sister nuns thought she looked fetching in it; yet it was accompanied by the vows of poverty, chastity, and obedience. Her veil, like those of the unproductive and therefore superfluous Tahitian women, was black. Like them, in Diderot's parallelism, she and her kind were utterly useless in a society where childbearing was woman's noblest prerogative.

If the two works are to be considered companion pieces, they also have as a main point of reference the French eighteenth century. If the backgrounds of both lie partly in pass-

ing events of the period, they also reflect controversies that
were of extreme actuality at the time of writing. A number of
comparisons may be made with this duality in mind.

In the first place, both works deal explicitly with a protest
against the Judeo-Christian view of man. "Plus que la morale qu'il ne peut ruiner tout entière," says Jean Thomas,
"c'est l'explication chrétienne de l'homme que Diderot prétend dénoncer."[13] Though Georges May and Robert Mauzi
are right in saying that *La Religieuse* preaches neither anti-
religion nor anti-Christianity,[14] there are passages in the novel that suggest both ironic skepticism and outright criticism
of certain religious beliefs. Sœur Suzanne wonders how it is
that "le même mal vient, ou de Dieu qui nous éprouve, ou du
diable qui nous tente" (A.-T., 5:20). When praying for guidance, Suzanne-Diderot remarks: "On n'invoque la voix du
ciel, que quand on ne sait à quoi se résoudre; et il est rare
qu'alors elle ne nous conseille pas d'obéir" (A.-T., 5:31). Here
the will of God would seem to prescribe passive obedience
to an order that is fundamentally opposed to nature and that
in consequence is destined to bring unhappiness. M. Manouri, a thinly disguised spokesman for the author, poses a
whole series of questions: Are convents essential to the state?
Did Christ advocate the establishment of religious orders?
Why does the Heavenly Spouse need so many "vierges folles"?
How can God, who created man so fragile and fickle, author-
ize or even tolerate the rash effrontery with respect to his
vows? Instances of speculation along such lines could easily
be multiplied.

Orou in the *Supplément* adds to these questions, supplies
a few tentative answers, and, in fact, openly attacks Christian dogma. M. Manouri, in *La Religieuse*, argues against the
binding power of religious vows in general. Orou, with the
grudging assistance of the almoner, does what he can to undermine the vow of chastity and especially the sanctity of
the marriage vows. One of the more famous passages is
Orou's statement to the effect that constancy can hardly be

238

expected of a couple who—though swearing eternal fidelity —live in a world of flux under a sky that itself is never for a moment the same. From this what are we to conclude? That if the institution of marriage is condemned in the natural state, how much more so is the perversion of marriage that religious vows constitute! The apparent atheism of the Tahitians and their evident state of relative happiness even casts doubt on the necessity for believing in the very existence of God.

Another factor common to both works is the repeated protest against other social institutions besides marriage that are propounded at once by religious laws and civil legislation. Conventual life and the laws of the state deliberately subvert these norms.

Prior to the arrival of Europeans on the soil of Tahiti, any civil law had been merely an affirmation of the laws of nature. One aspect of this is the fact that both works are replete with legal connotations. The leitmotif of the trial runs throughout *La Religieuse*. Wherever Sœur Suzanne turns, she is either instigating a lawsuit or undergoing trials.[15] Legal overtones are also everywhere in evidence in the *Supplément*, whether revealed in the old man's farewell—itself a prosecutor's indictment of European criminality—or by the almoner's faltering defense of his religion and his office. These same overtones are readily apparent as Orou argues in behalf of the laws of nature and most certainly in the concluding forensic summation offered by those two algebraic personages, A and B. All this shows that Diderot, in every fiber of his body, was very much a corporate and sexual being.

Finally, both works may, as companion pieces, be regarded as an attempt to exteriorize the inner conflicts in social man in general, and in the individual—perhaps Diderot himself— in particular. The two basic drives that he sees as the primary source of conflict in man—one has been discernible from the outset—are sex and aggression. Sexual activity in *La Religieuse* reveals itself in a highly licentious and insidiously covert manner, which is generous in erotic detail. When it is homosexual, it becomes a sterile, hypocritical activity in conflict with man's natural inclination. When it is not, it can result in bastardy, with its attendant opprobrium in modern society. This is how the story of Sœur Suzanne begins. It ends with her escape from the convent into a Paris of prostitutes, panderers, rakes, brothels, and darkness—and everywhere, the spirit of aggressiveness.

Since on Diderot's Tahiti proliferation of the species is socially and economically imposed as the islanders' most pressing aim, sexuality is taken as a matter of course. In Orou's idealized family erotic play and emotional appeal are reduced to a minimum, and the resultant free love is described with an almost clinical objectivity. But if we are to believe "Les Adieux du vieillard," it is with the arrival of the aggressively ambitious and wicked Europeans that these children of nature are contaminated by disease and the notions of crime, of shame, and of guilt.

We see Diderot's insistence upon the energy of the sex drive, his concern over the unleashing of hidden instinctual and executive forces to the detriment or, possibly, advantage of the individual himself or of the social unit of which he is a member. We see Diderot's desire to bring to the surface the internal conflicts of both undercivilized and overcivilized man. This insistence, this concern, this desire suggest that Diderot anticipated Sigmund Freud more than is commonly assumed. And it was, after all, Freud who, with a handful of other advanced thinkers, was sufficiently perceptive to doff his hat to Diderot in passing.[16] Moreover, there is a touch of the Freudian in almost all Diderot wrote—including his correspondence. Freudian too was Diderot's conviction that at the more complex levels of society both aggressive and erotic energies are more inexorably directed inward and can lead to an agonizing civil war in society as a whole and in the individuals who constitute that society. By bringing man's instincts of sex and aggression into the open light of reason, these conflicts might be reduced if not dispelled entirely. But

Diderot, like Freud, knew that there was no simple solution to the problem. Any solution would, in fact, be slow and difficult; still there was hope, and the hope was the *raison d'être* of his humanism.

The presence of Diderot as a man of letters is readily apparent in both works, but it is the artist in Diderot who has the upper hand in *La Religieuse*. In the *Supplément* the writer's aesthetics is secondary to the ideas of the moralist and philosopher. Yet each work is, after its fashion, a criticism of eighteenth-century French life; for as a humanist, Diderot was striving to reach beyond generally accepted definitions of good and evil. Then, too, it should doubtless be kept in mind that eleven years separate the original composition of *La Religieuse* from that of his piece on Bougainville's *Voyage*, yet it is all the more noteworthy that a number of Diderot's most basic thoughts as a humanist and moralist remained unchanged. Neither the France he knew so well under the *ancien régime* nor the Polynesian community of his dreams could, in Diderot's mind, present a total answer to the question of man's happiness.

It is then hardly astonishing that, like many of his contemporaries, Diderot had faith in the power of better laws to ease the malaise of modern society. Once the eighteenth-century European has broken away from an arbitrary civil code —Diderot seems to be telling us in both works—he or she can, with some assurance of success, attempt to pursue the most essential undertaking of all, that of becoming a person in the true humanistic sense; the harmonious realization of physical, intellectual, and social potentialities in the individual, or, in modern psychological terms, the attainment of complete self-actualization.

1. Quotations from Diderot's works will be taken from the Assézat-Tourneux edition of the *Œuvres complètes*.

2. *Diderot et La Religieuse* (New Haven, Conn.: Yale University Press, 1954), p. 6.

3. A *Literary History of France: The Eighteenth Century, 1715-1789* (London: Ernest Benn, 1970), p. 215.

4. *L'Idée du bonheur au XVIIIᵉ siècle* (Paris: Colin, 1960), pp. 253-55. In this connection, Ellen Marie Strenski's provocative article, "The Problem of Inconsistency, Illustrated in Diderot's Social and Political Thought," in *Diderot Studies* 14 (1971):197-216, should also be mentioned.

5. Letter of 27 septembre 1780, in *Correspondance*, ed. Georges Roth and Jean Varloot (Paris: Les Editions de Minuit, 1970), 15:190.

6. Georges May, in *Diderot et La Religieuse*, and in his essay, "Une certaine Madame Madin," this volume, scrupulously indicates how this took place.

7. Louis-Antoine de Bougainville, *Voyage autour du monde par la frégate La Boudeuse, et la flûte, L'Etoile. En 1766, 1767, 1768, 1769* (Paris: Saillant & Nyon, 1771). This work will henceforth be referred to as *Le Voyage*.

8. See "*La Préface-Annexe* of *La Religieuse*" in *Diderot Studies* 2 (1952):21-147. Professor Dieckmann writes (p. 23): "The very title, which was evidently invented by Assézat indicates a contradictory trait: the work is to be a preface which precedes the novel and an annex which follows it."; (p. 30): "The *Préface-Annexe* is part of the novel, it is as much invention and fable as the novel itself."

9. Denis Diderot, *Œuvres complètes. Edition chronologique.* Introductions de Roger Lewinter (Paris: Le Club français du livre, 1971), 10:139.

10. *Le "Bon Prêtre" dans la littérature française* (Geneva: Droz, 1951), p. 308.

11. "Je fis dans la même année trois pertes intéressantes: celle de mon père, ou plutôt de celui qui passait pour tel; il était âgé, il avait beaucoup travaillé; il s'éteignit; celle de ma supérieure, et celle de ma mère" (A.-T., 5:41).

12. Recent studies showing Diderot's debt to, and knowledge of, ancient Greece and Rome are Raymond Trousson's *Socrate devant Voltaire, Diderot et Rousseau—La Conscience en face du Mythe* (Paris: Minard, 1967), his "Diderot helléniste" in *Diderot Studies* 12 (1969): 141-326, and Donal O'Gorman's *Diderot the Satirist, "Le Neveu de Rameau" and Related Works: An Analysis* (Toronto, 1971).

13. *L'Humanisme de Diderot* (Paris: Belles Lettres, 1938), p. 99.

14. Georges May, *Diderot et "La Religieuse"*, p. 184; Denis Diderot, *La Religieuse*, ed. Robert Mauzi (Paris: Colin, 1961), p. xxvii.

15. Sometimes alone, and sometimes with the help of a M. Manouri or a dom Morel.

16. Forcibly struck by the following sentence from Diderot, Freud quoted it on three separate occasions: "Si le petit sauvage était abandonné à lui-même, qu'il conservât toute son imbécillité, et qu'il réunît au peu de raison de l'enfant au berceau la violence des passions de l'homme de trente ans, il tordrait le cou à son père et coucherait avec sa mère." It is of interest to see how, on each occasion, Freud introduced the sentence; all three instances are drawn from *The Standard Edition of the Complete Works of Sigmund Freud* (London: Hogarth Press and the Institute of Psycho-Analy-

sis, 1953-66). In one of his shorter writings, *The Expert Opinion in the Halsmann Case*, Freud presents the Oedipus complex as follows: "Its essential characteristics, its universality, its content and its fate were recognized, long before the days of psycho-analysis, by that acute thinker Diderot, as is shown by a passage in his famous dialogue, *Le Neveu de Rameau*" (21 [1962]: 251). In his twenty-first lecture on *The Development of the Libido and the Sexual Organizations*, Freud says: "Among the writings of the Encyclopaedist Diderot you will find a celebrated dialogue, *Le Neveu de Rameau*, which was rendered into German by no less a person than Goethe. There you may read this remarkable sentence:" (16 [1963]: 337-38). In his posthumous *Outline of Psycho-Analysis*, we read: "Yet more than a century before the emergence of psycho-analysis the French philosopher Diderot bore witness to the importance of the Oedipus complex by expressing the difference between the primitive and the civilized worlds in this sentence:" (23 [1964], p. 192). Thumbing through Freud's *Complete Psychological Works*, a *Diderotiste* is impressed by many other striking concepts that had already been voiced by Diderot; there is no proof, however, that Freud was acquainted with any other of the philosopher's works except the abovementioned *Neveu*.

Diderot's Artist: Puppet and Poet

DOUGLAS BONNEVILLE

Of Diderot's works none is more controversial than the *Paradoxe sur le comédien*. Opinion is sharply, perhaps permanently, divided on most of the questions raised in this protean dialogue. Actors and critics still debate hotly the thesis of the actor's emotional disengagement from his role; among actors even the prestigious voices of Copeau and Jouvet have failed to settle the argument. As to the critics, Yvon Belaval sees the *Paradoxe* as a unified work, consistent with Diderot's over-all aesthetic theory,[1] but Lester Crocker apparently views it as another example of "Diderot's characteristic fragmented thinking."[2] Or, from a slightly different bias, Robert Niklaus decides that the essential paradox of the piece is philosophical, in that the artist is both determined by his heredity and milieu and a determinant in the world where he exists,[3] whereas Giorgio Cerrutti construes the aesthetic paradox as a social one: the philosopher as both dreamer and activist.[4] Considering the extent of disagreement, we can indeed be grateful to Joseph Bédier for quelling at least the once-raging controversy over the text's authenticity. So disparate is critical opinion, in fact, that we breathe a sigh of relief at anything that hints of concensus among commentators on the *Paradoxe*. This eagerness for comparative agreement is perhaps responsible for the traditional classification of the work as a pivotal text, a turning point in Diderot's aesthetic theory, separating the young, enthusiastic, and sensitive artist, represented by Dorval of the *Entretiens*

245

sur le Fils naturel, from the older, more mature theorist, cast as the "Premier Interlocuteur" in the *Paradoxe*.[5] Neat as this division appears, it is specious, as an interrogation of the texts will show. The *Paradoxe*, I believe, is not so much a turning point in Diderot's aesthetics, or a contradiction of previous notions, as simply a recognition of the artistic principles underlying his literary production. These principles are fairly consistent throughout Diderot's career and are recognizable in such apparently diverse writings as *Entretiens sur le Fils naturel*, *Jacques le fataliste*, *Le Neveu de Rameau*, *Rêve de d'Alembert*, and *Essai sur les règnes de Claude et de Néron*.

Diderot opens the *Paradoxe sur le comédien* with a debate between two critics as to whether a published work of criticism should be criticized. The dispute is occasioned by the fact that the "Second Interlocuteur" is a personal friend of the published critic (Antonio Sticoti); it is settled by an agreement that any published work must be judged quite independently of its author and that any criticism of it is therefore dispassionate. From the idea that criticism is depersonalized to the notion that the best actor is "un spectateur froid et tranquille" of his own performance (306),[6] and finally to the general conclusion that the greatest artistic expression is devoid of immediate sensitivity, is a natural if not inevitable progression. But it is in no way paradoxical. Mere disagreement with the rather puerile notion that art is the spontaneous expression of emotion does not constitute a paradox; nor does the opinion that the greatest actor imitates with absolute *sang-froid* the sensitive man (335). Though debatable, they are merely common-sense conclusions to a certain line of reasoning. It is only later, when Diderot opposes the two flagrantly contradictory conceptions, both articulated by the "Premier Interlocuteur" (Diderot's *porte-parole*), of the actor as puppet and the actor as creator (348) that, as Niklaus has said, we seem to be faced with a paradox. And at that, this creative puppet may be considered as a prefiguration of

246

Jacques, who lives in a determined universe but in his actions creates the illusion that he is free.

The ultimate expression of this paradox is probably made by Diderot the author describing the feelings of Diderot the critic in regard to the latter's reaction to a role he interpreted in one of his own plays (*La pièce et le prologue,* later *Est-il bon? Est-il méchant?*), based on his own experience. Diderot, in short, is the model for a stage character, the playwright, the actor, the spectator, and the critic. No confusion is created by this protean activity simply because each of the artistic functions is separated from the others in time. When Diderot the critic declares, "Le grand comédien observe les phénomènes; l'homme sensible lui sert de modèle" (335), he is merely developing a previous statement: "L'homme sensible obéit aux impulsions de la nature et ne rend précisément que le cri de son cœur; au moment où il tempère ou force ce cri, ce n'est plus lui, c'est le comédien qui joue" (335). In other words, the "homme sensible," or the model, and the "grand comédien," or the artist, can be one and the same person, but at different points of time. So that the statement, "Ce n'est pas dans la fureur du premier jet que les traits caractéristiques se présentent, c'est dans les moments tranquilles et froids, dans des moments tout à fait inattendus" (309), which is an early and rather academic formulation of the Wordsworthian notion that art arises from emotion recollected in tranquillity, may be applied to any of the artistic incarnations of Diderot.[7] But the Encyclopedist goes beyond this concept and introduces the element of the unexpected or the spontaneous during the act of creation, adding, "C'est lorsque, suspendus entre la nature et leur ébauche, ces génies portent alternativement un œil attentif sur l'une et l'autre; les beautés d'inspiration, les traits fortuits qu'ils répandent dans leurs ouvrages, et dont l'apparition subite les étonne eux-mêmes, sont d'un effet et d'un succès bien autrement assurés que ce qu'ils ont jetés de boutade" (309). There is in the *Paradoxe* no denial of the importance of sensitivity to creation. On the contrary, as in the *Entretiens sur le Fils naturel*, enthusiasm is still at the heart of the work of art.

The control that the artist is supposed to exercise in his expression of a great passion is in many cases only the result of the passage of time. Even during the process of creation there is room for inspiration, as "la mémoire se réunit à l'imagination, l'une pour retracer, l'autre pour exagérer la douceur d'un temps passé" (333), and we have intimations of Proust. Rather than standing in contradiction to Diderot's earlier thought, the *Paradoxe* merely restates in an aesthetic work the typically Diderotian concept of the individual as a succession of entities bound together by the thread of memory. It seems, in fact, that this work resolves more paradoxes than it poses. In a determined universe all artistic creation is hindsight. The only way to render experience intelligible is to be detached, by the passage of time, from the immediate context in which the experience occurs. Then, ironically, it may become meaningful to others, but only by moving them emotionally.[8] The intensity of audience participation is, in one of Diderot's favorite expressions, in inverse proportion to the artist's emotional pitch at the time of expression. Thus the emotionally charged moment, unintelligible to the individual who lives it and, moreover, meaningless because it is determined, may be transformed by the appropriately distanced artist into lucid commentary on the human condition. The audience is led by the artist to perceive some or all of the relationships grasped by the latter. As if in anticipation of some of his twentieth-century heirs, Diderot is placing a premium on lucidity: if you understand your plight, you are somehow superior to it.

From the opening debate, in which the work of art is declared independent of its creator, Diderot develops the concept of the autonomy of the various phases of aesthetic experience. The writer is detached from the original inspiration, the actor from the play, the critic from the work of art. The famous "perception of relationships" is not immediate but at a considerable remove from the stimulus. Only the nonprofessional spectator, completely removed from the creative process, is left to participate emotionally in the artistic production. I suggest that this aspect of the *Paradoxe*, at least, is perfectly consistent with the rest of Diderot's aesthetic and philosophical thought. It has become more or less standard procedure to point out that in the *Entretiens sur le Fils naturel* Diderot is defending enthusiasm and that in the *Paradoxe* he is doing quite the opposite. The latter work has thus come to represent a drastic change in the current of Diderot's aesthetic thinking. The flaw in this interpretation is, of course, Dorval himself, who chronologically precedes the "Premier Interlocuteur" by some thirteen years and who talks with sometimes utter detachment about himself as model, author, and actor. Dorval is playing, then, the same roles as the First Interlocutor: he participates in the whole existence of the play. In fact, if the *Entretiens* are read with the *Fils naturel,* the final effect is quite the same as that achieved by Tieck, Pirandello, Unamuno, Wilder, and the host of authors who make a fetish of the autonomy of dramatic or fictional characters.[9] In the context of Diderot's own work, Dorval, in his various entities, is very much like Jacques, whose acts and thoughts, we are constantly reminded, are totally dependent on an author who insists that Jacques is free. Consider the paradox in Dorval's reply to Moi's objection to the theatricality of one of the scenes of the *Fils naturel*: "C'est que ce n'est pas une fiction, mais un fait. Il serait à souhaiter, pour le bien de l'ouvrage, que la chose fût arrivée tout autrement" (94). Dorval admits to being a prisoner of his past; he has already confessed to being restricted by certain aesthetic demands as well as by moral considerations; in addition, it has previously been made clear that his thoughts are distorted by Moi's memory and lack of talent. And yet, in other parts of the dialogue, Dorval asserts and vigorously defends his independence.

It would seem that the apparent contradiction between

statements made by Dorval in the *Entretiens* and the general statement of the *Paradoxe* disappears when the structure of the two works is taken into consideration. To be sure, Dorval says, "Le poëte sent le moment de l'enthousiasme; c'est après qu'il a médité. Il s'annonce en lui par un frémissement qui part de sa poitrine, et qui passe, d'une manière délicieuse et rapide, jusqu'aux extrémités de son corps. Bientôt ce n'est plus un frémissement; c'est une chaleur forte et permanente qui l'embrase, qui le fait haleter, qui le consume, qui le tue; mais qui donne l'âme, la vie à tout ce qu'il touche" (98). But those who point only to these words are ignoring the structure of the work. They forget not only that the Moi of the dialogue has already confessed that his transcription of the interview consists of "des lignes faibles, tristes et froides," but also that Dorval himself, upon completing his impassioned description of the role of enthusiasm in creation, awakes as if from a dream, asking "Qu'ai-je dit? Qu'avais-je à vous dire? Je ne m'en souviens plus" (98). Dorval is unaware of the emotionally aesthetic experience he has undergone. Only the dispassionate observer is capable of judging and transcribing the truths that Dorval is here unwittingly reflecting, whether that observer is another person than the model or the same person at a later time. This awakening from a dream state is a device Diderot uses effectively in at least two other works, the *Neveu de Rameau* and *Rêve de d'Alembert*. Rameau, after an exhausting pantomime, is described as "epuisé de fatigue, tel qu'un homme qui sort d'un profond sommeil ou d'une longue distraction . . . semblable à celui qui verroit à son réveil son lit environné d'un grand nombre de personnes, dans un entier oubli ou dans une profonde ignorance de ce qu'il a fait."[10] Then, without a full realization of what he has just done, he adds, obviously unaware of the value of his statement, "Voilà ce qu'on doit appeler de la musique et un musicien." This statement of alienation, which has often been singled out for commentary, represents an incomplete grasp of the implications of one's own experience. It is up to the

artist, to Diderot, the dispassionate observer and man of genius to give meaning to this madness. So does Bordeu inter-
pret d'Alembert's dream and so does Diderot arbitrarily
summon d'Alembert, Bordeu, and Mlle de L'Espinasse together to give intelligible expression to Diderotian materialism. As brilliant as Rameau, d'Alembert, and Bordeu are,
they are not artists. The artist is he who, by chance or by habit, is capable of transcribing his thoughts and actions, of trans-
forming them into significance.

A statement from the *Essai sur les règnes de Claude et de
Néron* (1782), to the effect that Diderot would rather be considered "un homme sensible" than a man of genius or a great
writer,[11] is sometimes taken as a second reversal of thought
and a return to *sensiblerie*. Since he has never renounced
sensitivity as such and is in the *Essai* simply stating a prefer-
ence for one of the three outstanding qualities he has been
told he possesses, there is evidently no such reversal. Once
again, specious differences of thought are eliminated by a
consideration of the form of the work. The narrator of the
Essai, like Dorval, the First Interlocutor, and Jacques, is at a
carefully regulated distance from his subject. In the latest of
these works the author is in fact revising an earlier work, the
Essai sur la vie de Sénèque, in which, it is generally concluded, there are strong parallels between Diderot and Sen-
eca. So he actually is recasting an implicit comparison between himself and a man long dead. Whatever the effect of
the final work, this touching-up of corpses, in form and in content, is a plea for objectivity.

The somewhat surprising conclusion to be drawn from this
discussion is that some of the most disparate and outwardly
conflicting of Diderot's works are characterized by a substantial consistency of form. Michael Cartwright, in a remarkable
study of *Diderot critique d'art et le problème de l'expression*,[12] states that Diderot is incapable of the act of distancing,
yet it would appear that in all of the crucial works mentioned
here there is one viewpoint, stated or implied, that is emo-

tionally detached from the work itself, and that this view-point may be associated with a fundamentally dispassionate critic.[13] And if, as David Funt's excellent work concludes,[14] Diderot has no constant theory of aesthetics, he does follow, consciously or unconsciously, some fairly consistent practices. It follows that the substantial disagreements among Diderot critics as to his aesthetic theory might well be mitigated by a closer examination of his techniques.

1.   Yvon Belaval, *L'Esthétique sans paradoxe de Diderot* (Paris: Gallimard, 1950).

2.   Lester Crocker, *Two Diderot Studies: Ethics and Esthetics* (Baltimore: The Johns Hopkins Press, 1952), p. 67.

3.   Robert Niklaus, "Observations sur le style expressif de Diderot," in *Diderot critique d'art et le problème de l'expression*, by Michael T. Cartwright, *Diderot Studies* 13 (1969): 5.

4.   Giorgio Cerrutti, "Le Paradoxe sur le comédien et le paradoxe sur le libertin, Diderot et Sade," *Revue des sciences humaines*, fasc. 46 (1972): 243.

5.   Cerrutti, ibid., does take issue with this generality.

6.   All numbers in parentheses refer to Paul Vernière's edition of Diderot's *Œuvres esthétiques* (Paris: Garnier, 1962).

7.   This has already been pointed out by Margaret Gilman in "The Poet according to Diderot," *Romanic Review* 37 (1946): 52. Cf. David Funt, *Diderot and the Esthetics of the Enlightment, Diderot Studies* 11 (1968): 61.

8.   Cf. Crocker, *Two Diderot Studies*, p. 73.

9.   Funt compares *Jacques* with Pirandello's *Six Characters* (*Diderot and the Esthetics of the Enlightment*, pp. 119-20).

10.   *Le Neveu de Rameau*, ed. Jean Fabre (Geneva: Droz, 1950), p. 85.

11.   *Essai sur Sénèque*, ed. Hisayasu Nakagawa (Tokyo: Takeuchi, 1966-68), 2:189.

12.   Cartwright, *Diderot critique d'art*, p. 19.

13.   Cf. Roger Laufer, *Style rococo, style des Lumières* (Paris: Corti, 1963), p. 115.

14.   Funt, *Diderot and the Esthetics of the Enlightment*, p. 172.

Une certaine Madame Madin

L'ouvrage connu sous le nom de *Préface-annexe* de *La Religieuse* est fait de textes de deux natures distinctes: des lettres, d'une part, et, de l'autre, un récit narratif qui relie ces lettres les unes aux autres. Les lettres elles-mêmes sont de deux sortes: d'une part, celles du marquis de Croismare, qui ont bien été écrites par lui, tout au moins dans la version originale qui ne nous est pas parvenue; et, de l'autre, celles que le marquis reçut de la prétendue religieuse et de la prétendue protectrice de celle-ci, lesquelles sont de la main de Grimm, de Diderot et de leurs amis: "Vous voudrez bien vous souvenir que toutes ses lettres ainsi que celles de sa recluse ont été fabriquées par nous autres enfants de Bélial, et que toutes les lettres de son généreux protecteur sont véritables et ont été écrites de bonne foi."[1] Il résulte de là une certaine confusion qui n'est pas involontaire, puisque l'intention de Diderot et de ses amis était, comme on le sait, de mystifier monsieur de Croismare.

Afin de ne pas être à notre tour victimes de "cette insigne fourberie" et de ne pas perdre notre chemin comme monsieur de Croismare dans le labyrinthe résultant de "ce complot d'iniquité,"—ces expressions sont de Grimm (D 82-83, M 180),— il importe donc tout d'abord de savoir qui furent tous ces personnages et surtout lesquels existèrent vraiment et lesquels sont imaginaires. Le seul d'entre eux qui n'ait pas été identifié jusqu'ici est madame Madin, la protectrice de la pseudo-religieuse évadée, celle qui, dès la première lettre de celle-ci au marquis de Croismare, est appelée "digne femme" et "bonne amie" (D 92, M 184). Or, quoiqu'elle n'ait donc pas écrit les lettres qui furent signées de son nom,—"Elle ne savait rien de notre coquinerie, ni des lettres que nous lui fîmes écrire à elle-même par la suite," affirme la *Préface-annexe* (D 93, M 184)—elle a véritablement existé, comme ont aussi existé, ainsi qu'on le sait depuis longtemps, le marquis de Croismare et Marguerite Delamarre, la religieuse de Longchamp au sort de laquelle il prit intérêt.

Les quelques renseignements sur madame Madin qu'on peut extraire de la *Préface-annexe* sont, du reste, généralement exacts, tout au moins ceux qu'il a été jusqu'ici possible de contrôler. A commencer par son adresse, qui était évidemment aux yeux de Diderot et de Grimm l'élément le plus important de sa personnalité, puisque le rôle qu'ils firent tenir à cette femme dans la mystification de monsieur de Croismare fut celui d'une simple boîte aux lettres: "Nous avions besoin d'une adresse pour recevoir les réponses, et nous choisîmes une certaine Madame Madin." (D 92, M 184). Dans la première lettre qu'il reçut en 1760 de la prétendue religieuse le marquis de Croismare pouvait lire, en effet: "Voici l'adresse de Madame Madin: *A Madame Madin, au Pavillon de Bourgogne, rue d'Anjou, à Versailles*" (D 93, M 184), indication réitérée à la fin de la première lettre qu'il reçut de la pseudo-madame Madin: "J'attends, Monsieur, votre réponse, toujours au Pavillon de Bourgogne, rue d'Anjou, à Versailles" (D 103, M 189). Or, si l'on se rend aujourd'hui rue d'Anjou à Versailles, on y repère sans aucune difficulté un assez grand immeuble ancien, fait de deux corps de bâtiment, occupant les numéros 5 et 5bis, et portant sur la façade l'inscription peinte: "Pavillon de Bourgogne—1750."[2]

Nous n'avons retrouvé aucun document attestant de façon certaine que madame Madin habitait bien le Pavillon de Bourgogne en 1760; mais il n'y a aucune raison d'en douter. En effet, dans un acte notarié de 1758, elle est dite habiter la paroisse Saint-Louis à Versailles, dont la rue d'Anjou faisait et fait encore partie. De plus, un des témoins qui signèrent l'acte en question donne lui-même pour domicile rue d'Anjou à Versailles.[3] Du reste, madame Madin ne devait plus, semble-t-il, quitter cette paroisse ni ce quartier. En effet, lors de son décès, survenu le 16 mars 1779, elle habitait, non loin du Pavillon de Bourgogne, une maison de la rue de l'Orangerie;[4] et son nom figure sur le registre des sépultures de la paroisse Saint-Louis, où elle fut inhumée le 17 mars.[5]

Qui était cette madame Madin? et pourquoi Diderot et Grimm eurent-ils recours à elle en 1760? Ce sont là les questions auxquelles les pages qui suivent vont essayer de répondre. Or, comme on le verra, nous ne sommes encore qu'incomplètement renseignés sur elle, ce qui fait qu'il ne sera possible de répondre à la deuxième de ces questions que par des hypothèses jusqu'ici non démontrées.

Michelle Moreau—c'est son nom de jeune fille et c'est ainsi que son prénom est le plus souvent orthographié—dut naître vers 1714 et sans doute en Franche-Comté. En effet, le registre des sépultures dont il vient d'être fait mention la dit "âgée d'environ soixante-cinq ans" lors de son décès en mars 1779. D'autre part, les deux premiers légataires qui figurent sur son testament, à savoir sa sœur Marie Thérèse Moreau de Russy et les enfants de sa seconde sœur Charlotte Marguerite Moreau épouse Capitenet, habitaient tous Besançon lors de la mort de madame Madin, ainsi qu'en fait foi la procuration qu'ils signèrent en 1780 pour donner à un banquier de Paris pouvoir d'accomplir en leurs noms les formalités nécessaires à la délivrance des legs.[6] De plus, un autre témoignage, antérieur de trente-six ans, vient confirmer l'impression que cette famille Moreau était établie à Besançon ou aux environs dès la jeunesse de la future madame Madin. En effet, selon la convention de 1758 mentionnée ci-dessus (voir note 3), Michelle Moreau avait été la bénéficiaire d'un "contrat de rente viagère de cent soixante livres au principal de deux mille livres constituée à son profit par le sieur Jean Claude Chalon greffier au Parlement de Besançon passé devant Me

Archeret notaire audit Besançon le dix mai mil sept cent quarante-quatre."[7] Il convient de noter, toutefois, que les registres de baptêmes de la Ville de Besançon ne révèlent pas trace de Michelle Moreau de 1713 à 1715.[8]

Quoi qu'il en soit donc de la date et du lieu de naissance précis de madame Madin, sa présence à Paris est attestée dès 1745, alors qu'elle était donc âgée d'environ trente-et-un ans. En effet, selon le témoignage de la même convention de 1758 (voir ci-dessous note 3), c'est le 6 avril de cette année qu'elle épousait en la paroisse Saint-Germain-l'Auxerrois Jean Madin, et ce "sans avoir préalablement fait aucun contrat de mariage."[9] Ils étaient alors l'un et l'autre orphelins de pères et mères, ainsi qu'il est rappelé dans ce même document.

Il est dit dans la *Préface-annexe* que madame Madin était la "femme d'un ancien officier d'infanterie" (D 93, M 184). Ceci est parfaitement exact: son époux Jean Madin avait servi pendant une dizaine d'années au régiment de Lorraine Infanterie. Nommé lieutenant en second le 1er janvier 1734, il avait été reçu parmi les officiers du régiment le 1er février de la même année.[10] Par la suite on trouve son nom dans le *Contrôle collectif des officiers d'infanterie* pour 1734-38 et pour 1738-43, mais il ne figure ni dans le registre antérieur (1727-34), ni dans le registre postérieur (1745-48).[11] Il semble donc qu'il ait quitté le service peu avant son mariage. Il avait atteint alors le grade de capitaine.

Lors de la mort de sa femme en 1779, Jean Madin habitait Verdun avec sa fille Catherine Gabrielle, ainsi qu'en fait foi la procuration qu'ils signèrent l'un et l'autre le 21 mars 1779 devant Me Dognon et Me Thiébaut, notaires à Verdun, constituant un avocat de Versailles le représentant de leurs intérêts quant à la succession de madame Madin.[12] On est donc en droit de se demander si Jean Madin n'était pas peut-être originaire de cette ville ou de cette région où il se retira vers la fin de sa vie. Quoiqu'on ne connaisse, en effet, pas jusqu'ici la date de sa naissance, il ne semble pas, étant donné sa nomination au grade de lieutenant en second en 1734, avoir été beaucoup plus âgé que sa femme, et on peut supputer qu'il avait sans doute entre soixante-cinq et soixante-dix ans lorsqu'il devint veuf en 1779. Rien ne permet cependant d'affirmer jusqu'ici qu'il ait été en fait de Verdun ou de la région, car malheureusement aucune trace de lui n'a été jusqu'à présent retrouvée dans les archives locales.[13] Toutefois son appartenance au régiment de Lorraine ajoute à la présomption qu'il était très probablement originaire de cette province.

Quant à la date de naissance exacte de la fille des Madin, Catherine Gabrielle, elle ne nous est pas connue non plus, mais elle doit être de 1747-48, puisque la convention signée par ses parents le 28 février 1758 et déjà mentionnée plusieurs fois (voir ci-dessous note 3) la dit alors "âgée de onze ans." Au moment de sa naissance les Madin habitaient probablement encore Paris où ils s'étaient mariés, comme on l'a vu, en avril 1745. En tout cas ils n'étaient pas encore établis à Versailles, car ce n'est pas en cette ville que leur enfant est née. En effet, les registres de baptêmes de Versailles, qui, à la différence de ceux de Paris, nous ont été conservés, sont muets à son égard.

En réalité on ne sait rien jusqu'ici des faits et gestes des époux Madin pendant la douzaine d'années qui s'écoulèrent entre leur mariage en 1745 et la convention qu'ils signèrent en 1758 et que l'ordre chronologique que nous observons ici nous engage maintenant à examiner. Cet acte, reçu le 28 février 1758 par Me Louis Robineau, notaire à Paris, avait pour but d'effectuer la séparation de biens entre les époux Madin. C'est un long document qui commence par noter que les intéressés "ont sans aucune contrainte consenti à ladite séparation" pour toute une série de raisons, parmi lesquelles il est dit "qu'ils n'ont aucun commerce, que tous leurs biens consistent en rentes viagères, et que leur revenu est borné, sur le point même de vivre assez éloignés l'un de l'autre pour un long temps par un voyage de long cours que ledit sieur Madin est obligé de faire, après mûre délibération, de l'avis et conseil de personnes prudentes. . . . " Suit une série de huit articles où sont précisées les conditions dans lesquelles devait se

259

faire le partage de leurs biens en deux parts égales; où il est convenu que, tant que leur fille Catherine Gabrielle demeurerait à la charge de sa mère, son père verserait à celle-ci une pension annuelle de trois cents livres; et où il est enfin stipulé que madame Madin serait désormais légalement émancipée et autorisée à jouir pleinement de tous ses droits juridiques comme si elle n'avait jamais été en puissance de mari.

Et pourtant, malgré l'abondance de détails présents dans ce document, les causes réelles ayant amené les époux Madin à cette séparation de biens nous échappent. Nous ignorons notamment pour quelle raison l'ancien capitaine Madin dut effectuer un voyage au long cours, et rien n'indique pourquoi les Madin avaient quitté Paris pour Versailles où ils étaient établis au moment de leur séparation. En effet, dans l'acte en question, Jean Madin est désigné sous le titre de "bourgeois de Versailles" et l'acte de séparation, quoique reçu par un notaire de Paris, est libellé "fait et passé en ladite ville de Versailles." Aucune allusion n'est faite non plus aux occupations peut-être rémunérées auxquelles pouvaient alors se livrer l'un ou l'autre des deux époux et qui auraient pu expliquer leur présence à Versailles.

Ce qu'on y apprend, en revanche, c'est la modicité des ressources de cette famille. Les biens meubles des Madin s'élevaient, selon cet acte, à 2300 livres, plus 1500 livres d'argent liquide, pour un total de 3800 livres, somme de laquelle il convient de défalquer 700 livres de dettes alors à leur charge. Sur leurs rentes viagères l'acte est muet, sinon pour observer, comme on l'a vu, que celles-ci constituaient "tout leur bien." On regrette d'autant plus cette absence de renseignements capables de nous donner une idée plus claire de leur mode d'existence, que nous n'avons retrouvé aucun document concernant madame Madin qui soit plus rapproché que celui-ci du moment où Diderot et ses amis firent choix d'elle pour recevoir rue d'Anjou à Versailles les lettres que le marquis de Croismare devait écrire de son château de Lasson en Normandie.

Or, lors de son décès en 1779, madame Madin était à la tête d'une fortune qui nous semble sensiblement plus considérable que la part qui lui était revenue un peu plus de vingt ans plus tôt, lors de sa séparation d'avec son mari. Sans tenir compte une fois encore des rentes viagères auxquelles il sera fait allusion plus loin, on observe, en effet, que l'exécuteur testamentaire de madame Madin put faire état d'une recette en liquide de 9325 livres 8 sols et 8 deniers à l'actif de la succession.[14] Et, si l'on examine l'inventaire de ses biens, établi après son décès,[15] on ne peut manquer de conclure que, vers la fin de sa vie, madame Madin vivait en petite bourgeoise aisée.

Son logement, au troisième étage d'une maison de la rue de l'Orangerie appartenant au marquis de Forget et dont les loyers étaient perçus par Augustin Prat, apothicaire du roi, consistait en deux pièces donnant sur la rue, une cuisine donnant sur la cour et un grenier. Elle avait à son service une domestique, Catherine Deschamps, femme d'un palefrenier du prince de Poix nommé Jacques Laroche, à laquelle elle légua une rente viagère de quarante livres. Elle était abondamment et confortablement meublée et possédait en particulier deux petites bibliothèques pourvues de livres, tant reliés que brochés, un grand clavecin prisé cent vingt livres, plusieurs tableaux encadrés et glaces de Venise, une grande quantité de linge et de vêtements, et des couverts d'argent qui réalisèrent 158 livres et 12 sols lors de la vente après décès, sans parler des ustensiles de cuisine et de ménage qu'on imagine.

Madame Madin avait aussi, à ce qu'il semble, des relations flatteuses. Son exécuteur testamentaire fut, en effet, "M. François Joubain de Doisu, avocat au Parlement de Paris, jurisconsulte des Affaires étrangères, seigneur de Doisu, les Mouchoirs, les Volveaux et autres lieux." L'un des témoins présents lorsqu'elle dicta son testament au notaire Barat était le prêtre Pierre Astoin, ou Astouin, chanoine de Péronne, "chapelain ordinaire de la Reine et de Madame." Parmi les papiers qu'on trouva chez elle après sa mort et dont on dressa l'inventaire se trouvaient, d'une part, plusieurs reconnaissances de dettes totalisant près de huit mille livres et signées par madame de Cagny et par messieurs Asselin, de Quinjay et de Mard, ce dernier commis à la Marine, et, de l'autre, diverses pièces témoignant des services qu'elle semble avoir été à même de rendre à des personnes en place. En plus d'"une rente viagère de soixante-huit livres neuf sols sur les revenus du Roi," madame Madin possédait, en effet, "un brevet en date du quinze avril mil sept cent soixante seize signé Louis et plus bas Lamoignon [. . .] pour lequel Sa Majesté a fait don à ladite femme Moreau femme Madin d'un terrain sis dans l'ancien prieuré de Clagny contenant en superficie quinze perches environ." De plus, selon le compte d'exécution testamentaire signé par monsieur Joubain de Doisu le 30 août 1780 (voir ci-dessous note 14), la défunte avait également bénéficié d'une "pension de trois cents livres que lui faisait madame la comtesse d'Artois et qui doit être payée par madame de Roquemont première femme de chambre de la princesse." Enfin la marquise d'Havrincourt avait constitué à madame Madin en 1775 une rente viagère de deux cents livres "pour remplir les intentions que la comtesse de Gergy lui a témoignées avant son décès."[16]

On peut donc se demander en récompense de quels services madame Madin avait reçu un terrain du Roi, une pension de la comtesse d'Artois et une rente viagère de la marquise d'Havrincourt en souvenir de la comtesse de Gergy sa mère. Et on ne peut s'empêcher d'observer de prime abord que c'étaient là de bien grands personnages, comparés à la petite bourgeoise qu'était Michelle Moreau Madin.

Une hypothèse qui se présente tout naturellement est qu'elle avait pu faire partie à un moment donné du nombreux personnel au service de la famille royale. Ceci expliquerait les récompenses du Roi et de la comtesse d'Artois sa belle-sœur; et ceci rendrait possible que madame Madin, en raison de ses accointances avec ce monde, ait été à même de rendre service à la comtesse de Gergy. Malheureusement les documents que nous avons pu consulter aux Archives nationales pour vérifier cette hypothèse sont muets sur le compte de madame Madin.[17] En revanche, il est possible que la dame de Cagny à qui elle avait prêté 2100 livres—somme qui fut, du reste, remboursée par madame de Cagny et versée par elle au compte de la succession—ne fût autre que Julie Charlotte Marin de Cagny, dont le nom figure plusieurs fois dans ces documents et qui fut pendant plusieurs années une des femmes de chambre au service de madame Élisabeth, la sœur du futur Louis XVI et du comte d'Artois.[18]

Si l'on rapproche cette observation du fait que l'un des chapelains ordinaires de la Reine et de Madame servit de témoin en 1779, comme on l'a vu, lors de la signature du testament de madame Madin, on commencera peut-être à voir se dessiner l'image hypothétique d'une femme qui, sans être régulièrement employée par la Maison du Roi, en connaissait et fréquentait le personnel et rendait à l'occasion service aux uns et aux autres. Il n'est pas exclu, du reste, qu'elle ait eu à un moment donné, peut-être au début de son séjour à Versailles, un emploi régulier dont nous n'avons simplement pas réussi à retrouver la trace. En effet, lorsque la marquise d'Havrincourt lui constitua une rente viagère en 1775, il est dit de madame Madin qu'elle demeure "ordinairement à Versailles," ce qui peut vouloir dire que, n'étant plus astreinte alors à un emploi fixe, elle était suffisamment libre de ses mouvements pour se déplacer à son gré. Notons, du reste, que c'est bien ainsi qu'elle nous est présentée dans la *Préface-annexe* de *La Religieuse*, faisant sans difficulté apparente la navette entre son domicile de Versailles et le refuge où la pseudo-religieuse se cache à Paris. Une fois seulement un empêchement survient: "Mon état, qui m'attache à Versailles, ne m'a point permis de venir plus tôt à son secours" (D 99, M 187); mais c'est là une exception: la plupart du temps le personnage donne l'impression de faire l'aller-et-retour Versailles-Paris chaque fois qu'elle l'entend. Cette image hypothétique cadrerait donc assez bien avec le rôle qui fut celui de l'authenti-

263

que madame Madin en 1760 dans la mystification dont fut victime le marquis de Croismare.

Comme on le sait, madame d'Épinay fit partie du complot dont Grimm et Diderot étaient les membres les plus actifs; et c'est chez elle qu'aux dires de la *Préface-annexe* le marquis de Croismare finit par rencontrer un jour madame Madin: "Le hasard voulut que M. de Croismare, après son retour à Paris, et environ huit ans après notre péché, trouvât Madame Madin un matin chez une femme de nos amies qui avait été du complot" (D 94, M 185). Était-elle connue de madame d'Épinay dès l'épisode de 1760? et est-ce donc elle qui eut l'idée de se servir de cette femme pour recevoir les lettres de monsieur de Croismare? C'est ce qu'on est en droit de se demander, mais non pas d'affirmer. Par une des nombreuses personnes qui fréquentaient chez madame d'Épinay, d'abord à la Briche, puis à la Chevrette, l'amie de Grimm et de Diderot était, en effet, en principe bien placée pour avoir entendu parler de cette femme qui habitait seule à Versailles, qui devait avoir la réputation d'être une personne serviable et de confiance et à qui on pouvait donc s'adresser pour un service discret.

Il convient peut-être de faire observer ici qu'à part madame d'Épinay, une autre femme joua, elle aussi, un rôle dans cette affaire, et que, tant qu'on ne l'aura pas identifiée, on devra se demander si ce n'est pas elle qui fit connaître madame Madin aux amis de monsieur de Croismare. Grimm note, en effet, après avoir transcrit le premier "Billet de la Religieuse": "Ce billet était écrit de la main d'une jeune personne dont nous nous servîmes pendant tout le cours de cette correspondance" (D 48, M 182). Et l'auteur du compte rendu paru dans la *Décade philosophique* du 21 octobre 1796 renchérit, sans qu'on puisse vérifier le bien fondé de son assertion: "Les lettres de la Religieuse et celles de madame Madin [. . .] étaient recopiées par deux femmes leurs complices."[19]

Il est probable en tout cas que le nom et la réputation de madame Madin parvinrent aux oreilles de Diderot et de ses amis par l'entremise d'une personne à qui elle avait rendu service. On songe, par exemple, à la marquise d'Havrincourt et à sa famille qui étaient tous gens très en vue à Paris. De toute évidence madame Madin avait été l'objet d'une dette de gratitude de la part de la mère de celle-ci, la comtesse de Gergy. Or le mari de cette dernière, Jacques Vincent Languet, comte de Gergy appartenait à une famille connue et nombreuse et avait eu en particulier deux célèbres frères cadets: Jean-Baptiste (1675–1750) qui avait été curé de Saint-Sulpice de 1715 à 1748 et avait alors présidé aux travaux de construction et de décoration de l'église telle que nous la connaissons; et Jean-Joseph (1678–1753), prélat de renom, défenseur de la Bulle *Unigenitus*, membre de l'Académie française et archevêque de Sens. Diderot emménagea trop tard dans la paroisse Saint-Sulpice pour avoir avec le curé Languet de Gergy les démêlés qu'il avait eus un peu plus tôt avec le curé de Saint-Médard; mais il le connut assez bien, tout au moins par réputation, pour en dire le plus grand mal. En effet, lorsqu'il vit sa statue sculptée par René Michel Slodtz au Salon de 1765, il se déclara partagé entre son admiration pour le travail du sculpteur et son aversion pour le défunt curé, "le plus grand charlatan de son état et de son siècle. La tête en est de toute beauté, et le marbre demande sublimement à Dieu pardon de toutes les friponneries de l'homme."[20]

Bref, il ne devait pas manquer à Paris ou à Versailles de connaissances communes entre l'humble madame Madin et les cercles que fréquentait Diderot. Mais, dans l'état actuel des connaissances, on ne peut pas identifier avec certitude la personne qui mit les amis du marquis de Croismare en contact avec la femme de l'ancien capitaine au régiment de Lorraine.

Ce qui est sûr, en revanche, c'est qu'ils la connurent assez bien. On remarque, en effet, dans la *Préface-annexe* que les lettres qu'elle est censée avoir écrites sont toutes signées du double nom "Moreau Madin," qui est bien la signature qu'on trouve au bas des actes notariés signés par la véritable ma-

265

dame Madin. On imagine que Diderot, Grimm ou madame d'Épinay avaient sans doute reçu d'elle des lettres signées de la sorte. Du reste, les lettres écrites par la pseudo-madame Madin s'harmonisent dans l'ensemble fort bien avec le personnage authentique tel que nous pouvons le reconstituer aujourd'hui. Un exemple suffira: dans la "Lettre ostensible" du 16 février 1760, Diderot fait dire à madame Madin qu'elle n'hésiterait pas à engager elle-même Suzanne Simonin comme gouvernante, si celle-ci n'était pas obligée de quitter la région parisienne. Or, ce que nous savons de la vraie madame Madin, de ses ressources et de sa manière de vivre rend vraisemblable un pareil train de maison.

En revanche, Diderot et ses amis semblent avoir été moins bien renseignés sur la famille de madame Madin. En effet, dans cette même "Lettre ostensible," Diderot lui fait dire: "J'ai deux filles" (D 104, M 189), affirmation reprise implicitement dans la lettre du 13 avril où le personnage parle de "la plus jeune de mes filles" (D 129, M 199), alors que la vraie madame Madin n'eut jamais, à ce qu'on sache, qu'une seule fille, dont on n'est même pas sûr qu'elle habitât encore avec elle à Versailles en 1760. De plus, dans cette même lettre du 13 avril, la pseudo-madame Madin se dit veuve—"Quand je perdis M. Madin, tous les médecins m'assuraient qu'il en reviendrait" (D 133, M 201)—alors que, nous l'avons vu, Jean Madin était encore en vie près de vingt ans plus tard, lors de la mort de sa femme. Il n'est pas impossible, toutefois, que, vivant séparée de son mari pour des raisons qui nous échappent, situation qui n'était sûrement pas fréquente à l'époque dans son milieu social, madame Madin ait passé pour veuve aux yeux des gens qui ne la connaissaient pas intimement. Il n'est pas même impossible qu'elle ait encouragé cette erreur qui lui évitait des explications peut-être embarrassantes. On observe, par exemple, que le clerc du notaire Barat qui écrivit l'inventaire après décès du 12 avril 1779 qui nous a été conservé (voir ci-dessous note 15) donne pour titre abrégé à ce document: "Inventaire de Dame Michele Moreau veuve du sieur Madin." Il convient donc de ne pas trop faire fonds sur ce genre de preuves internes, tant qu'on n'en saura pas davantage sur l'authentique madame Madin.

On en vient même à se demander si le peu que nous savons de sûr au sujet de ce personnage suffit à justifier l'étude qui précède et les recherches sur lesquelles elle est fondée. Autrement dit, un travail strictement historique comme celui-ci, surtout lorsqu'il n'aboutit qu'à des résultats fragmentaires comme c'est le cas, ajoute-t-il vraiment à la connaissance qu'on a de l'œuvre littéraire qui lui a servi de point de départ, ou n'a-t-il pour principale fonction que de flatter la manie de l'amateur de vieux papiers qui s'y livre? Nous sommes trop évidemment juge et partie pour trancher la question et en tirer des considérations applicables à d'autres cas. Bornons-nous donc à remarquer en manière de conclusion que, lorsqu'il s'agit de bien des romans, et surtout lorsqu'il s'agit de ceux de Diderot et en tout cas de *La Religieuse*, la question du mélange du réel et de l'imaginaire se pose de façon à la fois très pressante et très évidente. Or, comme on le sait aujourd'hui, la *Préface-annexe* de ce roman, qui était à l'origine un récit anecdotique autonome, fondé sur la réalité historique et destiné à divertir les lecteurs de la *Correspondance littéraire*, devint plus tard, de par la volonté même de Diderot, qui n'en était pourtant pas l'auteur exclusif, une partie intégrante du roman. De ce fait, le dosage de la vérité et de l'invention se pose à son propos comme elle se pose à propos du roman auquel elle est annexée.

Dans la *Préface-annexe* deux personnages écrivent au marquis de Croismare afin de le mystifier: celui qui signe Suzanne Simonin et celui qui signe Moreau Madin. De même qu'on sait depuis longtemps que le premier repose en partie sur un être authentique qui s'appelait Marguerite Delamarre, de même il n'est pas sans intérêt de savoir désormais que le second repose sur un être non moins authentique, plus même peut-être en ce qu'il ne se dissimule pas, comme celui de la religieuse, derrière un pseudonyme. Et pourtant ce person-

267

nage n'en est pas moins imaginaire pour cela, puisque la vraie madame Madin "ne savait rien [. . .] des lettres que nous lui fîmes écrire à elle-même."

Autrement dit, le marquis de Croismare n'est pas le seul à être en danger de se tromper ou d'être trompé. Lorsque Grimm raconta l'histoire de sa mystification aux lecteurs de la *Correspondance littéraire* en 1770, ceux-ci aussi furent victimes d'une "insigne fourberie," s'ils prirent pour parole d'Évangile, ainsi qu'ils étaient invités à le faire, l'aventure telle que la leur présentait un récit qui n'était exempt ni d'inexactitudes, ni de faits controuvés: le nom de l'héroïne, l'affirmation que le roman de Diderot "n'a jamais existé que par lambeaux," etc. Enfin le lecteur moderne de *La Religieuse* et de la *Préface-annexe*, celui auquel Diderot s'adresse dès 1780-82 alors qu'il révise, remanie et récrit l'une et l'autre, est à son tour mystifié en bien des cas et surtout si, ajoutant trop foi aux dires de la *Préface-annexe*, il prend pour pure imagination le récit autobiographique de sœur Suzanne.

Même donc si Diderot n'avait pas écrit *Les Deux amis de Bourbonne* et surtout *Jacques le fataliste et son maître*, dans lesquels la question des rapports ambigus du roman avec la réalité est reprise et approfondie, on saurait par le seul exemple de *La Religieuse* et de sa *Préface-annexe* que pour lui tout roman résulte d'un jeu complexe et subtil entre le réel et l'imaginaire et participe donc nécessairement de la mystification.[21] Or, comme celle-ci s'exerce, on l'a vu, à plus d'un niveau et avec plus d'un degré de subtilité, afin de ne pas être à notre tour victimes de l'un en voulant éviter l'autre, la meilleure planche de salut semble bien être d'essayer de cerner avec autant de précision et de certitude que possible la vérité historique à partir de laquelle s'est exercée l'imagination du romancier. C'est en tout cas ce que nous nous sommes efforcé de faire ici à propos d'un élément soigneusement circonscrit de cette réalité. Nous n'avons donc aucunement l'illusion d'avoir résolu le problème du vrai et du faux qui gît au cœur même du phénomène de création littéraire qui donna naissance à *La Religieuse* et à sa *Préface-annexe*. Tout au plus avons-nous peut-être réussi à le poser avec un peu plus de précision.

1. D 46. Tel est l'état le plus ancien du texte, originellement de la main de Grimm et qui fut ensuite corrigé, au moins à deux reprises par Diderot. Voici le dernier état résultant de ces corrections: "Vous voudrez bien vous souvenir que les lettres signées Madin, ou Suzanne Simonin ont été fabriquées par cet enfant de Bélial, et que toutes les lettres du généreux protecteur de la recluse sont véritables et ont été écrites de bonne foi" (D 86, M 181-182). Le sigle D renvoie à l'édition de la *Préface-annexe* donnée par Herbert Dieckmann (*Diderot Studies* 2 (1952); et le sigle M à l'édition de *La Religieuse* et de la *Préface-annexe* donnée par Robert Mauzi ("Bibliothèque de Cluny," [Paris: Colin, 1961]). L'orthographe a été normalisée. Les recherches dont les résultats sont présentés ici furent entreprises pendant la préparation de l'édition de *La Religieuse* qui doit paraître dans les *Œuvres complètes de Diderot*, t.XI (Paris: Hermann, 1975).

2. A un moment donné l'immeuble occupa les numéros 5 et 7, selon J.-A. Le Roi, *Histoire de Versailles* (Versailles: Oswald, 1868), 2:355.

3. "Convention Jean Madin Michelle Moreau," reçue le 28 février 1758 par Me François-Louis Robineau, notaire à Paris. Minutier central des notaires de Paris, étude XXVII, liasse 286. Nous tenons à exprimer ici notre reconnaissance envers Me André Lamé, notaire à Paris, qui nous a autorisé à consulter ce document reçu par son prédécesseur.

4. "Testament Michelle Moreau femme de sieur Jean Madin," reçu le 15 mars 1779 par Me Barat, notaire à Versailles, Archives départementales des Yvelines et de l'ancien départment de Seine-&-Oise. Étude Gayot. Au cours des recherches dont nous donnons les résultats ici et dont une grande partie eut lieu en ce dépôt d'archives de Versailles, nous avons reçu de la part des archivistes et conservateurs un accueil d'une grande amabilité et des conseils précieux. Nous tenons à exprimer ici notre reconnaissance particulière envers monsieur Marcel Delafosse, Directeur des services d'archives des Yvelines, et envers monsieur Pierre Lions, Adjoint d'archives.

5. "Registre des sépultures de la paroisse royale de Saint-Louis de Versailles pour 1779," Archives des Yvelines.

6. Procuration reçue le 15 mai 1780 par Me Henry Viguier, notaire à Besançon, dont la minute est annexée aux "Quittance et constitution" reçues le 31 juillet 1780 par Me Jean Maupas, notaire à Paris. Minutier central des notaires de Paris, étude CI, liasse 646. Nous tenons à exprimer ici notre reconnaissance envers Me Pierre Huas, notaire à Paris, qui nous a autorisé à consulter ce document reçu par son prédécesseur.

7. Ce contrat de rente de 1744 n'a malheureusement pas pu être retrouvé, la plupart des minutes de l'étude Archeret de Besançon ayant disparu. Nous tenons à exprimer ici notre reconnaissance envers monsieur Jean Courtieu, Directeur des services d'archives du Doubs, qui a bien voulu répondre à nos questions à ce sujet.

8. Ces registres ont été aimablement dépouillés pour nous par madame

O. Paris, Bibliothécaire de la Bibliothèque municipale de la Ville de Besançon, à qui nous tenons à exprimer ici notre reconnaissance.

9. Les archives d'état-civil de Paris ayant été détruites lors de l'incendie du Palais des Tuileries en 1871, il n'a pas été possible de retrouver d'autres traces de ce mariage. La reconstitution partielle de l'état-civil de Paris, disponible aux Archives de la Seine, est muette sur le compte des Madin. En l'absence d'un contrat de mariage dont la minute aurait pu être retrouvée au Minutier central des notaires de Paris, on ne semble pas pouvoir aller plus loin.

10. "Tableau des officiers qui composent le Régiment de Lorraine avec les dates de leurs commissions et lettres et celles de leurs réceptions, du 15 janvier 1735." Services historiques de l'Armée. Château de Vincennes. Xb6 (carton: Régiment d'infanterie de Lorraine).

11. Services historiques de l'Armée, Yb85, 86, 87 et 88.

12. La minute de cette procuration est annexée à l'inventaire après décès de madame Madin. Voir ci-dessous note 15.

13. Nous tenons à exprimer ici notre reconnaissance envers monsieur Bernard Lemée, Directeur des services d'archives de la Meuse, comme envers les services de la Mairie de Verdun des recherches qu'ils ont bien voulu entreprendre à notre demande sur Jean Madin et qui sont malheureusement demeurés infructueuses.

14. "Compte d'exécution testamentaire Madin," reçu le 30 août 1780 par Me Barat, notaire à Versailles. Archives des Yvelines, étude Gayot.

15. "Inventaire de Dame Michele Moreau veuve du sieur Madin," reçu le 12 avril 1779 par Me Barat, notaire à Versailles. Archives des Yvelines, étude Gayot.

16. "Constitution viagère," reçue le 29 novembre 1775 par Me Jean-Louis Bro, notaire à Paris. Minutier central des notaires de Paris, étude XCII, liasse 775. Nous tenons à exprimer ici notre reconnaissance envers Me Dominique Fontana, notaire à Paris, qui nous a autorisé à consulter ce document reçu par son prédécesseur.

17. Apanage d'Artois. R^1 304: emprunts; états des rentiers de la Maison d'Artois—XVIIIe siècle; R^1 306; relevé des traitements, gratifications annuelles, pensions (1773-87); R^1 375: état des maisons de Mgr. le comte d'Artois, de Mme la comtesse d'Artois, de Mgr. le duc d'Angoulême (1774-78). Maison du Roi. O^1 3744: Maison du Dauphin, fils de Louis XV; gages continués après son enfance ou depuis sa mort (1762-79); O^1 3771: états des gages du personnel (1766-74); O^1 682-83: pensions (Mab-Mu): O^1 637: état des pensions (1768-78); O^1 638: autre état analogue (1764-80); O^1 3922: titres de propriété, vente, échange (Clagny); et cartons mentionnés à la note suivante.

18. Maison du Roi. O^1 3715: maison des Enfants de France (1760-79); O^1 3786: maison du comte et de la comtesse d'Artois (1759-89).

19. Cité par J. Th. de Booy et Alan J. Freer, *"Jacques le fataliste" et "La Religieuse" devant la critique révolutionnaire (1796-1800)*, SVEC 23 (1965): 124.

20. Diderot, *Œuvres complètes*, ed. Assézat et Tourneux, 10:440.

21. Sur le goût de Diderot pour la mystification et notamment dans *La Religieuse*, on pourra consulter, outre les introductions aux éditions de *Mystification*, notamment celles de Jacques Proust et de Herbert Dieckmann,

les ouvrages suivants: Roger Kempf, *Diderot et le roman* (Paris: Le Seuil, 1964), pp. 212-22; Jean Mayer, "Le thème de la tromperie chez Diderot. *Vivat Mascarillus fourbum imperator,*" dans *Roman et Lumières* (Paris: Éditions sociales, 1970), pp. 321-30; Jean Catrysse, *Diderot et la mystification* (Paris: Nizet, 1970); et Jacques Chouillet, *La Formation de l'esthétique de Diderot* (Paris: Colin, 1973), pp. 495 et ss.

Subterfuges et stratagèmes, ou
les romanciers malgré eux

Les études sur le roman du dix-huitième siècle connaissent depuis une dizaine d'années surtout un renouveau impressionnant ainsi qu'en témoignent les beaux travaux de Henri Coulet, de Georges May et de Vivienne Mylne, la série des grandes thèses récentes, comme celles de Roger Laufer, Jean-Louis Lecercle, Charles Porter, Jean Sgard, Jacques Van den Heuvel et Laurent Versini et enfin le chapitre consacré au roman dans le Supplément à la bibliographie de Cabeen, chapitre qui, par le nombre et l'importance des notices qu'il contient, est l'un des plus riches du volume.

Dans la majorité de ces études, la part du lion est faite aux chefs-d'œuvre reconnus du genre, ainsi qu'à l'opinion des grands romanciers et au jugement des critiques contemporains. Ce qui est parfaitement raisonnable et d'ordre pratique aussi, car les œuvres des romanciers mineurs ne sont pas toujours facilement accessibles aux chercheurs. Préparant, depuis plusieurs années déjà, un complément à l'inventaire de S. Paul Jones pour les romans parus entre 1751 et 1804, j'ai eu l'occasion de consulter des milliers de romans de toute sorte et de lire, en particulier, les innombrables avant-propos, préfaces, introductions et autres pièces liminaires qui les accompagnaient. Aussi aimerais-je essayer de tracer ici un aperçu rapide des tendances générales et des attitudes les plus communes à la multitude de ceux qui pratiquent le roman avec un zèle et un enthousiasme inlassables dans la seconde

273

moitié du siècle. Les voix que nous allons entendre ne seront pas celles des virtuoses si bien connus, mais celles des romanciers de deuxième, de troisième, de dernier ordre et des anonymes de tout calibre.

Dans son *Dilemme du roman au XVIIIe siècle*, Georges May a admirablement montré combien le roman avait eu la vie dure—notamment entre 1715 et 1760—et comment, à un certain moment, il avait même été menacé d'extinction. Si les attaques, généralement conjuguées au nom de la morale et de la vraisemblance, deviennent de moins en moins virulentes dans la seconde moitié du siècle, la méfiance des âmes bien pensantes et des autorités civiles et religieuses à l'égard de ce genre pernicieux ne semble pas se relâcher tout à fait. Et, malgré l'immense succès de *La Nouvelle Héloïse*, le roman est loin de partager le prestige dont jouissent les genres dits nobles. Il n'est donc pas surprenant que les malheureux romanciers, ne sachant plus à quel saint se vouer, continuent à recourir à toutes sortes de subterfuges et tours de passe-passe. En fait, ils adoptent et perfectionnent avec une ingéniosité incomparable les procédés dont avaient fait usage leurs confrères ès romans depuis plus d'un siècle et ceci jusqu'en 1804, date terminale de mon enquête.

Puisque l'anathème a été jeté sur le roman, plusieurs alternatives se présentent aux romanciers et la première, d'où vont découler toutes les autres, consiste à renier tout simplement la paternité de leurs propres ouvrages. Le nombre des romans publiés de manière anonyme va sans cesse croissant. Après tout, peu d'écrivains peuvent se targuer, comme Baculard d'Arnaud par exemple, de la protection que confèrent l'approbation et le privilège royal. Fortifié sans doute par cette double bénédiction, ce dernier a fait imprimer sa modeste devise, "Je ne dois qu'à moi-même toute ma renommée," sur la page de titre de ses innombrables rhapsodies.

Le culte de l'anonymat amène ces écrivains à des prodiges d'invention. Nul n'est auteur, tous deviennent éditeurs et les manuscrits tombent miraculeusement entre leurs mains tout

comme la manne du Seigneur. L'époque où une simple mystification suffisait est révolue. On ne se contente plus de recevoir
les manuscrits des mains d'un ami expirant ou de les trouver
commodément dans quelque vieux bahut ou bibliothèque.
Même si une bibliothèque est invoquée, elle se trouve placée
dans une position éminemment stratégique et partant béné-
fique. Ainsi les lettres qui composent *Eugénie de Monclare*
ont été trouvées dans un "secrétaire placé à proximité de la
bibliothèque d'un château."[1] Les voyages sont, comme on le
sait, aussi instructifs que productifs et Mailhol, l'auteur du roman intitulé *Les Bonnets, ou Talemik et Zinera*, déclare en
avoir acquis le manuscrit au cours de ses voyages "dans une
île mystérieuse,"[2] tandis que celui de *Cléomène*[3] a été trouvé
chez les caloyers du Mont-Athos. Certains de ces prétendus
éditeurs font même preuve d'un manque de délicatesse insigne: celui de la *Correspondance d'un jeune militaire, ou Mémoires du marquis de Lusigni et d'Hortense de Saint-Just*[4]
avoue avoir trouvé les lettres dans le portefeuille d'un ami, et
l'éditeur du *Cabriolet*[5] transcrit tout simplement le manuscrit en question pendant que le véritable auteur est à l'opéra.
D'autres éditeurs-romanciers prennent franchement le parti
de la plaisanterie, comme Louet de Chaumont, qui nous fait
savoir qu'il a lu le manuscrit de l'histoire qu'il publie en rêve
et qu'il s'est contenté de le transcrire de mémoire à son réveil![6]
Ces quelques exemples de ruse sont relativement simples.
Un certain nombre d'auteurs, cependant, poussent le jeu si
loin qu'ils finissent par échafauder de véritables romans pour
expliquer l'origine des romans mêmes qu'ils sont en train de
publier. Il en est un si cocasse et si ridicule qu'il mérite d'être
rappelé en détail. Voici donc l'histoire du manuscrit de
L'Aventurier chinois.[7] Lors d'un séjour à Pékin un libraire
européen traduit le manuscrit en français. Il quitte Pékin et
va à Alexandrie où il achète une momie qu'il enveloppe des
feuilles de sa traduction avant de l'expédier à Paris. La momie
est confisquée par les commis qui gardent les portes de la capitale. Ne connaissant pas les momies, ils décident que celui

à qui elle appartient soit appréhendé comme assassin. La momie est envoyée à la morgue. Le malheureux libraire vient pour la réclamer et est arrêté. Il parvient à obtenir sa liberté, des dédommagements et sa momie. Pendant ce temps, les feuilles de sa traduction courent le monde et retournent en Chine dans un vaisseau de la Compagnie des Indes où elles servent à envelopper de petites miniatures indécentes. L'infortuné libraire retourne à Pékin, y voit ses feuilles imprimées, les revendique et les rapporte en Europe. Il peut enfin les publier! Des centaines et des centaines de préfaces et avertissements racontent les multiples variations de la même histoire monotone.

Cependant, quels que soient les moyens par lesquels ces manuscrits sont tombés entre les mains de leurs "éditeurs," les histoires qu'ils racontent sont évidemment toujours vraies. Ce ne sont que "mémoires vrais," "histoires véritables" dans lesquels le lecteur chercherait "en vain un roman" car, comme tout le monde le sait, "la vérité est au-dessus de la fiction."[8] Les abus amènent nécessairement la plaisanterie et ainsi un auteur facétieux intitule son roman: *Le Véridique, ou Mémoires de Fillerville, histoire véritable, par un menteur*.[9]

Ces histoires qui sont toujours vraies sont aussi le plus souvent traduites d'une langue étrangère, ce qui leur confère une garantie d'authenticité de plus. Dans la seconde moitié du siècle, le nombre des "traductions" s'accroît de manière vertigineuse. L'horizon linguistique et géographique s'étend en conséquence et côte à côte avec des histoires "traduites" de l'allemand, du portugais, de l'espagnol, de l'italien, sans parler du latin et du grec, on trouve des contes phrygiens, mongols, babyloniens, des traductions de l'égyptien, du chaldéen, du syrien, de l'éthiopien et même une histoire orientale traduite de la langue malabare![10] Tout ce qui n'est pas français étant naturellement plus apprécié, deux auteurs, Dujardin et Sellius, n'hésitent pas à intituler une de leurs coproductions: *La Double Beauté, roman étranger*.[11] Mais le nombre de ces traductions supposées n'est rien en comparaison à l'avalanche des imitations ou prétendues traductions de romans anglais. Rappelons que l'invasion du roman anglais qui commence peu après 1750 ira sans cesse croissant jusqu'à la fin du siècle. La grande difficulté consiste justement à distinguer les véritables traductions de celles qui sont données pour telles. Harold Wade Streeter s'était heurté à ce problème délicat lorsqu'il avait établi sa bibliographie des traductions de romans anglais du dix-huitième siècle. Le problème, déjà compliqué par le fait que les originaux anglais sont aussi très souvent anonymes et par conséquent difficiles à trouver, est aggravé outre mesure par la désinvolture désarmante qu'affichent les soi-disant traducteurs. Deux ou trois exemples suffisent pour nous donner une idée de l'étonnante liberté avec laquelle ils accomplissent leur tâche. "Suivant ma coutume," avoue l'un d'eux, "je n'ai rien retranché, mais j'ai changé tout ce qui m'a déplu."[12] Car ces traducteurs-apprentis sont d'accord pour trouver un manque de goût et de délicatesse insignes chez les nations étrangères et notamment chez leurs voisins d'Outre-Manche, ce qui excuse évidemment tous les changements et toutes les mutilations qu'ils effectuent. Certains de ces traducteurs ont parfois la bonne grâce de reconnaître qu'ils sont peut-être sortis des limites permises, et l'un d'eux a même l'obligeance de prévenir le lecteur, soit par honnêteté professionnelle, soit par orgueil d'auteur débutant: "La traduction finit à la page 142, j'ai composé le reste car le peu que j'ai pris de l'anglais ne vaut pas la peine d'en parler."[13] Dans les deux mille cinq cent romans et quelques que j'ai examinés, un sur trois et peut-être même davantage était une *imitation* ou une *traduction* de l'anglais. Cependant dans le concert quasi harmonieux de l'anglomanie, quelques voix dissidentes se font entendre. Ainsi l'auteur anonyme d'un curieux petit roman intitulé *De Langres et Juliette d'Est . . . anecdote française*, dénonce l'esprit moutonnier de ses compatriotes et proclame, non sans fierté, son indépendance:

> Intimement persuadé qu'on lit peu d'Avertissements, je n'en aurais point fait; mais je n'ai pu résister à l'envie de dire que ce petit ouvrage n'a été composé que pour faire diversion à

la manie de la plupart de ceux qui se mêlent à présent d'écrire dans le même genre. En effet, je ne sais quelle fureur les possède d'aller prendre tous leurs sujets chez une nation étrangère. On ne voit qu'*Imité de l'Anglais, Pris de l'Anglais, Traduit de l'Anglais, Histoire Anglaise, Anecdote Anglaise,* etc., etc. Le Français, si souvent original, veut être le singe de l'Angleterre. On s'habille, on veut penser *à l'Anglaise.* Il ne manque plus que de parler la langue britannique. Au reste, ce serait user de représailles. On sait qu'il fut un temps où les habitants de l'île de ce nom, se firent un point d'honneur de ne se servir que de la nôtre. Quoiqu'il en soit, je suis Français, j'ai puisé dans l'histoire de mon pays, et j'ai cru bien faire.[14]

L'anonymat et les traductions supposées assurent une certaine protection aux romanciers-caméléons—ils peuvent même être parfois des garanties de succès—mais ils ne suffisent pas à déjouer la vigilance de l'autorité. Car si les attaques au nom de l'invraisemblance sont en voie de disparition, les condamnations pour cause d'immoralité semblent toujours subsister. Parallèlement, on peut constater que l'on écrit de moins en moins de romans d'aventure, tandis que le nombre des romans de mœurs ou d'analyse psychologique va augmentant. La teneur des approbations qui ont été accordées à quelques rares romans de cette période permet de se faire une idée de la position officielle. Au lieu de la formule traditionnelle: "J'ai lu par ordre de Monseigneur le Chancelier un manuscrit intitulé . . . , et je n'y ai rien trouvé qui m'ait paru devoir en empêcher l'impression," nous lisons par exemple: "Le petit roman qui y est joint est rempli de bons conseils pour les jeunes gens, surtout pour les militaires. On y fait l'éloge de l'Ordre hors duquel tout est mal, et dans lequel tout est bien."[15] On ne saurait s'exprimer plus clairement. Il n'est donc pas surprenant que, si quelques auteurs avouent écrire pour le plaisir et l'amusement du lecteur, la majorité prétende le faire pour son éducation et son édification. Les temps sont corrompus, les mœurs relâchées, la vertu est sans cesse bafouée et le libertinage règne partout en maître. On présentera donc aux hommes le miroir de la vérité, on leur montrera les défauts et les ridicules du siècle ainsi que la meilleure façon de s'en corriger. Voilà les raisons le plus souvent invoquées. Hors du roman, point de salut. A en croire ces prédicateurs zélés, chacun de ces romans ne serait qu'un traité de morale mise en action, destiné à ranimer chez les lecteurs sensibles "le feu sacré de la vertu." Somme toute, ils prétendent faire œuvre d'utilité publique. L'un veut "mettre les jeunes personnes en garde contre le danger d'une correspondance secrète"—il écrit pour cela un roman par lettres—et "il s'estimerait trop heureux s'il pouvait arracher une seule victime des mains des infâmes séducteurs qui se font un jeu de porter le trouble et le déshonneur au sein des familles les plus respectables."[16] La popularité du roman épistolaire due à l'influence de Richardson d'abord, puis à celle de *La Nouvelle Héloïse* n'est plus à redire. Un autre, conscient de son devoir, exprime sa pensée avec la rigueur d'un théorème mathématique: "Peindre les mœurs, faire aimer les bonnes et donner de l'horreur pour les mauvaises. Tel est le devoir d'un écrivain, malheur à qui ne le remplit pas."[17] A la lecture de centaines de professions de foi de ce genre on ne peut s'empêcher de songer à la définition facétieuse de la Miss Prism d'Oscar Wilde: "The good ended happily, and the bad unhappily. That is what Fiction means."

Indépendemment des déclarations que l'on trouve dans les préfaces et avertissements, les titres seuls des romans sont révélateurs des préoccupations hautement moralisatrices des romanciers. Il serait difficile d'imaginer une liste plus austère et plus affligeante. Ce ne sont que dangers, désordres, écarts, écueils, égarements, erreurs, imprudences, inconstances, infortunes et malheurs qui semblent guetter les pauvres humains à chaque pas de leur triste existence. Ces termes reviennent avec une fréquence remarquable dans les titres des romans de la seconde moitié du siècle. Une petite comparaison avec la liste des romans établie par S. Paul Jones paraît intéressante. A titre d'exemple nous pouvons choisir le mot *danger*. Il ne figure dans aucun titre principal de la première moitié du siècle, tandis que dans la seconde, nous rencontrons des dangers de toutes les sortes possibles et imaginables. Au singulier d'abord:

> *Le Danger d'aimer un étranger*[18]
> *Le Danger d'une première faute*[19]
> *Le Danger de la satire*[20]
> *Le Danger des circonstances*[21]
> *Le Danger des liaisons*[22]
> *Le Danger des passions*[23]
> *Le Danger des préjugés*[24]

et au pluriel:

> *Les Dangers d'un amour illicite*[25]
> *Les Dangers d'un premier choix*[26]
> *Les Dangers de l'amour*[27]
> *Les Dangers de la calomnie*[28]
> *Les Dangers de la coquetterie*[29]
> *Les Dangers des correspondances*[30]
> *Les Dangers de la séduction*[31]
> *Les Dangers des spectacles*[32]
> *Les Dangers de la sympathie*[33]

et aussi:

> *Fanny de Varicourt, ou le Danger des soupçons*[34]
> *Aldouzin, ou les Dangers d'une mauvaise éducation*[35]
> *Alphonsine, ou les Dangers du grand monde*[36]

et encore:

> *L'Amitié dangereuse*[37]

sans oublier:

> *Le Paysan et la Paysanne pervertis, ou les Dangers de la ville*

280

et bien entendu:

Les Liaisons dangereuses!

Certes, le censeur le plus sévère aurait eu mauvaise grâce de condamner des ouvrages aussi édifiants, en apparence du moins. Car, en réalité, toutes ces protestations ne sont qu'un prétexte, qu'une ruse de plus qu'emploient les romanciers dans leurs efforts de se protéger des attaques d'immoralité et afin de pouvoir faire de la peinture des mœurs, aussi basses qu'elles soient, le sujet de leurs romans. Ici, comme ailleurs, la pratique dégénère et certains titres frisent le ridicule. Les libertins devenus vertueux et les courtisanes converties deviennent monnaie courante, preuve sans doute de la vertu purificatrice de ces romans. L'Abbé Dulaurens se moque franchement et joyeusement de tous ces abus en présentant son roman facétieux et galant, *Je Suis Pucelle*,[38] comme étant hautement moral.

Ces observations rapides sont évidemment purement descriptives et ne prétendent nullement à être qualitatives. J'ai tout simplement voulu relever les moyens de défense généralement pratiqués par les romanciers de la seconde moitié du siècle et dont il est peut-être permis de dégager quelques conclusions. Si les auteurs continuent à déployer toutes sortes de réflexes défensifs, cela signifie que le roman est loin d'être intégré de bonne grâce dans la cité littéraire aussi bien que dans la vie civile. S. Paul Jones a trouvé, par exemple, que le terme *roman* est employé quatre ou cinq fois seulement dans les titres de la première moitié du siècle. Le chiffre n'est pas sensiblement plus élevé dans la seconde, exception faite, bien sûr, des nombreux *contes* et *romans moraux*. D'autre part, cependant, les mesures prohibitives quelles qu'elles soient n'arrêtent nullement la production romanesque qui va s'accélérant. Ainsi, pour la période 1700-1750, S. Paul Jones avait dénombré 946 titres, mon compte pour les cinquante années qui suivent est trois fois plus élevé. Enfin, alors qu'au dix-septième siecle et durant la majeure partie du dix-huitième, le roman est considéré comme un genre roturier, bâtard, il est néanmoins réservé à un public essentiellement aristocratique. Par un mouvement de retournement, plus il conquiert ses droits, bien lentement il est vrai, plus il devient populaire et à la veille de la Révolution, le roman comme le théâtre connaît un succès sans précédent.

Dans les années à venir les chercheurs vont certainement faire de belles découvertes et révéler des romans de valeur injustement oubliés. Mais la majorité de ceux que j'ai eu l'occasion de lire me font songer à l'avis de Voltaire: ". . . pour faire œuvre parfait,/Il faudrait se donner au diable." Soucieux sans doute de leur propre salut comme de celui de leurs lecteurs, nos auteurs s'en sont apparemment bien gardés.

1.   Madame Moylin-Fleury, *Eugénie de Monclare, ou l'Histoire de la mère et de la fille, par C. M.* (Paris: Lavillette et Compagnie, 1801), p. 3.

2.   Gabriel Mailhol, *Les Bonnets, ou Talemik et Zinera* (Londres et Paris: J. F. Quillau, 1765), p. vii.

3.   Anon., *Cléomène, ou Tableau abrégé des passions, extrait d'un manuscrit trouvé chez les caloyers du Mont Athos* (Paris: Imprimerie de Monsieur, 1785).

4.   Louis-Alexandre-Marie de Musset ou Jean-François de Bourgoing, *Correspondance d'un jeune militaire, ou Mémoires du marquis de Lusigni et d'Hortense de Saint-Just*, 2 vols. (Yverdun et Paris: chez l'Auteur, 1778), 1:4.

5.   Gabriel Mailhol, *Le Cabriolet* (Amsterdam: Marc-Michel Rey, 1755), p. vi.

6.   Louet de Chaumont, *L'Amour et les Français, histoire héroïque et galante des Amazones* (Paris: Pigoreau, 1803), p. 4.

7.   Anon., *L'Aventurier chinois* (Pékin et Paris: Mérigot le jeune, 1773), pp. i–ii.

8.   Anon., *La Fille trouvée, ou la Sympathie paternelle* (Liège: D. de Boubers, 1776), p. 3.

9.   Jean-Henri Marchand, *Le Véridique, ou Mémoires de Fillerville, histoire véritable, par un menteur*, 2 parties. (Amsterdam: Changuion; Paris: Lejay, 1769).

10.   Antoine-Etienne-Nicolas Fantin-Desodoard, *Ander-Can, Raja de Brampour, et Padmani, histoire orientale, traduite de la langue malabare*, 3 vols. (Brampour et Paris: Briand, 1788).

11.   Bénigne Dujardin et Godefroy Sellius, *La Double Beauté, roman étranger* (Cantorbéry, 1769).

12. Madame de Montolieu, *Le Fils d'adoption, ou Amour et coquetterie*, traduction libre de l'allemand, 3 vols. (Paris: Debrai, an XII), p. iii.

13. F. J. Moreau, *Caroline de Montmorenci*, ouvrage en partie traduit de l'anglais (Tours et Paris: Debrai, an X), p. 4.

14. Anon., *De Langres et Juliette d'Est* . . . *anecdote française* (Londres et Paris: F. G. Deschamps, 1771), pp. v–vii.

15. Approbation de: *Les Derniers Adieux de la Maréchale de *** à ses enfants* par Louis-Antoine de Caraccioli (Paris: Bailly, 1769), p. 392.

16. T. F. A. d'Aymery, *Les Dangers des correspondances*, 2 vols. (Paris: Caillot, An X), p. vi.

17. Gatrey, *La Philosophe par amour, ou Lettres de deux amans passionnés et vertueux*, 2 vols. (Paris: Cailleau, 1765), p. ix.

18. Witart de Bézu, *Le Danger d'aimer un étranger, ou Histoire de milady Chester et d'un duc français*, 2 vols. (Londres: T. Hookham; Paris: Veuve Duchesne, 1783).

19. J. H. D. Briel, *Le Danger d'une première faute, histoire angloise* (Londres et Paris: Couturier, 1784).

20. Abbé de Sancy[?], *Le Danger de la satire, ou la Vie de Nicolo-Franco, poëte satirique italien* (Paris: Les Frères de Bure, 1778).

21. Pierre-Jean-Baptiste Nougaret, *Le Danger des circonstances, ou Lettres du chevalier de Joinville et de mademoiselle d'Arans* . . . , 4 vols. (Bruxelles et Paris: Defer de Maisonneuve, 1789).

22. Marquise de Saint-Aubin, *Le Danger des liaisons, ou Mémoires de la baronne de Blémon*, 3 vols. (Genève, 1763).

23. Marquis de Thibouville, *Le Danger des passions, ou Anecdotes syriennes et égyptiennes* (S.l., 1757).

24. Marie-Agnès Falques, *dite* Mlle de Fauque, *Le Danger des préjugés ou les Mémoires de mademoiselle d'Oran* (Londres et Paris: Bastien, 1774).

25. Anon., *Les Dangers d'un amour illicite, ou le Mariage mal assorti, histoire véritable*, 2 vols. (Londres et Paris: Gattey, 1788).

26. Nicolas Bricaire de la Dixmerie, *Les Dangers d'un premier choix, ou Lettres de Laure à Emilie*, 3 vols. (La Haye et Paris: Delalain le jeune, 1785).

27. Anon., *Les Dangers de l'amour, ou les Aventures d'un négociant portugais* (Lisbonne: Jouan Perezza, 1764).

28. Madame Beccary, *Les Dangers de la calomnie, ou Mémoires de Fanny Spingler, histoire angloise* (Neufchatel: De l'Imprimerie de la Société Typographique, 1781).

29. Madame de Gacon-Dufour, *Les Dangers de la coquetterie* (Paris: Buisson, 1788).

30. Voir note 16.

31. Pierre-Jean-Baptiste Nougaret, *Les Dangers de la séduction et les faux-pas de la beauté, ou les Aventures d'une villageoise et de son amant* . . . , 2 vols. (Paris: L'Auteur, Desenne, an VII). Réimpression de *Lucette ou les Progrès du libertinage*, 1765.

32. Chevalier de Mouhy, *Les Dangers des spectacles, ou les Mémoires de M. le duc de Champigny*, 4 vols. (Paris: L. Jorry, 1780).

33.   Pierre-Jean-Baptiste Nougaret, *Les Dangers de la sympathie, lettres de Henriette de Belval au baron de Luzi* . . . , 2 vols. (Londres et Paris: Bastien, 1785).

34.   P. Duputel, *Fanny de Varicourt, ou le Danger des soupçons* (Paris: Renard, 1802).

35.   Anon., *Aldouzin, ou les Dangers d'une mauvaise éducation,* 2 vols. (La Haye et Paris: Guillot, 1787).

36.   James Rutlidge, *Alphonsine, ou les Dangers du grand monde,* 2 vols. (Londres et Paris: Regnault, 1789).

37.   Anon., *L'Amitié dangereuse, ou Célimaure et Amélie, histoire véritable par l'auteur des Liaisons dangereuses,* 2 vols. (La Haye et Paris: Buisson, 1786).

38.   Henri-Joseph Dulaurens, *Je Suis Pucelle, histoire véritable* (La Haye: Frédéric Staatman, 1767).

Censorship and Subterfuge in
Eighteenth-Century France

EDWARD P. SHAW

The French Revolution has often been described as the most significant event of modern history. Although there were various causes for this tremendous upheaval, it had many intellectual forebears who propounded ideas hostile to the absolutism of government and church under the Bourbon dynasty. Yet ideas, in themselves, are ineffectual unless they can be disseminated, and the despotic power of French monarchs of the eighteenth century would seem to preclude any attacks upon their prerogatives. To govern the printed word, they had at their disposal a system of censorship, not entirely unknown in democratic societies, and strict regulation of the book trade. Nevertheless, critics of social, political, judicial, or religious institutions, together with those desiring freedom of expression in other areas, found it possible to reach the reading public. An answer to this seeming paradox may, I believe, be found in an examination of the adminstration of an official under whom many of the major works of so-called liberal thinkers were published.

During the period between 1750 and 1763, the task of supervising the publishing industry, including censorship, was entrusted to a young man of twenty-nine by the name of Malesherbes, born in a family of statesmen, whose legal career had already indicated a talent for leadership and sufficient diplomacy to cope with the temperamental inclinations of individuals forming the society of letters. During his thir-

287

teen years of stewardship, no single bureaucrat wielded more personal influence on the professional careers of authors or booksellers, on the progress of letters, or the dissemination of knowledge during the tumultuous formative years of the *esprit philosophique*. Despite Malesherbes's protests, Voltaire accurately described him in practice, if not in title, as the minister of literature.

The only compact, if loosely written, code for the supervision of the book trade had been approved by the Council of State as recently as 1723, and Malesherbes was forced to use as a basis for his administration this incomplete legal document, perhaps theoretically sound, but, as we shall see, practically inapplicable.

Certain of the major regulations are of interest. The Community of booksellers, printers, and those exercising related trades was legally governed by a Syndical Chamber, composed of members of the Community itself, whose activities were usually dictated by self-interest. They were expected to visit all establishments of the book trade and write a report, every three months, to the police, stating identities of workmen, number of presses, and quality and quantity of type characters. Print shops had to be open to inspection during hours of work or closed solely by a latched door. All books had to be taken, before offered for distribution, to the Chamber, to permit proper inspection. Foreign books had to pass through one of ten towns of entry where a permit would be given for their transportation to the Chamber. No individual was permitted to receive books other than booksellers.

Only thirty-six individuals were permitted to exercise the book trade, and they had to establish their business in a carefully defined geographical area, the University Quarter and inside the Palais-Royal. Only masters having seven years of training could own a shop. To receive this title, they had to pass an oral examination administered by their professional superiors, furnish evidence of good moral character, sign a certificate professing the Catholic faith, and obtain a testimonial from the rector of the university that they possessed a working knowledge of Latin and an ability to read Greek. Professors of emeritus standing might automatically become booksellers, although their number was fixed at three. If a bookseller also owned a printing establishment, both shops were supposed to be on the same premises. Only with special permission could storehouses be used outside his own home in so-called privileged places, such as schools or religious institutions. However, certain printed matter, such as edicts, decrees, almanacs, and the like could be sold by peddlers, one hundred and twenty in number, who agreed to wear a large copper disk labeled "peddler" and to carry their merchandise in a large, open carton. They could store their material only in their homes, which had to be located on certain designated streets near the Palais-Royal.

According to law, no book could be printed or reprinted for distribution without written permission being granted. At the beginning and end of the book, the privilege or permission had to be indicated, as well as the approval of the censor. Permissions were to be registered at the Syndical Chamber. The most flagrant infraction of the Code, one actually accepted by the administration, concerned the clause necessitating a printed endorsement of the censor. The latter had become increasingly hesitant about publicly approving books that other readers, from their personal point of view, might condemn for statements of an antireligious, antistate, licentious, or libelous nature. It was more convenient to incur the displeasure of an uninfluential author than the hostility of a member of the clergy or nobility. As a result, Malesherbes made use of what was known as the tacit permission. Originally it may well have been only a verbal authorization, but by 1750 it had become as common as a legal permission; and all books printed by this method had to be registered in written form. The official register of works given tacit permission was called "list of books printed in foreign countries, the sale of which is permitted in France," evidence of the fact that many of the countless books supposedly published in London, Amsterdam, and elsewhere were actually printed in France with the connivance of the government itself. Malesherbes tried to make use of tacit permission legal after being named director of the book trade. He ascribed his failure to the Frenchman's odd respect for the law. If he saw inconveniences in a law, rather than make a change, he preferred to circumvent it. Malesherbes was therefore informed by his superiors that, though they recognized the need for a tacit permission, no public sanction of it would be issued. Even members of Parlement, constantly in opposition to royal authority, were aware of its existence, but never prosecuted those publishing books fraudulently, provided they had a tacit permission, although they staunchly refrained from registering a law legalizing this procedure.

Other books might be printed with a simple tolerance or even with "assurances of impunity." If it was thought that a work might be tolerated, yet sufficiently dangerous so that no one would assume responsibility for approving it, even tacitly, the printer was told to undertake its publication secretly by the lieutenant general of police, who pretended to be ignorant of its existence and thus had no reason for seizure. This kind of permission had also become common under the administration of Malesherbes, but it was not officially registered. The printer had to make sure of himself in case of inspection, if the book aroused animosity, but his security was actually guaranteed by the police, who warned him when a raid was to take place.

Coupled with the practical impossibility of obtaining written endorsements, Malesherbes was constantly annoyed with arguments over privileges, which permitted authors, but more usually booksellers, the exclusive right to print and sell a book over a designated period of years. Many of the arguments concerned those who, unsatisfied with this exclusive right, desired that privileges become a permanent possession, even hereditary, like a piece of property. The exclusiveness of the privilege also brought about countless abuses. Some printers sought privileges, not to publish books, but to prevent others from doing so, presumably because the material might be competitive with that already printed by them, or solely through personal grudge. Others, in their greed, wished to profit financially by printing an edition of a successful book initiated by a competitor. Consequently, though the privilege was technically used to prevent counterfeits, actually it increased the number of illegal books. It also created monopolistic practices: a certain Courmont had obtained the right to print all public announcements, posters, and the like, not merely for Paris but for the provinces as well. Counterfeiting of French books with privilege in foreign countries simply could not be controlled. As an example, the County of Avignon, at that time a possession of the pope, sheltered many printers of illegal works, not merely because smuggling at this frontier was relatively simple, but also because printing costs could be maintained at a level below those of France. The fact that only successful books were counterfeited eliminated financial gamble. It was known to the officials that many French workers had migrated to Avignon to set up presses, of which, in 1754, there were about twenty, far more than necessary for the tiny county itself, but nothing was done about it.

Indeed, it is astonishing that Malesherbes, on his own initiative, took effective police action only once, at a time when he was forced to do so because of the open flaunting of the law forbidding counterfeiting. During a raid on the establishment of a bookseller named Ratillon, a huge cache of illicit books was seized in two large warehouses. The owner had been dealing in such books with numerous associates and had even formed an illegal company with partners in Paris and Versailles. The books were printed by a man named Machuel of Rouen, who used a fellow conspirator to transport the books to Paris by the use of carriages, including those of the nobility and diplomatic corps, such as the vehicles of the king's daughter and the ambassador of Malta. Machuel was actually the key figure in the affair, but, again, no prior action had been taken. Malesherbes writes, with little apparent concern, that he had long been known as the operator of a central agency for fraudulent publications. This time, he was temporarily placed in the Bastille, forced to sell his equipment, even, for a few years, losing his professional standing. Nevertheless, it is the only case of voluntary, energetic prosecution on the part of Malesherbes. Of the many suggestions for eliminating this abuse, all of them never seriously considered by the director, there was one of a curious nature. A plan was offered for the establishment of an illegal press to be run by the government, with the sanction of the police, supervised by a reliable printer who might locate genuinely clandestine presses by his contacts in the trade.

If counterfeiting remained an insoluble problem, control of the shipment of books, especially those arriving from foreign countries, caused no less concern. Although the Code of 1723 contained laws covering this aspect of the book trade, they were easily broken and served only to augment, by cumbersome administrative routine and an impractical system of inspection, the interminable delays suffered by bookdealers in their commercial activities. If books were to be imported, the Code stipulated that only ten towns might serve as ports of entry: Paris, Rouen, Nantes, Bordeaux, Marseille, Lyon, Strasbourg, Metz, Amiens, and Lille. It was a law both awkward and inefficient, forcing shipment of books to their destination by the most circuitous routes. Malesherbes notes in a memoir that many precautions had been taken to ensure that shipments arriving at ports along the English Channel be made directly to Rouen, although, in this city, the director admits, illegal activities are rife. It was also ruled that books printed in the County of Avignon must proceed to Lyon for inspection regardless of their final destination, but it was a plan actually unfeasible owing to the close relationships existing between the official supervisors in Lyon and their confederates in Avignon. Indeed, to create further complication, it appears that many of those hired for inspection duty at the ports of entry were illiterate and unable to execute their duties. Many intendants or governors of provinces were completely unaware of their responsibilities in this area. Yet, in one case, when an official at Dieppe assumed the role of book inspector in this city, which was not officially recognized as a port of entry, Malesherbes complimented him for his sagacity, since the law had created so much inconvenience for the inhabitants of that city. In addition to outright smuggling, other means were used to nullify the laws. The personal effects of travelers could not be inspected, and, even more surprising, the introduction of illegal books might readily be realized by the simple expedient of the postal service, which evidently was not checked. Cases of books were often substituted for boxes of other merchandise. Correspondents of Parisian booksellers covered illegal contents of cases with books having a permission or inserted in these books leaves of a prohibited edition. Customs inspectors in Paris had every opportunity to make substitutions. When Malesherbes gave verbal orders to return prohibited books to a foreign printer, they were usually delivered to a Parisian bookseller. The requirement that printed material should be immediately deposited in the Syndical Chamber, after inspection at the customs, was flagrantly broken when coaches of aristocrats, including princes of the blood, often containing contraband, refused to stop at the barriers for inspection. Few paid any attention to the law forbidding shipment of books to individuals, unless it was applied by officers of the Chamber for their personal profit. One daring bookseller even used the name and address of the lieutenant general of police to effect the entrance of prohibited books into the city. He was caught, but given only a small fine. Many efforts were made to avoid completely any inspection by a syndical chamber. One observer, noting the many prohibited books sold in Versailles, blamed the excessive number of booksellers functioning in that town, as well as so-called book agents. He advised that bookdealers be reduced to eight (four within the chateau) to ease supervision. The real villains were the agents, who rented their property close to Paris as depots for books. Their sole function was to circumvent the law, their excuse being that visits of the Syndical Chamber caused delays that were damaging to business.

From a psychological point of view, the most naïvely incredible law of the Code provided for the policing of the book trade by its own members. Businessmen with a sense of civic responsibility may have existed in the eighteenth century, but the average bookseller, whose major ambition was associated with monetary gain, found little satisfaction in forcing himself or professional friends to sacrifice profit in order to obey the law, or to inflict punishment upon himself or others for so doing. Although subject to higher authority, one syndic and four assistants shared the responsibility of governing their trade, and the gravity of illegalities committed under this system was no less than might have been expected. Obviously, the officers of the Chamber were both parties and judges in the examination of books. Knowing, in general, through correspondence, what each case contained, they inspected most superficially. If printed material was addressed to individuals, only those without foresight to warn or to cajole them were hurt. Even in these cases, the severity of the officers was quickly mitigated by sharing the seized books with the guilty. Agreements were made between them and the customs officers to substitute cases before their arrival at the Chamber. No register of prohibited editions was maintained, as was legally required. Indulgence with relatives or friends, undue severity with rivals, and preoccupation with their own interests reduced the inspection of these supervisors to a name only. All the most important booksellers, who at some time had acted as officers of the Chamber, traded in prohibited books. The fact that they had only once been given mild punishment accentuates the frequency of the practice; otherwise, because of their prominent position in the community, they would have been left untouched. As a result, control of the publishing industry and inspection of books by officers who were themselves booksellers engendered so many gross infractions that Malesherbes took steps to rectify the situation. Although one printer or bookseller may not have been more trustworthy than another, he endeavored to force approval of his own selection of candidates for supervisory duties in the Chamber. Indeed, he managed to appoint two inspectors in 1757 to check on the activites of these officers. However, two inspectors for the entire city of Paris were scarcely sufficient to control illegalities of the trade; furthermore, in the provinces such inspectorships were virtually impossible, since governors and police officers, despite their inefficiency, were already responsible for this type of duty. It should also be emphatically noted that the problem of controlling printers in cities or towns where neither a parlement nor governor existed remained unsolved, proving conclusively that large areas of the kingdom were without any supervision whatsoever.

Illegalities likewise occurred in the distribution and sale of books. In the provinces books printed in Lyon and other southern cities were taken to Italy or Spain by itinerant merchants who inhabited the mountains of Savoy. Since authors were forbidden to deal commercially with their own books, people of quality, especially women, did them the favor of selling copies for more money than the amount demanded by booksellers. Peddlers roamed around the countryside or sold "under the cloak," even in Paris and Versailles—in Malesherbes's own words, an everyday occurrence.

Among other laws openly violated, the regulation that one registered storehouse only must be owned by a single bookseller was necessarily broken by all fraudulent dealers, who were forced to possess at least two. The establishment of presses in officially identified locations ceased to aid supervisors when there existed more than one hundred small portable presses that were noiseless and easily hidden in closets. Privileged places for storing books, notably religious institutions, were admittedly never inspected, although there was nothing in the law to prevent such action. A knowledge of ancient languages, legally required for booksellers and printers, was no longer enforced unless it was used by officers of the Chamber to hamper the professional advancement of undesired candidates. Malesherbes confessed ignorance of procedure used to procure a certificate from the rector of the university, but stated with certainty that many members of the book trade could scarcely read French.

Although the director complained about the inefficiency of provincial governors, he nevertheless placed himself, without the slightest qualms of conscience, in the paradoxical position of being responsible for the application of regulations, yet personally suggesting or condoning their circumvention. If laws had to be broken to assist the publishing industry in general or those plying that trade, he did not hesitate. Approval of the city of Dieppe as a port of entry was based on a desire to expedite the shipment of books, although it lacked legality. Similarly, he violated regulations by permitting publication of prohibited books in Lyon to aid French printers. The sale of books "under the cloak" was generally accepted because it served as a means of distributing literature often offensive only to a small segment of the population, but without giving this system the official approval of the government. Malesherbes was prone to suggest the use of a foreign frontispiece to permit publication of a manuscript that could not otherwise be condoned. If an author were having censorship difficulties, Malesherbes often gave his personal approval. He frequently ruled that, though seizure of books in provincial cities was quite legal, no prosecution of those guilty should be forthcoming. His personal permission was given for at least one text even before censorship was completed.

The director's task as administrator was made no easier by the intervention of influential individuals who arbitrarily broke rules in their personal dealings with publishers. When

Malesherbes ordered the seizure of a memoir libeling the magistracy of Strasbourg, it was discovered that certain copies were stamped and addressed to the dauphin and to almost all the princes of the blood. Nothing could be done about preventing such people, above the law, from receiving prohibited material. In many cases, Malesherbes was placed in the awkward position of not being informed whether the king had expressly authorized the publication of a book, particularly since authors and printers were prone to use these so-called indirect permissions as an excuse to avoid legal formalities.

Innumerable technical irregularities were prevalent. Malesherbes received complaints that censors sealed manuscript rather than printed pages after approval, thus permitting censorable material to appear in the final copy that had presumably been sanctioned. Other manuscripts would be received with lines written so closely together that no space was available for corrections, necessitating the use of detached sheets, which might readily be mislaid. The director frequently ordered that shipments of books be taken neither to the customs nor to the Syndical Chamber. Or he informed individuals that the passage of a book to the Chamber was merely a matter of form. When Stanislas, the deposed king of Poland, asked that a shipment be delivered directly to a nobleman in Paris, obviously not a bookseller, he readily consented. When the bishop of Grenoble wrote that he did not want his books sent to the Chamber, stating that regulations applied only to books for sale and not to those given away, Malesherbes happily acceded to this interpretation. The most common but technically illegal practice of the director, utilized so much that it might be called a policy, was to suspend judgment of a book until a few copies were sold, so that their effect upon the public might be ascertained. His extensive use of the tacit permission, which could always be countermanded, may be partially explained by his fondness for this policy, particularly when a book dealt with matters of gov-

297

ernment or public law where official approval might create an undesired reaction on the part of the public.

Official indifference to, or actual sanction of, infractions of regulations and methods of circumvention, hypocritical insistence on arbitrary "rights," financial greed, and professional jealousy on the part of booksellers caused innumerable disputes, multiplied by indignant or self-pitying complaints of authors often victimized by a hypersensitiveness so commonly associated with their temperament. These disputes were frequently referred to the judgment of Malesherbes, adding another responsibility to his position, although he always refused to judge affairs that he considered legally contentious, generally endeavored to steer a neutral course in other cases, or ignored them completely.

Quarrels between authors and booksellers were often caused by the habit of publishers to use arbitrarily the authority of the director in declaring that an author's manuscript had been disapproved, in order that they might publish it later without being forced to expend funds for its purchase. Rarely were booksellers punished for printing works without the permission of the author. Others endeavored to lower the purchase price of a manuscript by threatening to print unauthorized editions. Even the greatest authors were not immune. Voltaire himself, through his agent, was vicitimized in this way when the proposed publisher of his famous history *Le Siècle de Louis XIV* hypocritically declared that a demand of four thousand livres for the manuscript was exorbitant. Nor were booksellers at a loss to quarrel among themselves. Such disputes may be illustrated by a conflict between a Parisian publisher, Garnier, and his professional counterpart in Lyon, a man named Bruyset. Garnier contended that Bruyset was counterfeiting some of his books and requested an order to raid his stores in Lyon to effect their seizure. The order was forthcoming, and Madame Garnier, probably accustomed to victory in domestic disputation, was dispatched to see that justice prevailed. The inspection, however, uncovered only sixteen copies of a work of an author named Collet for which Garnier had exclusive rights. Garnier voiced his dissatisfaction to the chancellor and finally instituted court proceedings, stating that despite Garnier's privilege for this work Bruyset had obtained copies of Collet's work printed in Avignon and had shipped them to Lyon contrary to the law prohibiting the entrance of counterfeit books into France. Meanwhile, in a letter exuding self-confidence to Malesherbes, Bruyset contended that the books were merely passing through Lyon en route to Frankfurt and were not intended for him. It was apparent that justice was on the side of Garnier. Bruyset, one of the most unscrupulous booksellers of the eighteenth century, unquestionably engaged in many illegal procedures. However, the self-confidence he always expressed in correspondence with Malesherbes indicates that the director protected rather than prosecuted him whenever possible.

In other arguments Malesherbes even received letters concerning disputes over payment for a book. In Marseille two priests inspected a copy of an official decree in the shop of a man named Isnard. They wanted to take the copy and have Isnard collect the money for it at their residence. Isnard said that the copy was theirs only if the money was immediately forthcoming, whereupon the priests pummeled the bookseller with their fists and even tried to make off with the remaining copies of the decree. The clerics threatened to inform Malesherbes of the argument, and Isnard actually wrote the director to defend himself in this petty, inconsequential squabble.

Authors also brought their quarrels to Malesherbes, although, rather than entailing interpretation of regulations, they usually were a matter of antagonistic attitudes concerning the contents of a book. Such arguments were most troublesome for Malesherbes; he was dealing, not with infractions of a stated law, but rather with the subjective opinions of sensitive personalities. Unless he evoked the law against libel, there was no legal basis for action, yet he was constantly requested to take a stand in disputes by those who wished satisfaction against hostile criticism. The director refused to accept these requests unless pressure was brought to bear from his superiors, but he continually tried to impart to literary opponents his own emotional stability and to exercise his natural quality of tact, together with elementary principles of psychology, in order to appease those who considered themselves victims of unjust attack. He believed the course left open to such individuals was simply to print their own rebuttal. In so doing, the director often exhibited tendencies toward liberalism, by his approval of free and open discussion and democracy, by his belief in the judgment of the public and his disinclination to establish despotic control over literature. Even theologians brought their debates to Malesherbes for arbitration, but, in this highly delicate area, he utterly refused to assume responsibility, basing his decision on what he must have considered, at least in his official capacity, as a happy state of ignorance.

Incredible as it may seem, others, with wounded sensitivities, came to the director to obtain redress for equivocal dedications. Before dedications could be printed, regulations required approval by the recipient. Some, however, did not take the trouble to read the actual dedication before granting approval, believing that it must, by definition, contain words of praise. Shocked to discover that eulogy could degenerate into ridiculous flattery, they came mourning to Malesherbes.

Complaints based upon pride in ancestry brought the director additional woes. Although he always tried to assuage ruffled feelings, he realized that problems arising from the publication of genealogies were insoluble because censorship in this specialized area remained essentially ineffective. In one case, a marshal of France became infuriated when a certain Madame de Lismore inserted an article in a genealogy claiming that she was related to him. He demanded the elimination of the insertion in all unsold copies, together with the printing of a public notice containing his protests. Malesherbes calmly explained to the marshal that the censor could not be held blameworthy and hinted that the matter was being given too much importance. More critical problems concerning genealogical publications arose when a large number of families were involved. What should be done with a proposed genealogy of the nobility of Lorraine that would expose the false claims to ancient aristocratic ties of those only recently ennobled? The censor stated that the work should be prohibited, but Malesherbes permitted publication, believing that authentic genealogies hurt only those who had assumed titles to which they had no right. As a true aristocrat, he sympathized with noblemen who, through impoverishment, had begun to doubt the legitimacy of their extraction, and condemned those who usurped honors belonging only to the old nobility.

The position of director of the book trade assigned to Malesherbes in 1750 included the assumption of responsibility for executing censorship regulations and supervising the activities of the royal censors.

Before 1741 censors were appointed without permanent title and, for the most part, lacked efficiency. Consequently, in 1741, hoping to render the censorial system more effective, the authorities increased the number of censors to seventy-nine and granted them permanent status. By 1762 the list had been augmented to one hundred and twenty-two names, divided into the various areas of learning. Of the sixty names in the general field of literature and history, there are scarcely more than half a dozen who have the most modest claim to renown. In addition to these individuals, other high authorities, notably ministers and obviously the king, assumed this prerogative. At least one minister permitted his secretary to do his censoring for him, and, if Malesherbes approved, an author might choose his own censor, even though the man chosen had no official status. In principle, a book was assigned to a censor presumably specialized in the subject matter of the book, although this procedure could not always be carried out when manuscripts in one particular area were submitted simultaneously.

There were, however, few attractions to induce competent individuals to assume the function of censor. Despite the award of permanent tenure in 1741, poor pay scarcely outweighed the antagonism of noted authors or their aristocratic supporters incurred by disapproval of a manuscript. Unlike many other governmental positions, pensions were not automatically granted. Their distribution was often based upon such factors as impoverishment; there is no mention of efficiency as a necessary condition for the receipt of a pension.

During his thirteen-year tenure of office, Malesherbes's relationships with his censors remained excellent. Lacking the arrogant attitude so often displayed by officials of the *ancien régime*, the director shielded his assistants as much as possible from public and private enmity, never censured them openly and seldom privately, disliked to intervene in their labors or to question their decisions, and gave them unqualified support in clashes with others, unless thwarted by superiors, even to the point of endangering his own status. Only occasionally, when he believed that a censor was biased or unnecessarily strict, did he override his decision; even in these cases, the director usually appointed a second censor. Indeed, when a censor hesitated to make a decision, he frequently assumed this responsibility. Nevertheless, despite the attractions of a benevolent supervisor, some financial return, and a position of authority, the profession of censor involved psychological problems as well as delicate decisions over and above judgments based on censorship regulations. Foremost in the mind of most censors was fear of reprisal for adverse criticism. They refused to have their identity revealed to authors if their censorial reports contained hostile comments. Others declined giving public approval to manuscripts because of a belief that such approbation might witness their lack of literary taste. If one were appointed to censor a journal, it was found impossible to verify the accuracy of all quotations with the original sources.

Custom dictated that censorship be performed by those residing in Paris. Although Malesherbes favored delegation of authority in the provinces, he found it difficult to achieve owing to utter confusion or ignorance in regard to established regulations. He may, indeed, be partially blamed for lack of action in ameliorating this situation; directives could have been dispatched to responsible officials; a more rigorous policy might have been adopted to check overt acts of illegality; he might have forcefully appealed for additional supervisory personnel under his authority (there were only two provincial inspectors of the book trade). Governors of provinces, whose help was needed, often showed indifference, and their official rank precluded domination by Malesherbes unless he applied pressure through the chancellor, which he was temperamentally unprepared to do. Yet the director, conscientious within the self-imposed limitations of his responsibilities, had inherited a system traditionally accepted, and it would be difficult to censure him if he had concluded that a truly effective method of supervision could not be realized through the efforts of a single individual who lacked the support of publishers, writers, the public in general, and even superiors in administration or society, who occasionally showed interest in his functions, not to improve conditions, but only to intercede in isolated, individual cases.

We have noted that the Code of 1723 provided punishment for those who permitted the appearance of books containing libels against individuals or families, attacks against the church, state, or king, and licentious, immoral material.

When concerned with complaints of real or supposed victims of libels, Malesherbes usually stated that he could do nothing about them, except to determine whether they had been printed in defiance of a censor's disapproval, or to place an offcut over the disputed passage. Having endeavored originally to make the delicate decision between legitimate

303

criticism and defamation, it became his firm policy, despite commiserative notes to complainants, never to intervene in contentious cases where printed libel might be involved, unless forced to do so because of the rank of the individual supposedly maligned. He did, however, take the trouble to explain his position and indicate possible courses of action to those who appealed to him, though always counseling restraint. He was of the belief that disputes, unless defamation of character was obviously involved, should be advocated rather than forbidden, particularly as a means of furthering the progress of knowledge. In his words, the use of print in disputation had never hurt people of true merit. However, unless under the form of allusions, only rarely were libels condemned through the censorship. Authors realized that defamatory passages could easily be detected and consequently associated themselves with unprincipled French printers or foreigners in the publication of their material, gambling that the appearance of their libels in Paris would arouse no public clamor and thus reducing to a minimum any likelihood that Malesherbes would take action.

Similarly, manuscripts composed solely to appeal to man's baser instincts infrequently reached the censor because of the ease of detection, although there were a number of borderline cases that were generally passed unless there happened to be a more compelling reason for disapproval. Literary licentiousness seldom troubled Malesherbes.

On the other hand, a state of confusion existed in the censorship of books treating religion. It is common knowledge that Malesherbes's personal policy, in dealing with Voltaire, Rousseau, and others, favored liberalism, which, one may safely hypothesize, extended to complete freedom of expression in the field of theology. He was compelled to contrary action only through the intervention of superior authority or when he believed that he must abide by the law for the maintenance of public order. In this policy he was supported by a number of censors, as well as by a large segment of the populace. The average Parisian eagerly sought prohibited books ridiculing the church. In his manuscript diary of 1760 a book inspector noted that a few copies of such a work entitled *Praise of Hell* were circulating in Paris, a book badly written but anxiously sought because religion, priests, and monks were so maltreated. Neither did Malesherbes endeavor to prohibit the sale of Protestant works, often using the argument that, though official permission might seem to sanction independent expressions of opinion, verbal tolerance should be granted, since the book would appear anyway, the sale of which might fill the coffers of foreign rather than native booksellers. A discourse on irreligion by Haller, despite open disparagement of the church, was tolerated, even though the censor was a professor at the Sorbonne. In similar spirit a treatise was banned for supporting the authority of a monarch to force adherence of his subjects to ecclesiastical decisions. Other texts, however, were prohibited for an unseemly intermingling of devotion and gallantry. Malesherbes himself permitted attacks on liberal thinkers in keeping with his beliefs that there should be free expression in debate. But, above all, censors were particularly sensitive about approving treatises supporting the church unless their quality equaled that of antagonistic texts. Many manuscripts precluded official approbation because of their general mediocrity, although the contents were innocuous. It was generally believed by the censors that a mediocre work in the field of religion did more harm than good; it would be little read by the common folk and ridiculed by the incredulous.

Because of the delicacy of censorship, responsible officials also disliked to approve political works if they had any doubts concerning the contents. Books that might arouse the ire of foreign countries currently friendly or at peace with France were rejected. Similarly, those that seemed to oppose government foreign policy were never approved unless Malesherbes had the permission of a minister. During the Seven Years' War, attempts were made to ban the many books expressing anglophile opinions. In the case of a proposed translation of two English pamphlets concerning the war, Malesherbes believed that no official sanction could be granted, but realized that if the foreign petitioner did not print the translations, one of his competitors would do so even without complying with the formality of seeking permission. Consequently, the director used another customary method in handling the affair: he simply did not reply to the request. The greatest problem of political censorship, however, was to stem the flood of anti-French propaganda through foreign gazettes, notably the *Gazette de Hollande*, which had already been given an exclusive privilege. Malesherbes realized that it would do no good to try to prevent the entry of copies into France, nor would the reprinting of the gazette, excluding censorable passages, be effective; such reprints would simply give greater value to the original. His solution was practical: suppress the exclusive privilege and make reprints selling in France for considerably less than the original. Once profits decreased, those responsible for printing objectionable material would abide by the wishes of the French government. Another affair concerned the abbé Coyer's *Histoire de Sobieski*, a work containing outspoken republican statements that had vexed Louis XV. The chancellor wrote Malesherbes that it was incredible how such a book could have appeared without permission and that the censor must be punished. The director was forced to admit that the book had been granted tacit permission and earnestly requested that the censor be given a hearing to justify himself—a request in keeping with his innate sense of justice. In this case, however, both author and censor received sentences. Malesherbes had covered himself by refusing an express permission, but the work would have appeared "tacitly," with the director's blessing, as did hundreds of other books, if it had not been singled out for attack by those in power.

There were other reasons for censorial disapproval not specifically covered by the Code of 1723. Often censors became self-appointed experts, not always with justification, in sub-ject-matter areas pertaining to the manuscript they were re-viewing. One book on arithmetic was banned because it was considered to instruct incorrectly. Another censor voiced dis-satisfaction with a *Mémoire sur la milice* merely because the author did not discuss the crucial problem of the appropriate size of a standing army in France. Publication of an apology for luxury was refused because the censor did not agree with the author. Similarly, a treatise on smallpox received disap-proval because it contained statements contrary to the opin-ion of the Faculty of Medicine. As we have seen, rejections could be based on the general mediocrity of a work, it appar-ently being a policy of some to "protect" the public from books of little literary value. On the other hand, a censor named Moncrif would approve works actually because of their mediocrity, believing them, for that reason, to be harm-less, though his pride as a man of letters prevented him from giving approval by name. Malesherbes himself was capricious in this matter of mediocrity. Although he rejected some books of inferior quality, he would approve others, primarily out of sympathy for impoverished authors. Other censors, believing themselves to be arbiters of good taste, banned books solely for stylistic reasons.

Complaints reaching Malesherbes against censors who de-manded excisions were not so numerous as might be expected, probably because authors generally accepted the unofficial, tacit permission having less stringent requirements than an open approval, or because the director, in most cases, was known to support the censor, or because arrangements be-tween author and censor were made verbally. The greatest source of irritation was the slowness of the reviewer. One au-thor complained that his censor had read only one-twentieth of his manuscript in eighteen months, a rate of speed that would require fifteen years before censorship was completed.

In general, then, the form rather than the spirit of censor-ial laws was obeyed. Censors found it useful to suggest sale of books under the cloak, an illegal procedure. A reviewer of licentious tales was willing to follow the policy of ignoring the fact that they existed. Permitting the illicit distribution of an obviously lascivious tale, he added the curious statement that, except for a few lines describing the lubricity of a monk, one could not write more decently on such an indecent subject. It concerned prostitutes, and the place of debauchery where they are found is described, but even ladies could read the story without blushing. Censorship of journals seems to have been nonexistent at times, and, at the most, superficial. Censors wrote to Malesherbes that a manuscript should not be printed by express approval, but might be distributed by peddlers as if the book were printed in a foreign country. In more than one case the director informed the author that permission had been refused, but that he had instructed his inspector not to be severe if the book appeared without sanction. Finally, execution of regulations was hampered by the indifference of censors in forcing obedience to their orders or by actual collusion between censor and author or printer. At least once, Malesherbes himself gave oral approval for a book without taking the trouble to ascertain its contents. When copies were seized, he admitted, with embarrassment, that he had even forgotten that he had granted such permission.

Although a lawyer himself, Malesherbes may be said to have failed as director of the book trade and as chief of the royal censors if one interprets his function as being that of a strict administrator of existing regulations, but he was temperamentally unfitted and philosophically unwilling to act in that capacity in many cases. He remained normally unworried, calm in conscience despite countless violations, by nature prone to forget, to forgive, to tolerate, rather than to punish. Yet, in his case, equanimity was the final product neither of apathy nor indifference. Impelled to write his reflections on the book trade in 1758, he attacked certain laws held sacred by privileged groups and condemned others that

308

in his opinion were more damaging than beneficial. Nor can the fact that no concrete steps were taken to ameliorate conditions by using his logical proposals serve as evidence of the director's irresponsibility. The hierarchy existing within the monarchy was such that superiors could scarcely be prodded to action. Legal changes in France were difficult to effect. Consequently, Malesherbes followed the only course available, even though it involved personal judgment rather than objective application of regulations. In his own words, bad laws could be made harmless through circumvention. The Code of 1723, except in the *principle* of censorship, rarely coincided with his liberal philosophy of administration. When conflicts arose, he preferred to follow personal conviction rather than to act as an automaton, judging in strict adherence to injurious laws.

Thus, the attitudes of officials, the power of privileged individuals or groups, incompetency of booksellers policing their own trade, cumbersome administrative procedure in transportation, abuses of laws openly violated and seldom punished, in sum, a crass lack of respect for the Code of 1723, resulted in complete, incredible chaos. License in the book trade had reached the point where sale of prohibited books took place under the eyes of the king at Versailles. Only two months before Malesherbes's retirement in 1763, an observer wrote that the book trade was a completely unrestricted business of brigandage. Nothing could be more conclusive than the director's own opinion, stated in 1759, that there was little regulation and less consequence in what had been done, up to that date, in the management of booksellers and censors. Louis XV found himself totally powerless to prevent freedom of expression, which was to sweep the *ancien régime* to its ultimate doom.

Bibliographical Notes on the Beaumarchais-Goezman Lawsuit

When the fourth *mémoire* was published, Voltaire told d'Alembert, "De tous les ouvrages dont on régale le public le seul qui m'ait plu est la quaterne de ce Beaumarchais" (Best. D18819). And he added, "Quel homme! il réunit tout, la boufonerie,[1] le sérieux, la raison, la guaité, la force, le touchant, tous les genres d'éloquence; et il n'en recherche aucun; et il confond tous ses adversaires; et il donne des leçons à ses juges." I must confess that I find this praise excessive, but the master's word is law. Over the years I acquired Beaumarchais *factums* whenever the opportunity arose, and gave them to the Institut et musée Voltaire.

Recently, however, after I was unfortunately obliged by the city of Geneva to discontinue my gifts to the Institut, I had the good luck to acquire a contemporary volume containing no fewer than twenty-seven printed documents concerning the Beaumarchais-Goezman affair, including one or two borderline *factums*. What is more, when I came to check them against the section devoted to these famous documents by Henri Cordier in his *Bibliographie des œuvres de Beaumarchais* (Paris, 1883), I found that several of these pamphlets (more than one is as long as a book) were partly or wholly unknown to the bibliographer. It would have been useless merely to list these new pamphlets, for Cordier's descriptions are extremely imprecise, and even incorrect. Indeed, by modern standards they are useless. And to establish a critical bibliography of the case would be possible only after prolonged

311

research by a Beaumarchais specialist. It would be necessary, for instance, to collate the documents in their original editions, and even in the collected *Mémoires*, which do not by any means contain all the *factums*.

For these reasons I have adopted an intermediate procedure: a detailed catalogue of my volume as it stands. The references to Cordier are to his nearest equivalents, but it is impossible always to be sure of this. It must also be borne in mind that Cordier's order is only nominally chronological.

[1: Unknown to Cordier]

[*ornamental typographic border*] / *MÉMOIRE* / A CONSULTER / *POUR* Pierre-Augustin Caron de / *BEAUMARCHAIS*, *Ecuyer, Conſeiller-Secré-* / *taire du Roi, & Lieutenant-Général des Chaſſes* / *au Bailliage & Capitainerie de la Varenne du* / *Louvre, grande Vénerie & Fauconnerie de France,* / *Accuſé.* /
[*colophon:*] De l'Imprimerie de VALLEYRE l'aîné, rue de la / vieille Bouclerie,[2] à l'Arbre de Jeſſé. 1773. /
pp. 42; sig.A-E[4], F[1]; cm.23.3[3].

This edition has a frontispiece, the engraving by Saint-Aubin after the portrait of Beaumarchais by Cochin, which was added to a few copies of the *Mémoire*, no doubt those intended for presentation.

[2: Cordier 332]

The bibliographic transcription of the title is identical with [1], but in fact it is from a different setting, as is the whole pamphlet.

[*colophon:*] De L'Imprimerie de C. SIMON, Imprimeur de / LL. AA. SS. Meſſeigneurs / le Prince de Condé, le Duc de Bourbon & de l'Archevêché, / rue des Mathurins, 1773. /

[3: Cordier 333]

Same remark as for [2]:

[*colophon:*] A PARIS, de l'Imprimerie de Ph. D. *PIERRES,* / rue Saint-Jacques. 1774. /

[4: Cordier 334]

[*ornamental typographic border*] / SUPPLÉMENT / AU MÉMOIRE / A CONSULTER, / Pour PIERRE-AUGUSTIN CARON DE / BEAUMARCHAIS, *Écuyer, Conſeiller Secre-* / *taire du Roi & Lieutenant-Général des Chaſſes au* / *Bailliage & Capitainerie de la Varenne du Louvre,* / *Grande Venerie & Fauconnerie de France, accuſé* / *en corruption de Juge & calomnie.* /
[*colophon*:] De l'Imprimerie de QUILLAU, Imprimeur de LL. AA. SS. Mgrs. le / Prince de Conti & Comte de la Marche, rue du Fouarre, 1773. /
pp.64; sig.A-H⁴.

The "consultation" is dated 17 November 1773.

[5, 19: Cordier 335]

[*ornamental typographic border*] / ADDITION / AU SUPPLÉ-MENT / DU MÉMOIRE / A CONSULTER, / POUR PIERRE-AUGUSTIN CARON DE / BEAUMARCHAIS, Écuyer, Con-ſeiller-Secré / taire de Roi, & Lieutenant-Général des Chaſſes au / Bailliage & Capitainerie de la Varenne du Louvre, / Grande Venerie & Fauconnerie de France, accuſé: / *SERVANT de Réponſe a Madame* GOEZMAN / *accuſée; au Sieur* BERTRAND D'AIROLLES, / *accuſé; aux Sieurs* MARIN, *Gazetier de France,* / & DARNAUD BACULARD, *Conſeiller* / *d'Ambaſ-ſade, aſſignés comme témoins.* /
[*colophon*:] De l'Imprimerie de J. G. CLOUSIER, rue Saint-Jacques, / vis-à-vis celle des Mathurins. /
pp.78; sig.A-I⁴, 4³.

Needless to say, the *Supplément* is longer than the *Mémoire*, and the *Addition* longer than either; it is dated "Délibéré à Paris par nous Avocats au Parlement, le 18 Décembre 1773."

[6: Cordier 336]

There is another edition, from a different setting, but with an identical title, except that D'AIROLLES reads DAIROLLES.

[*colophon*:] *A PARIS*, DE L'IMPRIMERIE DE PH. D. PIERRES, 1774. /

[7: Cordier 337]

The *Addition* was preceded by a document, dated 17 December 1773, which Cordier recorded out of chronological sequence:

REQUÊTE / D'ATTENUATION / *POUR* / LE Sr CARON DE BEAUMARCHAIS. /
[*colophon:*] A PARIS, de l'Imprimerie de KNAPEN, au bas du / Pont Saint-Michel, 1773. /
pp.[ii].28; sig.[ ]^1, A-C^4, D^2.

[8: Unknown to Cordier]

This pamphlet was issued in another edition, largely from the same setting and with the same colophon.

[*ornamental wood-cut border*] / REQUESTE D'ATTENUA-TION, / *POUR LE Sr CARON DE BEAUMARCHAIS.* / pp.28; sig.A-C^4, D^2. The woodcut is signed V. LIS.

[9: Cordier 338]

The *Mémoire, Supplément,* and *Addition* being regarded as three distinct *factums* (as in the *Arrest de la cour du parlement,* pp. 22-3), a fourth, still larger, followed a few weeks later. This time the rapidity with which these documents were passed through the press becomes directly evident, the *factum* itself being dated 7 February, the printed publication as shown below. The description given by Cordier is particularly inaccurate.

[*ornamental triple rule*] / QUATRIÈME / MÉMOIRE / A *CONSULTER,* / POUR PIERRE-AUGUSTIN CARON DE / BEAUMARCHAIS, Écuyer, Conſeiller-Secré / taire du Roi, Lieutenant-Général des Chaſſes, &c. / Accuſé de corruption de Juge. / *CONTRE M.* GOEZMAN, *Juge accuſé de* / *ſubornation & de faux; Madame* GOEZMAN, / *& le Sieur* BERTRAND, *accuſés; les Sieurs* / MARIN, *Gazetier;* DARNAUD-BACULARD, / *Conſeiller d'Ambaſſade; & Conſorts.* / [*two-line* *epigraph between rules*] / *ET réponſe ingénue à leurs Mé-moires, Gazettes, / Lettres courantes, Cartels, Injures, & mille & / une Diffamations.* / [*two-line epigraph between rules*] / [*colophon:*] De l'Imprimerie de J. G. CLOUSIER, rue Saint-Jacques, / vis-à-vis celle des Mathurins, 10 Février 1774. / pp.108. [i]. [i blank]; sig.A-N⁴, O³.

The additional leaf at the end of this booklet is a stop-press complaint about the suppression of the *Barbier de Séville.*

[10: Cordier 325]

[*wood-cut border*] / PRÉCIS SIGNIFIÉ / POUR le ſieur CARON DE BEAUMARCHAIS; / *CONTRE le Comte* DE LA BLACHE. /
[*colophon:*] A PARIS, chez P.G. SIMON, Imprimeur du Parle-ment, / *rue Mignon Saint-André-des-Arcs,* 1774. /
pp.24; sig.A-C⁴. The woodcut is signed "Papillon 1773."

[11: Cordier 356]

[*wood-cut border*] / ARREST / *DE LA COUR* / DU PAR-LEMENT, / EXTRAIT DES REGISTRES DU PARLE-MENT. / *Du 26 Février mil ſept cent ſoixante-quartorze.* /
[*colophon:*] A PARIS, chez P.G. SIMON, Imprimeur du Parle-lement, / *rue Mignon Saint-André-des-Arcs,* 1774. /
pp.24; sig.A-C⁴. The woodcut is signed "Papillon Inv. 1762."

This pamphlet must date from about 10 March 1774, because it records not only the order of the court to lacerate and burn nos. [1–4] above, but the execution of that order on 5 March.

[12: Unknown to Cordier]

This *factum* is similar to Cordier 327, but differs from it in the title and collation.

MÉMOIRE / POUR / *PIERRE-AUGUSTIN* / CARON DE BEAUMARCHAIS. /

[*colophon*:] De l'Imprimerie de J. G. CLOUSIER, rue Saint-Jacques, 16 Janvier 1775. /

pp.[i]. [i blank]. viii.84.[i].[i blank]; sig.[ ]¹, *a*, A-K⁴, L³.

The additional leaf at the end contains *errata*.

[13: Unknown to Cordier]

[*wood-cut border*] / ARREST / DU CONSEIL D'ÉTAT / DU ROI, / *Qui ſupprime un Écrit ayant pour titre*: Mémoire / à conſulter & Conſultation pour Pierre-Auguſtin / Caron de Beaumarchais. / Du 4 Février 1775. /
[*colophon*:] A PARIS, DE L'IMPRIMERIE ROYALE. 1775. /
pp.2. The woodcut is signed "Papillon fecit."

[14: Unknown to Cordier]

[*double rule*] / NOTES / SUR le *Mémoire du ſieur* DE BEAU-MARCHAIS, / *contre le Comte* DE LA BLACHE. /
[*colophon*:] De l'Imprimerie de STOUPE, rue de la Harpe. 1775. /

pp.4.

[15: Cordier 339]

SUITE / DE LA JUSTIFICATION / *DU SIEUR* / DE BEAUMARCHAIS. /
[*colophon*:] De l'Imprimerie de QUILLAU, Imprimerie de S. A. S. Mᵍʳ / le Prince DE CONTI, rue de Fouare 1776. /

pp.[i]. [i blank]. 64; sig.[ ]¹, A-F⁴,G⁵, H³ [probably misprints for G-H⁴].

At the head of page [1] is a woodcut signed "Le Brun." This booklet contains the *Jugement* (26 February 1774), *Lettres-patentes du roi* (12 August 1776), *Extrait des registres de parlement* (27 August 1776), *Lettres de requête civile* (31 August 1776), *Consultation des avocats au parlement* (30 August 1776), *Plaidoyer pour le sieur Caron de Beaumarchais* (6 September 1776), *Arrest de la cour de parlement de Paris* (6 February 1776; confirmed 12 September 1776), *Requête du sieur de Beaumarchais* (11 December 1776).

316

[16: Unknown to Cordier]

[*wood-cut border*] / EXTRAIT / *DES REGISTRES* / DU
PARLEMENT, / *Du dix-huit Janvier mil ſept cent ſoixante-
dix-ſept.* /
[*colophon:*] A PARIS, chez P. G. Simon, Imprimeur du Parlement, / *rue Mignon Saint-André-des-Arcs.* 1777. /
pp.2. The woodcut is signed "? Hutuin."

[17: Cordier 342]

[*ornamental wood-cut border*] / OBSERVATIONS / *POUR*
Monſieur de Goezmann, Conſeiller de / Grand' Chambre. /
[*colophon:*] De l'Imprimerie de M. LAMBERT, rue de la
Harpe, / près Saint Côme, 1773. /
pp.38; sig.A-D⁴,E³.

[18: Cordier 354]

[*ornamental wood-cut border*] / PLAINTE / *CONTRE* / LE
SIEUR CARON DE BEAUMARCHAIS. /
[*colophon:*] De l'Imprimerie de MICHEL LAMBERT, rue de
la Harpe, 1774. /
pp.7. [i blank]; sig.A⁴.

[19: Duplicate of 5]

[20: Cordier 343]

[*ornamental wood-cut border*] / MÉMOIRE / *POUR* / Madame de Goezmann. /
[*colophon:*] De l'Imprimerie de Michel Lambert, rue de la
Harpe / près Saint Côme, 1773. /
pp.54; sig.A-F⁴,G³.

[21: Cordier 344]

MÉMOIRE / *A CONSULTER.* /
[*incipit:*] [*ornamental wood-cut border*] MÉMOIRE / *A
CONSULTER* / *POUR* Francois-Thomas-Marie d'Ar-

317

NAUD, / Conſeiller d'Ambaſſade de la Cour de Saxe, de / l'Académie Royale des Sciences & Belles-Lettres / de Pruſſe, &c, &c. / *CONTRE PIERRE-AUGUSTIN CARON, Ecuyer, / Conſeiller, Secrétaire du Roi, & Lieutenant-Général / des Chaſſes au Bailliage & Capitainerie de la Varenne / du Louvre, Grande Vénerie & Fauconnerie de / France, &c.* /
[*colophon:*] De l'Imprimerie de MICHEL LAMBERT, rue de la Harpe, près / Saint Côme, 1773. /
pp.15. [i blank]; sig.A-B⁴.

The "consultation" is dated 9 October 1773.

[22: Cordier 345]

MEMOIRE / *A CONSULTER* / ET CONSULTATION, / *POUR ANTOINE-BERTRAND D'AIROLES, / Accuſé.* /
[*colophon:*] De l'Imprimerie de L. CELLOT, rue Dauphine, 1773. /
pp.41. [i blank]; sig.A-D⁴, E⁵.

This document is dated 23 November 1773.

[23: Cordier 346]

[*ornamental wood-cut border*] / SUPPLÉMENT / AU MÉMOIRE DU Sʀ BERTRAND D'AIROLLES. /
[*colophon:*] De l'Imprimerie de M. LAMBERT, rue de la Harpe, 1773./
pp.24; sig.A-C⁴.

This *factum* is dated 22 December 1773.

[24: Unknown to Cordier]

[*triple rule*] / *A NOSSEIGNEURS* / DU PARLEMENT, / LES CHAMBRES ASSEMBLÉES. / SUPPLIE HUMBLEMENT, ANTOINE BERTRAND / D'AIROLLES; /
[*colophon:*] De l'Imprimerie de M. LAMBERT, rue de la Harpe, / près Saint Côme, 1773. /
pp.7.[i blank]; sig.A⁴.

[25: Cordier 350]

[*triple rule*] / *A NOSSEIGNEURS* / DU PARLEMENT, / LES CHAMBRES ASSEMBLÉES, / Supplie humblement Louis-Francois-Claude / Marin; / [*colophon:*] De l'Imprimerie de Michel LAMBERT, rue de la Harpe, / près Saint Côme. 1773. / pp.4; sig.A².

[26: Cordier 352]

[*ornamental woodcut*] / MÉMOIRE / *A CONSULTER,* / POUR le ſieur MARIN, en réponſe à ce qui le / concerne dans un Mémoire pour le ſieur Caron / de Beaumarchais. / [*colophon:*] De l'Imprimerie de D. C. COUTURIER pere, / aux Galeries du Louvre. / pp.36; sig.A-D⁴, E².

This *factum* is dated 30 November 1773.

[27: Cordier 353]

[*ornamental woodcut*] / MÉMOIRE / POUR le ſieur Marin, / EN RÉPONSE / *A ce qui le concerne dans un troiſieme Libelle du / ſieur C aron de Beaumarchais, intitulé:* / Addition, &c. / [*colophon:*] De l'Imprimerie de D. C. COUTURIER pere, / aux Galeries du Louvre. / pp.24; sig.A-C⁴.

The *Mémoire*, oddly enough, is not dated; the latest date in the accompanying documents is 13 January 1774.

1.   Beaumarchais did not like this word, so in the Kehl edition he altered it to *plaisanterie*, a normal editorial procedure in the age of reason (and much later), from which Voltaire suffered thousands of times.
2.   This seems an unlikely name, and must surely be a misprint (however odd it may seem that a typesetter should make such a mistake in his own address) for Boucherie; I have not found a street with this exact name, but there was a very ancient slaughterhouse opposite the Châtelet.
3.   As all the pamphlets here described were bound at the time into a single volume, now in my possession, this height applies to them all, and will not be repeated.

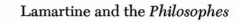

Lamartine and the *Philosophes*

Lamartine, the quintessential romantic poet, is not generally thought of as a disciple of the traditions of the Enlightenment. In fact, the Lamartinian *œuvre* is often presented as the rich antithesis of the allegedly dry and rationalist eighteenth-century neoclassicism. The rapport between the poet and the *philosophes* has not, however, gone altogether unobserved. Desvoyes[1] saw some similarity between Voltaire's *Monologue de Caton* and Lamartine's fifth meditation on the theme of immortality. Gaudon[2] has suggested that Lamartine drew some inspiration from his readings of the marquis de Sade, and there is, of course, a considerable body of critical commentary on Lamartine and Rousseau, most of which establishes what Fournet[3] has called "une parenté d'âme" between the two. This latter writer is one of the few who tries also to examine Lamartine's attitude toward Rousseau the political theorist as well as Rousseau the poet.

The relative paucity of comment on the Lamartine-*philosophes* relationship is all the more striking when one considers the immense volume of space Lamartine devoted to them not only in his *Histoire des Girondins* but in the *Confidences*, *Mémoires politiques*, *Histoire de la Turquie*, *Histoire de la restauration*, and several other works. Aside from the *Histoire des Girondins*, which contains a more or less systematic evaluation of eighteenth-century writers in the light of the Revolution, Lamartine's observations on the *philosophes* have the

321

quality of random thoughts; no attempt is made to establish an ordered critique of Enlightenment thinkers.

It is not surprising that Lamartine should have had an abiding interest in the philosophic currents of the age that immediately preceded his. He was born less than a year after the French Revolution and reached the age of discernment during a period when France was still undergoing the convulsions occasioned by the unprecedented upheaval in the social order.

Lamartine's preoccupation with the Enlightenment was not, moreover, merely an intellectual involvement based on a commonality of interests or the curiosity of an inquiring mind. He grew up in a family that had personal contacts with the literary luminaries of the prerevolutionary period. On his mother's side there was a grandmother and an uncle who had entertained Rousseau and Voltaire and many of their contemporaries.

Finally, one can posit Lamartine's political career (he entered the Chambre des Députés in 1834) as a factor in his observations about the philosophic coalition of the eighteenth century—members of which had produced trenchant critiques of society, and, in the specific case of Rousseau's *Contrat social*, elaborate formulas for the amelioration of the human collective. As a thinking politician, Lamartine could not but confront the vital, libertarian ideals that the *philosophes* brought to the fore during their century. It was entirely natural for the man who thought of himself as a poet-orator-leader of his people to have been preoccupied with those eighteenth-century figures who had altered not only the course of France but of Europe and the world.

I. PHILOSOPHES IN GENERAL

Development and Nurturing of Philosophes

As might be expected, the most thorough exposition of the *philosophe* movement appears in the *Histoire des Girondins*. There Lamartine offers some very percipient observations on the political and social ambiance that facilitated and accelerated the growth of Enlightenment thought. He mentions that the *foyer* of the duc d'Orléans provided a meeting place for the great thinkers of the age. There the cross-pollination of ideas helped produce the new spirit of the age. The duke's salon, moreover, was not parochial, including, as it did, guests from America (Franklin), England (Gibbon), and Germany (Grimm). Orléans's hospitality caused a melding of spirits, and both he and his children were the recipients of a blessing from the dying Voltaire (10:12).[4]

If the salon was the breeding ground for revolutionary thought, the presses of Holland, according to Lamartine, were responsible for its dissemination. "Tout ce qui avait une pensée suspecte à émettre," he writes, "un trait à lancer, un nom à cacher, allait emprunter les presses de la Hollande. Voltaire, J.-J. Rousseau, Diderot, Helvétius, Mirabeau lui-même, étaient allés naturaliser leurs écrits dans ce pays de publicité" (9: 271). This does not mean, of course, that all subversive writing was proscribed in France. A good deal of radical thought managed to reach print, reports Lamartine, thanks to the indulgent influence of the censor Malesherbes, who permitted the publication of the *Encyclopédie*, "cet arsenal des idées nouvelles en France." Lamartine quotes Dorat-Cubières to the effect that Malesherbes was himself a *philosophe* (12:21,24).

Role of the Philosophes

Lamartine makes few categorical assertions about the influence of the *philosophes* on the French Revolution. He does, however, permit others to see parallels between the Enlightenment posture, the Revolution, and political upheavals in early nineteenth-century Europe. Continental monarchs viewed the Revolution with almost unconcealed delight, states Lamartine, because they believed that the Revolution was nothing more "que la philosophie du 18ᵉ descendue des salons dans la place publique et passée des livres dans les discours" (9:252). In the *Mémoires politiques* he does concede that the Revolution was the realization of ideas found in the "catéchistes," Fénelon, Montesquieu, and Rousseau (28:13). This is not, however, the same as saying that those ideas created the Revolution. In the same essay Lamartine reinforces this view by alluding to the fact that the whole idea of human freedom (which the Revolution was supposed to be all about) and the rights of man were barely understood or grasped by the *philosophes*.

Lamartine sees evidence of *philosophe* ideology in some of the most brutal events in history. In his *Histoire de la Turquie*, for example, he indicts Voltaire, Diderot, and d'Alembert for having encouraged and applauded Europe's racist posture against Turkey. "Née dans une cour sceptique en Russie," writes Lamartine, "encouragée par un souverain athée en Prusse, . . . applaudie en France dans les correspondances de Voltaire, de Diderot, de d'Alembert, . . . elle fut une pensée de civilisation tendant à ruiner par la main de la Sémiramis du Nord les mosquées de Mahomet en Orient" (28:75).

The *philosophes* succeeded in influencing the texture of certain parts of France, and those areas in turn radiated the radical spirit of the Enlightenment. The physical proximity of the *philosophes* was apparently enough to spread the "infection." Such an area, affirms Lamartine, was Savoie, where Rousseau spent the early part of his childhood in the village of Annecy. Les Charmettes was near Chambéry. Voltaire lived out his old age at Ferney, "à la porte de Savoie." Lamartine feels that the presence of these individuals extended to Geneva, the Calvinist citadel of religious obscurantism, and turned it into the metropolis of modern philosophy (12:156).

As for the importance of the *philosophes* for individuals, Lamartine sees their hand either as positive or negative influences. Louis XVIII found in Voltaire an admirable model of clarity and grace, whereas the sophism and declamatory excesses of Rousseau repelled him (12:114). Emperor Alexander of Russia is alleged to have borrowed his ideas about constitutional government from Montesquieu and Voltaire (17:

324

169). The preponderant Galioni and Filangieri carried on the
Enlightenment spirit (27:119). De Maistre, on the other hand,
abominated the atheism of the age of reason, and turned Voltaire, says Lamartine, into a "terroriste sacré" (37:44).

The Personal Connection

Lamartine's exposure to the idea of the Enlightenment occurred early. In the *Confidences* he reveals that the childhood
tutorials carried on by abbé Dumont included the major
works of the eighteenth century. Nor were these books merely the subject of cursory examinations—they formed the basis
of interminable discussions and arguments (29:355). Dumont,
however, was prudent enough to have him also read counter-
revolutionary pamphlets and newspapers (29:100). This initial contact with the polarities in French intellectual and
political thought doubtless explains in part why he was constantly vacillating between his often fervent support of the
Revolution and his criticism of the society that followed it.

Lamartine's sensitivity to these issues was honed at Mâcon,
where his uncle welcomed many of the Enlightenment luminaries. In retrospect, Lamartine records that his uncle's *foyer*
was, for many years, a substitute for the Academy of Dijon,
the institution to which the names of Rousseau and Buffon
are inevitably linked (29:491). M. de Valmont, Lamartine's
uncle, mixed with the aristocracy, the literary fraternity, and
the clergy. He also claimed to have known Frederick the
Great (29:476). "L'abbé Sigorgne avait connu les écrivains et
les philosophes du 18e siècle," writes Lamartine about one of
the regulars of the Mâcon coterie (29:472). This singular cler-
ic had been the interlocutor of both Rousseau and Voltaire
and had discussed religion and philosophy with them "avec
talent, politesse, dignité, estime mutuelle" (29:472).

Catherine and the Philosophes

Lamartine is unusually severe in his indictment of the *philosophes* for their sycophancy toward Catherine the Great.
"Voltaire, Diderot, d'Alembert, le grand Frédéric, donnèrent

honteusement, les uns par vanité, les autres par cupidité, ceux-ci par engouement, ceux-là par faiblesse, l'exemple de l'adulation du succès, et l'exemple pire de l'estime au vice et de l'indulgence au crime" (31:240). It was their example that caused an otherwise distinguished literary generation to prostrate itself before a woman "qui s'était faite veuve pour régner en homme sur le trône, en courtisane dans son lit." D'Alembert almost went to Russia to tutor her son, but his love of Paris caused him to reconsider. Diderot went to Saint Petersburg ostensibly to instruct the tzarina in philosophy and legislation, but, as Lamartine wrily observes, she could have taught him much about the science of government. Her association with these writers, through personal contact and correspondence, had selfish personal ends, those of acquiring the luster that names like Voltaire and Diderot would add to her court (31:268). What is all the more ironic is that despite her familiarity with the most radical thinkers in France and her assiduous cultivation of them, Catherine's sympathy was a mere pose. She was in reality, asserts Lamartine, a counter-revolutionary and an implacable enemy of the anarchy that the *philosophe* ideology had allegedly engendered (31:3,9).

Lamartine is especially exercised by the fawning correspondence of Voltaire. He calls it "des railleries adulatrices" (28:109) and asserts that it was his worst weakness. "L'apothéose de Cathérine II par Voltaire est la plus grande faiblesse de ce philosophe," he writes scathingly, "car en faiblissant ainsi devant une femme dont toute la fortune était fondée sur un meurtre, il faisait faiblir avec lui toute la morale de l'humanité" (31:241). Lamartine elsewhere indicts Voltaire as an accomplice in Catherine's crimes. "L'adulation, quand elle descend si bas, n'est plus seulement lâche, elle est complice" (31:256).

II. VOLTAIRE

The Voltaire-Lamartine Rapport

We have noted briefly the family ties that joined Lamartine to the *philosophes*. In the *Nouvelles confidences* the poet speaks several times of the closeness of Voltaire in the structuring of his literary vocation. He records that his father was so enamored of Voltaire's poetry that he found it difficult to appreciate his own son's verses. On reading some of the latter he did not know whether to approve or to criticize them (29:503).

Lamartine's association with Voltaire goes back to his childhood days and the influences of both his maternal grandfather and uncle. His grandfather was intendant for the duke of Orléans and his grandmother a governess for the children. In these capacities they came in contact with the celebrities of the period. "Voltaire, à son court et dernier voyage à Paris, qui fut un triomphe, vint rendre visite aux jeunes princes," recalls Lamartine. "Ma mère, qui n'avait que sept à huit ans, assista à la visite, et quoique si jeune, elle comprit, par l'impression qui se révélait autour d'elle, que c'était quelque chose de plus qu'un roi." Voltaire's appearance, his accoutrements and words became indelibly marked in the consciousness of Lamartine's mother, or as the poet himself expressed it, "comme l'empreinte d'un être antédiluvien dans la pierre de nos montagnes" (29:29).

On his father's side there was M. de Valmont, who represented for the young Lamartine the example of the literary erudite who had read all the "haute litterature," and especially Voltaire. The fact that his uncle's estate was at Saint-Claude, near Ferney, afforded Valmont the opportunity of meeting the patriarch of Ferney. "Il ne partageait pas toutes les opinions philosophiques de Voltaire," Lamartine hastens to explain, "mais il aimait par similitude de nature, ce bon sens exquis qui exprime l'idée avec la même précision que le chiffre exprime le nombre. Il aspirait comme lui à la réforme des idées arriérées sur l'esprit humain de quelques siècles" (29:449).

The importance of Voltaire for the Lamartine household was reinforced by the poet's father, who made a practice of reading aloud such plays as *Mérope*. Reminiscing about this in the *Préface des Méditations*, Lamartine speaks rhapsodically about Voltaire's instinct for poetic symmetry and divine-like

327

rhythm. "Je me disais intérieurement: Voilà une langue que je voudrais bien savoir, que je voudrais bien parler quand je serais grand . . . la *Henriade,* toute sèche et toute déclamatoire qu'elle fût, me ravissait" (1:7,8).

Although he was later to surpass Voltaire as a poet, Lamartine sometimes credits the former with furnishing inspiration for some of his memorable poems. Just before writing the sixteenth *Recueillement,* he recalls having read some of Voltaire's letters along with those of Horace and Mme de Sévigné (5:202).

Voltaire's Influence

Lamartine's evaluation of Voltaire is a well-balanced one, alternating between accolades showered on the man's genius and criticism heaped on his personal ethics.

His influence, we are told, extends far beyond the borders of France—into Berlin, where academicians seek to emulate the genius of Voltaire (9:273). Lamartine feels that his incredible letter-writing activity helped spread the Voltaire ideology, for his correspondents spanned the continent (9:267).

In the *Histoire des Girondins* Lamartine observes that Voltaire had eighty years with which to do battle with time and with his century. Unlike Rousseau's disciples, who came mainly from the proletariat, Voltaire's were drawn from the highest echelons of French society. Voltaire's followers eventually overturned altars, and Rousseau's raised them. In the final analysis, Voltaire was a monarchist, and Rousseau believed in the republic (9:215).

Lamartine sees Voltaire as a conscious iconoclast who wished to abolish theocracy and establish the rule of reason and tolerance. His reputation in the post-Revolution period was so strong that Napoleon found it necessary to denigrate him in order to consolidate his own tyranny (9:220). An astute politician, Voltaire gained the support of kings by ceding them absolute powers and fighting for their freedom from

Rome. With the backing of the monarchy, the nobility, and the educated bourgeoisie, he felt secure enough to launch his lifelong assault on Christendom (9:224).

Although Lamartine recognizes Voltaire's invaluable contributions to the cause of religious freedom and to human reason, he does not sympathize with the latter's destructive cynicism. The end product of the Voltairean ideology is the skeptic, not the believer. Moreover, cautions Lamartine, impiety can never destroy a religion; only another faith can do that (9:226).

This failing, however, does not detract from Voltaire's luster as the leading mind of the eighteenth century. Lamartine is even moved in the *Ressouvenir du lac Léman* to celebrate that fame in verse.

> Voltaire! quelque soit le nom dont on le nomme,
> C'est un cycle vivant, c'est un siècle fait homme!
> Pour fixer de plus haut le jour de la raison,
> Son œil d'aigle et de lynx choisit ton horizon,
> Heureux si, sur ces monts où Dieu luit davantage,
> Il eût vu plus de ciel à travers le nuage.
>
> (4:165)

This accolade might seem excessive except for the fact that Lamartine asserts on several occasions that Voltaire is one of the great immortal poets (1:20).

Voltaire's name also appears in Lamartine's appreciative essay on John Milton. He sees him as an imitator of the Miltonian epic (36:19) but admits that the *Henriade* never approached *Paradise Lost* (36:32). Both, however, asserts Lamartine, lack real understanding of human emotion, and that is why "la *Henriade* est surannée et le *Paradis perdu* n'est plus qu'un monument de bibliothèque" (36:33).

Lamartine shares with Mérimée an intense admiration for *Candide*, especially chapter 26 and its deposed monarchs at the Venice festival. For Lamartine this portion is symbolic of the current state of affairs in the French legislature—with one significant difference. "C'est qu'à Venise on masquait son visage pendant ce carnaval de rois, et qu'à Paris on ne masque que son nom" (40:427).

Lamartine also sees Voltairean traits in individuals such as Paoli (10:78), the grand duke of Tuscany (37:212), and the marquis of Maisonfort (37:189).

III. ROUSSEAU

Rousseau-Lamartine Rapport

There has been no dearth of critical commentary on the "parenté d'âme" between Lamartine and his eighteenth-century "romantic" predecessor. Virtually every book on Lamartine contains sections tracing the poet's dependence on Rousseau as the precursor of the poetry of feeling. Most of these works, however, focus their attention on the elements in Lamartine's poetry that are seen as evocative of Rousseau's apotheosis of nature.

There is no doubt that it was this characteristic in Rousseau that led Lamartine to admire and later to seek to emulate the author of the *Confessions*. But in his readings of Rousseau, Lamartine soon realized that there was a lot more there than lyricism and poetic fervor. Lamartine perceived in Rousseau's political writings, especially the *Contrat social*, manifestoes for the direction of French society. Since he himself was actively involved in French political life, Lamartine could not help but confront Rousseau's vision of the utopian state.

As for the Rousseauean elements in his poetry, Lamartine acknowledges his debt often and in one or two instances speaks of himself as a kind of reincarnation. In referring to the *Méditations*, he states somewhat immodestly: "Le public entendit une âme, sans la voir, et vit un homme au lieu d'un livre. Depuis J. J. Rousseau . . . c'était le poète qu'il attendait" (1:19). Lamartine ranks Rousseau with Homer, Job,

330

and Milton, among those who spoke of him "dans la solitude de la langue de mon cœur; une langue d'harmonie, d'images et de passions" (1:30), and Rousseau is summoned by Lamartine in the *Ressouvenir du lac Léman*. "Je vois d'ici verdir les pentes de Clarens," he writes movingly of the Genevese lake, "Des rêves de Rousseau fantastiques royaumes" (1:164). In the *Préface aux recueillements poétiques*, Lamartine again models himself consciously on Rousseau when he tells Léon Bruys d'Ouilly to read his, Lamartine's, confidential thoughts, his confessions (5:184).

The association of Rousseau with Lake Léman again moves Lamartine, on 7 June 1833, to pen the following verses written at the Ermitage:

> Toi, dont le siècle encore agite la mémoire,
> Pourquoi dors-tu si loin de ton lac, ô Rousseau?
> Un abîme de bruit, de malheur et de gloire,
> Devait-il séparer ta tombe et ton berceau?
>
> (5:373)

In the subsequent stanzas, Lamartine expresses the hope that he, unlike Rousseau, will be interred in the place he loves so well.

Rousseau's gift for introspection is one of those qualities that attracts Lamartine. In the *Histoire des Girondins*, he alludes to this in a somewhat awkward self-complimentary fashion. "Mais si je n'ai pas reçu de la nature le style et l'éloquence de Jean-Jacques Rousseau, je n'ai pas reçu non plus sa féroce personnalité; et si le lecteur a quelque excès à craindre de ma plume dans ce jugement sur moi-même, ce n'est pas, à coup sûr, l'excès d'orgueil; ce serait plutôt l'excès de sévérité" (15:18). Lamartine makes another attempt to explain himself in terms of Rousseau in the *Préambule aux nouvelles confidences*, where he asserts that he, Rousseau, and others have quietly interrogated their soul and the result has been a dialogue with themselves, on the one hand, and with their century and the future, on the other (29:403). In the same work, however, he returns to disparaging himself for not having the genius of Rousseau (29:407).

The Family Ties

As with the other *philosophes*, Lamartine came to know of Rousseau through his grandmother, Mme des Roys and through his mother. In the *Confidence* he asserts that Mme des Roys knew Rousseau better than Buffon, Grimm, Gibbon, or d'Alembert. "Ma mère, quoi que très pieuse et très étroitement attachée au dogme catholique," declares Lamartine, "avait conservé une tendre admiration pour ce grand homme, sans doute parce qu'il avait plus qu'un génie, parce qu'il avait une âme. Elle n'était pas de la religion de son génie, mais elle était de la religion de son cœur" (29:30). Lamartine's mother was familiar with Rousseau's theories on the education of children (29:78) and doubtless transmitted aspects of the nature doctrine to her precocious youngster. She had observed a precedent for this in the Orléans household, where the duke had innovated in using Rousseau's techniques in teaching his own children.

Lamartine's infatuation with Rousseau, begun through the osmosis of family ties, was reinforced by visits to those haunts associated with Rousseau. He mentions a sojourn in Chambéry, near Les Charmettes, "ce berceau de la sensibilité et du génie de Jean-Jacques Rousseau," as the source for the nineteenth *Méditation* (6:174). In the *Confidences* he calls it a *"berceau fleuri"* (29:330). In the *Voyages en orient* we find corroboration of the importance to Lamartine of locales once frequented by Jean-Jacques. "Combien plus tard j'ai passé de matins et de soirs assis aux pieds des beaux châtaigniers, dans ce petit vallon des Charmettes, où le souvenir de Jean-Jacques Rousseau m'attirait et me retenait par la sympathie de ses impressions, de ses rêveries, de ses malheurs, et de son génie" (6:313). The *Confidences* provide additional evidence of Lamartine's attempts to derive inspiration from Rousseau's old haunts, this time Lake Geneva (29:310).

The Political Rousseau

Lamartine related directly to Rousseau in a much wider context than that of the literary disciple. He saw in the latter's *Contrat social* and other political documents regimens that were adopted by revolutionary figures such as Robespierre. Much of Lamartine's political *œuvre* is characterized by an intense struggle over whether Rousseau's utopian vision was indeed the panacea he claimed it was for resolving society's inequities.

In Lamartine's view, Rousseau was no political theorist but rather a dreamer in whom one could sense the hand of God (9:25). But in the *Histoire des Girondins* he makes but one of his many strictures about Rousseau. The latter, he asserts, was a very poor psychologist when it came to understanding man. He did not grasp man's innate weaknesses. On the other hand, Rousseau might have sensed that in order to inspire men you must set ideals before them; you cannot mingle illusion and reality. The church does just that. Rousseau saw the political ideal just as Fénelon had seen the Christian ideal (9:26).

Lamartine is always careful in assessing Rousseau's influence on the French Revolution. His writings, or at least "les maximes plus mâles de la philosophie de Rousseau," helped undermine the faith that the nobility once had in the monarchy (9:278). Rousseau's theories, we are reminded, were canonized by the revolutionary thinkers. "Les ouvriers de la Révolution," he writes, "rendaient toujours hommage à la pensée de leur œuvre dans l'auteur du *Contrat social*, qui aurait si souvent désavoué de tels disciples" (12:437).

In the *Histoire des Girondins* Lamartine praises the *Contrat social* as the harbinger of the rights of man, but with the *Entretiens littéraires* (1861) a heavy disenchantment has set in. There Rousseau is termed "ce faux prophète d'une liberté anarchique, d'une liberté sans limites, d'une égalité impracticable" (15:122). Lamartine asserts that both the *Contrat social* and the *Déclaration des droits de l'homme et du citoyen*

333

of 1789 "sont un catalogue de contre-vérités politiques. Ni l'un ni l'autre de ces apologistes," continues Lamartine, "ne comprenaient un mot de ce qu'ils écrivaient; du moins ils n'en prévoyaient pas les conséquences. Le peuple votait de l'enthousiasme, quoi? le néant" (15:122). There is another Lamartinian appraisal of the *Contrat social* in the essay on Fénelon. The latter's *Télémaque* is ranked with Rousseau's work, More's *Utopia*, and Plato's *Republic* as an example of vain speculation. Reading these works, observes Lamartine, reminds him of Frederick the Great's sally: "Si j'avais un empire à punir, je le donnerais à gouverner à des philosophes" (36:279).

Robespierre

Robespierre is seen by Lamartine as the disciple *par excellence* of Rousseau. "La philosophie de J.-J. Rousseau avait pénétré profondément son intelligence; cette philosophie, en tombant dans une volonté active, n'était pas restée une lettre morte; elle était devenue en lui un dogme, une foi, un fanatisme" (9:47). It was Robespierre along with Pétion who, basing themselves on the Rousseauean vision, created the popular movement, while Cazalès, Mirabeau, Maury and the clergy debated frivolously what form the government should take (9:369). Robespierre was the convinced and passionate pupil of Rousseau, according to Lamartine. The *Contrat social* was Scripture for him. War fought on behalf of this ideology was considered by Robespierre to be a glorious vocation (9:442).

"Si son maître J.-J. Rousseau eût quitté sa cabane des Charmettes ou d'Ermenonville pour être le législateur de l'humanité, il n'aurait pas mené une existence plus recueillie, plus pauvre que celle de Robespierre," asserts Lamartine about the Rousseau-Robespierre rapport (11:258). Like his model, Robespierre found solace in taking lonely walks on the Champs-Elysées (11:258). Of Robespierre's politics, Lamartine writes: "C'était comme nous l'avons dit, la politique de J.-J. Rousseau. En remontant plus haut, on en retrouve le germe dans le Christianisme mal appliqué" (11:375). Robespierre's conscious emulation of Rousseau was reinforced by frequent visits to the latter's onetime domicile at Montmorency. "C'est dans cette maison et dans ce jardin qu'il acheva son rapport, sur ces mêmes arbres où son maître avait si magnifiquement écrit de Dieu" (14:307). At a critical juncture in his career, Robespierre spent time meditating at Rousseau's Ermitage. "Venait-il chercher des inspirations politiques," asks Lamartine, "sous les arbres à l'ombre desquels son maître avait écrit le *Contrat social*? Venait-il faire hommage au philosophe d'une vie qu'il allait donner à la cause de la démocratie? Nul ne le sait" (14:400).

Lamartine feels that both Rousseau and Robespierre made fundamental errors when they promulgated their social axioms about the rights of man. They confused man's natural instincts with the legal rights created and guaranteed by society (12:347). "Mais, si la science manquait à la déclaration des droits de Jean-Jacques Rousseau et de Robespierre," writes Lamartine in mitigation, "l'esprit social respirait dans chacune de ces formules. C'était l'idéal de l'égalité et de la fraternité entre les hommes" (12:348). Robespierre is also seen to have modeled his educational theories on the prototype offered by Rousseau in the *Emile* (12:354).

In the final analysis, argues Lamartine, it was Robespierre who conferred much of the fame on Rousseau that posterity takes for granted. It was he who saw to it that Rousseau's remains were transported to the Pantheon, and in so doing he "donnait, par cet hommage à la philosophie religieuse et presque chrétienne de J.-J. Rousseau, son véritable sens à la Révolution" (14:316).

Rousseau and Others

Although Lamartine links Rousseau most often with the figure of Robespierre, there are several other historical and literary personalities whose names are joined with Rousseau, usually as his disciples. Aimé-Martin is one of those who "avait contracté parenté avec les âmes de Fénelon, de Jean-Jacques Rousseau" (9:217). Another is Mme Roland. "La lecture de l'Héloïse de Rousseau, qu'on lui prêta alors," comments Lamartine, "fit sur son cœur le même genre d'impression que Plutarque avait fait sur son esprit . . . Rousseau lui fit rêver le bonheur" (9:412). Even her marriage resembled the fictional union between Julie and Wolmar (9:416).

It is not surprising that Marat's name is also associated with Rousseau by Lamartine, who asserts that the revolutionary leader had a supernatural faith in Rousseau's principles (9: 274). Lamartine also alludes to an affinity between Rousseau and Lamenais, particularly in the latter's love of reverie (17:204). Of Mme de Staël, Lamartine also observes in the *Histoire de la restauration* that she had much of Rousseau's reverie in her. In fact, he calls her "le J.-J. Rousseau des femmes," with the demurer, "mais plus tendre, plus sensée et plus capable de grandes actions que lui" (17:188,191).

Another woman whom Lamartine links with Rousseau is Mme de Sévigné. He does this in an essay in which he deals with the transitory nature of political fame versus the permanence of literary reputation (41:41). It is Mme de Sévigné, asserts Lamartine, who after the separation from her daughter, "s'y plonge dans toute la poésie des larmes. . . . Elle découvre ces délicieuses sympathies entre la nature inanimée et l'âme vivante qui ont fait depuis le génie de Jean-Jacques Rousseau" (41:112).

Fénelon is another literary great whom Lamartine juxtaposes to Rousseau. Like Rousseau and other "grands esprits" Fénelon began by singing before thinking, says Lamartine (36:353). But his ideas on education were superior to those of the *Emile*, because Fénelon had a pragmatic orientation whereas Rousseau was utopian. Lamartine also affirms that when one tries to ascertain who was the pioneering spirit of French revolutionary thought, the first real tribune of the people, the first reformer of kings, the first apostle of liberty (in the Rousseauean sense), it is Fénelon whose name comes to mind (36:277).

Reference here should also be made to brief parallels drawn by Lamartine between Rousseau and Brissot de Warville (9:204), Girardin (9:340), and Mme de Staël's mother (9:295).

Lamartine, Critic of Rousseau

As with his attitude toward the *philosophes*, Lamartine, particularly in the later years, has some fairly mordant comments to make about his youthful idol, Rousseau. In the *Confidences* he calls Rousseau's *Confessions* "puérilités" (29:52); and, in *Raphaël*, Lamartine speaks of him as being more passionate than inspired and more "grand instinct . . . que grande vérité" (32:318). "Jean-Jacques Rousseau a dit un mot qui serait un blasphème, si ce n'était pas un paradoxe," writes Lamartine in order to amend Rousseau; "L'homme qui pense est un animal dépravé! Quant à moi, si j'écrivais comme lui des axiomes, je dirais: L'homme qui réfléchit est un homme qui commence, mais l'homme qui prie est un être achevé" (33:416). In the *Histoire des Girondins* there is little criticism save for a somewhat ambiguous allusion to Rousseau's middle-class parentage (9:300). But by the time of the *Critique de l'histoire des Girondins*, Lamartine is indicting Rousseau along with Mably, Robespierre, and Saint-Just for having preached the kind of social chimeras "qui mènent le peuple droit au crime par la fureur qui succède aux déceptions, et qui tuent bourreaux et victimes par la guerre anti-civique de la propriété qui refuse tout et du prolétariat qui anéantit tout" (15:88).

On the positive side of the ledger, Lamartine sees Rousseau's greatest contribution in sensitizing Frenchmen to nature. This modern Platonism, as he terms it, was an efficient antidote to the materialism and near atheism ("crime, honte et désespoir de l'esprit human") that had infested the French mind. In the *Histoire de la restauration*, Lamartine also credits Bernadin de Saint-Pierre, Ballanche, Jouffroy, Royer-Collard, and Aimé-Martin with working in concert to find a substitute for the Enlightenment's pernicious doctrine of irreligion (17:204).

By virtue of family ties Lamartine could almost be regarded as a nineteenth-century honorary *philosophe*. His mother and uncle transmitted to the impressionable young Lamartine personal anecdotes and stories about thinkers such as d'Alembert, Diderot, and Voltaire. Later this domestic influence was reinforced by the study, under the tutelage of abbé Dumont, of the major texts of the Enlightenment. This apprenticeship also exposed him to the postrevolutionary literature of reaction, which the abbé conveniently made available. As a budding poet it was quite natural for Lamartine to draw inspiration from Rousseau, the one *philosophe* with soul. As Lamartine became involved in France's political affairs and began to think seriously about the structure of society, the writings of the *philosophes* and their revolutionary interpreters were subjected by him to a new kind of scrutiny.

In the Lamartinian *œuvre* the image of the *philosophes* is judiciously balanced between praise for the accomplishments of the Enlightenment—notably the spread of tolerance and the concept of freedom—and severe criticism both of the philosophic coalition and its unrealistic theories about the reformation of mankind. In this Lamartine resembles Chateaubriand. Both are ready to heap encomiums on the *philosophes* for their contributions to the idea of constitutional government, but they also indict them for personal hypocrisy. Lamartine, in particular, was incensed by the way d'Alembert, Voltaire, and Diderot, ostensibly the *avant-coureurs* of progressive political thought, scurried to solicit the favor of Catherine, the northern Semiramis, and the woman who in later

338

years came to personify autocratic rule and political obscurantism.

In the case of Voltaire one finds in Lamartine the kind of respectful posture that a nineteenth-century writer would have for the Enlightenment's greatest giant. What is unexpected, however, is the debt that Lamartine claims to owe Voltaire as the model for poetic splendor. The esteem in which Lamartine held the *Henriade* is especially surprising. As for Voltaire's political program, Lamartine has many kind words to say about the application of reason in the conduct of human affairs. He also feels that, unlike Rousseau, Voltaire had a more mature approach in his assault on the establishment. Although his targets were controversial enough, the church and the monarchy, Voltaire was astute enough to act the role of Brahmin, and in so doing gained the support not only of the aristocracy but of the bourgeoisie as well. Lamartine does not, however, let Voltaire off without a condemnation of the latter's materialism and cynicism. He makes a telling critique of the whole idea of *écrasez l'infâme* when he points out that Voltaire failed to understand that you cannot make people give up a religious persuasion by subjecting it to abuse and ridicule. This can only be done by introducing them to a new and superior religious system.

There is little doubt that in the early years of his fame Lamartine thought of himself as Rousseau incarnate in a new century. He testifies to this in numerous passages describing the inspiration he derived from reading Rousseau and from frequenting the latter's haunts and residences, particularly Les Charmettes. Even in those passages in which Lamartine denies the possibility of a legitimate comparison, the impression is strongly conveyed that Lamartine is obviously searching for a felicitous contradiction.

Lamartine never lost his admiration for Rousseau the prophet of sensibility, but he did acquire severe reservations about Rousseau the political theorist. Rousseau, he admits, had an inspiring vision of the future, but that vision must be supplemented with a mature understanding of human psychology—a science totally lacking in the author of the *Contrat social*. This is why, claims Lamartine, it is possible to see Rousseau's writings leading logically into anarchy and violence—which is precisely what happened when Rousseauean disciples like Robespierre tried to apply his master's utopian ideas to postrevolutionary society.

Despite his strictures on Rousseau's "vain speculations" Lamartine recognizes in him the man who did the most in teaching the world about the rights of man and the ideal of liberty, equality, and fraternity. But his real contribution, according to Lamartine, was helping to reorient French literature from the sterile intellectualism of the mainstream *philosophes* to a modern Platonism in which soul and heart and nature assumed the preeminent roles.

1. A. Desvoyes, "Voltaire et Lamartine," *RHLF* 19 (1912): 911-12; J. Sareil's section on Lamartine and Voltaire, in *Voltaire et la critique* (New York, 1969).

2. J. Gaudon, "Lamartine lecteur de Sade," *Mercure de France*, No. 343 (1961), pp. 420-38.

3. C. Fournet, "Lamartine et Rousseau," *Annales de la Société Jean-Jacques Rousseau* 28 (1939-40): 7-17.

4. All quotations from Lamartine are from the *Œuvres complètes* (Paris, 1860-66). Lamartine also cites the salon of Mme de Staël's mother as another *foyer* for the *philosophes*. He calls it "le cénacle de la philosophie du dix-huitième siècle," where Voltaire, Rousseau, Buffon, Diderot, Raynal, Bernardin de Saint-Pierre, Condorcet, "avaient joué avec cet enfant [Mme de Staël] et atisé ses premières pensées" (9:295).

Stendhal and the Age of Ideas

Stendhal remained all his life a man of the eighteenth century, and it is my purpose to indicate the crucial role the Age of Ideas and its writers played in crystallizing some of the novelist's most profound attitudes and beliefs. I shall not attempt to present a complete survey of those authors and books that are discussed at some length in Stendhal's personal writings; obviously the scope of such a study would necessitate a book-length essay. But I should like to delineate the essential features of Stendhal's affinity with the eighteenth century.[1]

Paul Valéry, in his typically tentative and skeptical manner, alluded to Stendhal's indebtedness to the eighteenth century by emphasizing the writer's lightness of touch and vivacity of mind: "Beyle tenait heureusement du siècle où il naquit l'inestimable don de la vivacité. La prépotence pesante et l'ennui n'eurent jamais de plus prompt adversaire. Classiques et Romantiques, entre lesquels il se mut et étincela, irritaient sa verve précise."[2] Whereas Valéry envisaged Stendhal as a man of the eighteenth century primarily because of his style and temperament, Georg Lukács defined the affinity in ideological terms: "Stendhal's attitude to romanticism is . . . a complete rejection. He is a true disciple of the philosophers of the Enlightenment."[3] We shall see, however, that Stendhal was never the docile, respectful type of disciple, for even when dealing with authors he most admired —Montesquieu, Voltaire, Diderot, and Rousseau—he adopted a resolutely independent, irreverent stance, an eminently eighteenth-century attitude.

To begin, the Revolution was the most dramatic and exciting feature in the otherwise gray and uneventful landscape of Beyle's lonely and precocious childhood in his native Grenoble. In *La Vie de Henry Brulard* Stendhal quite obviously takes keen pleasure in evoking his revolutionary zeal and jubilation and in contrasting his secret feelings of joy and enthusiasm with the utter consternation and dismay of his family, especially of his father, Chérubin Beyle. To be sure, Grenoble was fortunate in escaping the excesses of the Terror, and young Beyle was spared the experience of persecution or the spectacle of mass arrests and executions. And Chérubin Beyle, despite his notoriously royalist opinions, never paid for these with the loss of property, or worse.[4]

In a particularly vivid scene in *Henry Brulard*, Stendhal depicts his feelings upon learning of the execution of Louis XVI from his distraught father: "Je jugeais la cause entre ma famille et moi lorsque mon père entra. Je le vois encore en redingote de molleton blanc qu'il n'avait pas ôtée pour aller à deux pas à la poste. 'C'en est fait, dit-il, avec un gros soupir, ils l'ont assassiné.' Je fus saisi d'un des plus vifs mouvements de joie que j'ai éprouvés en ma vie. Le lecteur pensera peut-être que je suis cruel mais tel j'étais à dix ans tel je suis à cinquante-deux."[5] But when young Beyle sneaked into the local Club des Jacobins in order to witness a meeting, which was open to the public, this experience turned out to have a sobering effect on him. He was frightened and repulsed by the unruly and foul-smelling mob of spectators and disappointed by the orators.[6] Recalling this scene, the older Stendhal mused that this ambivalent reaction was to typify his politics for the rest of his life. A sincere democrat by conviction, he would nevertheless retain aristocratic tastes and leanings and, when confronted with political tactics or ideology, found it hard to rid himself of doubt, skepticism, and a desire to remain aloof and independent.[7]

344

At the Ecole Centrale in Grenoble, where Beyle was a student from 1796 to 1799, the professors were all imbued with the philosophy and ideology of the Enlightenment. What he learned from the works and theories of such late Enlightenment thinkers as Condorcet and Helvétius has already been demonstrated.[8] But the most persuasive spokesman for the eighteenth century was the kindly Dr. Henri Gagnon, young Beyle's maternal grandfather and favorite relative, a man of vast culture, exquisite manners, and a great admirer of the *philosophes* and especially of Voltaire, whom he had personally visited in Ferney and of whom he always spoke with immense respect and affection. A bust of Voltaire adorned his study. Dr. Gagnon's skepticism, fine sense of irony, and aristocratic charm stood out in stark contrast against the somber background of the Chérubin Beyle household.

By reading books surreptitiously borrowed from the libraries of his father and grandfather, young Beyle came into contact with a number of eighteenth-century authors. Henri Beyle had a special predilection for the historians, chroniclers, memorialists, novelists, and dramatists who could enlighten him on the manners and mores of the Regency. Saint-Simon, Lesage, and Montesquieu were among his favorite authors. He particularly admired Saint-Simon: "J'ai adoré Saint-Simon en 1800 comme en 1836."[9] Through the works of these writers he discovered fascinating new sociological types: the nouveau riche, the financier, the woman of intrigue, the adventurer, the rake. In an increasingly unstable society a new class of men and women made their appearance, and Beyle saw in them qualities that he considered necessary for social success: daring, resourcefulness, and ambition unencumbered by too many moral scruples. He noted in his *Journal*: "L'histoire de la Régence doit être le morceau de celle de France le plus agréable à étudier. Lire Voltaire pour les faits officiels, Duclos, Saint-Simon, Marmontel et le morceau de Chamfort sur les mémoires de Richelieu et ceux de Duclos."[10]

The future apologist of strong passions studied with par-

345

ticular care those authors—especially novelists, memorialists, and moralists—who could probe and analyze human character and social behavior. Of the two major moralists of the eighteenth century, Vauvenargues and Chamfort, he undoubtedly preferred the former for the importance he attached to energy, action, and feeling.[11]

But what about the major figures who dominated the eighteenth century: Montesquieu, Voltaire, Rousseau, and Diderot? Let us pass in review, without attempting to be exhaustive, these writers as they appear in Stendhal's personal works.

Montesquieu occupies a special, privileged place. Stendhal, who generally liked to treat even his favorite authors with a total lack of reverence, was always respectful when speaking of Montesquieu. In *Henry Brulard* the aging novelist, in a moment of melancholy and self-doubt, quipped: "S'il y a un autre monde, je ne manquerai pas d'aller voir Montesquieu, s'il me dit: 'Mon pauvre ami, vous n'avez pas eu de talent du tout,' j'en serais fâché mais nullement surpris."[12] Dr. Gagnon, Henri Beyle's grandfather, probably aroused the boy's interest, for he always spoke of Montesquieu in the highest terms of praise. To be sure, Henri could not make sense out of the *Considérations sur les causes de la grandeur des Romains et de leur décadence* when he first read it, but he was immediately won over by the *Lettres persanes*, which he took along with a few other select books when he departed Grenoble for Paris in 1799.[13] He was to read *L'Esprit des lois* at a somewhat later date, in 1803, and copied long selections from it. Eventually, however, he expressed one reservation concerning Montesquieu's great work: he felt that it revealed too much willingness to compromise with established traditions.[14] It is especially as a stylist that Montesquieu fascinated Stendhal, who considered him even superior to Voltaire in this respect and did not hesitate to rank him in the select company of seven other French writers whom he regarded as the supreme masters of style: Montaigne, Molière, La Fontaine, Corneille, Racine, Voltaire, and Rousseau.[15]

346

Voltaire was greatly revered, not only in Dr. Gagnon's household, but also at the Ecole Centrale in Grenoble. Beyle was therefore introduced to Voltaire at an early age. "Prie mon g(rand)-p(ère) de te lire *Zadig* de la même manière qu'il me le lut il y a deux ans," he wrote to his sister Pauline in March 1800.[16] Even Chérubin Beyle, despite his conservative philosophy and strong religious sense, owned a complete set of Voltaire's works, which he kept in the library of his country house in Claix:

> Claix me déplaisait parce que j'y étais toujours assiégé de projets d'agriculture, mais bientôt je trouvai une grande compensation. . . . Je volai des volumes de Voltaire dans l'édition en quarante volumes. . . . J'en prenais deux et écartais un peu tous les autres, il n'y paraissait pas.[17]

And yet Stendhal has frequently repeated that he disliked Voltaire: "Du plus loin que je me souvienne, les écrits de Voltaire m'ont toujours souverainement déplu," and "Je méprisais sincèrement et souverainement le talent de Voltaire: je le trouvais *puéril*."[18] He himself found it difficult to explain this antipathy, since there were so many reasons why he should have been an admiring disciple of Voltaire.[19]

Like so many members of the post-Enlightenment generation, Stendhal had a certain image of Voltaire that was far from fair to the *philosophe*. He regarded him as a witty writer and storyteller, a talented historian and competent playwright, but as a superficial thinker and a man who knew nothing about the finer, more delicate feelings of which the human heart is capable: "Le conte espagnol le plus commun s'il y a de la générosité me fait venir les larmes aux yeux, tandis que je détourne les yeux du caractère de Chrysale de Molière et encore plus du fond méchant de *Zadig, Candide* . . . et autres ouvrages de Voltaire."[20] But if Stendhal professed never to have loved Voltaire, he was a constant and attentive student of his works, especially of his *contes*, which he considered as a perfect antidote against what he detested most in

347

the style of his contemporaries: bombastic verbosity and flatulence.[21]

Young Beyle's revelation of Rousseau was through *La Nouvelle Héloïse*, which he also read in secret and with such intense rapture that he later viewed this experience as one of the most memorable and ecstatic in his life.[22] Interestingly enough, Chérubin Beyle was a devout Rousseauist: "Dès l'âge de six ans, je crois, mon père m'avait inoculé son enthousiasme pour J.-J. Rousseau, que plus tard il exécra comme *anti-roi*."[23] Despite his strong feelings of resentment against his father, upon whom he looked as the very embodiment of bourgeois pettiness and chicanery, he was willing to give him some credit for sensitivity because of his sincere devotion to Jean-Jacques: "Il faut rendre cette justice au goût de mon père, il était enthousiaste de Rousseau."[24]

Beyle's veneration of Rousseau was to reach a high point when he sought guidance and solace in books as a shy and lonely youth in Paris in 1799, and when, as an eager if inexperienced horseman following Bonaparte's army in Italy in 1800, he beheld for the first time the beauties of mountains and lakes in Switzerland and Lombardy. Although his initial enthusiasm was to cool considerably in the light of a more critical and dispassionate study of Rousseau, he remained a loyal disciple of Jean-Jacques the dreamer, hapless lover, wanderer, and man of exquisite feeling. Rousseau the thinker and theorist, on the other hand, left Stendhal unmoved and unconvinced, and on many occasions he took the author of *Le Contrat social* and *Emile* to task for what he viewed as an unrealistic, impractical, and utopian approach to political and social problems.[25]

For Stendhal, Rousseau was primarily the autobiographer, novelist, and analyst of the human soul and its more noble aspirations. He even attributed to his excessive enthusiasm for Rousseau's idealistic vision of men and women his own difficulties in coping with reality:

348

Il y a un autre défaut que j'ai eu longtemps dont je cherche à me guérir chaque jour. Ne voyant personne chez mon gr(and)-p(apa), je portais toute mon attention sur les ouvrages que je lisais; Jean-Jacques eut la préférence; je me figurai les hommes d'après les impressions qu'il avait reçues de ceux avec qui il avait vécu. . . . Cette folie me donna quelques moments de la plus divine illusion . . . mais, en g(énér)al, elle me donna une existence mélancolique, j'étais misanthrope à force d'aimer les hom(mes). C'est-à-dire que je haïssais les hom(mes) tels qu'ils sont, à force de chérir des êtres chimériques, tels que Saint-Preux, milord Edouard, etc.[26]

On the positive side, however, Stendhal credits *La Nouvelle Héloïse* for having effectively counteracted the effect of the eighteenth-century libertine novels he was devouring in secret: "La lecture de la *Nouvelle Héloïse* et les scrupules de Saint-Preux me formèrent profondément honnête homme; je pouvais encore, après cette lecture faite avec larmes et transports d'amour pour la vertu, faire des coquineries, mais je me serais senti coquin. Ainsi c'est un livre lu en grande cachette et malgré mes parents qui m'a fait honnête homme."[27]

Many references to Diderot show that Stendhal was thoroughly familiar with those works by the Encyclopedist that had thus far been published. Both his father and grandfather owned complete sets of the *Encyclopédie*: "Mon père et mon grand-père avaient l'*Encyclopédie* in-folio de Diderot et d'Alembert. . . . Mon père ne me voyait feuilleter l'*Encyclopédie* qu'avec chagrin. J'avais la plus entière confiance en ce livre."[28] Other comments scattered in Stendhal's writings allude to Diderot's plays and essays on the theater, to his *Salons*, to his novels and *contes*, and to his correspondence. On 15 September 1832 Stendhal inscribed Diderot's name among "les douze premiers, parmi les gens qui donnent du plaisir en français par du noir sur du blanc."[29] Although sometimes criticizing Diderot for lapsing occasionally into what he called "le style emphatique," he nevertheless exonerated

349

him by confidently predicting that, by 1850, the Encyclopedist would appear far "supérieur à la plupart des *emphatiques actuels*."[30] In *De l'amour* Stendhal analyzes amorous jealousy in women and remarks: "Je ne connais d'autre remède à un mal si cruel que la mort de qui l'inspire ou de qui l'éprouve. On peut voir la jalousie française dans l'histoire de Mme de La Pommeraie de *Jacques le Fataliste*."[31] When Stendhal undertook to become an art critic and *salonnier*, he became especially aware of the important role Diderot played as the first man of letters who succeeded in treating that genre in an original, creative fashion.[32] In January 1805 he noted in his *Journal*: "Je lis la *Vie de Sénèque* par Diderot, bon ouvrage"; and in December of the same year he wrote: "Lire la *Poétique* de Diderot et, en général, ses œuvres. Jacques me paraît charmant."[33] In the *Courrier anglais*, Diderot is proclaimed as an "homme d'un génie et d'un jugement peu ordinaires,"[34] no small compliment from the pen of such a highly critical and independent-minded writer as Stendhal.

There is another angle from which Diderot helped Stendhal to formulate his own ideas, and it concerns the role of passions and emotions in the creative process. Although wholeheartedly subscribing to Diderot's rehabilitation of the passions as an irreplaceable source of productive energy, Stendhal, in a personal evolution of his thought on the subject that closely parallels that of Diderot, came to the conclusion that emotion untrammeled by judgment and the critical faculties hinders more than it stimulates the writer or artist. Obviously thinking of the *Paradoxe sur le comédien*, he determined to reject Rousseau's concept of the act of writing as a spontaneous outpouring of feeling and thought: "Je trouve froid ce que j'ai écrit dans l'enthousiasme. Je pense que la dissertation de Diderot sur les acteurs, pourrait bien être vraie (qu'on peut jouer, imiter la passion, étant pour le moment très froid, et ayant seulement le souvenir que tel jour qu'on était très agité, on faisait ainsi). Mon extrême méfiance me rend froid."[35] Through Diderot, Stendhal increasingly

350

adopted the Wordsworthian aesthetic that emotion is best expressed when it is recollected in tranquillity. Hence his irritation with his Romantic contemporaries, who placed such complete faith in the direct, uninhibited outflow of feeling and passion: "Il est bon d'avoir de ces états de *maximum* de passion, car sans ça il ne serait pas possible de les peindre; mais ces moments de *maximum* ne sont pas les meilleurs moments pour écrire. Les meilleurs sont ceux où l'on peut écrire les choses les plus émouvantes; il faut *tranquillité physique* et *sérénité d'âme.*"[36]

It should be apparent from Stendhal's comments on Diderot that his attitude toward the Encyclopedist was eminently positive, objective, and free from the kind of emotional, subjective involvement that marked his reactions to Voltaire and Rousseau. Neither unduly hostile and sharply peremptory, as when he spoke of Voltaire, nor oscillating between extremes of adoration and rejection, as when he dealt with Rousseau, he approached Diderot in a remarkably calm, unprejudiced, and open-minded manner and, in general, preferred to comment upon specific aspects of Diderot's thought and works rather than to make sweeping generalizations.

The good Dr. Gagnon also owned a complete set of Buffon's *Histoire naturelle*, which young Beyle read with great curiosity and amusement and which he recommended to his sister Pauline: "Tu peux demander au grand-papa les *Lettres persanes* de Montesquieu et l'*Histoire naturelle* de Buffon, à partir du sixième vol(ume), les premiers ne t'amuseraient pas."[37] In Paris, he enjoyed reading aloud certain sections of the work to Adèle Rebuffel, the mistress of Martial Daru, and noticed that she blushed when certain physiological features of apes were described and compared to those of humans. On the whole, his appreciation of Buffon is real, and if he occasionally disapproved of Buffon's *emphase*, he was grateful to the naturalist for having enlightened him on human physiology and matters of sex at a time when he could get no such information from his prudish and straitlaced relatives. And Buffon confirmed the lesson learned from Montesquieu concerning the importance of climate and geography in the development of laws, habits, and customs.

From a very early age Beyle became familiar with the novels of the eighteenth century. His uncle Romain Gagnon, the local Don Juan whose only interest in literature focused on the more spicy novels, had accumulated quite a collection; and it was not too long before Henri discovered the cache where the volumes in question had been stacked: "Je ne saurais exprimer la passion avec laquelle je lisais ces livres. . . . Je devins fou absolument, la possession d'une maîtresse réelle, alors l'objet de tous mes vœux, ne m'eût pas plongé dans un tel torrent de volupté."[38] Thus it was that young Beyle, his imagination set afire by visions of amorous conquest, went through Duclos, Crébillon fils, and more obscure specialists in the devious ways of *boudoir* life. And he naturally came upon Laclos's *Liaisons dangereuses.* He was convinced that the scandalous mores so mercilessly depicted in the *Liaisons* were those of social circles in Grenoble that he could see only from afar.[39] Even before reading the notorious novel, he had heard all kinds of rumors whispered about certain men and women of Grenoble who were the original models of the characters in the book, for had not Laclos, as an officer in the artillery, been stationed in that town?[40] In *Henry Brulard* Stendhal tells us that, as a child of nine, he liked to visit an elderly lady by the name of Mme de Montmaur, who was a neighbor of Dr. Gagnon and who always treated him to candied nuts, a delicacy of which he was very fond. It was whispered that this Mme de Montmaur was none other than Mme de Merteuil, now an old woman who walked with a limp. All this greatly intrigued the inquisitive and precocious young boy: "J'ai donc vu cette fin des mœurs de Mme de Merteuil, comme un enfant de neuf ou dix ans dévoré par un tempérament de feu peut voir ces choses dont tout le monde évite de lui dire le fin mot."[41] If Stendhal was, as he asserts, nine or ten when he first heard about the "scandales greno-

352

blois" that formed the basis for the *Liaisons dangereuses*, it was in 1792 or 1793, and Laclos had left Grenoble in 1775. Scholars have generally confirmed the reliability of the *clef* proposed by Stendhal with regard to the historical basis of the main characters and events portrayed in the *Liaisons*.

There is no doubt that the novel, and the aura of scandal and secrecy that surrounded it, made a great impression upon young Beyle. Later, in 1801, he reread the *Liaisons* while in Milan and even met Laclos himself, by then an elderly general in Bonaparte's artillery; the encounter probably took place at La Scala.[42] This was shortly after the victory at Marengo, and Beyle, his mind filled with dreams of emulating Valmont as a successful and cynical seducer, was elaborating a quasi-military strategy of amorous conquest. Although he admired Mme de Merteuil's tactic of dissimulation and hypocrisy, which he viewed as a legitimate means of defense for superior women in a male-dominated society, he remained totally unmoved by the virtuous and hapless Présidente de Tourvel's demise: "C'est uniquement pour ne pas être brûlée en l'autre monde, dans une grande chaudière d'huile bouillante, que Mme de Tourvel résiste à Valmont. . . . Combien Julie d'Etange, respectant ses serments et le bonheur de M. de Wolmar, n'est-elle pas plus touchante?"[43]

But though admiring the elegance, clarity, and economy with which Laclos had depicted a corrupt and disintegrating society, though recognizing in Mme de Merteuil and Valmont ruthless, cunning, strong-willed individuals admirably equipped to survive in a world that follows the law of the jungle, in his own outlook on love and life Stendhal felt greater affinity with the philosophy expressed through *La Nouvelle Héloïse*. His secret sympathies would always go to those incorrigible dreamers and sensitive souls whose idealistic notions made them unfit to cope with reality. At the same time, however, he evidently felt that Laclos and other novelists of this ilk showed the world, not as it ought to be, but as it really is. It is noteworthy that, when he decided to become his sister Pauline's intellectual mentor, he tirelessly cautioned her against the danger of viewing society through the embellishing prism of youthful naïveté and enthusiasm. He advised her to become acquainted with the treacherous ways of the world by reading the eighteenth-century novelists: "Le tableau le plus ressemblant de la nature humaine, telle qu'elle est en an 13 en France, est encor le vieux *Gil Blas* de Lesage, réfléchis sur cet excellent ouvrage."[44]

As for Marivaux, Beyle appreciated his novels more than his plays, which he found too *précieux*; he had the heroine of *La Vie de Marianne* in mind when he selected the theme for *Lamiel*. In both instances the sentimental education of an independent-minded young girl is sympathetically analyzed. Apropos of Prévost, also an author he read with keen pleasure, he noted in his *Journal* on 17 June 1811: "Je lis . . . les *Mémoires d'un homme de qualité*. Le style en est un peu trop périodique, mais il y a dans cet ouvrage une vraie noblesse, bien au-dessus de la plupart des romans. Il y a même des peintures de mœurs."[45]

Thus, although Rousseau as novelist occupied a very special place in young Beyle's heart, Lesage, Prévost, Marivaux, Duclos, Crébillon fils, and Laclos were prized as more accurate and realistic analysts of manners and mores. When, in 1839, Stendhal established a list of the best French novels, it is noteworthy that, with the exception of *La Princesse de Clèves*, all the works enumerated belonged to the eighteenth century and that not a single nineteenth-century novel was included: Lesage's *Gil Blas*, Prévost's *Manon Lescaut*, Marivaux's *La Vie de Marianne*, Voltaire's *Zadig* and *Candide*, Duclos's *Les Confessions du comte de *****, Crébillon fils's *Les Egarements du cœur et de l'esprit*, Rousseau's *La Nouvelle Héloïse*, and Laclos's *Les Liaisons dangereuses*.[46]

More and more, as Stendhal grew increasingly disappointed with the turn of events in his own century as well as with the ideology and aesthetics of the Romantics, he tended to look upon pre-Revolutionary France as an age in which he would

354

have felt in his element. Refinement of taste, lightness of touch, the art of leaving certain things unsaid, the secret of being erotic without being vulgar, the aptitude for hiding one's melancholy and sadness behind a smile or a witticism, all these attributes of *politesse, bon ton,* and *délicatesse* had been lost, he felt, with the triumph of a materialistic bourgeoisie, a class he loathed as much as he empathized with the common people and admired the old aristocracy. His frequent denunciations of the Romantics were but the manifestation of his profound malaise. His exasperation knew no bounds when he was confronted with bombastic verbosity, emotional self-indulgence, religious sentimentalism, and complacent exhibitionism. The public display of private emotions always struck him as obscene, and he could never sympathize with the Romantics' unabashed self-revelations. Chateaubriand especially, the hero of his times, was constantly singled out for sharp reproof or outright ridicule. And no wonder, for in the eyes of Stendhal the author of *Le Génie du Christianisme* was the very embodiment of the obscurantist spirit of his age. For Stendhal, who so greatly prized clarity of thought and expression and economy of words, the sumptuously orchestrated sentences of Chateaubriand, their slow and solemn progression, represented everything abhorrent to him in the way the French language had evolved since *Les Lettres persanes.*

---

1. A number of helpful studies of influence and affinity have already been made. See Pierre Moreau, "Les Stendhaliens avant Stendhal," *Revue des cours et conférences* 28 (1927): 301-9, 656-64, 734-46; Ferdinand Boyer, *Les Lectures de Stendhal* (Paris: Editions du Stendhal-Club, 1925); Jules C. Alciatore, *Stendhal et Helvétius; Les Sources de la philosophie de Stendhal* (Geneva: Droz, 1952); Jules C. Alciatore, "Stendhal lecteur de La Pucelle," *Stendhal Club* 3 (15 July 1960): 325-34; Jules C. Alciatore, "Stendhal et les romans de Voltaire," *Stendhal Club* 4 (15 January 1961): 15-23; Haydn T. Mason, "Condorcet et Stendhal," *Stendhal Club* 10 (15 April 1967): 255-58; Victor Brombert, "Stendhal lecteur de Rousseau" *Revue des Sciences humaines,* n.s. 92 (October-December 1958): 463-82; Gita May, "Préromantisme rousseauiste et égotisme stendhalien," *L'Esprit Créateur* 6 (1966): 97-107; and

especially V. Del Litto, *La Vie intellectuelle de Stendhal; Genèse et évolution de ses idées, 1802-1821* (Paris: Presses Universitaires de France, 1962).

2. Paul Valéry, "Stendhal," *Variété*, in *Œuvres*, ed. J. Hytier (Paris: Gallimard, 1957), 1: 556.

3. Georg Lukács, *Studies in European Realism* (New York: Grosset and Dunlap, 1964), p. 68.

4. *La Vie de Henry Brulard*, in *Œuvres intimes de Stendhal*, ed. H. Martineau (Paris: Gallimard, 1961), p. 97. Hereafter, all references to Stendhal's autobiographical and personal essays will be to this edition.

5. *Henry Brulard*, p. 94.

6. Ibid., p. 143.

7. See Michel Crouzet, "Misanthropie et vertu: Stendhal et le problème républicain," *Revue des sciences humaines*, n.s. 125 (January-March 1967): 29-52.

8. See Alciatore, *Stendhal et Helvétius*; Mason, "Condorcet et Stendhal"; and Del Litto, *La Vie intellectuelle de Stendhal*.

9. *Henry Brulard*, p. 368. See Théo Gieling, "Stendhal lecteur de Saint-Simon," *Stendhal Club* 7 (15 July 1964): 284-95; 8 (15 October 1964): 21-38; 8 (15 January 1965): 100-112.

10. *Journal* (25 April 1804), in *Œuvres intimes*, p. 691.

11. See V. Del Litto, *La Vie intellectuelle de Stendhal*, and G. Saintville, *Stendhal et Vauvenargues* (Paris: Divan, 1938).

12. *Henry Brulard*, p. 7.

13. "Catalogue de tous mes livres," in *Œuvres intimes*, p. 442.

14. See V. Del Litto, *La Vie intellectuelle de Stendhal*, p. 196.

15. F. Boyer, *Les Lectures de Stendhal*, p. 8.

16. Stendhal, *Correspondance*, ed. H. Martineau and V. Del Litto (Paris: Gallimard, 1962), 1:2. Also see Paul Arbelet, *La Jeunesse de Stendhal* (Paris: Champion, 1919), 1:168, and Jules C. Alciatore, "Stendhal et les romans de Voltaire."

17. *Henry Brulard*, p. 78.

18. Ibid., pp. 23, 260 (cf. also p. 1497 for a similar comment).

19. Ibid., p. 352.

20. Ibid., p. 180.

21. Cf. Boyer, *Les Lectures de Stendhal*, p. 15.

22. *Henry Brulard*, p. 153.

23. *Essais d'autobiographie*, in *Œuvres intimes*, p. 1495.

24. *Henry Brulard*, p. 224. For more detailed studies of the impact of Rousseau on Stendhal, cf. Brombert, "Stendhal lecteur de Rousseau," and Gita May, "Préromantisme rousseauiste et égotisme stendhalien."

25. Cf. Michel Crouzet, "Misanthropie et vertu: Stendhal et le problème républicain."

26. *Correspondance*, 1:161 (letter to Pauline Beyle of 29 October-16 November 1804).

27. *Henry Brulard*, p. 168.

28. Ibid., p. 299.

29. *Du Style*, in *Œuvres complètes*, ed. H. Martineau (Paris: Le Divan, 1927-37), 26:130.

30. Ibid.

31. *De l'amour*, ed. H. Martineau (Paris: Classiques Garnier, 1959), p. 115.

32. Cf. Gita May, *Diderot et Baudelaire, critiques d'art* (Geneva: Droz, 1959), pp. 17-27.

33. *Œuvres intimes*, pp. 563, 712.

34. *Œuvres complètes*, 67: 318.

35. *Journal* (9 October 1814), *Œuvres intimes*, p. 1266.

36. *Journal* (11 February 1805), p. 586. See also *Journal*, 15 September 1813: "Je suis le contraire de J.-J. Rousseau en beaucoup de choses sans doute, et en particulier en celle-ci, que je ne puis travailler que loin de la sensation. Ce n'est point en me promenant dans une forêt délicieuse que je puis décrire ce bonheur; c'est renfermé dans une chambre nue . . . que je pourrai faire quelque chose" (*Œuvres intimes*, p. 1241).

37. *Correspondance*, 1:30 (letter of 6 December 1801). In his fifties Stendhal was to take renewed pleasure in rereading Buffon: "On dit Buffon pompier et cependant quel naturel, quelle simplicité, comparé à nos benêts de 1840" (Boyer, *Les Lectures de Stendhal*, p. 17).

38. *Henry Brulard*, p. 151.

39. See Libero Solaroli, "Stendhal et la clef des *Liaisons dangereuses*," *Stendhal Club* 2 (15 October 1958): 109-13.

40. See ibid. for details on Laclos's stay in Grenoble.

41. *Henry Brulard*, p. 59.

42. *Souvenirs d'égotisme*, in *Œuvres intimes*, p. 1478. See also H. Martineau, *Le Cœur de Stendhal* (Paris: Albin Michel, 1952), 1: 147.

43. *De l'amour*, p. 221.

44. *Correspondance*, 1:255 (letter written at the end of November 1805).

45. *Œuvres intimes*, p. 1042.

46. Boyer, *Les Lectures de Stendhal*, p. 17.

Readership in the American Enlightenment

PAUL M. SPURLIN

More than a decade ago now, a distinguished American historian wrote, "With something of a shock, I have lately realized how little we know about the literacy and actual reading (not book-ownership) of the eighteenth-century Americans. How few Americans of that age are there whose reading we can describe with any confidence!"[1] In the field of French-American intellectual relations, I too must confess to a similar puzzlement—mine running back over many years. Would that there were statistical standards on which to rely! Unfortunately there are none. Hence I for one am skeptical, for example, of *ex cathedra* pronouncements as to the influence of various thinkers on "the Americans" of the formative years of the nation's history. He who would play the pontiff should possess a modicum of sound knowledge concerning the American reading public in the early years. And this, as one will see, is not easy to come by.

I propose, then, to probe in this essay the matter of readership during that movement of ideas in this country known as the Enlightenment. I take as my definition of readership one from *The American Heritage Dictionary of the English Language*: "the readers of a publication or publications." And for all practical purposes, the period of the American Enlightenment is here understood to be the last half of the eighteenth century. I shall deal first with the question of literacy, then with the readers and their number, and hardly at all with the titles of things read.

John Adams did not beat about the bush. "A native of America who cannot read and write," he said in 1765, "is as rare as a comet or an earthquake. . . . And I have good authorities to say, that all candid foreigners who have passed through this country, and conversed freely with all sorts of people here, will allow, that they have never seen so much knowledge and civility among the common people of the world."[2] Distinguished contemporaries backed up Adams's opinion. In 1793 Noah Webster affirmed that "a greater proportion of the people are *readers* than in any other country."[3] Royall Tyler, who was to become a chief justice of the Supreme Court of Vermont, maintained in the preface to his novel, *The Algerine Captive* (1797), that "in no other country are there so many people, who, in proportion to its numbers, can read and write." And in 1800 the French economist, Du Pont de Nemours, in a treatise on education in the United States written at Jefferson's request, said this: "Most young Americans can read, write and cipher . . . while in Spain, Portugal, Italy, only a sixth of the population can read; in Germany, even in France, not more than a third; in Poland, about two men in a hundred; and in Russia not one in two hundred."[4] Du Pont grounded his opinion of young Americans on the large number of primary schools here and on "paternal affection [which] protects young children from working in the fields . . . a condition which does not prevail in Europe."

Present-day research findings tend to substantiate the opinions of Adams, Tyler, Webster, and Du Pont. With reference to New England, J. H. Shera wrote that "there is abundant correlative evidence to indicate that the proportion of the public able to read and write was very large. The school had become entrenched in the Colonial folkways, and in countless homes patient mothers and fathers pored with their children over crude primers and spelling books."[5] In Philadelphia, according to the Bridenbaughs, the "spread of education brought an increasing demand for textbooks, and it is probable that in actual number of copies printed this category exceeded all others combined."[6] In a study devoted to the principal southern colony, investigators state that though "Virginia did not provide as much educational opportunity for the people as did a colony such as Massachusetts, there were educational facilities available even for the poor."[7] There are many problems concerning education and literacy in eighteenth-century America,[8] and we shall never have all the facts and figures needed. But there is another barometer by which one can, to some extent, measure literacy: the ownership of books, however few.

Michael Kraus writes that "recent studies show that a considerable proportion of New Englanders of all classes owned books."[9] In Maryland an investigator found "that nearly sixty percent of the free white population possessed books. Although three-quarters of the book collections contained less than ten books, often only a Bible and a few religious books, there were colonists who owned comparatively large and interesting libraries."[10] And in Virginia, according to T. J. Wertenbaker, "large collections could be afforded only by the wealthiest, while the small planters and even the moderately well-to-do had to content themselves with from ten to a hundred volumes."[11]

There were, here and there, large private libraries,[12] but not many. At the very end of the century, there are dolorous complaints from two prominent Americans concerning libraries generally. Noah Webster wrote in 1800 that "as to libraries, we have no such things. There are not more than three or four tolerable libraries in America, and these are extremely imperfect."[13] And the well-informed Samuel Miller expressed himself in this manner: the American student, he said, "has often to spend as much time and thought to obtain a particular book, as the reading it ten times would cost. Our public Libraries are few, and, compared with those of Europe, small. Nor is this defect supplied by large private collections; these are also rare."[14] My immediate concern, however, is with broad-scale readership, not libraries. A vast amount of research has been done on the various types of libraries in the early days, and one can pursue the study in excellent books.[15]

Literacy, it goes without saying, does not imply readership. But the growth and spread of the reading habit in eighteenth-century America was revolutionary.[16] In the 1920s Bernard Faÿ, the French historian, called attention to the "great demand for books and newspapers in America" and expressed the opinion that in the last thirty years of the century "the average man seems to have read more than was the case in Europe."[17]

The American penchant for newspapers did not escape sharp-sighted French visitors who were here in the time of Enlightenment. Brissot de Warville came to the United States in 1788. He was impressed by the number of gazettes in Boston and Philadelphia. Moreau de Saint-Méry carefully recorded in his *Voyage aux Etats-Unis, 1793-1798* that Philadelphia had "14 gazettes" including one French and one German. And La Rochefoucauld-Liancourt, who traveled here in the years 1795-97, noted that at his stopping place in Marlborough, Massachusetts, "from the landlord down to the housemaid they all read two newspapers a day."

With reference to the eastern states, and speaking of the diffusion of knowledge among the working people, Noah Webster wrote in 1800 that "they read not only the Bible, and newspapers, but almost all read the best English authors."[18] Indeed, La Rochefoucauld-Liancourt had commented only a few years before on the habit of referring to the United States as "the most enlightened nation in the world."

But paradoxically, "the great majority of the people seldom saw a letter or even a newspaper," Albert J. Beveridge wrote in his book *The Life of John Marshall*. Beveridge was referring precisely to the years 1783-90, the years that John Fiske denominated the critical period of American history. Even those Americans who did read newspapers were more

362

or less wasting their time, in the opinion of Henry Adams. For in his *History of the United States during the First Administration of Thomas Jefferson,* he voiced vigorously his lack of appreciation of the American gazette around 1800. In Adams's view "the education supposed to have been widely spread by eighteenth-century newspapers was hardly to be distinguished from ignorance."

All these assertions and counterassertions concerning the reading of Americans in the formative years of the Republic shed little or no light on readership. Where, one wonders, were all those readers reported by John Adams's "candid foreigners"? Who was Faÿ's "average man"? The broad-scale identification and number of readers of newspapers, pamphlets, magazines, and books, should be matters of great consequence to the intellectual historian.

The phrase "average man," as used in the context above, seems to imply a more or less homogenous mind. And it does not suggest the possibility of what has been called "cultural cleavage." There was no uniform mind in eighteenth-century America. There were aristocrats and artisans, businessmen, bakers and candlestick makers, farmers and frontiersmen, sailors, scholars, and soldiers. Reading opportunities varied extremely. A few facts and figures will show the impossibility of anything approaching cultural unity in the early days.

In 1790, the year of the first census, the population of the United States totaled 3,929,625. This figure included whites, free negroes, and slaves. The white population amounted to 3,172,444. The southern states had 48.5 percent of the entire population, the remainder being distributed almost equally between the New England and the Middle Atlantic states. Virginia had the greatest number of people. Massachusetts was second and Pennsylvania third in the number of inhabitants. Philadelphia, New York, Boston, Charleston, and Baltimore were, in order, the five largest cities. Along with Annapolis and Williamsburg, they were, to use an expression of Thomas J. Wertenbaker, "crucibles of culture." Merle Curti has indicated the importance of the way towns had grown for the development of intellectual life in America. "The towns were the chief centers of intellectual activity because they enjoyed closer relations with Europe and because they offered great opportunities for social contacts and the discussion of events and ideas."[19] The startling fact, however, is that in 1790 only 5.4 percent of the people lived in towns. The combined population of the five largest cities came to 123,475.[20] The urban population was trifling in comparison with the rural and rustic.

One can but wonder who and where were the "hundreds of thousands" of men whom John Dos Passos mentions in his book *Tom Paine* as having bought *Common Sense* (1776). This calculation of the number of copies of Paine's pamphlet sold brings us directly to the problem of readership. To say that pamphlets were cheap is in no way a denigration of the powerful appeal of *Common Sense*, about which more later. It seems to me, however, that the only way to get an idea of readership in bygone days is to gather a few statistics on the output of the presses. And this I have endeavored to do, not as an authority on such matters but simply as one anxious to clarify a subject that is extremely murky.

The production of the early American printing presses seems astonishing, even though the majority of books, until the nineteenth century, were imported. For the years between 1639 and 1800, Frederick R. Goff writes, there were "more than 50,000 recorded titles in the Evans-Shipton-Bristol bibliographies . . . books and pamphlets, newspapers and journals, broadsides and other ephemera."[21] As to sizes of editions at the beginning of the American Enlightenment, Lawrence C. Wroth wrote, "If there needs to be stated an average figure for editions of books and pamphlets of a literary or political character in the early and middle years of the eighteenth century, it would not be far out of the way to suggest 300 to 500 copies as probable. Such a figure does not apply to the exceptional books, long awaited and of known general interest."[22] It would be both tedious and pointless to consider here sizes of editions of pamphlets, almanacs, and broadsides. Statistics on some of these can be found in Wroth's first section in *The Book in America*. The almanac and the Bible, presumably, were ubiquitous. As time moved on, the reading habit, as already noted, grew rapidly and spread popularly. What, then, of the readership of newspapers, magazines, and books at the end of the American Enlightenment?

The newspaper is certainly one of the least expensive forms of reading matter. One is almost tempted to make it a common denominator of culture. Newspapers were published from Maine to Georgia. Frank Luther Mott found that "in all, 202 papers were being published January 1, 1801."[23] According to Mott, "Circulations were still small, however. The semiweekly *Columbian Centinel* probably topped the list, with over 4,000. *Porcupine's Gazette*, a daily, claimed over 2,000 early in 1799; this was as large a circulation as that of any English daily. . . . But the average for dailies, semiweeklies, and weeklies was very low even at the end of the [eighteenth] century—perhaps between 600 and 700."[24] The *Centinel* was published in Boston, which had a population of 18,038 in 1790. *Porcupine's Gazette* was published in Philadelphia, the capital of the United States and the country's largest city, with a population in 1790 of 42,444. The following observation by the editor of another Philadelphia newspaper of that time may come as even more of a shock. John Ward Fenno declared in the powerful federalist *Gazette of the United States* on 4 March 1799 that "more than nine-tenths of the scanty literature of America is made up of newspaper reading."

The magazines provided a second form of fairly inexpensive regular reading matter. Mott states that "there were about seventy-five different magazines begun during the years 1783-1801, inclusive. Most of them were short-lived, and only a few had any considerable importance."[25] Concerning circulation figures, Lyon N. Richardson, in *A History of*

Early American Magazines, 1741-1789 (1931), writes that "only occasionally did subscription lists attain one thousand to sixteen hundred names, and probably the average list did not exceed beyond five hundred; so doubtless the total copies of magazines printed at any one time did not exceed twenty-five hundred until the decade of the 1780s, when the lists expanded rapidly and the number of magazines increased." Mott thought it "extremely doubtful if the aggregate number of copies of magazines circulated in America reached five thousand at any one time in the period under consideration [i.e., 1741-1794]."[26]

Eighteenth-century Americans could acquire books in a number of ways. They were to be had not only in the bookstores but from the printers, from peddlers, at book auctions, and by subscription.[27] In passing, I might mention an instance of publication by subscription and a proposal for publication that are germane to the matter of readership. Rousseau's *Social Contract* was published in Albany in 1797. A count of the names in a copy preserved in the Peabody Library shows 207 subscribers, not including two people who ordered six copies each, another person who took seven, and two others two copies each. An advance order of only two hundred and thirty copies! Montesquieu's *Spirit of Laws* did not fare so well. This book had become an "American" classic by 1787. But a proposal to publish it in the United States in 1775—300 subscribers in "various parts of the country" were desired[28]—came to naught. The first American edition of the *Spirit of Laws* did not appear until 1802.

Bookstores were not lacking in the cities and towns. Russel B. Nye writes that "Boston in the 1770's had fifty bookstores, Philadelphia probably thirty or more, and peddlers hawked almanacs, chapbooks, broadsides, and standard books through every city street and backwoods hamlet."[29] In the latter part of the eighteenth century, "every sizable town had one or more booksellers," according to E. B. Greene.[30] And Noah Webster wrote in 1793 that "the booksellers are everywhere extending their business—a sure proof of increasing demands for books."[31]

The majority of books sold during the American Enlightenment were imported. This fact, coupled with the common practice of borrowing and lending books, makes the problem of readership exceedingly complex. The mind boggles at the thought of arriving at any meaningful conclusion with regard to the number of books sent here from abroad. But there are a few figures available—not nearly enough—concerning the sizes of editions and sales of books published in the United States.

Mathew Carey, born in Dublin, began in Philadelphia about 1790 what turned out to be a fruitful and influential career as publisher and bookseller. Rollo G. Silver[32] has supplied information as to sizes of editions of publications by Carey in his first ten years of business. Among nineteen items was John Bunyan's *Divine Emblems: or, Temporal Things Spiritualized. Fitted for the Use of Boys and Girls.* This book led with 4,250 copies. In one of the years Carey published two editions of Susanna Rowson's novel *Charlotte Temple: A Tale of Truth.* The number of copies in the first edition was 1,000, in the second, 1,500. This novel was later to enjoy a great vogue. The sizes of the editions of the nineteen titles averaged 1,565 copies. Presumably, Carey printed as many copies as he hoped to sell.

Especially pertinent to any study of readership is Frank Luther Mott's book *Golden Multitudes: The Story of Best Sellers in the United States* (New York, 1947). His concern is with the first editions of books published in America. As a criterion for the designation of a book as a best seller, he sets the sales figure at one percent of the entire population of the continental United States for the decade in which the book was published. To be an "over-all best seller" in the decade 1790–99, he stipulates as a requirement total American sales of 40,000 copies. Eleven books are judged to have had such a sale in this decade. They include Franklin's *Autobiography,*

Paine's *The Age of Reason*, Mrs. Rowson's *Charlotte Temple* (but see Hart, *The Popular Book*, p. 63), Shakespeare's *Plays*, and Volney's *The Ruins*, a deistic book and the only French work to achieve the best-seller distinction here in the eighteenth century.

The most successful best seller during the American Enlightenment was not a book, however, but a seventy-nine-page pamphlet: *Common Sense; Addressed to the Inhabitants of America*. In making this statement, I exclude the Bible, for which I have no figures. Paine's pamphlet was published initially by Robert Bell in Philadelphia. Mott states, "It appeared within the first few weeks of 1776, and was very soon reprinted in the leading cities and towns. Within a year probably 150,000 copies had been sold; reckoned on the basis of increased population, that would represent a distribution today [i.e., about 1947] of close to eight million copies."[33] Hart estimates that "one copy was sold for every twenty-five people in the colonies—men, women, and children—Whigs and Tories alike."[34] Paine himself, A. Owen Aldridge writes, "believed that 150,000 copies were sold in America—'the greatest sale that any performance ever had since the use of letters,—exclusive of the great run it had in England and Ireland.'" Aldridge adds, "There may be more self-satisfaction than truth in this declaration."[35] Be that as it may, *Common Sense* was an extraordinary success. But even more successful in the United States—phenomenally so with the passing of the years—was Noah Webster's *American Spelling Book*. It first appeared in 1783. In 1791 the author wrote that the sale of it by a Philadelphia printer "has been about 7000 a year."[36] Just twelve years later, in the preface to an edition of the work —a preface dated 1803—Webster affirmed that "the sales of the *American Spelling Book*, since its first publication, amount to more than three millions of copies, and they are annually increasing." This statement sheds more light on literacy, of the high degree of which in eighteenth-century America I am convinced. But the *succès de librairie* of both the *American Spelling Book* and *Common Sense* leave us in the dark—except for the best sellers previously mentioned—as regards readership generally. What can one deduce from the data assembled here, data that I have reason to think are representative and comprehensive? The statistics hold significance for all who write about the influence of authors and books. For the number of readers of a publication or publications is, or should be, a meaningful factor in the final decisions of the intellectual and literary historians.

Readership of newspapers, magazines, and books at the very end of the first half-century of the American Enlightenment was small and restricted. The total white population, according to the second census in 1800, had grown to approximately 4,415,000.[37] Mott's optimum figures for the circulation of newspapers at the close of the century come to 141,400. There were, of course, more readers than subscribers. But if we can assume that ten persons read every issue of a paper, the readers would still number less than a third of this population. And "thousands who read them read nothing else," William Cobbett had declared when announcing in the *Gazette of the United States* on 1 February 1797 his intention to publish *Porcupine's Gazette* to combat the pro-French journals.

Even though the great majority of Americans did not read them, the newspapers played a considerable role, as did the pamphlets, in the development and crystallization of thought in those critical years. I do not share Henry Adams's opinion that the papers were educationally ineffective. The articles that dealt with political matters were endless. Quotations of key ideas of many thinkers lighted up their pages. Informative paragraphs here and there helped fan an interest in the writings of foreign and native authors. The gazettes are studded with the advertisements of booksellers who itemized their offerings. Editors printed literary extracts for the edifi-

369

cation and amusement of their subscribers, and sometimes, one suspects, to fill space. Newspapers and magazines frequently reprinted articles and essays from one another.

Among the subscribers to newspapers there was a smaller, more select group—the readers of pamphlets, magazines, and books. Mott, to my way of thinking, makes an important point when he says, "There is doubtless some difference in the quality of a readership concentrated in time—and that of a readership dispersed over a long term."[38] The first part of this statement reminds me of Schopenhauer's wish to assign every writer to one of three categories: shooting stars, planets, and fixed stars. Paine was a "shooting star," and *Common Sense*, with its ardent appeal to all sorts and conditions of Americans, was an example of "a readership concentrated in time." What needs to be said, then, concerning "a readership dispersed over a long term"? The general run of pamphlets and magazines reached a limited audience, and they require no comment. And only a few remarks seem necessary, in light of the figures already presented, as regards the readership of books. We shall forever be in the dark about the sum total of readers of books in the nonprivate collections. These include the circulating, college, and social libraries. The circulating library became increasingly important in the second half of the century. Kraus found that by 1800 there were more than a hundred libraries of this type in Connecticut alone.[39] The growing interest in novels was responsible in part for the flourishing of the circulating library. The social libraries were of two sorts, the proprietary and subscription or association. The latter was more democratic than the former, which appealed to more wealthy patrons. According to J. H. Shera, "the 1780's produced more new social libraries than the entire previous half-century."[40]

Books were not cheap, and private libraries usually were not large. Mathew Carey, one of the nation's principal publishers and for whom "Parson" Weems peddled books in the south, limited extremely the sizes of his editions, as was seen, even at the end of the century. Carey, of course, imported and sold books published in Europe. But the number of copies in his own editions published in the 1790s was insignificant when compared with the population. On the other hand, the sales of the best sellers on Mott's list, in the same period, are most impressive, and especially so if compared with the distribution of books in the United States today.

There were, obviously, different levels of readers during the American Enlightenment. These levels were not, however, mutually exclusive. But "cultural cleavage" did exist. Most of those readers reported by John Adams's "candid foreigners" lived, by and large, in the cities and towns. So did Faÿ's "average man." And "the Americans," whom inquirers into literary influences write about, were for the most part urban residents, those who were able to purchase books or who had fairly ready access to them—doctors and lawyers, merchants and ministers, scholars and statesmen, tradesmen and members of the middle class generally.

The Enlightenment was one of history's greatest ideological revolutions. It began in seventeenth-century Europe and stopped at no frontiers. Its "seeds," wrote one scholar, were present in England, France, and Germany, but the time and manner of their germination were different. It is difficult to generalize about this highly complex revolution in thought. At the risk of oversimplification, one can say that its leaders deposed faith and enthroned reason and science. Eighteenth-century France was its principal theater. Rationalism passed through that country like a tidal wave, followed by a heavy ground swell of sensibility.

In America, the Age of the Founding Fathers was the Age of Enlightenment. The climate of ideas here in the second half of the eighteenth century differed greatly from that of the first half. There are many reasons for this radical shift in opinion. The spreading of literacy and an ever-widening

371

readership were in part responsible. These factors strengthened the forces that, between 1750 and 1800, badly breached the dike of orthodoxy—religious, political, or whatever.

Readership in the American Enlightenment had far-reaching consequences. Everyone was involved in this rupture with the past—the users of almanacs in which, as Hart writes, "significant public documents and political tracts were synopsized, economic grievances were cited,"[41] as well as those who availed themselves of *Common Sense*, other pamphlets, and of newspapers and books. From aristocrats and planters to city dwellers, farmers and frontiersmen, from all this varied readership—*coupled with experience*—came a political Declaration of Independence and the "Miracle at Philadelphia."

1. Daniel J. Boorstin, *America and the Image of Europe: Reflections on American Thought* (New York, 1960), pp. 73-74.

2. *Works*, ed. C. F. Adams, 10 vols. (Boston, 1850-56), 3: 456.

3. *Letters of Noah Webster*, ed. H. R. Warfel (New York, 1953), p. 112.

4. *National Education in the United States of America*, tr. B. G. Du Pont (Newark, Del., 1923), p. 3. Cf. Carlo M. Cipolla, *Literacy and Development in the West* (London, 1969), pp. 92, 94.

5. *Foundations of the Public Library: The Origins of the Public Library Movement in New England, 1629-1855* (Hamden, Conn., 1965), p. 49.

6. Carl and Jessica Bridenbaugh, *Rebels and Gentlemen: Philadelphia in the Age of Franklin* (New York, 1965), p. 81.

7. Robert E. and B. Katherine Brown, *Virginia 1705-1786: Democracy or Aristocracy?* (East Lansing, Mich., 1964), p. 282.

8. See, for example, Bernard Bailyn's *Education in the Forming of American Society: Needs and Opportunities for Study* (New York, 1960).

9. *The Atlantic Civilization: Eighteenth-Century Origins* (Ithaca, N.Y., 1949), pp. 81-82.

10. J. T. Wheeler, "Books owned by Marylanders, 1700-1776," *Maryland Historical Magazine* 35 (1940): 353.

11. *The Golden Age of Colonial Culture* (New York, 1942), p. 113. See also George K. Smart, "Private Libraries in Colonial Virginia," *American Literature* 10 (1938-39): 33.

12. See Edwin Wolf II, "Great American Book Collectors to 1800," *Gazette of the Grolier Club*, New Series No. 16 (June 1971).

13. *Letters*, ed. H. R. Warfel, p. 212.

14. *A Brief Retrospect of the Eighteenth Century* (New York, 1803), 2: 409.

15. See, among others, James D. Hart, *The Popular Book: A History of America's Literary Taste* (New York, 1950) and J. H. Shera, *Foundations of the Public Library*.

16. See Hart, *The Popular Book*, pp. 25, 50; Kraus, *The Atlantic Civilization*, p. 86; Tyler, *The Algerine Captive*, pp. v-vii; Wertenbaker, *The Golden Age of Colonial Culture*, p. 72.

17. *Notes on the American Press at the End of the Eighteenth Century* (New York, 1927), p. 14.

18. *Letters*, pp. 210-11.

19. *The Growth of American Thought* (2d ed.; New York, 1951), p. 39.

20. For this figure and the preceding population statistics, I am indebted to the *Encyclopedia of American History*, ed. Richard B. Morris (New York, 1953). See also U.S. Bureau of the Census, *Historical Statistics of the United States: Colonial Times to 1957* (Washington, D.C., 1960), which gives figures in thousands. In his book *The Cultural Life of the American Colonies 1607-1763* (New York, 1957), p. 46, Louis B. Wright presents an analysis of a study of the white population in 1790, and gives the percentages of the various components: English, Scotch and Scotch-Irish from Ulster, German, Dutch, French, and Swedish. The only figures for the white population in the early period that I can cite are in Wright's book, *The Atlantic Frontier* (New York, 1947), p. 304. By 1760 it numbered 1,385,000.

21. Roger P. Bristol, *Supplement to Charles Evans' American Bibliography* (Charlottesville, Va., 1970), p. vi.

22. "Book Production and Distribution from the Beginning to the American Revolution." In Hellmut Lehmann-Haupt et al., *The Book in America* (2d ed.; New York, 1951), p. 40.

23. *American Journalism* (3d ed.; New York, 1962), p. 113 n.

24. *Ibid.*, p. 159. According to Faÿ, *Notes on the American Press*, pp. 21-22, William Cobbett, the editor of *Porcupine's Gazette*, announced around 1798 that his paper had 3,200 subscribers.

25. *American Journalism*, p. 138. See also his *A History of American Magazines 1741-1850* (Cambridge, Mass., 1957), 1:35 n. Wroth found that ninety-eight magazines and periodicals were published between 1740/41 and through 1800. (see *The Book in America*, p. 39).

26. *A History of American Magazines*, 1:14.

27. See Wroth in *The Book in America*, pp. 50-59.

28. Howard Mumford Jones, "The Importation of French Literature in New York City, 1750-1800," *Studies in Philology* 28 (1931): 241.

29. *The Cultural Life of the New Nation: 1776-1830* (New York, 1960), p. 250. See also Hart, *The Popular Book*.

30. *The Revolutionary Generation: 1763-1790* (New York, 1943), p. 135.

31. *Letters*, p. 112.

32. *The American Printer 1787-1825* (Charlottesville, Va., 1967), Appendix, p. 173.

33. *Golden Multitudes*, p. 51.

34. *The Popular Book*, p. 45.

35. *Man of Reason: The Life of Thomas Paine* (Philadelphia, 1959), p.

42. According to Aldridge (p. 41), there were 1,000 copies in the first edition; it was exhausted in two weeks.

36.   Emily E. F. Skeel, ed., *Notes on the Life of Noah Webster* (New York, 1912), 1:305.

37.   *Return of the Whole Number of Persons within the Several Districts of the United States* (Washington, 1802).

38.   *Golden Multitudes*, p. 10 n.

39.   *The Atlantic Civilization*, p. 81.

40.   *Foundations of the Public Library*, p. 68. I am indebted to Shera for this information concerning the social libraries. This book has also a chapter on the circulating library.

41.   *The Popular Book*, p. 42.

Encyclopedism and Its Conscience:
Evolution and Revolution

DOROTHY M. MC GHEE

Morning light from the Seine filters up the street to form almost a limned picture of the Arsenal, presently in part La Bibliothèque de l'Arsenal. A kind of fortress it has been in history and is to this day, though now rather one of ideas, of history that might seem to float interminably about the quarter. Its walls had formerly housed arms magazines and apartments both military and elegant (when Sully resided there) of the sixteenth and seventeenth centuries—a temporary residence of Richelieu, of M. le maréchal et Madame la maréchale de Meilleraye, then of the marquis d'Argenson through the Revolutionary period and into the early nineteenth century, to become a Nodier salon and increasingly a famous library and museum. The odd-shaped structure holds a fascination for us today. For those cultivating *le dix-huitième*, its confines harbor a dream equal to any *songe* or *dialogue* of the period. One lives out a Utopia within these walls, within the countless, often massive tomes. Looking up from a volume of Diderot, Buffon, Montesquieu, Voltaire, Marmontel, Rousseau, Mercier, one may evoke a usual recent scene also of revered moderns who have sat working here—of Professor Daniel Mornet entering, laying down a folio in businesslike fashion, and immersing himself in a century; of Professors Bellessort, Ascoli, Chinard, Morize, Havens, and many others who have penetrated "un siècle illuminé."

377

The eighteenth century for France witnessed a complex sequence of movement and thought, from an opening resolution and plea for liberalism and enlightenment into a heavy burden of guilt-ridden conscience, into the gory maelstrom of actual revolution, and finally into a surprisingly gradual emergence of a most green and gracious time. Inspiration from the striking pages of *L'Encyclopédie* and from the distilled vitriol of Voltairian *pâtés* had indeed remained throughout the years, but in retrospect the inspiration bespoke an admirable variety, for enjoyment rather than for immediacy or necessity.

Evolution and revolution had merged, and France had seen its relative Utopia in many shadings. Though man would be, forever and admittedly, insignificant and incapable of fulfilling his own ideals, there would be no concessions with regard to his thought and his endeavor. High adventure would become rash and daring in those realms, but cool moderation would tend to anneal the metal.

One may readily observe that Europe, rather as a whole, had early in the century declared its intention to think, to cast off certain shackles of a binding tradition, whether political or individual. It would intensify its feelings and assert its mental independence. Not only would France dare to pry relentlessly into human affairs and actions, but it would concoct practical methods by which such inquiry could prove relatively safe under the eyes of royalty or censors. Individuals and institutions alike could and must be attacked with guile. The attitude in the phrase *sous guise de* was to become a watchword for authors in almost any genre. Temerity allowed them tremendous scope in subjects; they proceeded to do battle with a valiant mixture of thought, sentiment, meditation, and craft. An essentially serious purpose of inquiry and reform underwent the guile of now fantasy, now realism, enhanced and rendered palatable under guise of pleasantry and often brilliance.

In a period of glaring social inequity, even cruelty, the purpose of most writing remained consistently and almost inevitably criticism, varying in tone, amusing, pungent, mordant, caustic, vitriolic, corrosive, virulent, or venomous, as the century approached its own Revolution. If we might formulate, from Diderot's definition of a *philosophe* included within *L'Encyclopédie*, the two terms "philosophism" and "Encyclopedism," we might approach cautiously this basic attitude of an enlightening era. It was reason at its best, applied to conditions at their worst.

Intriguing features mark the long, complex emergence of the philosophic ideal. Possibly today its intangibility challenges us most forcefully. Even the eighteenth century was familiar with a venerable doctrine of man's perfectibility, by which he might endlessly glimpse a goal in his world but never quite reach it. As the century progressed on French soil, the *philosophe* gradually became rather well defined as that being who could persistently bear his ideal in mind, then proceed to seize, analyze, and convey to others any new aspects that he might have gleaned. Experience must therefore evolve conscience.

The impertinent century was bound to know, and obliged to give. Its French prototype, the *philosophe*, must assume the burden of curiosity so implicit in his being, yet he must project knowledge and experience with a sparkle that would save "Encyclopedism" from dullness. The nervously impatient period must conceal its meanings, not only cautiously, but wittily, to save itself both physically and mentally. *L'Encyclopédie* was ever so successfully teaching its own scheme of clever cross-references that couched tremendous force beneath innocuous headings. On pages in every genre and subdivision of genre, authors of drama, novel, and tale were conveying their personages as artfully naïve yet delightfully suspicious of their entire world—as *naïfs* that were never naïve.

One observes French conscience evolving gradually, yet vehemently, for this was an age of slow and painful process encased within passionate vehicles of impudence and action.

Much of Europe had committed itself to the eager but difficult task of thinking, not alone for the ideas, but for their implementation, for the prime goal of amelioration, physical, mental, moral. France was early in the century becoming conscious of her individual responsibilities toward physical misery. In the wake of a Molière, a La Bruyère, a rather newly socialized literature was eagerly propelling ideals of improvement toward a public increasingly able to read and to ponder them. One is even prompted to observe that for much of the western continent an actual *littérature engagée* was taking firm hold. In the earlier courageous hands of a Bayle, Montesquieu, Diderot, d'Alembert, or Lesage rested much of the force that was later to become sternly and relentlessly applicable. On the part of authors the task required commitment far beyond a conscience, with clairvoyant glimpses into *lettres de cachet*, burning of volumes, exile, imprisonment, and death. But before them, too, lay the invitingly open field of liberalism, to teach all, to create an educable mass, to democratize all learning. And they in turn followed a growing ideal of curiosity, impertinence, and compassion. Salons were to be no longer a world apart; they would endure and suffer with the best and the worst of conditions. They would, in the best of utilitarian tradition, harbor new and daring ideas within their walls, even propagate entire doctrines to an eagerly reading public. Until their closing there would emanate from them a tremendous variety of types represented under the labels of treatise, dialogue, tale, dream, tableau, portrait, travel, and countless more. A serious conscience would prescribe for all authors, and in turn for all readers, combined tones of approach: there would be throughout the century the cruel, shameless laughter at man's folly, all the way from a Lesage to a Voltaire or a Beaumarchais; and there would be just as sympathetic and fully as shameless weeping over his plight, from a Rousseau to a Restif de la Bretonne. This Encyclopedic age must lash out for immediacy, as did Voltaire, or it could persuade and dissuade as did many before and after

380

him. Satire, irony, and nuances within them all produced their pungent effect,

Expressive of the idea of man's need for God, as also of God's need for man, certain eras of time have seemed to prove a consummate courage in the face of both opportunity and obstacle. One might find this true of the Age of Reason not only for France but for the entire Western world. As a period it sparkles among the constellations. One cannot fail to note similarities in the two centuries, the eighteenth and the twentieth. Though hesitantly, we might well dare to place our present period also among the stars. In both, mankind has witnessed evolution and revolution. Though under differing circumstances, he has insisted upon knowing, rather more daringly than respectfully; he has persisted in knowledge for all of a teachable and reachable world; he has deplored circumstances of his planet, tried to check its frequent madness and to alleviate its wounds. In both, he has emerged a most complex being, spectacularly happy and profoundly sad. In both, he has developed almost a mania of social conscienceness.

The Age of Ideas insisted, most of all, upon analysis. Authors would continue to point the way toward man's motives, but especially must they examine the springs of his action in order to suggest effects upon himself, upon society, upon government. The Encyclopedic ideal tended to evolve such practicality. Practicality in turn exacted a certain objectivity. But since man was the subject, not simply his surroundings or just his circumstances, objectivity alone could never suffice. Being, thinking, and writing, alike, must inflict vicarious suffering or unbearable joy, the better to suggest a duality that could encompass such ugliness allied with such beauty.

With the usual human propensity for reaction, the opening century seemed to glory in its disorder. It was desperately bound for a freedom that it could scarcely define. Literary genres reflected the disorder. But scientific approach and relativity had long passed the stages of Descartes and Pascal. One senses, as early as the twenties, a willing reconciliation

381

with regularity and plan. Historical treatises, narrative forms, drama, verse, all tended to reflect the furies of a dissatisfied society that either stormed or wept; but there, clearly and constantly on the page, under guise or not, were the reasons and motives for the fury.

It was a justifiable commotion for freedom's sake, and the natural human counterpart was concern. We may wonder whether administrators, authors, and public could possibly have foreseen the expansion of their own humanitarianism that would forever mark the century. Certainly commitment was an order of the day; suggestions must be implemented; determination would pursue every goal. By turn sensitive, sensible, and sentimental, the period made scarcely any claim to perfection. It did envisage, by exhortation or harshness or bitterness, necessary physical changes; it did dare to hope for a more generous society. One could, and must, become "philosophized." In turn, said de Tréogate, youth could be "brought back to Truth through Sentiment *and* Reason." A true *philosophe* would have profited and suffered under both auspices. "Cultivating gardens" was to become a preoccupation, in any one of many interpretations.

We are constantly reminded that this was a far from naïve century. It would concern itself, physically, with necessary environmental change, but also with an aspiration toward self-mastery. Mentally, it would whet its wit relentlessly upon social change. Morally, it must understand its soul. In many a volume of the period one senses all three aspects running and leaping confusedly and confusingly. One cannot fail to note, however, the aim and a seriousness of concern, often an intense remorse. From sensitivity, into sensuality, into licentiousness, then into reverse order, one interprets a cycle—*le cœur, le corps, l'esprit, le cœur.*

Subjects, then, had run throughout the era on both the analytical and the psychological sides, as well as on the sociological. Rage against the general condition of man pervaded a century of reason and progress. Pity and anger strode through

382

the years. Mesalliance in marriage, rehabilitation of the courtesan, the status of the natural child—such subjects had received a "harsh compassion," but prejudice, as well as ignorance, could be combatted. Modern forms of psychological and sociological understanding might recognize and concur in many aspects. But especially was the self, the "moi," to retain its essential dignity, its consciousness of a conscience.

As the embattled years wore on, this "philosophism" or "Encyclopedism" contributed to untold but useful confusion. One finds, especially in treatises and in tales, countless Utopias. Traced with either positive or negative pen, they frequently raise the question of whether they were pose or actuality; no matter, they exhorted physical, mental, or moral improvement. A Rousseauistic conception of pastoral themes tended to attract those who would see in a calmness of nature some of the much desired amelioration. Education, already ensconced in a certain amount of practicality, could advocate systems and procedures. Through an expanding journalism came a desire for *reportage*, for external detail as a means of teaching and of exerting reform. Because of conscience the "search for happiness" theme was evolving into reality. As proofs of reality, themes were even moving into laboratory techniques. One may half glimpse a coming Naturalism. Impertinence, impudence, and temerity constituted their own benefits, based upon reason.

France was extremely busy with her undertakings. Well-considered utopias of human qualities must precede or accompany those of a reformed society. As in any restlessly discontented ambiance, individual and institutional features must fulfill an ideal. *L'Encyclopédie* had indeed sought to improve the human being upon whom its knowledge might descend. Freedom was therefore to be construed not only as a liberation *toward* certain ideal aspects of one's living, such as improved institutions, but just as importantly as a liberation *from* the vanity or lack of moderation that would inevitably deter implementation of them.

Since understanding still remains for us often elusive, it is interesting to note the persistence of the theme in every genre of the eighteenth century. Persons languished in prison while an issue was being decided; matters of peace among nations awaited minute details of wording. We know that calumny was one of the sharpest thorns of a period in which even caustic writers flayed its detestable power. Ill-content for its own sake was capable of crushing all endeavor, but contentment that rested upon class alone would be equally reprehensible. Abuses were apparent, and conscience must hold its place.

These reasonable beings of the period were eminently fulfilling both roles within their improving years: they were painters of the ideal and sculptors of its forms. In both they appeared at times almost unbelievably clairvoyant. For their corner of a universe they claimed relatively little but expected much, and whether on promenades or at the workbench they proved determined and indefatigable. One evokes the picture of a nervously intense, often erratic Diderot pursuing his goal despite all discouragement or danger. His was one determination among many in a vigorous, soaring and volatile age.

Again placing the two centuries together, one notes that both have demonstrated a contrasting admiration, on the one hand, for a decidedly mechanistic progress reaching into ordinary living as well as into institutions, and on the other, for aspects of a completely ephemeral intangibility. Both have inordinately loved man, yet have shockingly mistreated him. Naturally, in viewing any historic section of our planet, one must concede the possibility that many of the later recognized discernments may have been accidental. Yet the eighteenth was a precocious century and far from timid. One cannot refrain from labeling certain phases of those years as "psychological," "sociological." Even many of the intricacies that we tend to call modern are very surely on the page. Novels and tales divide the "introspective," "extraspective," and

384

"interspective" long before our present uses of these terms. The human processes, it is true, may have been ancient, but still we note with interest the amount of space here allotted to them. Moderation in all sorts of fields, of action or of thinking, would exact the "delayed reactions," the "subconscious retreat," "living substitution," "escapism," of which we speak today.

Nor were these discerning moments exclusively of mental projection. A century that so actively knew fear could scarcely help conveying it physically. Again journalism offered effective means; caricatures often became venomous beneath their ingratiating lines. A reading public had been taught to read between cross-references; now it could apply itself to drawings. An ancient idea of frequent connection between moral good or evil and physical ease or suffering found interesting application in a "roving reporter," Restif de la Bretonne. His graphic sketches, running from pungency to horror, made the public increasingly conscious of correlated squalor and delinquency. As must be so, if an era were to envisage implementation of its ideals, the Age of Reason placed due stress upon its youth. Though in the thousands of pages of its literature, the century would endlessly, often tediously, admonish its youth or warn against dangers, yet it worshiped the same tumultuous curiosity that could allow advancing years to retain their glow. It would profitably export into the following century a Rousseauistic idea that learning seemed good only when it was being conveyed. Above all, it saw an educational evangel in induction. Some few keenly perceptive members even espoused the cause of coeducation, as a means of rendering the sexes more understanding toward each other. Important as were facts, with regard to change and progress, they could be overemphasized. One is amused to read of Dorat's enjoining upon his public not to live with the facts alone or·one will surely emerge "un peu plus bête le lendemain."

The confusion, rage, and grief that had accompanied the

emission of an *Encyclopédie* evolved both a philosophic and an actional ideal. The century recognized that in order to cope with life, it must attack abuses with determination, but also with laughing disrespect, and especially with a will to practicality. Utilitarianism would be by no means just a doctrine; "Encyclopedism" could never remain simply "philosophism." Twilight years were to witness a diminishing need for the virulence of opposition, the acerbity of tone that had so actively produced their effect. As with countless heroes and heroines of its drama or novel, the era was to accede to a maturity, a graciousness of being. Quiet conviction would supplant the perturbed agitation of its beginning and middle years. Immediacy was to be of lesser importance than permanence. And again, as in an eternal cycle, the self would be of utmost concern. But whether it might be for environment or for self-analysis, one transcendent difference would be evident—the individual would forever work upon his group knowledge. Nothing indeed could be more difficult than coping with this, or any other existence, but he found himself encouraged to imagine and to enforce his visions. A period of immoderation had profoundly coveted moderation.

Together with an ambitious ideal, reasonableness could next proceed to certain subtleties of refinement. A century that had somewhat doubtfully viewed asceticism would naturally incline toward an extroverted future, in which the constructive forces so ardently pursued might become actualities. It may even occur to us that this ideal of never living unto one's self alone, of groups assuming entities in and of themselves, has lived a rather fascinating existence during the years. A term of Unanimism has evolved within our time.

The evening of a century is drawing to a close. At the Arsenal desk huge tomes and series of the small volumes side by side bespeak a Utopia developed through social conscience. And now it is a fading but softly penetrating light coming up from the Seine.

386

A Bibliography of the Writings of George R. Havens

1918

"The Date of Composition of *Manon Lescaut*." *MLN* 33 (March): 150-54

1919

"Rabelais and the War of 1914." *RR* 10 (January-March): 79-83.

"The Sources of Rousseau's Edouard Bomston." *MP* 17 (July): 125-39.

"The Abbé Prévost and Shakespeare." *MP* 17 (August): 177-98.

1920

"The Abbé Le Blanc and English Literature." *MP* 18 (December): 423-41.

1921

The Abbé Prévost and English Literature. Elliott Monographs No. 9. Princeton: Princeton University Press; Paris: Champion. 135 pp. Reviews: F. Baldensperger, *Rcr* 88 (1921): 431-32; P. Hazard, *Etudes critiques* (Chicago, 1929): 85-86; V. Klemperer, *Archiv* 146 (1923): 272-74; D.G.L., *MLR* 17 (1922): 438; D. Mornet, *RHLF* 29 (1922): 369-70; P. Van Tiegham, *RSH* 34 (1922): 143.

"The Theory of Natural Goodness in Rousseau's *Nouvelle Héloïse*." *MLN* 36 (November): 385-94.

Review: A. R. Riddle, *Flaubert and Maupassant: A Literary Relationship*, *MP* 18 (March): 617-19.

1923

"The Theory of Natural Goodness in Rousseau's *Confessions*."
MLN 38 (May): 257-66.

"James Madison et la pensée française." *RLC* 3: 604-15.

A Minimum Requirement for Elementary French. Columbus,
Ohio: College Book Co. 18 pp.

Review: A. Schinz, *Vie et Œuvres de J.-J. Rousseau*, *MLN* 38
(March): 174-75.

1924

"La Théorie de la bonté naturelle de l'homme chez J.-J. Rousseau."
RHLF 31: 629-42.

"General Reading for Undergraduates." *AAUP* 10 (October):
480-92.

Reviews: Stewart and Tilley, *The Classical Movement in French
Literature*, *MLJ* 9 (November): 123-25. G. Chinard, *Volney et
l'Amérique*, *MLN* 39 (December): 499-502.

1925

*Selections from Voltaire, with Explanatory Comment upon His
Life and Works*. New York: Century Co. xxv + 434 pp. Review:
Anon., *RLC* 6 (1926): 350.

"La Théorie de la bonté naturelle de l'homme chez J.-J. Rousseau."
RHLF 32: 23-37, 212-25. Review: L. Pinvert, *AJJR* 17 (1926):
282-83.

"The Nature Doctrine of Voltaire." *PMLA* 40 (December): 852-
62.

"The Department of Romance Languages, Founding of the Department by Elliott." *JHA* 14: 50-54.

1928

Selected Stories from Guy de Maupassant, with Olin Moore. Boston: Ginn. xxiv + 252 pp. Review: B. Jordan, *MLJ* 14 (1929):
259-60.

"Voltaire's Marginal Comments on Pope's *Essay on Man*." *MLN*
43 (November): 429-39.

388

"The Private Library of Voltaire at Leningrad," with N. L. Torrey. *PMLA* 43 (December): 990-1009.

1929

"An Eighteenth-Century Royal Theater in Sweden." *MLN* 44 (January): 22-23.

"Leningrad Glimpses." *Sewanee Review* 37 (January): 59-72.

"Voltaire's Books: *A Selected List*," with N. L. Torrey. *Fortnightly Review* 126 (September): 397-405.

"Voltaire's Pessimistic Revision of the Conclusion of his *Poème sur le désastre de Lisbonne*." *MLN* 44 (December): 489-92.

"Rousseau's Doctrine of Goodness According to Nature." *PMLA* 44 (December): 1239-45.

Reviews: Mercier, *French Pronunciation and Diction, JEdR* 20 (October): 210-11. Church and Young, *French Literature in Outline, FR* 3 (October): 66-69.

1930

Selections from Voltaire. . . . New York: Appleton-Century Co. Revised Edition. xxvii + 437 pp.

Review: M. Barr, *A Century of Voltaire Study: A Bibliography of Writings on Voltaire, 1825-1925, MLN* 45 (May): 347.

1931

Reviews: N. L. Torrey, *Voltaire and the English Deists*, and Georg Brandes, *Voltaire, YR* 41 (Summer): 851-53. M. E. Robertson, *Abbé Prévost: The Adventures of a Man of Quality, MLN* 46 (June): 420-21.

1932

"A Corrected Reading of One of Voltaire's Notes on *Emile*." *MLN* 47 (January): 20-21.

"The Composition of Voltaire's *Candide*." *MLN* 47 (April): 225-34.

"Voltaire's Note on *Emile* Once More." *MLN* 47 (May): 325.

"Voltaire's Marginal Comments on Rousseau." *SAQ* 31 (October): 408-16.

"University Library in Peril." *OSUM*, October, pp. 6-8.

Reviews: M. Josephson, *J.-J. Rousseau*, SR 8 (January 30): 488; Reply to Josephson, *SR* 8 (February 27): 557. N. L. Torrey, *Voltaire and the Enlightenment*, *MLJ* 16 (January): 378-79. P. Trahard, *Les Maîtres de la sensibilité française au XVIIIe siècle (1715-89)*, Tomes I-II, *MLN* 47 (December): 534-36. F. C. Green, *Eighteenth-Century France*, *MLJ* 17 (December): 225.

1933

Voltaire's Marginalia on the Pages of Rousseau: A Comparative Study of Ideas. Columbus: Ohio State University Press. x + 199 pp. Reviews: G. Mongrédien, *NL* (March 17, 1934); D. Mornet, *RHLF* 41 (1934): 135-36; A. Schinz, *AJJR* 22 (1933): 259-61.

"Les Notes marginales de Voltaire sur Rousseau." *RHLF* 40: 434-40.

1934

Voltaire, *Candide ou l'optimisme*. Ed. with Introduction, Notes, and Vocabulary. New York: Holt. lxiv + 149 + lxi pp. Review: B. M. Woodbridge, *MLJ* 20 (1935-36): 250.

Review: P. Trahard, *Les Maîtres de la sensibilité* . . . , T. III. *MLN* 49 (April): 268-69.

1936

Easy French Readings, with Olin Moore. New York: Holt. xx + 518 + cxvii pp.

"University Library under Veto Axe." *OSUM*, February, pp. 21-22.

Review: K. Weis, *Das antiphilosophische Weltbild des französischen Sturm und Drang*, *MLN* 51 (June): 413.

1937

Reviews: M. S. Libby, *The Attitude of Voltaire to Magic and Sciences*, *PR* 46 (March): 232-33. Lovejoy and Boas, *Primitivism and Related Ideas in Antiquity, MLN* 52 (June): 421-22. E. P. Dargan, *Anatole France, RR* 28 (December): 369-71.

1938

Reviews: M. L. Buchner, *A Contribution to the Study of the Descriptive Technique of J.-J. Rousseau, RR* 29 (February): 89-90. H. Hastings, *Man and Beast in French Thought of the Eighteenth-Century, MLN* 53 (June): 466. G. Le Roy, *La Psychologie de Condillac, PR* 47 (September): 554.

1939

"The First Course in Literature." *MLJ* 23 (May): 563-71.

"Diderot and the Composition of Rousseau's First Discourse." *RR* 30 (December): 369-81.

Reviews: R. Naves, *Voltaire et l'Encyclopédie, MLN* 54 (December): 617. W. Müller, *Die Grundbegriffe des gesellschaftlichen Welt in den Werken des Abbé Prévost, MLN* 54 (December): 628.

1940

Selections from Voltaire. New York: Appleton-Century. 2d Revised Edition. xxviii + 439 pp.

"The Dates of Diderot's Birth and Death." *MLN* 55 (January): 31-35.

"Romanticism in France." *PMLA* 55 (March): 10-20, 55-56.

"Rousseau, Melon, and Sir William Petty." *MLN* 55 (November): 499-503.

Twelve New Letters of Voltaire to Gabriel Cramer." *RR* 31 (December): 341-54.

Reviews: R. Naves, *Le Goût de Voltaire,* and E. Carcassonne, *Le Temple de goût, RR* 31 (February): 77-78. C. Engel *Figures et aventures du XVIIIe siècle: voyages et découvertes de l'abbé Prévost, RR* 31 (April): 176-78. N. L. Torrey, *The Spirit of Voltaire, PR* 59 (May): 375-76.

1941

"The Modern Language Teacher in a Troubled World." *MLJ* 25 (January): 306-13.

"The Conclusion of Voltaire's *Poème sur le désastre de Lisbonne*."
MLN 56 (June): 422-26.

"Voltaire's Letters to Pierre Pictet and His Family." *RR* 32 (October): 244-58.

"E. Preston Dargan: A Career in Scholarship (1879-1940)." *BA* 15 (Autumn): 412-15.

Reviews: R. R. Palmer, *Catholics and Unbelievers in Eighteenth-Century France*, *PR* 50 (January): 85-86. D. Schier, *Louis-Bertrand Castel*, *MLQ* 2 (December): 639-40.

1942

"Rousseau's First Discourse and the *Pensées philosophiques* of Diderot," *RR* 33 (December): 356-59.

Reviews: I. O. Wade, *Voltaire and Mme du Châtelet*, *RR* 33 (February): 81-82. J. E. Barker, *Diderot's Treatment of the Christian Religion in the Encyclopédie*, *MLN* 57 (May): 397-98. L. C. Cohen, *From Beast-Machine to Man-Machine: Animal Soul in French Letters from Descartes to La Mettrie*, *MLN* 57 (December): 681-83.

1943

A travers les âges, with Olin Moore. New York: Holt, xiv + 488 + clx pp. Review: A. Langellier, *MLJ* (1944): 311.

"French Criticism: Eighteenth Century." In *Dictionary of World Literature*. New York: Philosophical Library, pp. 265-68.

Reviews: R. E. Cowdrick, *The Early Reading of Pierre Bayle*, *RR* 34 (February): 79-80. L. S. Gaudin, *Les Lettres anglaises dans l'Encyclopédie*, *MLN* 58 (April): 303-4. D. R. Mc Kee, *Simon Tyssot de Patot and the Seventeenth-Century Background of Critical Deism*. *MLN* 58 (November): 573-74. M. Waterman, *Pascal, Voltaire, and Human Destiny*, *PR* 52 (September): 526.

1944

"The Chronology of Diderot's Journey to Langres in 1759." *MLN* 59 (January): 33-37.

"Voltaire, Rousseau, and the *Lettre sur la Providence*." *PMLA* 59 (March): 109-30.

"Voltaire and English Critics of Shakespeare." *ASLHM* 15 (Summer): 176-86.

1945

"Why Literature?" *SAQ* 44 (April): 177-84.

Review: E. P. Shaw, *Jacques Cazotte, MLN* 60 (April): 276-77.

1946

Jean-Jacques Rousseau, *Discours sur les sciences et les arts.* Edition critique avec une Introduction et un Commentaire. New York: M. L. A. 278 pp. Reviews: O. Fellows, *RR* 38 (1947): 277-79; F.T.H. Fletcher, *MLR* 42 (1957): 269-70; A. François, *AJJR* 31 (1946-49): 262-64; A. C. Keller, *MLQ* 11 (1950): 125-26; D. Mornet, *RHLF* 49 (1959): 178-79; P. Spurlin, *MLN* 63 (1948): 423-25; R. Shackleton, *FS* 4 (1950): 161-64; I. Wade, *FR* 21 (1947-48): 509-11.

"Diderot and the Actor's Art." *ASLHM* 18 (Winter): 601-8.

1947

"The Beginning of Voltaire's *Poème sur le désastre de Lisbonne.*" *MLN* 62 (November): 465-67.

"Voltaire Today." *ASLHM* 18 (Winter): 380-90.

Review: M. Trudel, *L'Influence de Voltaire au Canada, BA* 21 (Winter): 60-61.

1948

"Reply to Wade on the edition of Rousseau's *Discours sur les sciences et les arts.*" *FR* 22 (October): 58-59.

Review: I. O. Wade, *Studies on Voltaire, RR* 39 (April): 164-67.

1949

Reviews: Gordon and Torrey, *The Censoring of Diderot's Encyclopédie and the Re-established Text, RRel* 13 (January): 199-202. G. Bonno, *La Culture et la civilisation britanniques devant l'opinion française . . . (1713-1734), AHR* 54 (April): 582-83. A. R. Oliver, *The Encyclopedists as Critics of Music, RR* 40

(April): 144-45. J.-J. Rousseau, *Lettre à d'Alembert sur les spectacles*, ed. M. Fuchs, *RR* 40 (December): 292-96.

1950

"The Road to Vincennes." *ASLHM* 21 (Autumn): 201-8.

1951

Editor, with D. F. Bond, *A Critical Bibliography of French Literature*, Volume 4: *The Eighteenth Century*. Syracuse, N.Y.: Syracuse University Press. Contributions: "Historical and Political Background" (with D. C. Cabeen), "Prévost," "Voltaire." Reviews: J. Bonnerot, *MerF*, No. 1170 (February), pp. 338-39; F. C. Green, *MLR* 48 (1953): 347-48; R. Shackleton, *FS* 6 (1952): 367-69.

"The Archbishop and the King." *ASLHM* 22 (Autumn): 213-24.

1952

Review: M. B. Ellis, *Julie ou la Nouvelle Héloïse: A Synthesis of Rousseau's Thought (1749-59)*, *RR* 43 (April): 129-34.

1953

"Beaumarchais on the Eve of the Revolution." *ASLHM* 24 (Spring): 43-57.

1954

"The Translator Enters." *ASLHM* 25 (Spring): 53-63.

"H. C. Lancaster (1882-1954)." *MLN* 69 (December): 541-44.

Review: B. Gagnebin, Voltaire, *Lettres inédites à son imprimeur*, *RR* 45 (October): 207-11.

1955

The Ages of Ideas: From Reaction to Revolution in Eighteenth-Century France. New York: Holt; London: Peter Owen. x + 474 pp. Reviews: D. F. Bond, *MP* 53 (1955): 130-31; V. Buranelli, *JHI* 18 (1957): 128-34; H. Cairns, *Washington Post* (24

April 1955); F. Crowley, *CL* 8 (1956): 359-60; C. Frankel, *PR* 55 (1955): 568-70; L. Gershoy, *SR* 38 (1955): 20; F. C. Green, *RHLF* 57 (1957): 254-55; A. Guerard, *NYT* (24 April 1955); P. Langellier, *FA* (May 15, 1955); J. Lough, *MLR* 51 (1956): 268; M. Lowenthal, *NYHT* (10 July 1955); B. Morrissette, *St. Louis Post* (29 June 1955); J. Powers, *Boston Globe* (19 June 1955); O. Prescott, *NYT* (25 April 1955); J. S. Schapiro, *New Leader* (20 June 1955): 21-23; R. Shackleton, *FS* 10 (1956): 177; *TLS* (31 January 1958), N. Torrey, *ASLHM* 26 (1955): 181-82, *RR* 46 (1955): 299-301; F. Vial, *FR* 29 (1955-56): 268-70; A. M. Wilson, *AHR* 61 (1955): 118-19; [Anon.,] *YR* 44 (1955): vi.

"Anatole France and the French Revolution." *ASLHM* 26 (Autumn): 229-39.

Review: *Montesquieu (1689-1755)*. *RR* 46 (December): 293-94.

1956

Reviews: Fontenelle, *Entretiens sur la pluralité des mondes* and *Digression sur les anciens et les modernes*, ed. R. Shackleton, *FS* 10 (January): 71-73. H. Roddier, *L'Abbé Prévost, l'homme et l'œuvre*, *RR* 47 (February): 60-62. W. H. Barber, *Leibniz in France*, *MP* 54 (August): 63-64. C. Rowe, *Voltaire and the State*, *RR* 47 (October): 218-20.

1957

"A Reply to Dr. Buranelli on *The Age of Ideas*." *JHI* 18 (January): 135-37.

Reviews: A. M. Wilson, *Diderot: The Testing Years*, *AHR* 63 (October): 106-8. D. Frame, *The Complete Works of Montaigne*, *NYT* (17 November): 56.

1959

Voltaire's Catalogue of His Library at Ferney, with N. L. Torrey. Studies on Voltaire and the Eighteenth Century, No. 9. Geneva: Institut et Musée Voltaire. 258 pp. Reviews: W. Bottiglia, *RR* 50 (1959): 292-94; J. Brumfitt, *FS* 14 (1960): 70; J. R. Loy, *MLN* 75 (1960): 453-55.

Reviews: I. O. Wade, *The Search for a New Voltaire*, RR 50 (April): 133-37. D. B. Schlegel, *Shaftesbury and the French Deists*, MLQ 29 (June): 204-6.

1960

"Further Comment on Voltaire's *Catalogue*." RR 51 (April): 156-58.

1961

"Diderot, Rousseau, and the *Discours sur l'Inégalité*." DS 3:219-62.

"Hardiesse de Rousseau dans le Discours sur l'Inégalité." *Europe*, nos. 391-92 (November-December), pp. 149-58.

1962

Review: J. Sareil, *Anatole France and Voltaire*, RR 53 (October): 236-38.

1965

"Pre-Romanticism in France." *L'Esprit Créateur* 6 (Summer): 63-76.

"Helvétius, A Philosopher with More Enemies Than Friends." DS 8:301-7.

Review: P. M. Jones, *The Assault on French Literature*, MP 62 (May): 370-74.

1966

"Gustave Lanson Reconsidered." RR 57 (December): 277-84.

"Foreword" to Nuçi Kotta, *L'Homme aux Quarante Ecus: A Study in Voltairian Themes*. The Hague: Mouton, pp. 11-14.

"Bayle," "Diderot," "Montesquieu," "Voltaire." *Collier's Encyclopedia*.

1967

"The Road to Rousseau's *Discours sur l'Inégalité*." YFS 40: 18-31.

"Introduction" to Hilde Freud, *Palissot and Les Philosophes*. DS 9: 15-19.

396

1968

"European Unity in the Eighteenth Century." *DS* 10: 201-12.

1969

Frederick J. Waugh, American Marine Painter. Orono, Maine: University of Maine Press. xii + 361 pp. Review: M. S. Young, *Apollo* 97 (April, 1973): 439-40.

Selections from Voltaire. New York: Holt. Revised Edition. xxxi + 447 pp.

Voltaire, *Candide ou l'optimisme*. New York: Holt. Revised Edition. lxvii + 148 + lxi pp. Review: C. Fleischauer, *MLJ* 54 (1970): 200.

A History of the Department of Romance Languages at the Ohio State University. Ohio State Centenary Pamphlets. 72 pp.

1971

Review: M. Barr avec la collaboration de F. A. Spear, *Quarante Annees d'études voltairiennes*. *DS* 14: 345-48.

1972

"Voltaire's *Micromégas* (1739-52): Composition and Publication." *MLQ* 33 (June): 113-18.

"Voltaire's *L'Ingénu*: Composition and Publication." *RR* 63 (December): 261-71.

1973

"Edward Cooke Armstrong." *Dictionary of American Biography*, Supp. 3: 21-22.

"Some Notes on *Candide*." *MLN* 88 (May): 841-47.

"Candide Returns," *DS* 18: 347-59.

Review: R. Niklaus, *A Literary History of France: The Eighteenth Century, 1715-1789, RR* 64 (May): 234-35.

1974

"Voltaire and Alexander Pope." In *Essays on Diderot and the En-*

lightenment in Honor of Otis Fellows, ed. J. Pappas. Geneva: Droz. pp. 124-50.

Voltaire, *Sept Discours en vers sur l'homme.* A Critical Edition with Introduction, Notes, and Variants. *The Complete Works of Voltaire,* ed. T. Besterman. To appear.

Abbreviations

AAUP	*Bulletin of the American Association of University Professors*
AHR	*American Historical Review*
AJJR	*Annales de la Société Jean-Jacques Rousseau*
Archiv	*Archiv für das Studium der neuren Sprachen und Literaturen* (Herrig)
ASLHM	*American Society Legion of Honor Magazine*
BA	*Books Abroad*
CL	*Comparative Literature*
DS	*Diderot Studies*
FA	*France-Amérique*
FR	*French Review*
FS	*French Studies*
JEdR	*Journal of Educational Research* (Ohio State University)
JHA	*Johns Hopkins University Alumni Magazine*
JHI	*Journal of the History of Ideas*
MerF	*Mercure de France*
MLJ	*Modern Language Journal*
MLN	*Modern Language Notes*
MLQ	*Modern Language Quarterly*
MLR	*Modern Language Review*
MP	*Modern Philology*
NL	*Nouvelles littéraires*
NYHT	*New York Herald Tribune Book Review*
NYT	*New York Times*
OSUM	*Ohio State University Monthly*
PMLA	*Publications of the Modern Language Association of America*

PR   *Philosophical Review*
Rcr   *Revue critique d'histoire et de littérature*
RHLF   *Revue d'histoire littéraire de la France*
RLC   *Revue de littérature comparée*
RR   *Romanic Review*
RRel   *Review of Religion*
RSH   *Revue des sciences humaines*
SAQ   *South Atlantic Quarterly*
SR   *Saturday Review*
TLS   London *Times Literary Supplement*
YFS   *Yale French Studies*
YR   *Yale Review*

Notes on the Contributors

ARNOLD AGES, University of Waterloo, has written numerous articles on Voltaire. His dissertation on Dom Calmet was directed by Professor Havens.

THEODORE BESTERMAN, The Voltaire Foundation, Banbury, Oxfordshire, is editor of Voltaire's *Correspondence* and *Notebooks*, general editor of the definitive edition of his complete works, and director of *Studies on Voltaire and the Eighteenth Century*. His most recent book is the biography *Voltaire* (1969).

DOUGLAS BONNEVILLE, University of Florida, wrote his dissertation on La Harpe under the direction of Professor Havens. He is the author of *Diderot's Vie de Sénèque: A Swan Song Revised*.

RICHARD A. BROOKS, Richmond College, City University of New York, is the author of *Voltaire and Leibniz* and the general editor of the supplementary volume to the *Critical Bibliography of French Literature: The Eighteenth Century*.

HARCOURT BROWN, Brown University, Emeritus, has specialized in the history of science in seventeenth- and eighteenth-century France. His work on Maupertuis will be continued in *Science and the Human Comedy*, to be published shortly by the University of Toronto Press, and in a projected separate volume on Maupertuis's life among scientists.

J. H. BRUMFITT, University of Saint Andrews, has written extensively on Voltaire's historical writing. He is the author of *Vol-*

taire, Historian (2d edition, 1970) and editor of *La Philosophie de l'histoire* and *The Age of Louis XIV and Other Selected Writings.*

ROBERT D. COTTRELL, Ohio State University, has published articles on baroque style, Brantôme, and Montaigne. His *Brantôme, the Writer as Portraitist of his Age* appeared in 1970.

ALESSANDRO S. CRISAFULLI, Catholic University of America, is an editor of the *Studies Presented to Helmut Hatzfeld.* A specialist on Montesquieu, his dissertation on Montesquieu was written under the direction of Professor Havens.

HUGH M. DAVIDSON, University of Virginia, has written on Pascal, Boileau, and the *Encyclopédie.* His *Audience, Words, and Art: Studies on Seventeenth-Century French Rhetoric* appeared in 1965.

OTIS FELLOWS, Columbia University, is founder and coeditor of *Diderot Studies.* A collection of his essays, *From Voltaire to La Nouvelle Critique: Problems and Personalities,* was published by Droz in 1970. His most recent book is *Buffon* (2d edition, 1974).

DIANA GUIRAGOSSIAN, Indiana University, is author of *Voltaire's Facéties* and coeditor of *Diderot Studies.*

JAMES F. HAMILTON, University of Cincinnati, has published several articles on Rousseau and is presently working on a study of Rousseau and literature.

GEORGES MAY, Yale University, has most recently published a critical edition of Diderot's *La Religieuse,* François Hemsterhuis's *Lettre sur l'homme et ses rapports avec le Commentaire inédit de Diderot,* and *Le Dilemme du roman au XVIIIe siècle.*

GITA MAY, Columbia University, has studied the development of French art criticism in her *Diderot et Baudelaire, critiques d'art* (2d edition, 1967). Her last book, *Mme Roland, étude sur une sensibilité révolutionnaire* (1970) will be followed shortly by a study of Stendhal.

DOROTHY M. MCGHEE, Hamline University, Emerita, received her Ph.D. under the direction of Professor Havens. She is author of *Voltairean Narrative Devices, Marmontel and the contes moraux,* and *The Fortunes of a Tale.*

JEANNE R. MONTY, Tulane University, has most recently published *Les Romans de l'abbé Prévost* (1970). Her dissertation, *La Critique littéraire de Melchior Grimm,* directed by Professor Havens, appeared in 1961; her *Etude sur le style polémique de Voltaire: le Dictionnaire philosophique,* in 1966.

JEAN SAREIL, Columbia University, is author of *Anatole France et Voltaire, Essai sur Candide, Voltaire et la critique,* and most recently, *Les Tencin* (1971).

EDWARD P. SHAW, State University of New York at Albany, Emeritus, has explored the intrigues of the eighteenth-century book trade extensively in his *Problems and Politics of Malesherbes as Directeur de la Librairie (1750-1763)* and his recently published study of the journal of Joseph d'Hémery. His other books include biographies of Moncrif and of Cazotte.

PAUL SPURLIN, University of Michigan, Emeritus, has specialized in Rousseau's writings and influence. His recently published *Rousseau in America,* continues his special interests in intellectual relationships.

VIRGIL TOPAZIO, Rice University, has examined extensively the relationships of Diderot, D'Holbach, and Helvétius and has written on Diderot's art criticism and on Rousseau. His book *D'Holbach's Moral Philosophy and Development* appeared in 1956; *Voltaire: A Critical Study of His Major Works,* in 1967.

IRA O. WADE, Princeton University, Emeritus, has published most recently *The Intellectual Origins of the French Enlightenment*

403

(1971), the first of a three-volume study, and *The Intellectual Development of Voltaire* (1969).

CHARLES G. S. WILLIAMS, Ohio State University, is completing a biography of Valincour and an edition of his collected correspondence.

Index

Académie des Inscriptions, 21–22

Académie des Sciences, 71, 72, 73, 74, 76, 77, 79, 84, 88, 91

Académie française, 6, 32

Acta Eruditorum (Leipzig), 71, 74

Acta Sanctorum (Bollandists), 15

Adams, Henry, 363, 369

Adams, John, 360, 363, 371

Addison, Joseph, 169, 203

Aimé-Martin, Louis, 336, 338

Aldridge, A. Owen, 368

Alembert, Jean Le Rond d', 18, 156, 210, 216–17, 311, 324, 325, 326, 332, 338, 349, 380

Alexander I (czar), 324

Algarotti, Francesco, 116

Amelot de Chaillou, Jean-Jacques, 136

Andry, Charles-Louis-François, 112

Annales (Benedictines), 16

Argens, Jean-Baptiste de Boyer, marquis d', 141–42

Argenson, Marc-Pierre de Voyer de Paulmy, comte d', 135

Aristotle, 7, 116, 180

Arnauld, Antoine, 36

Artois, comtesse d' (Thérèse of Savoy), 262

Assemblée du clergé, 37, 38

Aubigné, Agrippa d', 39, 43, 45, 47

Aulnoy, Marie-Catherine, comtesse d', 66 n.9

Aventurier chinois (anon. novel), 275–76

Aymery, T. F. A. d', 279

Bacon, Francis, 102, 105, 106

Baculard d'Arnaud, François-Thomas-Marie, 274

Bailyn, Bernard, 361

Ballanche, Pierre-Simon, 337

Baluze, Etienne, 15

Barrême, François, 292

Bayle, Pierre, 15, 17, 20, 21, 23, 25, 26, 33, 39, 46, 53, 102, 103, 104, 105, 106, 108, 109, 114, 115, 117, 380

Beaufort, Louis de, 21

Beaumarchais, Pierre-Augustin Caron de, 165, 220 n.13, 311, 312, 313, 314, 315, 316, 317, 318, 319

Beausorbe, Isaac de, 114, 115, 158, 163

Beauvoir, Simone de, 209, 210, 216, 227

Bédier, Joseph, 245

Belaval, Yvon, 245

Bell, Robert, 368

Benoist, Elie, 53

Bernoulli, Jakob, 73

Bernoulli, Johann I, 71, 72, 73, 74, 75, 76, 77, 78, 79, 80, 81, 82, 83, 84, 85, 86, 87, 88, 89, 90, 91, 92

Bernoulli, Johann II (or Jean), 73, 88, 90, 91

Haller, Albrecht von, 305
Hardouin, Jean, 16
Hart, James D., 368, 372
Havens, George R., ix–xvi, xvii, 98, 387–98
Hazard, Paul, 21
Helvétius, Claude-Adrien, 210, 323, 345
Hendel, Charles W., 187
Herodotus, 15, 19
Horace, 8, 10, 328
Houdetot, Elizabeth-Françoise Sophie, comtesse d', 216
Houtteville, Alexandre-Claude, abbé, 111
Huygens, Christiaan, 104

Isnard (Marseille printer), 299

Jaucourt, Louis, chevalier de, 156, 157, 158–60, 163
Jefferson, Thomas, 360
Jones, S. Paul, 273, 279, 281
Jones, William, 70
Jouffroy, Claude, marquis de, 338
Journal des Sçavans, 59–60, 61, 63, 64
Journal Helvétique, 116, 120, 122
Jouvet, Louis, 245
Julian the Apostate, 158
Jurieu, Pierre, 45
Jussieu, Bernard de, 69
Juvenel, Félix de, 22

Kraus, Michael, 361, 370

La Bruyère, Jean de, 7, 17, 23, 280
Laclos, Choderlos, 352-53, 354
La Condamine, Charles-Marie de, 73, 78, 92
Lafayette, Marie-Madeleine, comtesse de, 34, 354
La Fontaine, Jean de, 199, 201, 202, 346
La Forge, Dr. Louis de, 109

La Harpe, Jean-François de, 126
Lamartine, Alphonse, 321–40; Catherine II condemned by, 325–26, 338–39; *Contrat social* criticized by, 333–34, 337, 340; Mme des Roys (grandmother), influenced by, 327, 332; and Diderot, 324, 326; on dissemination of Enlightenment ideals, 323–24, 325; on *La Henriade*. 328, 329, 330, 339; as politician, 322; on Revolution, 323–24, 333–34, 335, 336, 337; on Robespierre, 334–35; Rousseau and, 321, 325, 328, 330–39; Sade and, 321; M. Valmont (uncle), influenced by, 325, 327; Voltaire and, 324, 325, 326–30, 339; *Confidences*, 325, 332; *Entretiens littéraires*, 333; *Histoire de la restauration*, 336, 338; *Histoire de la Turquie*, 324; *Histoire des Girondins*, 321, 322, 328, 331, 333, 337; *Mémoires politiques*, 324; *Ressouvenir du lac Léman*, 329, 331
Lamennais, Félicité-Robert de, 336
La Mettrie, Julien Offray de, 147
La Mothe le Vayer, François de, 19, 20
Lanson, Gustave, xiii–xiv
La Rochefoucauld-Liancourt, François-Alexandre, duc de, 362
La Sablière, Marguerite Hessein, dame de, 4
Lavisse, Ernest, 41
Le Blanc, Jean-Bernard, abbé, 97, 98
Le Bossu, René, 169
Lebrun, Charles, 9, 10
Le Clerc, Jean, 66 n.2, 109, 117
Leibniz, Gottfried Wilhelm: and Cartesianism, 71; Cuenz and, 108, 109, 118–19, 122, 123; Voltaire and, 102, 103, 106, 108, 119, 112
Le Long, Jacques, 22
Le Maistre, Antoine, 7
Lémery, Nicolas, 4
Le Moyne, Pierre, 17, 18
Le Nain de Tillemont, Sébastien, 16

413